LIFE SENTENCE

LIFE SENTENCE

The Memoirs of Lord Shawcross

CONSTABLE · LONDON

First published in Great Britain 1995
by Constable and Company Limited
3 The Lanchesters, 162 Fulham Palace Road
London W6 9ER
Copyright © 1995 by Lord Shawcross
The right of Lord Shawcross to be
identified as the author of this work has
been asserted by him in accordance with
the Copyright, Designs and Patents Act 1988
ISBN 0 09 474980 9
Set in Monophoto Poliphilus 13pt by
Servis Filmsetting Ltd, Manchester
Printed in Great Britain by
St Edmundsbury Press Ltd
Bury St Edmunds, Suffolk

A CIP catalogue record for this book
is available from the British Library

And the stately ships go on
  To their haven under the hill;
But O for the touch of a vanished hand,
  And the sound of a voice that is still!

Break, break, break,
  At the foot of thy crags, O Sea!
But the tender grace of a day that is dead
  Will never come back to me.

Alfred, Lord Tennyson

Contents

1	The Beginning	11
2	Gray's Inn – Marriage	18
3	The Bar	22
4	The War	35
5	Politics – How It Started	57
6	The Traitors	78
7	Nuremberg and the Nazi Criminals	85
8	Politics, 1945–46	138
9	Politics, 1947–48	158
10	Politics, 1949–51	181
11	Opposition and Practice, 1951–52	203
12	Politics and After, 1952–57	220
13	Into 'The Morgue'	266
14	Other Business	282
15	Disaster	288
16	Picking up the Pieces	298
17	Aftermath	304
18	At the End	321
	Index	331

Illustrations

between pages 96 and 97

My parents and myself soon after my birth in 1902
My mother in 1940, shortly before she died
With Alberta, my first wife, in Cornwall
As a young lawyer
With Joan, my second wife
Outside Peckhams in Sussex
Clement Attlee (*Hulton Deutsch*)
Ernest Bevin (*Hulton Deutsch*)
Herbert Morrison (*Hulton Deutsch*)
Hugh Dalton (*Hulton Deutsch*)
The British prosecution team at Nuremberg (*Hulton Deutsch*)
Handing down the indictments (*Hulton Deutsch*)
The Nazi criminals in the dock (*Hulton Deutsch*)
The Nazi criminals in the dock (*Hulton Deutsch*)
Hermann Goering (*Hulton Deutsch*)
Rudolf Hess (*Hulton Deutsch*)

between pages 224 and 225

William Joyce (Lord Haw Haw) (*Hulton Deutsch*)
John George Haigh (*Hulton Deutsch*)
With Joan and our children
Shaking hands with Winston Churchill at Bristol University (*Central Press Photos*)

With Joan (*Imperial War Museum*)
Vanity V
Fun and games on Vanity V in the early fifties
Stephen Ward (*Hulton Deutsch*)
Christine Keeler (*Hulton Deutsch*)
On elephants in Cambodia with Tony and Christiane Besse
With Joan and her horse at Friston in Sussex (*Sussex Life*)
Three cartoons
90th birthday party
Still sailing, on my last boat, Talisker, in 1994

Acknowledgements

I refreshed my memory of the Nuremberg trials by consulting John and Anne Tusa's *The Nuremberg Trial*; Bradley F Smith's *Reaching Judgement at Nuremberg*; Airey Neave's *On Trial at Nuremberg*; and Telford Taylors' *The Anatomy of the Nuremberg Trials*.

I am grateful to Lavinia Greacen for permission to quote from her biography *Chink* (Macmillan, 1989).

I am most grateful to Greta Kinder, my long time secretary, for deciphering my handwritten text and typing the manuscript. Subsequent versions were then efficiently typed by Coral Pepper. My thanks to them both. My old friend Kenneth Rose, historian and wit, suggested the title. Douglas Matthews kindly did the index.

I would like to thank my agent Graham Greene for getting me together with my publisher Ben Glazebrook, who has been a pleasure to work with.

CHAPTER I

The Beginning

SOON after I was elevated – if that is the correct description of so moderate a levitation – to a life peerage, the lowest form of peerage life, Burke published a short account of me accompanied by a pedigree going back at least to 1533 based on a book on the Shawcross family published in 1905. It was considered odd to include me in Burke because I was suspected of being a Socialist, and indeed once was. The editor defended himself by saying it was a perfectly good yeoman pedigree.

Looking through my ancestry to the fourteenth century, the family seems to have come from Denmark to the High Peak district of Derbyshire. There is a small village there called Shallcross (one of many variations on the name) and a Shallcross Hall, a respectable Tudor residence which I had hoped to purchase but which was demolished in 1945 before planning restrictions forbade such vandalism. There is little detail about that early period to be found from studying the family tree, but we seem to have been armigerous from the fourteenth century and I am entitled to the identical arms today.

My father was the youngest son, the thirteenth child, of a mill-owner in Rochdale. The family seems to have had a sense of public responsibility; my grandfather was three times Mayor of Rochdale, apparently a reasonably benevolent employer who bequeathed his home to be converted into a hospital. The eldest son became the first chairman of the National Housing and Town Planning Association. My father was educated at Giggleswick and University College, Oxford where he took a good degree and became a fluent linguist. He intended joining the Foreign Service, and took a high place in the examination for the first division of the Service, but was rejected in the medical examination. Fortunately, he was also rejected for compulsory military service in the First World War, for he would have been hopeless as a soldier. He lived to the age of ninety-five, with no serious health problems. So much for medical examinations.

My mother was, in an unpretentious way, beautiful. She was also gifted and, like my father, completely trilingual. My father had met her in Rochdale in the 1890s. She was the daughter of a Danish mother and an English businessman and at that time was living with the family of John Bright, the local MP, where she was his personal assistant.

These, then, were my parents. They married quietly in Tatsfield, Surrey, in 1900 and went to live in Giessen, then a small university town in Germany, where my father obtained the position of Professor of English Literature. And there, on 4 February 1902, I appear to have been born. I say 'appear to have been' because the evidence is slender. With typical professorial lack of *savoir faire* my birth was not registered with any British consulate or embassy, although it presumably was at the local town hall, which the American Air Force later destroyed during the Second World War. Up in flames went any evidence of my birth. Years afterwards, I paid a formal call on the Burgomaster, who received me courteously with a drinkable bottle of local wine and (having heard of my problem) a framed certificate confirming that the records of the university showed that on 4 February 1902 an English professor of my name did have a son born to his wife.

My father was an academic, very shy and retiring. He and my mother lived very modestly – they had very little money. During my father's life, he published several literary papers, most importantly his edition of Coleridge's *Biographia Literaria*, which the Oxford University Press continued to publish in new impressions year by year until 1989. In 1981 it occurred to me to enquire about the royalties and I was sent a copy of a letter my father had sent the OUP in October 1928 accepting £20 as 'a very fair settlement' of all his rights. It was a mere equivalent of £550 today. He was a German scholar, and one of the leading English authorities on Goethe and Schiller. At the age of eighty-five he published a translation of Goethe's *Faust* in rhyme. He was something of a poet: on the tenth anniversary of his marriage he published privately a collection of ten very moving and very beautiful sonnets dedicated to my mother. To the end, they were very deeply in love with each other, and their example and influence did much to shape the course of my own life.

Soon after my birth my parents returned to live in England, first in a house that later became the Hydro Hotel at the top of Boars Hill, Oxford, and later in a house on Clapham Common. But although they continued to keep a house in London, very early in my life they acquired a cottage in the heart of the Ashdown Forest and, for most of the years that followed, this became the real family home. It was an idyllic place perfectly suited to my parents' introspective natures, although my mother, pursuing her social responsibilities as she saw them, established a small co-operative village industry making jams, cakes and cream toffees. And very good they were.

My mother demonstrated her remarkable strength of character and personal courage even before her marriage. While she was with the Brights, a German maid in their employment was seduced by a visitor and had a male child which the girl registered in her own name and that of the putative father. To be the mother of an illegitimate child was in those days a matter of serious shame and disgrace; for a young unmarried woman to adopt someone else's illegitimate baby was virtually unheard of. Yet my mother showed the compassion and courage that characterized her life and she adopted the child (although there was of course no legal system of adoption in those days). George Bruce grew up and lived as a much-loved member of my family until my father's death.

Nor was that an isolated instance. In the depression following the First World War, my parents adopted a little girl from the East End of London and brought her up as my adopted sister Emily Shawcross. In a quiet way they devoted much of their lives to helping those less fortunate than themselves. I remember how, in the early days of the First World War, my mother helped organize the reception of refugees from Belgium and was responsible for those drafted into the Clapham/Wandsworth area of the city. After the collapse of Germany, where they had been treated with great kindness at the time of my birth, they travelled extensively there (I went with them), and were so moved by the suffering they saw that on returning to England they established a 'German Distress Relief Fund'.

It was in the Ashdown Forest that I and my brother Christopher grew up. Of my education, little can be said for, indeed, there was little of it. It was a free-range business. Certainly, my brother and I were allowed to range free in the Ashdown Forest. We built our tents, played Red Indians, cooked meals and, I fear, sometimes started vast forest fires.

My parents had odd – or should I say 'advanced' – ideas on educa-tion. They seem to have pursued a sort of do-it-yourself technique; cer-tainly I cannot recall any organized lessons before I was ten years old. I remember how one day I was stopped while walking in Clapham by a man who said he was a school inspector. He asked why I was not at school and I told him I did not have one. He seemed astonished and asked peremptorily for my father's name and address. On my giving the address (which was middle-class) he said, 'Oh – that's different,' and quickly walked away. It was pure snobbery. I am sure he would have touched his forelock if he had had one. My brother and I had a most happy, if undisciplined childhood.

I do not remember being taught to read. But read I did. And write. By the age of about ten I had taken up journalism and was writing a monthly 'journal' – an exercise book in which, using the editorial 'we', I expressed my critical views on home and foreign affairs and, later, the war, the misconduct of the Government, and everything else. No doubt, I perverted the views I had heard my parents express, my mother being a non-militant suffragette and my father a Liberal in the John Bright tradition. I circulated this journal to members of my family for sixpence a month, which kept me in sweets.

I recall my first two visits abroad, in 1912 and 1913, accompanying my parents, who were going to 'take the waters' at the hot sulphur springs in Baden, Switzerland. On the way we stayed in Paris at a respectable family hotel. But not for long. My brother and I behaved so badly that we were asked to leave. In Baden things went better. In the Schweizerhof Hotel the electric lift system had been thoughtfully fitted with all-floor buttons on each landing as well as inside the lift, and my brother and I kept ourselves constantly amused by sending passengers up and down. We were obviously odious children; how my poor father must have suffered! He remained tolerant, however, and although I was only about twelve years old I was allowed to go to the local casino where I won forty francs.

At about this time life changed somewhat: I was given a tutor and I sat for the Common Entrance examination at Dulwich College. I recall it well, for I was moved up to the head of the candidates' form on the strength of two simple answers. I was asked to translate 'How are you?' into German. All the other candidates said '*Wie sind sie?*' or '*Wie bist du?*' So I said '*Wie geht es ihnen?*' – and got full marks. I was next asked how to say 'a gentleman' in French. The general consensus amongst the candidates was '*un gentilhomme*' but I preferred '*un homme comme il faut*'. I was admitted to the Lower IV Form Modern. Otherwise, I recall little of my school days – apart from one memorable occasion when a fleet of German Gotha bombers flew across London towards us in broad daylight. We were ranged round the walls of the form, under the instructions of a German form master, an admirable man whom I was frequently able to convince that I had a bad headache and should be allowed to go home.

In the latter part of my time at Dulwich, I started interesting myself in politics and, moving further Left than my parents, joined the local Labour Party and became Ward Secretary for Wandsworth Common, then a pretty solidly Tory area. I actively canvassed it – at the age of sixteen! – during the 1918 general election. I hardly think my political activities benefited me much at Dulwich, except perhaps for the essays I wrote on current affairs, a subject in which I rather fancied myself. Nonetheless, more by luck than learning, I did pass the Matriculation Examination.

This was soon after the end of the World War and two events arose at this time which were to affect my subsequent life. The first was that at the general election in 1922 I became (with doubtful legality, for I was still under age and the post was a responsible one) the official election agent for one Lewis Silkin, the candidate of the Labour Party in Wandsworth. He was a fairly young solicitor, very fat as I remember (I drove him around at reckless speeds on a motor cycle and sidecar) and a man of character and ability who eventually became Minister of Town and Country Planning in the Attlee Government. Needless to say, Lewis Silkin was heavily defeated by the Tory, Sir John Norton Griffiths, or 'Empire Jack' as he was called. Griffiths was an agreeable candidate, though a man of little intellectual ability, and I would sometimes attend his meetings in order to heckle. Twenty-three years later, when I sought selection as a rather improbable Labour candidate in the 1945 election, that early apprenticeship in Labour politics stood me in good stead. Unknown to me, the local Labour Party in St Helens communicated with Wandsworth where I was still remembered, fortunately, and appear to have been given a glowing testimonial.

Once the excitement of that election was over, I had to decide what I was going to do. It was then that I made one of the many mistakes of a misspent life. I should have gone on to Oxford. My parents, although living on 'private means' which were steadily declining, would at some sacrifice have supported me, as they later did my younger brother, and I believe I would have benefited greatly from three years at my father's old college. But I was in a hurry and felt that it was better to commence a directly vocational training than to spend time at Oxford. It was a mistake that I have deeply regretted since, for I now realize how much I have missed in life through not having had the advantage of a university education: residence in a university seems to me now a marvellous introduction to a civilized life. This decision made, however, I had to decide what walk of life I would choose. My parents hoped that I might choose medicine, or the law, for my mother's grandfather had been a senior judge (I think Chief Justice) in Denmark. I decided on medicine, no doubt thinking that I should have an excellent bedside manner, and entered myself to commence studies at Barts (St Bartholomew's Hospital).

The new term did not begin until the autumn, nine months ahead. During that interesting period I was sent to Geneva, to live with a French family and to study French at Geneva University. I recall a very happy summer mostly spent sitting in cafés watching the young Genevese girls passing by.

In a very different sense, the nine months did prove a most important gestatory period for me. Towards the end of the summer the first postwar meeting of what was called the 2nd Socialist International – a gathering of leading Socialists from many countries – took place in Geneva. I offered my services free of charge, as a French/English interpreter, and was quite readily accepted. It is conceivable that the presence of this young English schoolboy acting as an interpreter may have caused some amusement to the English delegation, which included Ramsay MacDonald, Herbert Morrison and J. H. Thomas. At all events, to reward me for having acted in this way, I was invited to join a special steamer excursion on Lake Geneva. During the trip Herbert Morrison kindly concerned himself with me and I confided to him my political interests. Did I want to go into Parliament? On my saying that indeed I did, he advised me against being a doctor. He advised me to go for the Bar.

The next day I sent a telegram to my doubtless surprised parents to say that I had changed my mind. Medicine was not for me. I was going to become a barrister. In due course I returned to London and joined Gray's Inn. I do not think I saw Herbert Morrison again until the Second World War, though we later became firm friends.

Some years later still, it was my friendship with Herbert Morrison which prompted me not to stand for the leadership of the Labour Party, and thus I missed the opportunity of the highest office. I do not regret this, though I sometimes think I may have lacked the ambition to do worthwhile things. This book is about some of the things I have done.

CHAPTER 2

Gray's Inn – Marriage

AND so I became a member of Gray's Inn. Intensely shy, as I still am, I nonetheless managed soon to enter into student life, although at first I did little study. Life was fun. I joined the Debating Society and well remember my first attempt at a speech. I was tongue-tied, inarticulate, and very emotional. The debate was about German reparations and I had just returned from the trip through Germany with my parents which had prompted them to set up a relief fund. I, too, had been moved by the obvious privations – communal feeding, soup trolleys, and so on – under which most of the people of that defeated country were still living. However, the Debating Society was very informal and its members were kind to me. In due course, I became its Secretary and for some years its President. It provided excellent – and in those days, the only – training in public speaking. For a time, I was also President of the Field Club. I am delighted to know that both societies still flourish. Gray's Inn was small but it was noted – as it still is – for its sociable atmosphere and the interest it took in its students.

One practical circumstance led me to develop my preference for dining with young women rather than men. Dinner in Hall is one of the features of life at the Inns of Court. Indeed, it was compulsory then for students to dine at least six times a term. I dined as often as I could afford. At dinner, the members are organized in 'messes' of four, sitting at long tables, and one of the traditions is for the Senior of each mess to toast the members of the messes above and below his own. For this purpose each mess of four was given a bottle of red wine (often quite drinkable claret) and a decanter of port. In those early days of women's emancipation female students did not usually drink wine, or drank very little. Accordingly, I adopted the practice of organizing my mess to include three girls. This meant that I had a bottle of claret and ample port more or less for myself – as well as three pretty girls. Moreover, when dinner was over, members of Hall in those days usually stayed on for some time in convivial conversation with each other. This was an occasion for staid frivolity during which, if he so wished, a member (student or barrister) could bring a charge against another that he had broken some ancient tradition of the Inn. It was a rule that members dining must wear dark suits. I frequently spotted diners who were, in my rather colour-blind view, not so attired. This was always an easy ground for a charge.

One of my frequent victims was David Maxwell Fyfe, a man with whom I was later to share a room and lead at Nuremberg. He eventually became Lord Chancellor. He was a man entirely lacking any sense of humour and invariably wore black pin-striped trousers. 'Mr Senior, sir,' I would stand up and say, 'I deeply regret to have to draw your attention to a grave breach of the ancient traditions of our House. There is present tonight a Mr Maxwell, also calling himself Mr Fyfe, or Maxwell & Fyfe Limited, or whatever. The name is of no significance but what will, I fear, shock you as it has shocked me is that he has had the temerity, the rashness, nay the effrontery to come here tonight wearing white trousers with a black stripe. I submit that he should be severely fined.' After the defendant had replied to the charge, the Senior gave his decision, which was usually, and regardless of the justice of the matter, to find the charge proved and to impose a fine of a bottle of wine, usually awarded to the mess whose Senior had brought the charge. I found this a most useful way of supplementing the wine ration during the course of a long evening. And it also gave one a little practice in impromptu speaking with a lightheartedness that I have never been able to display elsewhere.

Another happy incident that I recall from the Gray's Inn days was winning a motorcycle for half a crown in a raffle. Half a crown was, incidentally, the most useful of coins – a largish silver piece worth what in those days was called two shillings and sixpence. Never did I spend a half-crown to better purpose than in that raffle. It was a second-hand Douglas motorcycle. I took it to pieces many times; usually I found when fitting it together again that there were parts left over, but the

Douglas seemed to go better without them. I fitted a more noisy exhaust. Why do motorcycle-owners always favour noisy exhausts? I thought at the time that mine made a splendid noise. Now, of course, I think that they should be altogether forbidden by law. I fitted a comfortable pillion seat, and spent many a happy day driving along the then almost empty roads for a country picnic with a pretty girl on the back. Since then I have owned cars and yachts but I doubt whether I ever got as much fun out of them as I did from my half-crown Douglas.

And so at Gray's Inn life went on, carefree and cheerful, until an event occurred which set me on a more serious course: I fell in love.

I remember the occasion quite vividly. We had a Summer Ball at Gray's Inn, the ancient Hall decked out with roses, when I saw, coming through the doorway into the Hall from the Benchers' rooms, a girl who immediately attracted my attention. Not perhaps a classical beauty: a little frail; not particularly sophisticated; not extravagantly dressed – but with a simple loveliness and charm, a sweetness all her own. Alberta Rosita Shyvers was the sister of a student of the Inn, one of the girls who regularly dined in my mess, the eldest of nine daughters of a Roman Catholic family. Her father was a ship-broker. She lived with her family in the country, and despite her frailty and her slight limp, which I was told was due to a mild attack of polio in early childhood, she had a horse and rode a little, although she did not hunt. Within a few weeks we were engaged; within a few months, in May 1924, we married – on a joint income of £300 a year.

That ball at Gray's Inn marked the point at which I at last turned to serious and hard work. The Bar examinations in those days must have been much easier than they are now, for I obtained first-class honours in each of them and won a prize of £100 (which I gave proudly to my mother) for the best paper in Criminal Law and for being the top First with a Certificate of Honour in the Bar Final. I was called to the Bar in 1925.

Sadly, however, life was not treating the person I loved quite as well. I had realized that Alberta was frail but neither she nor I knew before we married how ill she was. There were varied problems. One was that some congenital malformation incapable of remedy by operation – although she bravely submitted to one – made her unable to bear children or have sexual intercourse. My wife and I were good companions.

The absence of sex made no real difference; the important thing in my marriage, as it must be in all successful marriages, was mutual love, understanding and companionship. As time went on, she had to submit to one serious operation after another including, quite unnecessarily by modern practice, a double mastectomy. She bore all this far more courageously than I did.

We lived together first in a small flat in Elm Park Gardens in Chelsea. Alberta looked after it and did the cooking, and I obtained some parttime lectureships in law to supplement our meagre income. Eventually I bought a Morris Cowley to which I added an aluminium bonnet and aluminium disc wheels, and we toured about the country in this vulgar barouche at weekends, accompanied by an enormous St Bernard dog. Wildly extravagant, I soon acquired another car, a very flashy LeaFrancis sports car which was white with long front wings in red, and which I drove at reckless speeds. Before long, we acquired a lease of a little Tudor cottage in the causeway close to the church at Cuckfield in Sussex, and close enough to my parents' home in the Ashdown Forest to visit them most weekends. During the week I 'commuted' to London and we lived happily together in spite of my wife's illhealth. Neither of us realized then the darkening cloud of illness that hung over her.

CHAPTER 3

The Bar

FOR the first three years I practised in London. Or tried to. Although I was in the same excellent chambers where I had been a pupil of St John Field, a leading Junior, and where Gerald Gardiner (eventually a Labour Lord Chancellor but at that time thought – wrongly – to be rather attracted by the Fascists) was also a pupil, I got no work. Indeed, even today, I have still not been paid for my first case, which I won for an important firm of City solicitors. During this period, in order to eke out our meagre income, I did a little coaching for the Bar examinations.

I had in all perhaps six pupils and of these I remember three young men who, I was vaguely aware, came from Asian countries. Alas, during the time I coached them, none of them passed his examinations. I felt that they were very charming and agreeable but perhaps inclined to be playboys. I was reminded of their existence many years later in the 1950s when I had occasion to write to the then Prime Minister of Malaysia, Tunku Abdul Rahman. He promptly sent a detailed reply to my letter and then added in a postcript in his own hand, 'I suppose you remember that in the 1920s I was one of your pupils for the Bar examina-tions.' I had indeed quite forgotten. In fact, the three young men were all Malaysian princes, one of the others being the first Agong – King of the Malaysian States. After receiving this letter I naturally called on him when I was next in Malaysia and we became quite close friends. He sometimes lent my wife and myself a house on the beach near Penang, where he himself had his main home, and whenever we were in Malaysia he insisted on giving a dinner party that invariably included not only caviar but also, as an acknowledgement of our English associations, roast beef which he always cooked himself. The Tunku also enjoyed the more simple things in life; he kept racehorses and was a keen gambler until the end of his long life. Although not very successful in his Bar examinations he was a very great man who played the leading and critical role in the development of Malaysia as a free democracy and who, together with General Templer, saved the country from being overrun by the Communists. Certainly Malaysia owes a great deal to him. He was a giant, his successors comparative pygmies.

But coaching was not my line and, as the London Bar seemed to hold out no hopes, I let it be known to the benchers of Gray's Inn that I might, reluctantly, have to switch to an academic career. There soon followed an invitation to take an appointment to teach law at Christ Church, Oxford. This was on the recommendation of Lord Birkenhead, to whose notice I had first come when I had spoken for the students in a toast in his honour on the occasion of a dinner to celebrate his earldom. I remember comparing him to an earlier Master of the Bench – the famous Francis Bacon – and I called him a jurist. He replied that he had never been so insulted in his life. He said Bacon had entered Gray's Inn as a bankrupt – this was rather near the bone since there was gossip about his own financial stability. As for 'jurists' they were foreign people, possibly from the Continent, who knew nothing of the principles of English law – or any other principles. Nonetheless, 'F.E.' very kindly interested himself in my career.

However, the job at Christ Church would have meant giving up the Bar altogether, and at about the same time a part-time lectureship at Liverpool University became available. I applied, and entirely through the influence of another bencher of Gray's Inn, then the Chancellor of the County Palatine Court, who happened to be the Chairman of the Selection Committee, I was given the appointment, although far less qualified than other candidates, one of whom is now President of the International Court of Justice at the Hague. It suited me well. The hours of my lectures I fixed late in the afternoons so that I could be free for court work, however inconvenient this was for the students. I taught Roman Law, of which I knew nothing but taught myself from lecture to lecture, as well as Constitutional Law, in which I was interested, and Private International Law.

My real practice at the Bar began in late 1927 when I joined the

Northern Circuit and 'localized' in Liverpool. This was in itself a formidable step, for the Northern Circuit was then – as indeed it always has been – very strong. Among those in practice then as Juniors were several who were soon to become Silks and then judges, like Lynskey, Sellars, Gorman, Pritchard, Nield, and many others. There would, I knew, be the strongest competition.

I was afraid that it would also mean a break for my wife from her family and friends. However, the risks had to be taken and the general circumstances were good. A minimum subsistence was assured by the salary from my part-time lectureship. In addition we were fortunate indeed in that a cousin, Harold Darbishire, who had married Hester, one of the Bright family, very kindly lent me what had been a lodge cottage on their beautiful estate on Windyhill, Caldy, on the Wirral peninsula. Moving into a strange environment, our lot was made the more agreeable by the fact that my father, whose declining private means compelled him to add to his income, was, by a very happy coincidence, also appointed at the same time to a lectureship in English literature at Liverpool University. He was able to live with us during term time, returning to my mother in Susex for vacations, and so life was less lonely both for him and for my wife. Fortunately, Professor Raleigh Batt, the Dean of the Law School, who had frankly told me that he had voted against my appointment, also became a great and life-long friend, and he was most helpful to Alberta.

Before going up to Liverpool I had made enquiries about chambers, and John Singleton, a leading KC soon to become a High Court judge, proposed me for membership of the circuit. I was duly elected with the traditional toast, 'Congratulations or condolences, as the case may be.' He also suggested the chambers of David Maxwell Fyfe, where there were only two or three other barristers.

Fyfe had not forgotten the Gray's Inn badinage, but he readily agreed to take me, for the first six months nominally as a pupil and later as a tenant. I had a desk in his room which I shared with him throughout the time he remained a Junior. From my point of view – and perhaps his – it turned out to be a good arrangement.

It was a very mixed practice: like most at the local Bar we took any-thing on the common law/criminal side – or indeed anything on any side! – which came along. Local solicitors frequently came in for confer-

ences, and I was introduced to them. This helped the clerk to the chambers to pick up briefs for me, and these did come in at an encouraging
rate.

I got to know David Maxwell Fyfe well and became friendly with
him, although never intimately so. He was the most intensely ambitious
man I ever knew, and he had married an extremely clever and equally
ambitious Liverpool woman, the daughter of a local businessman. Both
were members of the Conservative Party and David eventually became
a Cabinet Minister at the Home Office. His wife, Sylvia, became the
chairman of the women's section of the Party. They both worked
extremely hard to further their ambitions. One practice that amused me
was that they regularly had seats at the Liverpool Empire Theatre, and
were to be found there almost every Saturday evening, the object of the
exercise – so it was said – being not so much to enjoy the plays as to ingra-
tiate themselves with local notables. At the interval they would stand up
and look round the auditorium. 'That is Alderman Snooks,' David
would apparently say to Sylvia, 'you should bow to him.' Or 'That is
Mr Smith, senior partner in Smith and Brown, leading solicitors. They
ought to be clients. Bow to him.' The only people they did not bow to,
on the rare occasions we went to the theatre, were my wife and myself.

David's political ambitions prospered, and he was adopted as the candidate for Spen Valley, though in a by-election in that constituency he
very wisely stood down in favour of John Simon, as the eventual Lord
Chancellor then was. This later helped to secure his adoption for the
Liverpool constituency of West Derby, and Fyfe himself eventually
ended up as Lord Chancellor. There was a small problem when the
election came in 1935. The local Party required a financial subvention
of up to £1,000 from its candidate. David at the time had no money
available. We talked about the problem and it happened, as far as I recall
for the first and almost the only time in my life, that I had a small credit
balance in the bank and was able to lend him £300 or £400, a sum that
sounds small enough now but which was quite significant for both of us
then. He was duly elected and did in the end pay me back, although not
without being reminded.

Nobody, I think, would have considered David Fyfe a great lawyer.
When, in later years, I was sometimes asked to propose his health at
public functions, and wished to tease him, I used to say that all the law

he knew was what I had taught him when we shared a room – for in those days I had 'devilled' many of his more difficult Legal Advices. This toast could then be taken one of two ways. Either that I was myself a brilliant lawyer and Fyfe was in the same tradition, or that I knew no law and so he could know none. The latter was the better view.

My first case in Liverpool was an affair before Mr Registrar Cripps of the Court of Passage. This was a local but historical court with unlimited civil jurisdiction, and much civil litigation went there rather than to the High Court. It was presided over by perhaps the most distinguished judge I have known, Sir Francis Kyffin Taylor, who later became Lord Maenan. He was a gentleman of the old school and a great lawyer, and he taught me all I know of the art and responsibility of advocacy. This case was a trivial enough affair, although I spoke of it later as an important commercial case. It concerned a parrot that my Chinese client had sold but had not been paid for, the defence being that the parrot did not talk, as it had been warranted to do. In court, however, the bird did give voice and the Registrar gave judgement for my client, remarking that he liked the parrot's way of loyally repeating the name of his former owner, Ah Fook.

Some time later I took on the case of a Mr Inman, a man of somewhat violent habit who, although he had already received one sentence of flogging, was inclined to board the local omnibus with a beer bottle which, when emptied, he was wont to use to knock other passengers on the head in a more or less friendly way. He did this rather severely on one occasion with the result that his victim was hospitalized and he was indicted for causing grievous bodily harm. I was briefed to defend him in what would normally have been a very minor case. Unfortunately, however, the victim died in hospital and the indictment became one of murder; David Fyfe was prosecuting. I was still very young and I foolishly got it into my head that the man had died through medical neglect. This was tantamount to an attack on the doctors, a very unwise course unless there is overwhelming evidence. And I added to my offence by having all professional witnesses out of court – thus implying that they were potential liars. The judge did not like my tactics at all and rebuked me personally in summing up for a conviction. As it was, the jury brought in a verdict of manslaughter. It was a lesson for both Mr Inman and me. He was, I hope, more careful in his future use of beer bottles, and I learned never to identify myself with my clients – itself a most important rule for a barrister.

Not long after this there was a case that became the sensation of the local press. In Liverpool at that time there was a certain Canon Fraser who had a great reputation for being against things. He was a man of very strict principles. He always opposed applications for liquor licences – which happened to be a regular and lucrative source of briefs for both Fyfe and myself. If there was any kind of local 'beano' or jollification, the Canon could be trusted to lead the opposition to it. He had a son, whom he had brought up very strictly, and also a maid. In due course the maid gave birth to twins of which she alleged Canon Fraser's son was the father. He denied it and she brought bastardy proceedings. The brief for her was offered first to David Fyfe, who refused it, explaining to me that the publicity would be very damaging – for him. In the event the case was first heard by the local magistrates, a solicitor appearing for the maid. The magistrates found against her, whereupon she exercised her right of appeal to quarter sessions. I was briefed to appear for the young woman.

The Recorder of the City, Hemmerde, was a most distinguished Silk and certainly the most cultured one on the circuit at that time. He presided at the Appeal and the case received great publicity as 'The Fraser Twins Case'. I had the plaintiff and her twins brought into court and placed in the front row under the very eyes of the Recorder, arguing that the physical appearance of the twins closely resembled that of the Canon's son and was admissible evidence that he was the father. His counsel, Fred Pritchard, a leading Junior and afterwards a High Court judge, argued strongly that this was not legal evidence and that the question as to whether there was any facial resemblance, which, he contended, there was not, was legally irrelevant. The Recorder said he accepted this argument and would completely reject the physical characteristics of the twins as a factor in the case. The general evidence was strongly contested on both sides. One thing I believed at the time did carry some weight – although it was entirely prejudicial – namely, that the Canon, in the course of evidence he chose to give attacking the character of the girl, brought out the fact that she had herself been illegitimate. I cross-examined him as to how he knew this was so and he was forced to admit that it was because he had himself baptized the girl.

I then asked him whether he thought he had acted in a Christian way in revealing her illegitimacy when he himself had known of it only because he was her priest. The wretched Canon collapsed in the witness box. Eventually, the Recorder found that the twins were indeed the Fraser twins and allowed the appeal. A sizeable crowd outside St George's Hall, where the case had been heard, cheered me as I left the court. Hemmerde, Pritchard and I proceeded to have dinner together that evening at the North Western Hotel, and Hemmerde remarked that he had never seen babies who were so much the spitting image of their father as the two Fraser twins. The evidence of personal resemblance in this case was certainly arguable or I would not have introduced it: I have always had a strong view that it is the duty of the Bar to assist the court and not to mislead the judge in any way as to the relevant law or the facts. In this case, in any event, there was abundant other evidence to justify the Recorder's decision.

My wife's health received another setback. The specialists diagnosed that she had a form of glandular tuberculosis and she was sent to Leysin in Switzerland for sunlight treatment under the care of the famous Dr Rollier. After two long winters there, during which I frequently visited her, she was much better, having put on weight and appearing, for her, really well. Thus encouraged, in about 1930 we acquired a delightful old house in Cornwall, at Treath on the Helford river.

Things seemed to be going well again. We had a good house in Liverpool and Alberta enjoyed a sporty little MG car; I had a splendid Railton coupé capable of great speed; and the holiday home in Cornwall was on a famous yachting river where I had, first, a cut-down six-metre yacht and then a fully rigged eight-metre, bought specially to beat the local sailing grandee in the regattas. Yachting had always been a favourite hobby – I had taught myself to sail in Poole harbour when I was about ten. My mother's sister was partner in a girls' school at Bournemouth, called Redmoor, and my family had always spent the summer holidays in one of the school houses, hence my love of the sea.

In addition, I bought from British Power Boats a beautiful mahogany sea-going speedboat with a splendid dual-ignition Meadows engine. We acquired a wonderful skipper, Walter Paull, a brilliant sailor who remained with me as skipper and friend until he died aged over 80. But the almost carefree respite was short-lived: this happiness was not to last.

More serious work began to flow in. This included, to my gratification, cases for the Crown where I had been nominated by the Attorney
General of the day. The practice was for the Attorney to nominate
counsel to appear in all cases for Government departments or for the
Director of Public Prosecutions. Whether the Attorney General still
does this, or indeed whether he now does anything connected with court
work, I am not sure. The office has greatly changed. But in those days it
was the recognized rule and a matter of some satisfaction to know that
one was on the Attorney's list. How one got on to it was never stated.
Sometimes no doubt it was by political influence: kissing goes by favour.
Sometimes no doubt it was because some judge or other, or possibly
several, had noted that a young barrister was doing well and reported the
fact to the Attorney.

A number of prosecutions in murder cases came my way, as well as
the occasional important case for the Bank of England or the like. In
1935 I was thus appointed Junior in a murder prosecution in which I
was led by J. C. Jackson, KC, a well-known and engaging Northern
Circuit Silk who gave me the coveted Red Bag for my help. And the
next year came the Junior brief in the murder trial of Doctor 'Buck'
Ruxton, which excited great public interest.

Ruxton was of Indian extraction and was a very popular doctor in
Lancaster. He killed his wife and cut her body up into small pieces,
doing the same for a maid who had apparently interrupted the process.
To these remains he added a Cyclops eye which he had preserved as a
specimen of medical curiosity, and proceeded to transport the lot in his
car to a bridge on a road near Dumfries, from which he dumped it into
a ravine, where it was found by some wandering tourist. Ruxton was
eventually arrested and tried for murder at Lancaster Assizes. He was
defended by Norman Birkett, the leading criminal advocate of the day,
who did not call Ruxton as a witness, perhaps because he had admitted
his guilt to him, or perhaps because Birkett attached the greatest importance to having the last word before the summing-up. He did make a
remarkable and memorable speech for the defence. I listened in admiration, if not in awe, never having seen before so many bricks made without
straw. I know that Norman had no doubt as to Ruxton's guilt, but he
knew, as all good advocates must, that he should never allow his personal
view to affect his advocacy. This was a gift I could never quite acquire.

In spite of the brilliant defence, Ruxton was convicted and hanged. Although he said that he was innocent – 'As God is my judge' – it turned out after his execution that he had sold a long confession to a Sunday paper, which paid Birkett's fees. I played little part in the case myself, being a Junior to J. C. Jackson, KC, and Maxwell Fyfe. My main recollection of it now is that the Lancashire police, in a fit of unnecessary enthusiasm, insisted on driving me up to Dumfries to see the ravine, which had been emptied of the bodily remains. It was the fastest drive I ever remember, and we crossed through every red light on the way, but somehow I emerged, shaken but undamaged.

In all, on one side or the other, I was involved in about twenty murder trials. I had always been against the death penalty but at that time my task was simply concerned with the administration of the law as it existed. Later on, when I was Attorney General, I took a leading part in the movement to abolish capital punishment, which eventually was suspended in 1965. Today I am not quite so confident about it, but I think that the very grave increase in the number of murders is the result of the general increase in violence throughout the world, itself partly the result of war and partly of the fact that the criminal feels that he will not be caught anyway, which makes the penalty irrelevant.

In the mid-1930s I was trying gradually to avoid having to do criminal work so as to concentrate on civil work. In 1933 Fyfe took Silk and the chambers split up. Basil Nield, who later became a High Court judge, remained in Harrington Street and I established a new set, beautifully furnished and with smart, newly bound Law Reports to match the furnishings, at 43 Castle Street, together with Dick Trotter and Melville Kennan (who both became County Court judges). We were also joined by Rose Heilbron, later to become the first woman appointed to the High Court Bench. We were a progressive and successful set of chambers and I soon had my first pupil, Daniel Brabin, who later became a High Court judge. Very sadly, he died prematurely of a heart problem, thus cutting short a brilliant career. I missed his friendship and support greatly, but still enjoy that of his widow, Mary, who has to this day been a marvellous, loving friend to me and my children. By this time I was able to give up the university job, having in the meantime been awarded a degree by Liverpool University, in order to concentrate entirely on the Bar.

Being the head of my own Chambers no doubt added to my standing and encouraged the flow of work. I had already been doing licens-
ing cases for Bents and other breweries. This was lucrative work,
particularly in connection with the applications for liquor licences in
new housing estates. There was almost a tradition in the Liverpool of
those days that the head of Bents Brewery was also the leader of the City
Council, which was then Conservative. This resulted in a remarkable
ability to foresee where a new housing estate would be built and what
public houses might be required in it – profitable work all round. This
sort of commission led to my being briefed from time to time by local
businessmen and industrial leaders. Thus Sir Thomas White, then
Conservative leader of the City Council, once instructed me in a libel
action he insisted on bringing against Randolph Churchill, who later
himself became a friend and client of mine. I have quite forgotten what
the libel was. Randolph apologized but said Sir Thomas had called him
a Casanova and he should also apologise. White instantly replied,
'Certainly. I don't know what a Casanova is, but if anyone called me
one I should be much flattered.' The discomfited Randolph had to join
in the laughter.

Soon after establishing myself in the new chambers, there occurred a
terrible event in which I became professionally involved. This was the
Gresford Colliery disaster in 1934 in which 265 miners lost their lives
as a result of a gas explosion. In due course a Government inquiry was
set up under the Chief Inspector of Mines, and I was briefed to represent the mine-owners, a North Wales family company. I already had
some little knowledge of mining techniques, having been down several
pits in connection with cases in which I had been briefed on behalf of
the owners. This could not be said of the Silk who was brought in to
lead me, A. T. Miller, KC. He was probably the leading commercial
Silk of that time, a man of great distinction and a specialist in his field.
My brother Christopher, who followed me to the Bar, was in his
Chambers. But Miller's field had nothing to do with mining accidents.
He came to Gresford and went down the remaining and little-damaged
part of the pit for a view. He did not enjoy it, and realized at once that
the case was not for him. He therefore quite rightly immediately with-
drew and returned his brief. The owners decided not to seek another
Leader and to let me do the case on my own. This was the classical

opportunity for which Juniors are supposed to hope. I found myself arrayed against the famous Stafford Cripps, who was giving his services free to the Miners Union, and thus I was obviously confronted with a considerable challenge. The Inquiry lasted about thirty days and at the end of it Cripps and then I made speeches lasting, I think, over three days each. I can only say that somehow I managed to hold my own.

Although grossly exaggerated, accounts of the disaster with pointed political innuendo have since been published. It must be admitted that this was a bad case of negligence involving cost-cutting economies on safety matters and breaches of the innumerable statutory regulations. On the other hand, the numerous miners called as witnesses tended, as perhaps the Welsh are occasionally inclined to do, greatly to exaggerate the dangerous conditions in the mine, which to some extent discredited their own evidence. The Chief Inspector's Report was followed by a prosecution of the owners and manager before the Wrexham magis-trates for a number of quite serious offences. There were forty-two sum-monses in all. The Government considered the case sufficiently important (as indeed it was) to justify the Solicitor General, Sir Terence O'Connor, KC, MP – a charming Irishman – coming down to pros-ecute. In turn, I was led by Sir Patrick Hastings, the famous Silk whose Chambers I was later to join. He was brilliant. I recall he made the shortest cross-examination I have ever heard. A witness, an expert in mining technology, gave fairly detailed and elaborate evidence about the inadequate system of ventilation in the mine. When he had finished his evidence in chief, Patrick Hastings rose to cross-examine. He said, 'You are a lecturer, are you not?' The witness agreed that he was indeed a lec-turer. 'I thought so,' said Patrick, and sat down. It was of course quite unfair, but it left the magistrates with the impression that they had been lectured to.

What perhaps finally turned the case generally more in favour of the mine-owners was a curious incident with a miner's lamp. These little oil-fed lamps are carried by every miner underground, their purpose being not so much to light the way, for they give out little light, as to detect the presence of methane. This gas is given off by the coal and ought to be carried away by efficient ventilation. If the gas is present in danger-ous quantities the lamp goes out, thus warning the miner. During the Inquiry, miner after miner gave evidence that the lamps were constantly going out. This evidence was somewhat tainted by the fact that the miners and their safety officials had done nothing about it. We sought to suggest by cross-examining the witnesses that the lamps would go out for other reasons, such as careless handling, being knocked against the walls, and so on. The Solicitor General, having been told of this line of explanation, attempted to destroy it. On the third day of the trial, when we went into court, there was a miner's lamp, lit, on the bench between him and the magistrates.

'It is quite nonsense,' the Solicitor General said to the magistrates, 'that these lamps go out accidentally. They are designed not to, their purpose being to extinguish themselves only in the presence of gas. They are robust instruments made for that purpose.' He then picked up the lamp, quite gently. It immediately went out. A shade nonplussed, he secured and lit another lamp. On his picking it up it also immediately went out. A third lamp was produced, and we could hardly believe our eyes when that also went out. In the end most of the summonses were dismissed. Ten were left and the only penalty imposed was a fine of £140 against the company for failing to keep a proper record of some detail or other and £15 against the manager. I can understand why many people were shocked at the outcome.

After this case I was regarded as something of an expert in industrial accidents and was subsequently briefed in one or two other mine disasters, although none nearly so serious as Gresford. To my gratification, for it showed the Union had not taken amiss my appearance for the owners, I was also briefed to go 'special' (meaning on a different circuit) for the Miners Union in an accident at another pit. Although the Gresford case had kept me away from my more normal practice for several weeks, cases continued to come in.

But then came the blow. In 1937, while I was at my practice in Liverpool, Alberta was spending part of the summer in Cornwall, in the garden and 'messing about' in a little boat. Then a new symptom developed. She telephoned me about it and after consulting Henry Cohen, the famous physician who was then Professor of Medicine at Liverpool University and my best friend, I had her flown up. Henry had no doubt about the diagnosis. It was the dreaded multiple sclerosis – possibly a recurrence after an unusually long remission – which had caused her earlier lameness. He told me she might possibly live for seven years, but would be increasingly disabled. It was a terrible blow. I took her to specialist after specialist for a different diagnosis or some hope of a cure. There was none. I had to make the best plans I could to meet this heartbreaking situation which she continued to face far more bravely than I could.

In 1938, I am sorry to say that at first I rejoiced in the Munich settlement, for although I felt that nothing would, ultimately, stop Hitler, Munich did at least postpone the evil day and gave me a little further time to make plans to meet my domestic problems.

I asked to see Sir Francis Kyffin Taylor, told him I was thinking of applying for Silk (i.e. to become a KC who wears a silk gown) but that I doubted whether I was fit. 'You are fit,' he said. 'Go forward.' Accordingly, I applied for a silk gown with the recommendation of Sir Francis and of several judges and was awarded Silk early in 1939. I was the youngest of a small handful awarded silk gowns at the time. It was then very much more of a distinction than now; there were 845 Silks in 1994, which seems a terrible depreciation of the currency.

Soon after I got Silk I was elected to be a Master of the Bench at Gray's Inn, which was most gratifying. We moved to Horsham, nearer to my wife's family and friends, and I obtained Chambers in London and started on the second stage of my professional career. It was something of a gamble, for a successful junior barrister is not always good in the front row. And in my case, because of my wife's illness, I was doing it a year or two earlier than I otherwise would. As it turned out, however, I was lucky at least in this, that the briefs continued to flow in.

CHAPTER 4

The War

AT the outbreak of war Alberta and I were at our Cornish home. It was the long vacation in the Courts. I had always managed to take the whole two months of the long vacation, which I rarely allowed to be interrupted.

In 1939, I realized very well that war was imminent. The Nazi/Soviet treaty had made it inevitable. War was declared on a Sunday, and I recall sitting on the quay at Treath with a portable radio and listening with a sense of inevitable fatality to Neville Chamberlain's speech.

My skipper, Walter Paull, reacted differently. He was a splendid man, brought up on the sea. His father had been a coal merchant in Falmouth and had owned a small coasting vessel, originally all sail, which plied up and down the east coast bringing coal back from Newcastle. Walter had been brought up on the boat from early childhood, when his father used to send him up the mast in every kind of weather to attend to the gaff rigging and so on. What he did not know about sailing, the weather, the ways of the sea, was not worth knowing. And he was an experienced racing tactician also, having regularly sailed in the J Class and other large yachts during the racing season. As I have said, he was my most loyal skipper and friend in a succession of boats which he kept in excellent shape, most of them beautiful wooden yachts built by the famous Fife yard of Fairlie.

On that particular Sunday we were preparing for a regatta to be held the next day. It was, of course, at once cancelled. I rowed out to my boat, the eight-metre *Caryl*. Paull was putting her sails in stops and getting ready for the race. We hoped, for the first time, to beat the only other eight-metre in those waters, a boat owned by the elderly, vain and intensely jealous Commodore of the Royal Falmouth Yacht Club. I told Paull the news. He was shocked. But not about the war. 'Fancy cancelling a regatta for a thing like that,' he exclaimed, a true believer in the Francis Drake tradition.

It was not only the Regatta which had to be cancelled. I reached, as I often do, hasty and wrong decisions. In 1937, believing that a war was most likely to occur, I had put my name down for what was called the Emergency Reserve of Officers, indicating a preference for the Navy. My brother Christopher did the same. When war finally broke out I expected that I would soon be called up. In any event, I thought, we would have to leave Cornwall and were unlikely to see it again. We sold up, lock, stock and barrel. I should have held on. We laid the boats up in Falmouth (the Navy later commandeered the speedboat), and moved back to Horsham. There we were joined by Geoffrey Vickers, VC, a leading solicitor, and his wife, an old friend of my wife's. We had already built an air-raid shelter in the garden, but I do not recall that it was ever used.

I had received, within a day or two of the declaration of war, a letter from Sir Claude Schuster, the head of the Lord Chancellor's Department. He requested me to take charge of one of the many tribunals that the Government was about to set up to examine enemy aliens: in the preceding few years refugees from Hitler's anti-Semitic policies had come over in great numbers and the Government was worried that their number might include spies or other undesirables. He also asked me to advise on the suitability of other Silks, all senior to myself, for this work. It was remarkable that I, the youngest Silk, should have come to the notice of so august a figure. But some years earlier, in about 1937, I had been one of a deputation sent by the Liverpool Bar to the Lord Chancellor to complain about a certain County Court Judge in Cheshire whom I will call RW. His conduct was a scandal. He had favourites among the advocates who appeared before him. One in particular, a barrister believed to be a relation but with no notable ability, invariably won his cases before this judge. This fact soon got around, with the result that local solicitors with cases in this judge's court sent this barrister all their briefs, although his practice in other courts remained non-existent. If one had the temerity to disagree with any of the judge's rulings, he would adjourn the case to the bottom of the day's list so that it would not be reached at all. He was a consistently unjust judge.

The deputation consisted of a very senior member of the local Bar, O. G. Morris, and me, still young and not yet in Silk. We were received by Sir Claude Schuster. He was a most distinguished man: very able and in the old tradition. He appeared very shocked that the Bar should have the temerity to complain about a judge. He said that he assumed we had told the Press and that there would be a public scandal. My senior companion rather shrank under this attack and the argument fell to me. I assured Schuster that we had done no such thing and that we appreci-ated the delicacy of the situation; but we feared that the Press would soon unearth the scandal for itself. We finished the interview feeling we had been issued with a rebuke. However, our argument must have recom-mended itself to Schuster in some way. RW soon ceased to be a Presiding Judge and the clients of his barrister friend seemed to fold their tents like the Arabs and as silently stole away.

I was appointed to preside over the Tribunal which was set up for the Golders Green/Hampstead area of London. It contained far more refugees than any other area. I was supplied with a service gas mask, which I did not need, and a police Inspector, whom I did. We started work together immediately and interviewed a very large number of aliens. Each one I questioned a little, studied whatever records existed, and discussed with my police colleague what he thought. In many cases those brought before us were able to exhibit concentration camp numbers which the Nazis had branded into their arms, although spies could of course have done this as a deception. As far as I remember, out of many hundreds I only ordered the detention of one man whose case I thought required further enquiry. He was a brilliant German photog-rapher working for *Picture Post*, who was promptly released by an appeal tribunal.

This process went on until about Christmas, during which my Bar practice was left more or less in suspense. We were still in the days of the so-called 'phoney' war, but I was getting anxious about my commission in the Emergency Reserve. I was determined not to take an Army commission in the Judge Advocate General's Department, which was

attracting a large number of barristers, as I had been asked to do. I did
not like to think of myself dressing up in an officer's uniform but continuing to do what in effect was an ordinary civilian legal job. No doubt
people were needed for such work but I felt they should have been those
above ordinary service age. After a little agitation on my part I was at last
granted an interview in an office in Grosvenor Place. It was a most
formal and formidable occasion. Seated around a long table seemed to be
almost all the Admirals in the King's Navy. They were courteous, asked
a lot of questions, and then solemnly adjourned. The Lord High
Admiral announced the decision: they would offer me a commission in
the Navy if I insisted. But they felt that I would be a round peg in a square
hole and that it would perhaps be better if like other citizens I waited
patiently for 'the Government' to direct me to whatever it thought was an
appropriate employment, as the Government then had power to do.

I was content to remain in my shabby pin-stripes if I was to do civilian work. My brother Christopher was more fortunate. He was only
thirty-four and not yet a Silk. He had a similar interview, was given a
commission and a ship at once, and ended the war very creditably as a
lieutenant-commander in the 'wavy navy', as the Royal Naval Volunteer
Reserve was known. Meanwhile, I had to exercise patience and, after
some interruption while I was doing the Enemy Alien Tribunal work,
briefs started flowing in again. There was only one case from that time
which was accorded any general public interest: it was one much headlined in the Press as 'The Officer in the Tower' case. A Lieutenant-
Colonel Williams, MC, who had had a distinguished record in The
First World War and who at the beginning of The Second World War
had been put in command of a searchlight regiment, was taken into
custody by the military and held under close arrest for some weeks,
mostly in the Tower of London, without any publicly specified charges.
There were, not unnaturally, rumours of some grave treason, and there
were some who wondered whether the position of Executioner would
be re-created to cut off his head. Eventually, in May 1940, he was
brought up before a court martial at Chelsea Barracks to face trial by a
major-general, three brigadiers, and three lieutenant-colonels. The
charge was 'behaving in a scandalous manner unbecoming to an officer
and a gentleman by being unduly familiar with a sergeant in his unit.' I
was briefed for the defence, and when my initial suspicion of a back-

ground of homosexuality was disposed of, I allowed myself some fun in handling the case.

The prosecution knew when commencing the proceedings that the sergeant in question had, along with another boy, been brought up and educated by the Colonel. The Colonel himself said when he was first accused: 'This is ridiculous. He is my adopted son. I brought him into the Regiment.' But the trial went on. 'Did he', I asked of some distinguished officer who appeared for the prosecution, 'consider that the sight of a lieutenant-colonel and a sergeant dining together at the Compleat Angler in Marlow, both in mufti, really prejudiced good order and discipline in His Majesty's forces?' It would be hard to imagine anything more calculated to cause disaffection in the modern Army, so many members of which had been friends in civil life before joining up, than to convict such old friends of criminal conduct because they openly continued their friendship. In the end that view prevailed. It is difficult to understand how, in May 1940, on the very eve of the German attack in Europe, the authorities could have pursued the opposite philosophy.

I did not have to wait very long to become involved in the war effort. In the spring the summons came, and the white bundles of papers tied up with red tape and marked with tempting fees had to be returned to the solicitors. The Home Secretary, Sir John Anderson later Lord Waverley, wrote asking me – really he was directing me – to be the Legal Adviser to the Regional Commissioner for the South-Eastern No. 12 Region, which consisted of most of Kent and Surrey and all of Sussex, including the coastal area in which the threatened enemy invasion was expected to take place. This was all designated as a 'Defence Area'. I had not been anxious for a legal job, but the location suited me because the headquarters were in Tunbridge Wells and my wife and I were able to move to my parents' home in the Ashdown Forest.

The office of Regional Commissioner, of which there were twelve for the whole country including Scotland, was of a quasi-ministerial nature. It was established on appointment by the King, to provide for the continuation of civil government in the event of an invasion. In that event the Commissioner would in effect become the civil governor of the region, with full powers and in immediate liaison with the Army

Commander in the region at the time. An elaborate communications network was set up through which the Commissioner could send directions to the military and the police.

In the case of the SouthEastern Region the Commissioner could fall back on an alternative headquarters similarly equipped in the north of the region if Tunbridge Wells became untenable. If the emergency of actual invasion did not occur, as surprisingly turned out to be the case, the Regional Commissioners had complete charge of the whole civil defence and fire service organization in their regions, as well as a general responsibility for the police forces, which remained otherwise independent, and they had a direct liaison with the Army Commander through an officer at their HQ. Under the Defence Regulations, they had very wide powers, and could make detention orders and give all manner of directions. To a large extent these powers were deliberately undefined: the Regional Commissioners were there as the senior representatives of central government to do whatever was necessary in any wartime emergency which might arise. In the event of an invasion, they could do anything, with a promise of indemnification after the war; they were the twelve dictatorsinwaiting. In the meantime, they had a general surveillance and coordinating function over the machinery of government, the regional offices of the various ministries and the manufacturing industry. Once a month or so they met together in London under the chairmanship of the Home Secretary, reported on conditions and morale and discussed the general civil arrangements for carrying on the war. The Commissioners collectively constituted one of the most influential bodies in the country under the War Cabinet.

The Regional Commissioner in the SouthEastern Region to whom I was to become Legal Adviser was then Sir Auckland Geddes, a remarkable man. He had once been Professor of Anatomy at McGill University but had returned to business and political life in England. He was in every sense a big man – and a deliberate man. He had one of the best minds I have encountered; he spoke thoughtfully, but with much assurance. He strode round the warroom of our headquarters at Tunbridge Wells with its great map showing the airraid situation of the whole country at any given moment in a notably deliberate way. You could not hurry him. And you could not ignore him. I was proud to be his adviser, and later became a close friend.

I was not, however, his Legal Adviser for long. And I have no recollection on what, if anything, I gave legal advice. Legal niceties were not our major concern in the South-East just then. My first (and in view of what followed, a lasting) recollection is about cars. The senior staff at Regional Headquarters for the most part used their own cars, although some staff cars were available. For personal use, we were expected to stick strictly to the petrol rationing allowance. For official use, we were allotted the necessary petrol coupons and we normally had a driver. Sir Auckland Geddes had established a small corps of eight or ten girl 'dis-patch' riders who were dressed in a not very elegant military type of uniform designed, I suspect, by his secretary. These girls drove the senior staff and were very familiar with the region and its organization. Sir Auckland had his own driver, a personal friend, and I was told I could pick one of the corps to become my personal driver when I required one. It was a somewhat invidious task. They did not exactly line up as in a beauty parade, but the fact that I was to choose a driver became known, and there was a line-up of sorts. It was not, I regret to say, because of my personal charm, but because my Railton coupé was by far the most flashy and exciting car of any available to them to drive. I had a casual glance at them. They were all respectable-looking girls, aged about twenty-four, the daughters of local gentlefolk, selected no doubt with discretion by the Commissioner. Looking at a photograph of them now there does not appear to have been much to choose between them. But some hidden fate or instinct guided me. I noticed a young woman who was called Joan Mather, the only daughter of a retired banker from Yorkshire, and asked her if she would be my driver. She accepted, and a very good driver she turned out to be.

Two things about Joan attracted my interest in the first few days. On the second day she drove my Railton, she ran into a bird. Although I was on a duty visit, she immediately, and without asking, stopped the car and got out to see if the bird had been killed. I said nothing. But it hap-pened to be a thing that I always did myself. I don't like to think that I have left a bird injured and in pain. That was a small thing. A week later she was called off duty to be told that her brother, training as a pilot in the RAF in Canada, had been killed in an air accident. I was told that they had been very close to each other, the only children of possibly rather dull but most worthy parents. I thought I should not see her for some days. Next day, however, she was back on duty. There may have been no smiles, but there was no moaning, no visible reaction. There was 'a war on', and she felt that her duty was to carry on.

Some years later, Joan Mather became my second wife. But that is a later story.

The Regional Commissioners all had at least one Deputy Commissioner. Sir Auckland Geddes had as his only Deputy when I arrived Lord Knollys, a charming man with a beautiful house near Hartfield and a delightful wife. Both were high in society, with a royal association. Not very long after my arrival at Tunbridge Wells, Sir Auckland, who did not regard legal advising as the highest priority in what he knew would become a total war, recommended my appoint-ment as his second deputy. Herbert Morrison – who by then had become Home Secretary and Minister of National Security – readily agreed, possibly glad that at last there was someone of Labour persuasion in the chain of command, for almost all the Commissioners were titled and Conservative. The appointment of course considerably enlarged the scope of my activities. I was now entitled to a large flag on my car and was driven all over the Region, inspecting fire service premises and per-sonnel; taking the salute at parades; surveying new buildings; discussing with mayors and town clerks all sorts of problems on which they wanted advice or help, and making pep speeches.

There was an occasion when I visited Eastbourne, not far from where I now live. My task was to secure a reduction in the number of air-raid wardens. The Mayor and Councillors gathered round their long table and I explained to them that we considered the risk of raids in Eastbourne unlikely. At this point there was a loud rat-a-tat-tat noise with which I was then unfamiliar. But my audience suddenly vanished. They had all dived under the table. We were being machine-gunned by an enemy plane making a surprise daylight raid. Eastbourne kept its wardens.

I well remember being driven to Canterbury in the middle of the night following the so-called 'Baedeker' raid. The great cathedral stood out starkly against a background of flame. Although much havoc was caused in the town, the cathedral was little damaged.

In all this I got to know a good many people and not least among them was the then General Montgomery, who was at that time in command of XII Corps stationed in Tunbridge Wells. He already had quite a reputation. His favourite lecture, which he gave at the staff college originally and often repeated, was on 'The Registering of Personality'. One of his theories was that in uniform one officer is like another. To make sure that his soldiery knew their commander, he wore odd-looking berets with an unusual assortment of badges and often moved among the troops. They all knew him. Less popularly, he initiated the practice of having his staff officers run some considerable distance round the outskirts of Tunbridge Wells at an unearthly hour every morning. I think he joined in. Equally unpopular with many was his objection to alcohol and smoking. I recall an occasion when he was Army Commander with his corps at Reigate. He asked me to dinner in the mess. It was a large mess and everyone was seated at a very large round table in order of seniority. Except for me. I was on Monty's right and so was the first to be served by the butler. I was offered wine and without thinking, at once accepted. Have I ever refused? I then watched the wine going round the whole mess. Not a single officer accepted. Cowards! I felt I might as well be hung for a sheep as a lamb, and had my glass refilled more than once. And had some port. Monty made no comment.

Another well-known idiosyncrasy was his dislike of any sort of interruption – sneezing, nose-blowing or the like – when he was speaking. I recall a dreadful occasion with the Regional Commissioner. We had been invited by Monty to attend one of his frequent TEWTs (Tactical Exercise Without Troops) in which he demonstrated how battles should be won. His ADC told us it would commence in a local hall at 9.30 a.m., and at 9.25 we turned up. But in fact it had started at 8.30 and Monty was already in full voice. Our little procession entered. Monty stopped speaking. There was dead silence. The assembled officers gaped in awe as we walked very self-consciously up the aisle to our reserved seats in the front row. Gaped in awe not, be it said, at the Regional Commissioner, but at what they thought Monty would say. Or do. As it was, all he did say was, 'I will now go on for another twenty-five minutes rather than the usual twenty minutes, before giving you an opportunity to blow your noses or cough.'

He had considerable conceit. I remember sitting next to him at a dinner in his honour in Hastings. At the end he got up and, addressing the party, said, 'I expect you would like to have my autograph. Will you write to my ADC with your names and addresses and one will be sent to you.' Then, turning to me, he said, 'Hartley, you can have yours now: I will give you one.' And he wrote his name on the back of the menu card. I did, indeed, pocket it with such enthusiasm as I could muster.

He was a vain and sometimes insensitive man. But he was a great general. He never fought a battle until he had built up the forces and the equipment to win it. And he always did.

The Regional Commissioners were not, at this period, directly concerned with military measures; our task was to facilitate them. In the event of invasion it would have been different. I remember one occasion when we were able to point out to an incoming contingent that they had encamped literally on top of an area mined with remote control by the outgoing force, and nobody knew where the remote control was. They moved out quite quickly. There were, of course, problems between the military and the local authorities. These we had to resolve. But things went surprisingly smoothly.

The phoney war – which was also known as the 'bore war' – continued in the spring of 1940. Then came the invasion of France, Belgium and Holland, and their collapse, followed by the evacuation of most of the British Expeditionary Force from Dunkirk. On 10 June, Italy declared war on us. These events led to a realization by the British that they were alone in facing the Axis powers. Hugh Dowding, Commander of Fighter Command, publicly, and I thought sincerely, thanked God for it. The British sometimes exhibit their best qualities when they find themselves standing alone against the most formidable circumstances. Certainly, at that time only a tiny proportion of the population imagined that Britain could be defeated. But we might have been. The German army had an immense superiority. And although the British Fleet was greatly superior to the German, one danger seemed to be that the Germans might establish a strong box barrage by heavy gunfire and by mining each end of the Channel so as to protect each flank of a German invasion across the Channel. If the Royal Navy could by these means be kept out of the battle, the main task of defeating an invading Wehrmacht would be for the RAF, which we believed to be outnumbered, although not greatly, by the Luftwaffe. If the RAF were defeated the last line of defence would be the Army and the Home

Guard, but apart from our lack of training and a paucity of arms, a difficulty here was that we did not know where invasion might come. There were constant rumours, all untrue, of parachute troops being dropped; certainly the Wehrmacht had powerful parachute divisions. British Intelligence was unsure as to where the Germans intended to make their strongest efforts and it was expected that attempts might be made at almost any point along the East Coast and the Channel. This led to some differences between the British Army commanders. Field Marshal (later Lord) Sir Edmund Ironside, whilst he was GOC British Home Forces, considered that the best strategy was to concentrate his main forces on holding the enemy on the beach. Sir Alan Brooke (later Viscount Alanbrooke), on the other hand, who took over from Ironside in June 1940, favoured a lighter defence on the beaches but a highly mobile and strong force which could move to any point at which the enemy had succeeded in breaking through the beach defences and repulse him. This was also Winston Churchill's view.

In mid-June the Government put out a general instruction to the public about what to do if invasion took place. After consulting Geddes, I sent my wife and my parents away from the Ashdown Forest, which would have been in the battle area, to the West Country. By that time military and governmental sources fully expected that there would be an invasion. We knew only later that was not then Hitler's intention. He hoped and expected that the British would make peace and it was not until we had attacked the French fleet at Mers-el-Kebir that he became convinced that the British intended to fight on, however favourable the peace terms might be. On 12 July, Hitler issued a tentative directive for preparations to be made for the invasion of England, but on the 19th, in an address to the Reichstag (copies of which were dropped on our region), he made what in effect was a clear offer of peace, adding that he saw no reason why the war should go on.

So-called 'historians' writing today seem to think they have uncovered hitherto unrecognized opportunities for peace in 1940 and 1941, and are making all sorts of suggestions of mistakes and mismanagement by Winston Churchill in his conduct of the war. The fact was, of course, that Hitler's anxiety to make peace with Britain in 1940 and 1941 was well known to the British — and rejected with scorn. Of course we could have made peace. But not peace with honour. We could have ended the war and left Nazism and totalitarian systems of government to expand throughout the world – and thus given Hitler further oppor-tunities to break the solemn treaties of peace and friendship which were so often his prelude to war. As for other mistakes in the conduct of war, no doubt wisdom after the event indicates that many were made, and no doubt sometimes Winston Churchill relied on advice from certain indi-viduals who did not deserve the complete confidence he placed in them. But Winston's mistakes were as nothing compared with those made in the 1914–18 war – and we won the Second World War with compar-atively few casualties, grievous as the loss of military and civilian life was. Nor would the conclusion of the war in 1940–41 have prevented in the end the dissolution of the British Empire, as the new historians suggest. The movement for independence in the various dominions and colonies had already manifested itself before the war broke out.

As it was, in 1940 we made it very clear that we intended to fight on and on 1 August Hitler issued another directive confirming Operation Sealion but emphasizing that the Luftwaffe had first to destroy the Royal Air Force. The Battle of Britain had begun.

Much of the battle was over London and the South-East Region. From then on the clear summer skies were criss-crossed with the inter-twining vapour trails of the fighter aircraft, with here and there a para-chute slowly descending with the crew who had bailed out from a crashing plane – was it one of theirs or one of ours? Here the published figures were unreliable: our own losses were always stated accurately but those suffered by the enemy, although given honestly by us, were almost always exaggerated. We had a number of quite small airfields for fighter aircraft in the region. I used to visit the scenes of the almost daily inci-dents on my rounds and often called in at the mess at the local airfields. The indomitable and indefatigable courage of those young pilots was beyond belief. By all the ordinary rules of physical and mental endurance, and mechanical survival, we should have lost the Battle of Britain as the enemy quite confidently expected. But we won it.

The decisive defeat of the Luftwaffe is put at 15 September. By the end of October 1940 the massed daylight raids had ceased altogether. It was the winning of that battle, with the consequence that the Germans did not attempt the anticipated invasion, which was critical in our ability to win the war. There followed, however, sustained bombing attacks on

London and other large cities by night, which were intended to destroy our fighting capacity. In most of the attacks on London the German air-craft were routed over the South-Eastern Region and the air-raid warning soon after dark was an almost nightly occurrence – and it often went on until nearly dawn. There were times when literally every air-raid warning district light on our map of the whole of the United Kingdom in the regional headquarters turned red. Usually the bombloads were intended for London or other important centres, but almost every night there would be occasional 'incidents' in the region, often caused by bombers going back to base and unloading their bombs on the way. I recall more than once listening tensely with my wife (for by this time, the danger of invasion over, she and my parents had returned from the West Country) as we heard a bomb falling with a sound like tearing silk – and we would hear this only if it was very close – till the blast of the actual explosion reassured us that, this time at least, we were safe and had suffered only blown-out windows or slight damage to the house. I remember too how night after night I used to walk up to the Kings Standing Hill, which was the highest point in the Ashdown Forest, and watch the fires burning across London, following the sus-tained and systematic attacks with incendiary bombs. Searchlights all over the region were trying, usually unsuccessfully, to pick out enemy planes. At first the Luftwaffe seemed to be winning, although in London the spirit of the population remained extraordinarily good. Smaller cities, such as Coventry and Liverpool, where the bombing could be more concentrated, suffered more heavily.

The most sustained attack on Liverpool, largely incendiary, came on the nights between 3 and 10 May 1941. After that, surprisingly, they ceased, and there was only one more serious incident. It was somewhat typical of the German air attacks that just at the point where it was beginning to look to us as if these attacks were achieving a degree of success, they suddenly ended – we liked to think because of larger losses of aircraft than we were aware of at the time. Certainly in the case of Liverpool – which was shortly to come under my jurisdiction – the city was beginning to come under real strain. A significant proportion of the people in Liverpool and Bootle evacuated the built-up area at night and camped out in the countryside, often returning to find their houses destroyed. Had the Germans kept up their intensive attack for a further seven days the situation could have been very critical, but during the winter of 1940/41 we had been able to put airborne radar detectors on some of our night fighters, particularly the squadron led by Squadron Leader John ('Cat's Eyes') Cunningham, which raised the rate of enemy loss to a level that was significant for them.

Defeated in the Battle of Britain and suffering heavy casualties in night raiding, the German Luftwaffe was perhaps becoming demoralized. But the critical factor which led to the cessation of the bombing of England was Hitler's decision, actually taken in 1940, to attack Russia, which led to the formal cancellation of Operation Sealion and to the Luftwaffe being transferred to the Eastern Front in May 1941.

The last heavy attack on London was on the night of 10/11 May 1941. Although there were 'hit and run' raids from time to time, serious raiding was not resumed until after our invasion force landed in France in 1944, when we were attacked by the so-called V1 flying bomb. We had, of course, known for a considerable time that the Germans were developing some kind of flying or self-propelled bomb – largely at the Peenemunde establishment which we had been harassing with bombing raids as often as we could.

Fortunately it was not until June 1944 that the enemy was able to launch the first V1. I remember hearing the strange noise of its approach, and getting out of bed to watch it. It was a rather eerie sight; it flew low and comparatively slowly, with a great white flame belching out from its tail. It was frightening to watch its relentless progress, knowing that some mechanism within it timed the engine and that the bomb would cut out and fall at some predetermined moment. This cut-out system often failed. Thus two bombs dropped in the garden of the house I was later to buy in Sussex.

The development of the V1, however, came too late for the Germans. After various changes in defensive strategy, which included shooting down the bombs from our far-faster fighter aircraft, a range of anti-air-craft batteries was eventually assembled along the coastline, firing shells with proximity fuses which brought the bombs down into the sea before they crossed the coast. Eventually our invading forces overran the enemy launching sites.

The V2, a more formidable ballistic weapon against which we had no counter, was first launched in September 1944. Fortunately, the enemy were never able to put it into large-scale production, although sporadically they continued using the V2, with heavy casualties, until just before the end of the war. I say the 'end of the war', but of course, by the end of 1941, when the risk of invasion had passed and the USA had entered the war, we already had some reason for confidence in victory. The last V2 was nevertheless launched against us only a day or two before the end of the war.

Early in 1942 my mother died of cancer. Although I had been warned that she was ill, it was a sad blow. There could never have been so devoted a couple as my father and mother. We buried her at Fairwarp near our house on the Ashdown Forest. I have two recollections of the service: one that a loud single sob escaped from me during a short address by R. J. Campbell, the famous preacher from the City Temple, who so admired my mother; the other that a stray daylight raider dropped a bomb nearby.

Meanwhile, there had been changes in the regional organization. From the point of view of our war effort, the centre of importance and potential danger had moved from the south-east coast to the area of heavy industry in the Midlands and north-west — and of course to Liverpool, the port for the north-western approaches. Accordingly, Auckland Geddes, who had been given a peerage in the Near Year's Honours of 1942, had been moved up to the No. 5 Region which had its headquarters in Manchester, and Lord Monsell had been appointed to No. 12 Region to succeed him. Monsell was charming, but a very different person from his predecessor. He had been Chief Whip for the Tory Party in the Commons. Possibly a little vain himself, he had a beautiful Lagonda car to be vain about; it quite outclassed my Railton. He did not, perhaps, display the same wisdom in handling the local authorities as Lord Geddes had done, and probably in order to balance the situation a little politically a third Deputy Regional Commissioner was appointed. This was Arthur Bottomley, then a trades union official with NUPE who later became an MP for the Labour Party and held various ministerial posts, acquiring in the end great knowledge of our former colonies and dominions.

I continued to work in the South-East Region under Monsell until the early part of 1942, when Lord Geddes was compelled to resign from the North-West Region owing to increasing blindness which soon came to be total. To my surprise, I was asked to take his place. This important promotion was, I have no doubt, due to his strong recommendation. I hesitated for a day or two, uncertain whether to accept because of the difficulties related to my wife's illness, but she made light of these and insisted that to succeed Lord Geddes – 'the great Lord Geddes', as she exclaimed – was something I could not possibly reject. So we moved up to Manchester.

We both lived for a time in a small house there. But this was beyond her capacity; reliable staff were difficult to come by and short of a nursing home, which we were both anxious to postpone as long as possible, the best solution appeared to be for her to live at the Adelphi Hotel in Liverpool where she had comfortable accommodation and caring friends from her university days to visit her. I had to remain near the job and its 'war room' and made a small bedroom in the Regional HQ office.

I was shopping in the Kendal Milne store in Manchester one day when the importance of my position as Regional Commissioner in the No. 5 Region was quickly brought home to me. I heard a rather nice-looking young woman say to her companion, 'Look, that's the Regional Commissioner over there.' I preened myself. 'What?' said her companion. 'Do you mean him what stands outside the Regal in the green uniform with the silver braid?' Alas, we had no uniforms; I was still in my shabby 'civvies' – I had no choice. But those young women were not the only ones in doubt about our status. There was a reasonably awkward question of precedence – that cardinally important factor in British social life.

Theoretically it was said that the Regional Commissioner, appointed by the monarch, took precedence over Lords Lieutenant, Lords Mayor and the rest. Not all those thus downgraded accepted this view. Some of my colleagues allowed themselves to get into absurd and undignified squabbles. Thus the late Lord Dudley, in the Midland Region, insisted that he had the right and duty of being the first to greet the monarch on his visits to the region. The Lord Mayor took the view that this was his function. They almost came to blows. In my region, I always made it a rule to let the local notables take precedence. Of course, I always went to meet the monarch: I was responsible for organizing the royal visits and accompanying the visitors on their tours. I recall an agreeable occasion on a beautiful sunny day, driving the then Duke of Kent around in my open car to salute the crowds. Shortly afterwards he was dead, killed in an aircraft accident.

The North-Western Region was very different from the South-Eastern. By the time I moved north there was no longer any great anxiety about air attack and none about invasion. This was the heartland of our industrial war effort, and my job as Regional Commissioner was much changed. I seemed to have a finger in every pie. I frequently visited the great factories making Lancaster aircraft, bombs and tanks, where munitions were being produced under heavy pressure. I seem to have made an innumerable – and boring – number of pep talks to the workers. I also dealt with smallish problems of an infinitely varied kind in a quasi-ministerial way. I kept in close touch with the local authorities and tried to visit all the more important ones with regularity, discussing their difficulties and seeing whether there was anything to be done in Whitehall in regard to local problems. In this, I profited from the example of the great Lord Derby,* the then Lord Lieutenant who, even when quite crippled in his later years, called regularly once a year on every local authority in Lancashire. I covered Cheshire, Westmorland and Cumberland as well as Lancashire and despite my, to him no doubt odious, political leanings, we became good friends. He said, a trifle condescendingly, that it was good to have educated people amongst the Socialists! And so matters went on till the end of that year. Then the first great tragedy of my life occurred.

Alberta's condition continued to get worse and more distressing and at the end of 1942 she took an overdose of her sleeping pills and died. She left me a most loving and moving letter. 'Greater love hath no man than this . . .' I had realized that the end was near and inevitable, but part of me died with her. I did quite soon remarry and develop a new, active and happy life, as she had often told me she wished me to do. She had, as I found out later, corresponded on such matters with the young woman – Joan Mather – whom I did eventually marry. But although she sacrificed her own life for my future, I have never quite been able to recapture the unalloyed happiness I had enjoyed in some of those years before her last and incurable illness.

* The 17th Earl of Derby (1865–1948)

After Alberta's death I took a couple of weeks' leave and returned home to the Ashdown Forest. I explained matters as sympathetically as I could to Alberta's parents – and pondered on the future. Should I throw my hand in or could I bring myself to go back to the north-west and at least resume my duties there until the war ended. My father, in his very quiet and shy way, was a man of human sympathy and wisdom, but I had few friends who could counsel me.

But there was one, who knew my situation and who encouraged me. This was Stella, Lady Reading, who had great influence on my life then, and later. Stella was one of the most remarkable women in public life by any standards. She was the widow of a Viceroy of India who had also been the Chief Justice of England. Her great achievement was the establishment of the WVS, now the Women's Royal Voluntary Service, which gave part-time service of a hundred different kinds. This vast force of women helped the casualties and homeless after air raids, provided after-care and meals-on-wheels, looked after people in distress, and did whatever was needed to help our war effort then or to assist in social problems in peacetime. I saw a good deal of Stella Reading, first in the No. 12 Region, then in the north-west which had over 100,000 members of the WVS. We became close colleagues and after the war she joined the Council of Sussex University of which I was the Chancellor for twenty years. In her will, she left the University a beautiful Tudor house nearby in which she had lived.

Stella became a personal friend and adviser. She had known of my wife's grave illness and, later, the circumstances of her death at the end of 1942, and she hoped that her death would give me the opportunity of a fresh start in life. She had an extraordinary sensitivity to others and on 19 February 1943, six weeks after Alberta's death, she wrote to me.

I gather things are beginning to move a very little bit – but it will obviously be slowly – don't despair about it – that gallant lady will be aiding all along and I know a worthwhile job will be yours soon – and if there is ever anything I can do to help – you know I have only to become aware of it. I know that these must be the very hardest of days for you – but don't reject the biggest and most generous gift you have ever been given – even if it brought endless pain to you and was a mistaken idea – the vision here is so extraordinarily limited and wisdom must be seen as a whole – not just one face of it – to be real⁄ized. I wish I had met your wife – she always sounded so brave and noble and I can just gauge the empty loneliness of going home – Do let me know if you are likely to be in London and care to have a meal.

A little later I had a talk with her. This was partly about leaving the region and taking up other work. Auckland Geddes, who strongly opposed this, advised me to stick it out. So did Herbert Morrison. I was offered a top job on the new UNRRA* organisation which had been established to deal with the enormous and still⁄increasing problems of refugees in Europe and indeed all over the world, and I was also spoken of as a possible successor to Sir George Etherton as Clerk of the Lancashire County Council. Stella thought the UNRRA job could be interesting if I was convinced I must do something new. More impor⁄tantly, she had met Joan Mather at the Tunbridge Wells Regional Headquarters and, assessing my position more dispassionately and objectively than I was able to do at that tragic time myself, she strongly advised me not to wait upon convention but to marry again. So too did Auckland Geddes, to whom I suspect Stella had spoken and who, of course, knew Joan as one of the first recruits for his team of dispatch riders. Without that advice and support at that critical time I think I might never have recovered. As it was, I pulled myself together and in a quiet ceremony at Rotherfield Church in Sussex on 21 September 1944 I married Joan Mather. I never regretted it. Joan had to act without much enthusiasm from her parents. A widower sixteen years her senior, nearly penniless and a Socialist at that, could hardly be their ideal for their only daughter. But Joan had no doubts and her parents loyally accepted her decision, and I like to believe that although I sometimes treated her badly and took her goodness too much for granted, it was one she never regretted.

I continued with my regular visits, inspections and 'pep talks' to the various units of the civil defence organization all over the region, for although air raiding appeared to have ceased, we had to remain on the alert. As it turned out, only one moderately serious air raid incident occurred. That was on Christmas Eve 1944 when a squadron of

* United Nations Relief and Rehabilitation Administration

Heinkels, each carrying one V1, approached unexpectedly over the North Sea and launched their cargo from near the East Coast. The V1's were fuelled so as to cut out over Manchester; in fact they were widely dispersed and mostly fell on Oldham.

In 1943 I had been asked by Ernest Bevin, the famous trade union leader and then Minister of Labour, to become chairman of an organization called the Catering Wages Commission which the Government was setting up. The catering industry was almost completely unorganized; the trade unions had virtually no membership among its employees. In many of the less reputable establishments the employment and living conditions were shocking and the employees were liable to gross exploitation. We were also to consider the invasion of tourists who were likely to be expected after the war and the question of how our hotel and tourist facilities could be improved to cope with it.

It may seem absurd, but my colleagues and I also published a number of reports on ancillary matters, including one on tipping. We would have liked to have made tipping illegal but were convinced it would be useless as there would always be some tourists who, in order to get special service for themselves, would break the rules and give tips. It was an interesting and useful experience to chair a body of this kind, but unfortunately its work was by no means finished when the war ended and a general election was held. I was a parliamentary candidate and although the office of chairman was in fact unpaid, I was warned by telegram from the Department that it might be regarded as 'an office of profit under the Crown' which would thus disqualify me from election. I hastily resigned.

I had combined work for the Catering Commission with my regional work but by this time the end of the war was obviously approaching. Herbert Morrison told me that the Regional Civil Defence organization would be gradually disbanded and it was agreed that my resignation should take effect early in 1945.

The departure of the Regional Commissioners gave rise to a curious problem of how to reward them for their services — if indeed they should be specially rewarded at all. I myself took the view that no reward was called for. We had simply been doing our job as others did, under direction from the Government, and had been paid for it. No doubt we were paid less than we might have been had we continued in our normal occupations, but others had been obliged to leave their jobs and had given their lives. Although I was not consulted, I did volunteer this view to Herbert Morrison. It was generally considered that a knighthood would have been the appropriate thing. But this was unsatisfactory for, apart from myself, all the other Commissioners were already knights, or barons – or even earls. A typically English solution was found. Herbert Morrison, as Secretary of State, gave a dinner for the Commissioners which was attended by the King. In addition, the King sent a personal letter to each of us, signed in his own hand, thanking each Commissioner for his services to the state. At the dinner, in thanking us on his own behalf and that of the nation, the King recalled that he had often been brought into contact with us during the war and he remarked very truly that although he had met nearly all of us before, and some on numerous occasions, he had never seen any of us look so happy and so free from care. 'Usually,' he said, 'I have seen you standing anxiously at the exit to some factory in a north-easterly gale, looking feverishly at your watches and wondering how on earth we could make up a time-lag of forty minutes, or at the end of a long day on the platform of some draughty railway station with your faces wearing that quite unmistakable expression which can only mean, "Well, thank God that's over!"'

Then came the problem of what to do next. I had no private means. Anything I had saved before the war, when I had been earning about £5,000 a year, had been used up by heavy expenses, only partly recouped by my official salary of £2,500 during the war. I had to get back quickly into some gainful occupation. Herbert Morrison then offered me the position of Commissioner of the Metropolitan Police, a position about to be vacated by Sir Philip Game. I rather fancied myself riding on a horse with a splendid red-lined cloak over my uniform. But Lord Geddes was against it. He pointed out that it was by tradition a post of limited duration and, although pensionable, would probably prevent my returning to the Bar or going in for politics. He thought that the right course would be to go back to the Bar and at the same time see how my interest in politics might develop.

And that is what my new wife Joan and I then decided to do. How right Lord Geddes had been was at once demonstrated when I announced my return to the Bar. The briefs literally flowed in, most, it is true, for cases on the Northern Circuit where, because of my commissionership, I had become something of a public figure, but some came from London solicitors too, and altogether they held out the promise of a satisfactory career. And then there were also the political possibilities.

CHAPTER 5

Politics – How It Started

I had received several approaches in 1944 with a view to becoming a candidate in the general election, which would have to be held as soon as the war was over and which was already the subject of speculation and some political propaganda. Thus Herbert Morrison was criticized more than once for making speeches supporting the Labour Party while he was still a Secretary of State in the Coalition Government. Up to that time I had not made any clear declaration of a political affiliation since my early days as a campaigner in Wandsworth. My job as a Regional Commissioner was strictly non-party-political and on the whole I was able to avoid any pronouncements suggesting leanings towards the Labour Party.

In the summer of 1944, I was approached by the local Conservative Party to put my name forward for one of the Wirral constituencies. My recollection is that I said that at that time it was premature to take any such decision. I gave a similar answer in June 1944 to the Divisional Labour Party for Platting, Manchester, and in September of that year to the West Birkenhead Labour Party. That autumn, however, I had some contact with the St Helens Labour Party. The sitting Labour member was not to stand for re-election and I knew the constituency fairly well, not only as Regional Commissioner, but also from pre-war days when I had often appeared in the local courts. I was told that they planned to select a new candidate early in 1945 and I agreed to let my name go forward, although I did not seek any great publicity about it at that time. There had originally been a list of nine possible candidates. This was whittled down to three: Mr C. W. Bridges (from the NUR),

Mr George Catlin, and myself. Ellen Wilkinson, Chairman of the Labour Party, wrote to me about Professor Catlin. I had had some contact with Ellen in my job as Regional Commissioner; she was a remarkable and brave woman but was not then in any real sense a personal friend, although she later become one. She sent me a copy of a letter that Catlin had written to her, which she described as 'an incredible communication'; in it he asked her to support him and obtain union support for his candidature for St Helens, saying it was his best and possibly last chance of getting into Parliament. That was true. Most of the rest of the letter, which contained many defamatory allegations against me, was not. Ellen Wilkinson replied to him in no uncertain terms that she would do no such thing and that she favoured my candidature. To me she wrote '. . . I would like you to know how much in all my capacities (1) as Chairman [of the Labour Party], (2) as Parliamentary Secretary to the Ministry of Home Security, (3) as NUDAW official, (4) as an ordinary citizen, I hope that St Helens will choose you.'

All three candidates addressed a well-attended meeting of party delegates in January 1945. I remember telling them that I assumed they did not want a political speech from me on the aims and policies of the Labour Party, but that I supposed they would want to know something about myself, so as to judge whether I would be a suitable person to promote Labour interests. This was a typical piece of laziness on my part: I had not swotted up current Labour policies and was not sufficiently familiar with them to make a policy speech. The other two candidates made their speeches and the three of us then waited in an adjacent room for the result. We heard a burst of clapping from the meeting room. Catlin, who had had more experience than I of attending selection meetings (he could not have had less), said that he could not understand what was going on. It was the invariable practice, so he said, for one or more of the candidates to be recalled for further questioning before the final decision was reached. I felt a bit sorry for him, he was so painfully anxious. As it was, we were eventually all asked in together and it was announced that the lot had fallen to me to be adopted as the Labour candidate for St Helens. Catlin did not obtain a constituency, but later he was rewarded for his long and devoted service to the Labour Party by a knighthood. I am sure that he deserved it.

The Central Wandsworth Labour Party sent me a generous letter, saying that they remembered me well and wished me success at St Helens. I was not entirely full of rejoicing at being selected, however. At that time, although I thought that Labour would, with any luck, hold St Helens, I felt that with Churchill leading the Conservatives, they would be bound to win the election for the country as a whole. I assumed then that I would have to combine membership (at a salary of £400 a year) with my practice, and I feared this would be very difficult. Shortly afterwards Herbert Morrison told me that I ought to follow the example of Dr Salter, a Labour member of parliament who had given up his practice and had gone to live in a very humble home in his south-east London constituency so as to devote his whole time to his constituency duties. He sent his children to the local council school. I must admit that I could not have dedicated myself to such a life, and in fact had purchased another house in Sussex early in 1945. Nevertheless, behind my strident and excessive enthusiasm I was a sincere believer that Socialism would produce a more fair society and eliminate the gross poverty that I had seen in the poorer parts of London and in the 'back-to-backs' in the Midlands and the North. I was not in any sense a scientific Socialist. I still have not read Marx or the other left-wing writers, not even the Webbs. I had no theoretical knowledge of economics. I was moved by what I saw; the gap between privilege and poverty was too glaring. Moreover, my Bar practice had given me some experience of the conduct of business and industry. Some industries, like mining, were grossly inefficient, and others were carried on sometimes corruptly and often without any regard at all for the welfare of employees or the general public interest. To use the language later used by Brendan Bracken, a pretty shrewd observer, I thought then that many of the leaders of British industry were boneheads. Private interests had failed to do anything but serve themselves, so public intervention and control seemed the answer. On that evening at St Helens in January 1945 I was joining a vast number of splendid local people in the campaign for a better Britain.

My resignation from the office of Regional Commissioner took effect at about the same time as my adoption as a parliamentary candidate. I went back to the Bar, but occupied such spare time as I could find in going down to Sussex with Joan to decorate and settle into the house we had acquired: a rather attractive, small 16/17th-century house in the rural area south of Uckfield. As the employment of decorators was not then permitted since the Government restricted employment to repairing war damage and building new accommodation, Joan and I redecorated it from top to bottom, working from early in the morning until late at night. It was a charming house, in which our three children were born and where we lived in much happiness for some twelve years. I say 'we' lived there; my work often kept me in London or elsewhere, even at weekends, and we had to have a London apartment. My elder son William started his now close association with the Press when he was about five years old in a letter to a paper. 'I hardly ever see my father. But I know he drives like a bomb.'

My Bar practice in Silk was building up very encouragingly by the time Germany surrendered in April 1945. Soon after the Armistice, Parliament was dissolved and a general election was announced. The polling itself took place in the United Kingdom on 5 July, but because of the need to collect and count the military vote, the result was not declared until 26 July.

The serious campaigning had started in May. What a campaign it was! Glancing through the press cuttings now, I am appalled at the brash and intemperate way in which I conducted myself. Everything on the Conservative side was evil. All of Labour was good. I blush at the things I said then, but my Conservative opponent gave as good as he got; he was also a barrister, but he had a distinguished war record as a Group Captain in the RAF which I did not. No holds were barred on either side. I suppose we all took it seriously. But it was all great fun. The local leader of the Tory Party was a woman and I had to apologize to her for alleging that she always looked for Reds under her bed, a remark which she considered impugned her chastity! My wife and I had an apparently popular act in which we pulled up in our car (no longer the Railton!) – on which a loudspeaker had been fixed – in the local market or other well-populated place, got up through the sun roof and sat on top. There she acted the political ingénue, asking elementary questions – 'What does nationalization mean?' (not so elementary perhaps!), 'When can we get all the boys home from the war?', 'Why can't I find a house to rent?', and so forth, and I tried to give plausible answers. The local Press was hostile, but made one mistake at least. They accused me of hypocrisy in living off a large income from shares in companies while denouncing private enterprise. I had no shares at that time in anything and they were obliged to apologize and pay damages to the local hospital.

I went to a number of nearby constituencies to speak for local Labour candidates. One of them was Widnes where, by a complete coin-cidence, my brother Christopher had, quite unknown to me, been adopted as Labour candidate. I had not influenced him in any way.

Christopher was three and a half years my junior. Unlike me, he went to Oxford, to my father's old college, but unhappily wasted his time there by various extravagances like joining the Bullingdon Club, removing policemen's helmets and the like, and he came down without a degree. Then he went to the Bar. He did better than I had in his examinations, winning the studentship for the first place in the Bar Final, and other prizes, before entering the chambers of Mr A. T. Miller, KC, a leading commercial Silk. He started to do well there; his style, which was perhaps more, shall I say, 'deliberate' than mine, was better suited to commercial courts. He found time to write what was acknowl-edged as the leading authoritative textbook on motor insurance (which was then a very active subject in the courts before the insurance compa-nies had the good sense to operate their 'knock-for-knock' procedure between themselves), and another on air law. He had married a most amusing and intelligent daughter of a well-known solicitor. I certainly expected him to prosper. But then came the war. Unlike me, Christopher was welcomed into the Navy and at once given a commis-sion, first on the executive side, on a sea-going warship, and later in Naval Intelligence, eventually, I think, in Downing Street. He ended the war with the rank of Lieutenant-Commander in the RNVR. His ded-icated wartime service enabled him to be selected to fight Widnes, which at that time was a Conservative seat – in spite of being a most derelict place. Christopher and I were able to share posters, which saved us some money, a serious matter for us Labour candidates. We put out such shaming placards as 'Your cross for Shawcross', 'You can be sure of Shawcross', 'A Vote for Shawcross is a vote for the People' (this in reply to my opponent's 'A vote for Whitworth is a vote for Winston') – and so forth.

The election campaign went well. Herbert Morrison came and made a strong speech at my adoption meeting. I had letters of support from

Ellen Wilkinson, William Jowitt, Stafford Cripps, and other leaders. To my surprise, however, Maxwell Fyfe came and spoke on behalf of my opponent. I felt that in view of our previous relationship I would not have spoken against him; however, I little thought then that in a few weeks' time I would be offering him a job! The newspapers reported Christopher and me as 'Two Brothers whom the Tories fear'. And they had reason to. Christopher won Widnes from the Tories, and I had a majority in St Helens of just under 17,000–13,000 more than the previous member had gained in 1935. All over the country Labour had won a resounding and surprising victory.

There were rollicking celebrations in St Helens and Widnes on the evening of the election result, 26 July 1945, following which Christopher and I, together with Joan and Doreen, Christopher's wife, drove hilariously and, I fear, not very soberly to London for the assembly of the new parliament.

Christopher had won the seat with a good majority, too. Unfortunately, this final instance of his following the same career as myself turned out to be a great mistake. I was the elder; I was a KC; I was the better-known brother. The lot fell to me to be appointed to the Government. One Shawcross in Parliament was more than enough. In the event, Christopher – although he was made a Silk – was relegated to the back benches and, as so often happens with many able MPs, was left to sit silently there and spent too much of his time in the Smoking Room, a resort which has been the downfall of many an MP. The war too had unsettled his marriage. He fell in with the vivacious and attractive daughter of a well-known West End physician and his Chilean wife. He persuaded his wife to divorce him and married again. There were two children, Timothy and Christabel, but his subsequent career was unsettled. Eventually Christopher died in a fatal accident, falling down the stairs at his home. Not very long afterwards his second wife also died from ill-health. It was a tragic end to what could and should have been a brilliant career. I look back on it with great sadness and a feeling of inadequacy on my part.

Now the lobbying and intriguing for leadership or junior appointments in the new government began, although I was not part of it at the time and later heard rather differing personal accounts of it from the main participants. There is no doubt that Herbert Morrison wanted to be Prime Minister. In this he had the support of Stafford Cripps, who thought that he would be more malleable material than Attlee, and one or two others, including Ellen Wilkinson and Professor Harold Laski. Morrison had been the most prominent wartime minister to make speeches that clearly advocated Labour policies, despite the fact that he was a member of the Coalition Cabinet at the time and had, I knew, excited Winston's disapproval for that reason. Morrison could not expect to be appointed Prime Minister, however, unless the Parliamentary Party elected him first as its leader. Attlee had, after all, been the Deputy Prime Minister in the Coalition Government. Churchill would doubtless agree with the King that Attlee should be asked to form a government. Morrison was by no means satisfied with this position. He was somewhat blinkered by his own ambition. He had been canvassing with those he thought (not always correctly) were his friends for an election by the new Parliamentary Party of its leaders before any name was submitted to the monarch. He had told Attlee before the election that he would run against him as leader when the new parliament was formed. He pursued this idea vigorously in the period between the poll and the announcement of the result on 26 July, convinced that if such a poll were conducted he would be the leader named. It is by no means certain that he would have been proved correct. His activities aroused the intense annoyance of the leaders, particularly Ernest Bevin. Events forestalled him. Winston, although most surprised and even dismayed by the election result, acted promptly and properly. In the early evening of the 26th he went to the Palace, tendered his own resignation and advised the King to send for Attlee. At the same time, he wrote to Attlee to inform and congratulate him. Even then, Morrison told Attlee that he should not respond to the King's invitation – if it came – until the Parliamentary party had voted. The swearing-in process had not even begun, but events were moving faster than Morrison realized. The King, within a few minutes of saying goodbye to Churchill, sent for Attlee and asked him to form a government. Attlee said he would.

Attlee went straight from the Palace to a victory rally at the Central Hall, where his announcement of the King's request was greeted with prolonged applause. Morrison even then did not desist from his canvassing, but he had lost the day. His next problem was what post he should seek in the new government. His first choice was the Foreign Office. This was not because he had any particular knowledge of or interest in foreign affairs but, as he told me later, because he felt that next to the premiership it was the most important office and would therefore at least mark him out as Attlee's successor. Attlee thought otherwise and selected Bevin as Foreign Secretary. It was the wisest possible choice, and it was not because the monarch had demurred at the choice of Hugh Dalton as was rumoured. Dalton was made Chancellor of the Exchequer, and Morrison, Lord President of the Council, a position sometimes regarded as something of a sinecure, although it rarely is. This appointment was combined with the Leadership of the House to mark Morrison as the 'No. 2' in the Cabinet, a kind of overlord of nationalization on the home front, rather than as Deputy Prime Minister, a post that has no real constitutional status then. Morrison accepted. As a result, he did get what was ostensibly the most powerful position next to Attlee.

Attlee's firmness was underestimated. Unfortunately the 'Big Four' – Bevin, Morrison, Dalton and Cripps – all hated each other. Attlee was closest to Bevin, and Bevin was loyal to Attlee, although at the end there were curious stories of Attlee wishing to get rid of him. Morrison and Attlee disliked each other, to say the least. As we walked out of the Cabinet Room over to No. 11 on one occasion, I remember Morrison saying to me, 'I wish I could know when I could trust that man.' Later Attlee so manoeuvred and timed his own retirement from the leadership of the Labour Party as to make Morrison's succession impossible. There was no love lost between Morrison and Bevin either. There was a story that someone once remarked to Bevin that Morrison was his own worst enemy. 'Not when I'm around he isn't!' replied Ernie. As for Dalton, with his booming voice, his constant intrigues, and his cultivation of the younger members and some of the trade union leaders, I found few who really liked him. He was certainly critical of Attlee, and disloyal to him too. Attlee did not trust him and later seized on an incident that might have been overlooked in order to accept his resignation.

On 27 July 1945, however, I was naïve and innocent enough to think that we were all a happy band of comrades, determined to build

Jerusalem in England's green and pleasant land, and at that time I was rather more closely involved with the Lord Chancellor than with the political side.

The Lord Chancellor was William Jowitt. He had been a Liberal. He was much criticized for crossing the floor, but with the virtual demise of the Liberal Party it was a legitimate and realistic thing for him to do. A big and handsome man, articulate and with an excellent voice, he was well cast for the office of Lord Chancellor. In fact there was no other candidate. He had little influence in the Government and his sincerity was not always trusted, but he performed his duties well and made some excellent speeches. Perhaps I am prejudiced in his favour because he never once questioned the correctness of any of the legal opinions I expressed to the Cabinet! Stafford Cripps, a much more brilliant lawyer than Jowitt, was not quite so deferential.

Jowitt sent for me and said, 'As far as the Attorney Generalship is concerned, you choose yourself. You have the job – but whom should we appoint as Solicitor?' I suggested the name of a Scottish KC MP who specialized in Revenue work. Jowitt accepted this, but it later turned out that Stafford Cripps, while agreeing with my appointment, wanted to see Frank Soskice, a Junior I did not know, as Solicitor. I made some rapid enquiry about him and concluded that he would indeed be most suitable. It turned out to be an extremely happy choice from every point of view. Frank was the son of a Russian emigré who had been a well-known and active associate of Kerensky at the time of the abortive 'white' counter-revolution in 1920. He was himself British, an Oxford graduate, highly intelligent, absolutely loyal and trustworthy, and he became my constant friend, companion and alter ego (for that is what the Solicitor General is) for the next five years. When I ceased to be Attorney, he took my place for a brief period and in a subsequent Labour government he was Home Secretary. Most unhappily he died prematurely of an obscure and painful disease. I lost one of my best friends.

I fetched him out of the Commons chamber – where he was waiting to take the oath – to tell him of his appointment and then went with him to be formally invited by Attlee. Clem, his usual taciturn self, simply said, 'I want you, Hartley, to be my Attorney and you, Frank, to be my Solicitor General. Do you accept?' I readily agreed but then said – as

Frank and I had agreed to do in a very short talk on the way – that we would both prefer not to receive the customary knighthood awarded on the occasion of appointments to the law officerships. It was a naïve and foolish gesture. Herbert Bowden, who later became the Chief Whip of the Party, and still later Lord Aylestone, was present and immediately intervened.

'For goodness' sake don't do anything like that. The lads will be furious if you don't get your knighthoods,' he said.

'Of course,' said Clem, 'you must take your honours with good grace in the ordinary course – goodbye.' So there was no further argument about that and in due time we were kneeling before the monarch. Years later, in subsequent Labour governments, the Attorneys and Solicitors General further diminished their impact on the legal and political scene by not taking the knighthoods.

I cannot say that I was overjoyed at the appointment. Earlier Press comment had made it clear that I was the probable candidate, but although the post of Attorney General would keep me in close contact with my profession, my real hope had been not to be a mere political lawyer but to have a political and constructive role in the country's social and foreign affairs. I had to realize, however, that there was a scarcity of qualified lawyers in the Labour Party at the time – and that if I had refused to accept the invitation I should have been regarded as unhelpful and would probably not have been offered any other job.

The position of Law Officer in those days was one of high importance. I set out in detail the responsibilities of the office in a statement to the Commons on 29 January 1951. But as I write this memoir to describe my time as Attorney General, it appears that certain very significant changes have since taken place, some of them subtle and some not so subtle, without any public or parliamentary debate having taken place. These changes have had the result of reducing the office to something equivalent to that of a junior ministry and that, indeed, is how the Attorney's rôle is now regarded in the House. One of the more subtle changes is that, without any great publicity, the Attorney General's Chambers have been quietly moved from the Law Courts to, of all places, Buckingham Gate. This move to the Whitehall area seems first to have been promoted by Sam Silkin when he was Attorney General. But Silkin never left a mark on the Law Office, or anything else, and when Michael Havers succeeded in 1979 he promptly put his foot on the idea.

Traditionally, the Law Officers had a large suite of chambers at the Royal Courts of Justice, and this was appropriate and convenient as the Attorney and Solicitor General would normally have been appearing in the courts frequently if not almost daily to conduct important cases in the public interest. They also needed to be conveniently placed for close contact with the Treasury Counsel. The removal to Buckingham Gate seems to involve a departure from court duties and inevitably some detachment from the Treasury 'devils' which is in itself regrettable. After the elevation of Michael Havers to the House of Lords it became very noticeable that the Law Officers appeared personally in court with increasing infrequency, if at all. The then Attorney told me that in 1992 he had appeared once. Not once a week – but once in a year! Other counsel represent a Law Officer in cases that previously would have been handled by the Law Officer himself. Indeed, even that is becoming unusual: counsel now says he appears to represent the Director of Public Prosecutions, or the Senior Fraud Office or some particular ministry.

This change in the activities of the Law Officers is said to be due to the much greater volume of work in which they are now involved in advising ministers. There is no doubt that the whole mechanism of government is now much more complicated than it was in my day. On the one hand, European organizations are increasingly involved in the policies and legislation of individual states in the Community, in spite of any 'subsidiarity' we might have under Maastricht. And associated with E.U. laws are rules under the Universal Declaration of Human Rights and other international conventions. In these matters the policies and the legislation of the United Kingdom are liable to be passed upon by the European Tribunals or Courts of Justice. It must also be said that the approach of the European lawyers is often more a matter of philosophy than of obedience; the British, by contrast with some other Europeans, regard it as a duty to conform to the rules and practices of the European Tribunals. A system of judicial review by British courts of action taken by Government departments has now been established whereby the judges can pass upon the administrative propriety of ministerial decisions in particular cases. Because of these and other considerations – not least, I dare say, the desire of ministers to fortify themselves with the Law Officer's support if not, indeed, to have the Law Officers as an alibi – it seems that ministers do increasingly bring the Law Officer's department into consultation. These consultations do not, however, by any means always involve the personal attendance of a Law Officer outside his chambers. The request for advice will more usually be in writing and the advice will be given in a letter from the department's legal secretary stating the opinion of the Law Officer.

It is said that the pressure of work for ministers is now so great that court attendances are impossible save in the most exceptional cases. I find this surprising and regrettable. In the period immediately after the war, there was a very great deal of such work: we wrote Opinions for departments on legal aspects of policy or administration; we advised the Cabinet or particular Departments; we drafted, piloted or assisted in the passage of bills through the Commons, and so on. The Solicitor General and I invariably moved at six o'clock from the Law Courts to our rooms in the House of Commons, or to the Bench in the House itself, and stayed until the House rose, often after midnight. I find it difficult to believe that the Law Officers of today are more heavily involved on the governmental and parliamentary side than we were. Moreover, they now have fifteen legal assistants working on advices in their chambers. We had none!

At the same time as these changes in the activities of the Law Officers are occurring, other associated changes are taking place. Decisions for which the Attorney General would previously have taken public responsibility are now announced as having been made by the Director of Public Prosecutions or by the head of the Serious Fraud Office or some other body. These decisions are often of importance; it may be that the Secretary of State for this department or that is unable to publish in full the report of a statutory enquiry in view of a statement by the Serious Fraud Office that police enquiries are being conducted into the matter and subsequent proceedings might be prejudiced. In the event, after enquiries have been carried out in what may seem a dilatory way for perhaps a year, proceedings may not even be instituted. The report might then not appear at all, or might then be published, but would be stale and discredited because of the absence of criminal proceedings. Previously, when such decisions were taken by the Attorney General, he was answerable in Parliament. The Director of Public Prosecutions or the Serious Fraud Office is not so answerable, except through the Attorney. Even some of the previous and important duties of the Director of Public Prosecutions seem to have become absorbed by the Serious Fraud Office which, established by the Criminal Justice Act of 1987, acts 'under the superintendence' of the Attorney General who, as far as the public know, rarely appears to intervene and whose superin, tendence does not seem notable. And I believe the Law Officers are no longer answerable in the Commons for the Lord Chancellor's Department. There is now a parliamentary secretary in the Commons. These are important constitutional changes and I am not at all happy about them. They may be due to pressure of work.

One factor I know has no relevance. When I became Attorney the remuneration was by way of a salary of £5,000 per annum plus fees paid on actual legal work done. In my first year, although the fees then were far lower in nominal terms than they would be now, I could cer, tainly have earned more than the Prime Minister, whose salary was then £10,000. I thought at the time that my total earnings including the salary might easily be as much as £20,000 (which in real terms would only have been twice as much as I had earned in my last year as a Northern Circuit Junior). As the good Socialist that I was, I felt I could not justify this and after discussions Frank Soskice and I agreed to change the system so that the Attorney and Solicitor would, like other ministers, be paid a salary. I was immodest enough to fix with the Treasury that the Attorney's fee should be the same as the Prime Minister, £10,000, with the Solicitor at £7,000. This was significantly less than the Attorney had earned before the war. There was some crit, icism in the profession of this departure from tradition, it being thought by some that the absence of fees for court work might in the eyes of the profession and the public diminish the significance of such work as part of the Law Officers' duties.

If court practice had, up to the time the Law Officers virtually aban, doned it, been continuing at the old rate the Attorney's fees would surely have been in the hundreds of thousands. Had I been Attorney I confess I would not readily have given up such an income and moved to Buckingham Gate! What is more, the change from fees and court work would immediately have attracted publicity and certainly the protests of the Bar. As it was, I fear that what Frank and I did in 1946 in one sense did pave the way to Buckingham Gate, although not with bricks of gold.

As for Frank Soskice and myself, we were not in the least affected by the fact that we were no longer paid fees for the cases we appeared in. We really enjoyed court work; we thought it important to remain in close contact with the Bench and Bar and we continued doing as many cases as before. We were workaholics.

For the most part, the departments have their own solicitors; and very often their own standing counsel (appointed on the recommendation of the Attorney General) who deal with matters of ordinary everyday occurrence. The advice of the Law Officers used only to be sought where some problem arose of special importance, perhaps because of its legal difficulty, very often because of considerations of policy or public relations arising in connection with it, or possibly because there was a very large amount at stake, and the department concerned did not want to take any risks.

When matters arise of a constitutional nature or affect international relations, the Attorney General is often asked to advise either the Cabinet or the Prime Minister. Indeed, since he is collectively responsible for all legal or constitutional action that is taken, along with all other members of the Government, it is his clear duty when occasion arises to call attention to it, if need be in the strongest terms. A case in point, where I assume the Attorney would have volunteered his advice if not asked for it, was the Suez affair in 1956. What advice he gave we do not know! He sits as a member of many Cabinet committees whose work may have legal or constitutional implications, and he sees all relevant Cabinet papers. There is, in fact, no rule of law that prevents his being a member of the Cabinet, but for a long time now it has been considered more appropriate that the independence which is necessary to a proper discharge of his office should not be blurred by his inclusion in the political body that takes decisions on policy after receiving the legal advice he has given. The Attorney General is, I suppose, almost the only officer of State who can go, as I did more than once, to a meeting of the Cabinet and say, in effect: 'You cannot do that – it is contrary to the law' or 'It is contrary to constitutional principles.' A Cabinet might take the view that they were going to do it all the same, but as a rule, and certainly in my experience, when it receives advice of that kind, it generally abides by it.

Opinions that have historical interest may be published with the permission of the Law Officer of the time, but generally they are never made available to the public. There is an additional protection which Law Officers enjoy; the Speaker has ruled that a minister who faces criticism must defend his policy or action himself without attempting to hide behind the Law Officers' opinion. So when the minister is told 'You cannot do that', he has to get up and say: 'I cannot do this', but he cannot add, 'I cannot do it because the Attorney General tells me I cannot do it.' Nowadays, however, there is of course 'the Leak'.

There was another branch of the Attorney's duties in which his detachment from the party political aspects of government was complete. The Attorney in my day was responsible for all Crown litigation. The practice used to be that he would 'lead' himself in cases that were of constitutional importance or particular legal difficulty and in tax cases. He or the Solicitor would usually represent the Government in any case before the International Court of Justice. With respect to criminal cases the Attorney General would normally prosecute in cases of treason or other cases involving serious constitutional considerations or matters of public order. There is a tradition that he should always prosecute in a case of murder by poisoning; it is an offence that is rarely committed nowadays (or should I say rarely discovered?) but I assume that it still remains the rule that the Attorney General should prosecute. The Attorney General may also intervene in other murders if they are of great importance or in other criminal prosecutions that present very special features. In such cases he has to act with a certain amount of discretion because the appearance of a Law Officer in a criminal prosecution might perhaps seem oppressive. It would be only in very unusual cases – I do not think it happened when I was Attorney – that the Attorney would appear to prosecute a case in a magistrates' court. Nevertheless, in all cases conducted by the Director of Public Prosecutions, the Attorney General in my day had the task of nominating the counsel who was to conduct the prosecution, and occasionally he might consult with that counsel before the prosecution was proceeded with, even if he did not himself appear in the case.

In the administration of the criminal law, it is the Home Secretary who is, broadly speaking, answerable for the police in the House of Commons, but for the enforcement of the criminal law in the courts it is, or was in my day, the Attorney General who is responsible. The Director of Public Prosecutions – a civil servant – acts under his super-intendence and is subject to his directions. He can direct that a prosecu-tion should take place in a particular case or, on the contrary, he may prevent a case being prosecuted by entering a *nolle prosequi*. It is often said nowadays that the DPP or the Serious Fraud Office has decided this or that. Indeed, the Attorney General is hardly ever mentioned nowadays. But the Attorney General does not escape his ultimate responsibility for such decisions. This gives the Attorney General a wide discretion to see that the processes of the criminal law are not abused. Whether he still exercises that discretion or leaves it all to the Director I simply do not know. Where a private prosecution is commenced, the Attorney can either intervene by requiring the Director of Public Prosecutions to take the case over, or he may himself enter a *nolle prosequi* at any stage to stop the proceedings, which is by no means an acquittal. The Crown could always, although it rarely would, prosecute afresh. But the Attorney General has an undoubted right to stop criminal proceedings at any point he likes, and whether the defendants like it or not, although gener-ally, of course, they have no reason to object.

Akin to the power of entering a *nolle prosequi* is the right the Attorney has to decide, in cases that are referred to him, whether to prosecute at all. It is by no means in every case where he considers a conviction might be obtained. Sometimes there are reasons of public policy which make it undesirable to prosecute; perhaps the wrongdoer has already suffered enough; perhaps the prosecution would enable him to represent himself as a martyr; or perhaps he is too ill to stand his trial without great risk to his health, or life. There was the case of the theft from Westminster Abbey of the Stone of Scone, for example; I thought the public inter-est would not be served by what might have been turned into a kind of State trial for a bunch of unimportant zealots. It is of course open to a private citizen to institute proceedings himself. As a rule, however, it is not desirable that a private citizen should set the law in motion and there are a number of statutory offences in which there cannot be a prosecu-tion without the *fiat* of the Attorney.

Under the Criminal Appeal Act and the Courts-Martial Appeal

Act, no Criminal Appeal may be taken to the House of Lords except with the *fiat*, the certificate, of the Attorney General that the case involves a point of law of exceptional public importance. Sometimes it is said that such power ought to be vested in the courts rather than in the Attorney General. But Parliament has twice decided in recent years that the Attorney General may be in a better position to decide whether leave to appeal should be given. There are many applications for leave to appeal to the House of Lords in criminal cases, and many of them are rather frivolous and have to be rejected, but on the whole I think the system works reasonably well. It may sometimes happen that the application is for leave to appeal against a conviction that may have been secured by the Attorney General himself, which may put him in an invidious position.

In the case of the war-time traitor, William Joyce (Lord Haw-Haw), I prosecuted, and eventually there was an application for leave to appeal to the House of Lords. Of course, I gave it; although in a notorious Irish case of treason (Casement), involving the death penalty, the then Attorney General (Birkenhead) refused to give his assent to the appeal, which of course raised comments.

The true doctrine is that it is the duty of the Attorney General in deciding, for instance, whether or not to authorize a prosecution to acquaint himself with all the relevant facts. In order to do so he may, although he is not obliged to, consult with his colleagues in the Government; and indeed, as Lord Simon once said, he would in some cases be a fool if he did not. However, the responsibility for the eventual decision rests with the Attorney General, and he is not to be put, and in my experience never is put, under pressure by his colleagues to take a particular decision. The only such incident I remember clearly concerned a dockers' strike, incorrectly recounted in Michael Foot's otherwise excellent life of Nye Bevan. I had told Nye that I intended – if the strike went on – to prosecute the dockers who were engaged in a strike action that was clearly illegal. I bided my time as long as I could. One day I met Nye in the corridors. He said, 'They are on their knees – go for them now.' I had already so decided. Unfortunately the jury did not agree and, having returned a guilty verdict on one count in the indictment, disagreed on another owing to an unusual lack of clarity in the summing-up by Lord Goddard. I entered a *nolle prosequi*. Later, Nye bitterly attacked me for prosecuting at all. I then had a private meeting of the Cabinet Committee concerned and told them what had happened. Mrs Bessie Braddock, the redoubtable and delightful Labour politician, wrote in her autobiography that Nye had lied.

If political considerations, in the broad sense, arise, it is the Attorney General who, applying his mind as best he can judicially to them, has to be the sole judge of the weight of such considerations. That was the view that Lord Birkenhead once expressed on a famous occasion, and Lord Simon – a better Attorney General than Birkenhead – reiterated that the Attorney General 'should absolutely decline to receive orders from the Prime Minister or Cabinet or anybody else, that he shall prosecute'. And I would add that he should also decline to receive orders that he should not prosecute. That is the traditional and undoubted responsibility of the Attorney General in such matters. This English tradition – which nowadays is sometimes known as 'The Shawcross Doctrine' – is now generally accepted. At a ninetieth birthday dinner kindly given for me by Sir Patrick Mayhew, and attended by all those who had been involved in the Law Office, including the Lord Chancellor, Lord Mackay, it was set out in full in a framed document, and all the guests signed it. It would be difficult to have a more authoritative statement!

All this does not mean that the Attorney General is not entitled to his own political life; far from it. He may be denied a private life, very often members of the Government are, but that is politics. But he may engage, as I too often did, in contentious politics, the only essential qualification being that he must not allow them to affect his official actions. There is nothing startling or inconsistent with this British tradition. Many of the distinguished holders of the Attorney Generalship have engaged in the past in very active politics, even more violently than I have ever done myself; I do not think anyone would say that Lord Carson or Lord Birkenhead entirely succeeded in concealing their political inclinations when they were Law Officers. In truth, the real danger in non-political matters is that the Law Officer, in his conscientious anxiety to be impartial, may fall over backwards in favour of his political opponents.

So much for the position of the Attorney in relation to government departments and in the discharge of his functions as chief legal adviser. The Law Officers answer questions in the Commons in regard to legal issues that may arise in the course of government. They used to answer in the House of Commons for the various departments and interests for which the Lord Chancellor is responsible, but this no longer seems the position. They are *ex officio* members of all standing committees, and sometimes, as in the case of the Crown Proceedings Bill and the Legal Aid Bill and – alas – the Trades Disputes Bill, the Law Officers are in charge of a bill throughout its passage through the House of Commons. It usually falls to the Solicitor General – I am glad I was never Solicitor General – to assist the Chancellor of the Exchequer in regard to the committee stage of the Finance Bill, an extremely difficult task because no laymen and very few lawyers can have a complete knowledge of that branch of the law, except that it always raises the taxation we have to pay.

The Attorney General is the head of the Bar of England, although how long the Bar will be content with this position if the Attorney General ceases to appear regularly in court is certainly doubtful and will have to be looked at. The present position is most anomalous, but I do not think it would be well resolved by making the Chairman of the Bar Council leader. But who else? Not, one hopes, the self-advertising Silks whose conduct often seems addressed to the popular Press rather than to the court. The Attorney General is an *ex officio* member of the General Council of the Bar. In general, questions of professional conduct are usually discharged nowadays with the full consent and approval of the Attorney General by the Bar Council, but I suppose there are still occa-sions when the Attorney has to advise, as I had to do, on questions of professional etiquette, such as whether a barrister is bound to accept, without discrimination, briefs that may be offered to him.

Among laymen on both sides of politics there are some foolish and short-sighted enough to think that a barrister may and should pick and choose the cases in which he is prepared to appear. Socialist lawyers – and indeed I was one – have been subject to bitter attacks in extreme left-wing papers and by those who do not like the subject-matter of cases in which those lawyers have been briefed, or perhaps the politics or occupa-tions – in my case capitalists and mine-owners – of the clients they are representing. *Tribune* once wrote that I had invented the 'Cab Rank rule', as it is called, under which a barrister had to accept any brief ten-dered on behalf of a British litigant. Quite untrue. But it is well to remember that a barrister must always accept a brief on behalf of any client in any court or tribunal before which that barrister normally holds himself out to practise. This arose in 1792 in the case of the prosecution of Tom Paine, when he published a second part of *The Rights of Man*. Paine had attacked in strong language the constitution and the govern, ment of England, and an information was accordingly laid against him; he was to be prosecuted. The great advocate, Erskine, was sent a brief to defend. At this time Erskine was the Attorney General to the Prince of Wales, a position that entitled him to accept private work, but he was warned in advance that, if he appeared on behalf of Paine, he would be dismissed from office. Nonetheless, Erskine accepted a retainer as he was bound to do, and made a brave defence for his client. He was deprived of his office of Attorney General to the Prince of Wales, but in a famous speech he said: 'From the moment that any advocate can be permitted to say that he will or will not stand between the Crown and the subject arraigned in the court where he daily sits to practise, from that moment the liberties of England are at an end.' That was truly said because in totalitarian countries, Fascist, Communist or whatever, no lawyer dares to put forward any real defence on behalf of those accused of crimes against the rulers, and one sees the depths to which the profession can sink and the bogus trials which can result with lawyers discriminating between persons for whom they would act. There is a similar danger in some racial cases. In this country the rule reiterated by Erskine has pre, vailed and Erskine himself was ultimately vindicated and became a Lord Chancellor. Loyalty to one's party is fortunately not incompatible with loyalty to professional and constitutional principles, to justice or to one's country.

Finally – and this is a field of great significance – the Attorney General is in a way the protector of not only charities but of the public interest generally. This duty has a very early origin. He has for long been the proper person to take legal proceedings where the interests of the public are endangered or where acts tending to the public injury are taking place without authority. When somebody improperly blocks a highway (that is one instance, still quite common) the Attorney General either directly or on the relation of a private subject intervenes by court proceedings to keep the way open. A modern variation of that occurs in connection with aircraft accidents. When I was Attorney General, the practice was established that the Attorney might intervene in any investigation into the cause of an accident (as in the case of the 1952 'Comet' disasters, described later) and might also make representations to the minister concerned that a public inquiry should be held. I was also concerned with the tribunal presided over by Mr Justice Lynskey, which enquired into certain allegations of corruption, involving suspicion against certain members of the Government. I felt that it was of the utmost importance to maintain the position that it was the duty (however personally unpleasant) of His Majesty's Attorney General to represent the public interest with complete objectivity and detachment, and that to refuse to discharge that duty in a particular case in which the public interest might be suspected to conflict with the interests of certain of his friends or political colleagues would be tantamount to saying that the office itself was inadequate to represent and protect the public interest against whosoever might challenge it.

The Attorney General is, of course, assisted by the Solicitor General, who in the absence of the Attorney may discharge almost all of his functions. Although the responsibility remains with the Attorney General and he tends to attract the major praise or blame, he and the Solicitor work in the closest concert together, and those Attorneys who are fortunate enough to have, as I had, a good Solicitor, find him the very greatest help and support. Usually, of course, the Solicitor eventually succeeds to the office of Attorney General.

Like other offices, that of Attorney General is in some respects what its holder can make of it. Sometimes great lawyers have filled the office unexpectedly badly, and sometimes lesser lawyers have filled it well. An Attorney General may be rash and truculent, as I dare say I was, or he may pursue a pedestrian course, never intervening save when he is compelled to, and fearful ever of putting his foot down wrongly. A good Law Officer has to try and find a course between those two extremes.

I was sworn into the then great office of Attorney General in August 1945. It was not an office that I had sought, for my interest in those foolish days was political rather than legal. It was not an office for which I was particularly qualified. But it happened to be an office for which I was the only obvious candidate at the time. I entered it with modest confidence. I like to think that when I left it in 1951 the office had not diminished in stature.

CHAPTER 6

The Traitors

AFTER my appointment as Attorney it fell to my lot to deal with the trial for treason of British subjects and the intended trial of at least some of the leading Nazis. The former were of transient interest only; the latter was, or so we hoped at the time, to have a profound and lasting influence on the law of nations. We were starry-eyed still.

The very first case I had as Attorney was the trial of William Joyce for treason. It was a case that attracted enormous public and also legal interest at the time, but it remains in my mind as one of which I am not specially proud.

The facts as they emerged at the trial became clear enough. Joyce was born in 1906 in the United States of parents who were of Irish origin, but who had emigrated and become naturalized subjects of the United States as long ago as 1892. He was therefore a natural-born American subject. In 1909, the Joyce family returned to Ireland and lived there until 1922, when they came to England, following their son William, who, the year before, had settled in this country, at the age of fifteen. He and his parents were assumed, and probably still thought themselves, to be British subjects. In 1922, Joyce took and passed the London matriculation and then studied at Birkbeck College where he graduated in 1927. Soon after his matriculation he had applied for enrolment in the London University Officer Training Corps. In the letter of application he said that he was born in the United States but of British parents, had left America when two years of age and did not propose to return. He added, 'As a young man of pure British descent, some of whose fore-fathers have held high positions in the British Army, I have always been desirous of devoting what little capability and energy I may possess to the service of the country I love so dearly.' His father was asked by the OTC Commandant to confirm that he (the father) had never been naturalized American, and he did so. Joyce was duly enrolled in the OTC and remained with it until 1926. But far from joining the British Army, he became from 1923 to 1937 a member of the British Fascist movement, eventually led by Oswald Mosley. From 1928 to 1933, he was engaged in post-graduate study of philology and psychology, and it has rightly been written of him that he became a man of very high education. In 1933 he applied for a British passport, describing himself as a British subject 'having been born in Galway, Ireland.' The passport was duly issued and subsequently reissued. In 1937, he established his own National Socialist League and wrote articles and pamphlets in support of Fascism. Significantly, the final renewal of his passport was on 24 August 1939. A few days later he travelled to Germany with his wife and within a fortnight of his arrival he began his propaganda work for Nazi Germany as a radio broadcaster. He was specifically described as British: this was his value to the Nazis. Because of his pseudo-Oxford accent he had early become known as 'Lord Haw-Haw', and he had a call-sign that sounded like 'Jairmany calling'. In September 1940, he was granted German nationality and his propaganda talks were broad-cast throughout the war. In his last broadcast, from Hamburg on 30 April 1945, he said, 'Germany is sorely wounded but her spirit is not broken. Her people are conscious of their duty . . . in this hour of supreme trial they seem to understand the European position with a clarity which is unfortunately denied to the people of Britain and they realize that the great alternative lies between Civilization and Bolshevism.' I have no doubt that this is what he really believed.

After the collapse of Nazi Germany, he found himself on the run in the British Occupied Zone near the Danish frontier. There, by chance, he saw two British officers in a wood searching for timber for fires. Foolishly, he spoke to them in English. His voice betrayed him; one of the officers asked, 'You wouldn't be William Joyce, would you?' Joyce put his hand in his pocket, intending to pull out a passport with a false name. One of the officers, thinking he was going to bring out a revolver, shot him in the foot. He was arrested and in due time brought to England for trial.

The trial was set for the Central Criminal Court on 28 June 1945 but was postponed to 17 September. I was appointed Attorney General only at the end of July and had an enormous amount of other work to cope with, so there was little time to prepare the case for opening. But I worked hard in those days and burned much midnight oil. I well remember on 17 September 1945 walking up the street with my clerk, Matthew Robinson, to the Old Bailey. It was my first case as Attorney General and my first ever at the Central Criminal Court; I approached it with a definite feeling of awe, and certainly excitement. Inside the building we found that the Law Officers had their own very grand special Robing Room. I robed and walked into the Number One Court, which was packed with barristers, anxious to see the start of a trial that was the first for treason for a long time and was expected to be sensational. At the back of the Bench sat the Lord Mayor and two aldermen, magnifi-cently robed and with their gold chains. In addition, the court was filled with other spectators; the so-called 'City Lands' Benches, reserved for privileged guests, were full of such persons. I have always disapproved of spectators of that kind attending criminal trials in which they have no serious interest, particularly when a man's life was at stake, but the courts must be open to all, and the interest in this case was inevitable.

The trial was before Mr Justice Tucker, an able and distinguished judge who, however, I fancied rather felt the strain imposed by the immense publicity and the difficulty of the case. I led two very experi-enced Juniors, T. K. Byrne and Gerald Howard, who later became an MP and eventually a judge. The Defence was led by Gerard Slade, QC, with Mr Derek Curtis-Bennett and Mr James Burgess supporting him. The last was, I think, a little by way of being a Fascist; the first made it his proud boast that no drop of alcohol had ever passed his lips, but he was an able man who became a busy practitioner and eventually a judge.

My argument for the Prosecution was that although Joyce was a natural-born American subject, subjects of the British Crown were not the only ones who might owe a duty of allegiance to the Crown, and if these others broke that duty, they too might be guilty of treason. Those also could commit treason who were at the material time entitled to the *protection* of the British Crown, whatever such protection might be worth. The famous Chief Justice of the seventeenth century, Lord Coke, referred with approval in one of the cases he tried to what was already an established maxim, *Protectio trahit subjectionem et subjectio protectionem* (Protection draws allegiance just as allegiance draws protection). I argued that by deliberately applying for and obtaining a British passport and, most significantly, by asking for and being granted its renewal just as he was about to leave for Germany in 1939, Joyce had placed himself under the protection of the Crown and had thereby undertaken the correlative duty of allegiance so long as his right to claim the protection of the passport continued. I quoted the words with which a British passport then opened 'as not being idle words . . . sanctified and recognized as they are by international diplomatic usage . . .'

> We, Sir John Allsebrook Simon, a member of His Majesty's Most Honourable Privy Council etc. etc. etc., His Majesty's Principal Secretary of State for Foreign Affairs requests and requires in the name of His Majesty all those whom it may concern to allow the bearer to pass freely without let or hindrance and to afford him every assistance and protection of which he may stand in need.

And then I coined the perhaps picturesque phrase that 'Joyce had clothed himself in the Union Jack', whatever his nationality might be. The basic argument was fully canvassed by both sides; Gerald Slade and I dug out a number of ancient legal authorities, while emphasizing that such authorities ought not to be read in too literal and restrictive a sense and without regard to the matter in hand. It was not in this way that the principles of English Law were elucidated. The slavish search for exact precedent was always a somewhat sterile pursuit. The incalculable advantage of the whole system of British law was that its principles were capable of adaptation to new circumstances perpetually arising.

Eventually the judge ruled that in law there was no doubt that Joyce, because he had obtained the protection of the British passport, owed a duty of temporary allegiance to the Crown. After that the verdict of the jury was inevitable. It was pure theatre and, although the case was conducted coldly and prosaically, the atmosphere was bound to be dramatic when the trial culminated in the judge, the black cap placed over his wig, pronouncing the macabre death sentence which ended with the words 'and may the Lord have mercy on your soul', followed by 'Amen' from the Chaplain.

There could be no doubt that the broadcasts which Joyce made lent 'aid and comfort', as the legal phrase was, to the Crown's enemies. How much that aid and comfort was worth to the Nazis is less clear. The BBC carried out an elaborate study which purported to show that while Joyce's broadcasts were listened to by a large number and taken seriously during the 'phoney war' period, listeners shrank to insignificant numbers during the years of the real war and most regarded Joyce as 'so fantastic as to be funny'. Learned as this study was, it is nevertheless true to say that I and my acquaintances did find the Hamburg broadcasts disturbing at the time.

Joyce naturally appealed to the Court of Criminal Appeal, which was presided over by the already ailing Chief Justice, Lord Caldecote, and included Mr Justice Humphreys, then our most experienced crim-inal judge, as well as Mr Justice Lynskey from the Northern Circuit. The Court unanimously rejected the appeal. From there the appeal could only go to the House of Lords if the Attorney General gave his fiat to certify that the case involved a point of law of exceptional public importance and that it was in the public interest that a further appeal should be held. This fiat, of course, I at once gave.

The appeal was heard by a strong court of five: the Lord Chancellor and Lords Macmillan, Wright, Simonds and Porter. They gave their decision, dismissing the appeal by a majority of four to one, and announced that they would give their reasons later. That was on 18 December 1945. Joyce was hanged on 3 January 1946, before the reasons were announced. This attracted some criticism of the Home Secretary and surprised me a little. But Chuter Ede was as fair and humane a Home Secretary as I have ever known and as eight out of nine judges had been agreed on Joyce's guilt, nothing would have been gained by delaying the inevitable end. Yet I still feel it was a mistake. The dissenting opinion was on the part of Lord Porter who, while accepting the general legal posi-tion as put forward by the Crown, felt that the jury should have been asked whether at the time of the relevant broadcasts, Joyce's allegiance to the Crown because of his possession of a British passport still in fact con-tinued. I always considered that of the Law Lords concerned, Lord Porter was the most learned and responsible. His dissenting view may well have been correct, although no one can doubt that the jury would have given an affirmative verdict on the point, had it been put to them.

Anyone who doubts the justice from an ethical rather than strictly legal point of view should read the masterly discussion of the case by Rebecca West in her book *The Meaning of Treason*. She had no doubt at all – nor indeed had J. W. Hall in his volume on the trial in the 'Notable British Trials' series – that Joyce was morally guilty. Moreover, all nine judges accepted the correctness of the Crown's argument in law.

Why then, as a lawyer, do I now say that this legal success is one of which I am not particularly proud? It is because I fear the prosecution – which in this context means me – failed to give to the public a simple, straightforward legal basis on which to rest a capital charge. It was all too subtle and technical, not calculated to convince non-legal minds of the reality of Joyce's guilt in law and his moral culpability. After its conclusion, the case became the subject of much public discussion and some argument among the lawyers. The general opinion – among the less informed at all events, which is to say the great majority – was that Joyce's execution was not fair. Most people, it is true, had hated Joyce during the war. But what stuck in their minds after the trial was the fact that he was not, after all, a British subject, but an American, and that he could therefore not be guilty of treason against the British Crown. For them the Protection/Allegiance theory arising from the passport was a subtlety that had no meaning. It is one thing to persuade a court of a particular legal position. It is sometimes quite another to persuade the great British public that the legal position is also fair and just. They are two different audiences and I failed to convince each equally. It is of the greatest importance that the public accept the law as fair. *Mea culpa* in this instance.

After the Joyce case there were four or five other treason trials for which as Attorney I was responsible. Only one had any general interest and that was the case of John Amery, the son of Leopold Amery, the distinguished statesman who had been Secretary of State for India.

I will say little of the facts and circumstances of this case lest relatives for whom I have the greatest respect be further distressed. But some facts have recently been published in the release of wartime papers by the Public Records Office.

Amery, a would be film producer, was trapped in Vichy France when the Germans invaded. He offered his services to the Germans as a propaganda broadcaster. He also attempted to recruit British prisoners

of war into a German-run British Legion. He was captured by parti-
sans in Italy in 1945 and later that year pleaded guilty to an indictment
for treason though the consequence – death – was fully explained to him
by an apparently rather shocked trial judge, Sir Travers Humphreys,
before he gave his plea.

The papers show that shortly before his execution psychiatrists
engaged by his family delivered the opinion that he was 'morally insane'.
This opinion was endorsed by Home Office specialists who recommended that his sentence be commuted to life imprisonment. However
the government rejected this advice. I grieved for his family.

CHAPTER 7

Nuremberg and the Nazi Criminals

I

WHEN we think of war criminals nowadays we generally have in mind the Nazi war criminals, the leaders of whom were tried at Nuremberg, rather than British traitors. Indeed, a whole literature has been built up on this subject. I am incapable of making any significant addition to it and what I shall write now will relate only to my own part in the matter. I have hitherto taken the view that now the principles established by the Nuremberg Trial have become an accepted part of international law, the time has come to put all the terrible factual details behind us. In the years since those awful things were done, new generations have grown up in Germany unstained by any guilt borne by some of those that preceded them. The new German administration, recognizing the basic equality of all men, has shown its determination to build and maintain a real democracy, and make its contribution to the pursuit of peace and happiness. Great difficulties and dangers still confront the world and this is not a time for recrimination or the revival of bitterness against Germany for the past. However, the recent revival of neo-Nazism makes it clear that it is also not a time to forget.

I am sure, and the more so because of the recent flagrant disregard of international law in the Gulf and Yugoslavia, that the lessons of history should not be casually forgotten and that there is advantage in the new generations that had no personal contact with the horrors of the Second World War knowing, dispassionately, something of what happens when, in a thirst for power, aggressive wars are prepared and fought and nations divide against nations in seeking each other's destruction. I am confirmed in this view by the disturbing emergence in Germany of a new, small section of people with Nazi leanings. I have no doubt that the German people will know best how to deal with such odious crea/ tures. But it is well that these latter/day Nazis should know how evil were their spiritual forebears. Moreover, there are a few polemicists in Britain and the United States who seek to pretend that the Holocaust never took place.

I came to the problem of what to do about the war criminals only after I was appointed Attorney General in August 1945. I had, however, and somewhat to my distaste, heard my one/time colleague Maxwell Fyfe making speeches during the election campaign about what 'he' was going to do about Goering, and I knew, of course, that some concrete measures had already been decided upon. Indeed, as early as October 1941, while the United States was still neutral, President Roosevelt drew attention to the wholesale execution of French hostages. 'One day', he said, 'a frightful retribution will be exacted.' I am not sure whether the British had made any pronouncements on the matter up to that time; we had been too fully involved in our own struggle for survival to bother much about what we would do to our enemies when eventually we won. The point was, as Secretary Stimson, the US Secretary for War, was to write later, 'We did not ask ourselves in 1939 or in 1940 or even in 1941 what punishment if any Hitler and his chief assistants deserved.' But in August 1942 President Roosevelt, who played the major role in the final decision, solemnly warned the Axis powers that 'the time will come when they will have to stand in the Courts of Law in the very countries they are oppressing and answer for their acts.'

In October 1942, in the United Kingdom, a committee was formed under the Lord Chancellor, John Simon, to consider the problem of war criminals in all its aspects. That committee directed the Treasury Solicitor to collect material upon which charges might subsequently be laid, and a long list was indeed prepared. I think the matter first arose for inter/Allied discussion and agreement in October 1943 at the Moscow Conference of foreign ministers. There, Mr Cordell Hull expressed a forthright opinion: 'If I had my way,' he said, 'I would take Hitler, and Mussolini and Tojo and their accomplices and bring them before a drum head court martial and at sunrise on the following morning there would be an historic incident.' This idea of a summary court martial attracted much support. Mr Molotov was, perhaps less unexpectedly, in favour of 'stern, swift justice'. The British position was equivocal. At one stage Mr Churchill favoured summary justice, but at the Moscow Conference Mr Eden is recorded as saying that all legal forms should be observed, whatever that may have meant. The following month the big three, Roosevelt, Churchill and Stalin, met in Teheran. It was their first meeting together and of course there were many more important things to discuss. It was not until the final dinner party on 29 November that the question of war criminals was raised. It was perhaps an unfortunate atmosphere. Marshal Stalin said that at least 50,000 of the German general staff must be physically and summarily liquidated. President Roosevelt, presumably construing the suggestion as made in jest, however grim, said that the number should be only 49,000. Winston Churchill was shocked: he said the British would never stand for such mass murder. 'I would rather', he said, 'be taken out into the garden here and now and be shot myself than sully my own and my country's honour with such infamy.'

The actual communiqué left the matter somewhat in the air. Those Nazis who had been responsible for, or had taken an active part in, atrocities, mass murders and executions would be sent back to those countries in which their abominable deeds had been done and punished according to their laws. Major criminals, it was added, whose offences had no particular geographical locale would be punished by the joint decision of the governments of the Allies. This sounded like executive action, but in fact the question remained open and was the subject of much debate.

In the autumn of 1944 Secretary Stimson, who was a very distinguished member of the New York Bar, thought the matter was important as a war aim and delegated responsibility to the Assistant Secretary, Jack McCloy. In a memorandum of 9 September 1944, Mr Stimson wrote:

Under the plan proposed by Mr Morgenthau [the energetic and sometimes said to be aggressive Secretary of the US Treasury], the so-called arch-criminals shall be put to death by the military without provision for any trial and upon mere identification after apprehension. The method of dealing with these and other criminals requires careful thought and a well-defined procedure. Such procedure must embody, in my judgement, at least the rudimentary aspects of the Bill of Rights, namely, notification to the accused of the charge, the right to be heard and, within reasonable limits, to call witnesses in his defense.

At the Quebec Conference in that year, the question of judicial trial as against executive shooting was not decided, but Mr Stimson is said to have heard from Mr McCloy reports that the President had there expressed himself as definitely in favour of execution without trial. This was deeply disturbing to the War Department. Stimson and McCloy set up a group of military lawyers to study in detail the possibilities for a trial, who after a month of study concluded that as well as local tribunals to punish particular war crimes, an international tribunal to prosecute criminals whose criminal activities had extended over several jurisdictions could be established. Colonel Bernays of the JAGD (Judge Advocate-General's Department) suggested the possibility of bringing charges against the whole scheme of Nazi totalitarian war, which, for the promotion of its end, had used methods that contravened the established rules of war. This virtually amounted to the theory of conspiracy. Mr Stimson was much attracted by the concept of a conspiracy as being the guide to a proper course in trying the Nazi leaders, and he reported on it to the President. Stimson recorded that the President

> was greatly interested and gave his very frank approval to my suggestion when I said that conspiracy . . . with . . . representatives of all classes of actors brought in from top to bottom would be the best way to try it and would give us a record and also a trial which would certainly persuade any onlooker of the evil of the Nazi system.

The President was thus already shifting from his original position and he appointed Judge Rosenman, his personal counsel, to study the problem. In January 1945, the US Secretaries of State and War and the Attorney General submitted a detailed memorandum setting out a carefully reasoned argument in favour of a judicial trial on charges of conspiracy:

The German leaders and the organizations employed by them, such as those referred to above (SA, SS, Gestapo), should be charged both with the commission of their atrocious crimes, and also with joint participation in a broad criminal enterprise which included and intended these crimes, or was reasonably calculated to bring them about.

The allegation of the criminal enterprise would be so couched as to permit full proof of the entire Nazi plan from its inception and the means used in its furtherance and execution, including the prewar atrocities and those committed against their own nationals, neutrals, and stateless persons, as well as the waging of an illegal war of aggression with ruthless disregard for international law and the rules of war. Such a charge would be firmly founded upon the rule of liability, common to all penal systems and included in the general doctrines of the laws of war, that those who participate in the formulation and execution of a criminal plan involving multiple crimes are jointly liable for each of the offences committed and jointly responsible for the acts of each other. Under such a charge there are admissible in evidence the acts of any of the conspirators done in furtherance of the conspiracy, whether or not these acts were in themselves criminal and subject to separate prosecution as such.

This was the so-called Yalta Memorandum, but at the Yalta Conference no action was taken other than an agreement for later consideration by the governments there represented. The US President sent Judge Rosenman to Europe to conduct negotiations with the governments concerned. Judge Rosenman had long, separate talks with Winston Churchill (including a weekend at Chequers), the Lord Chancellor, Anthony Eden and others of the British War Cabinet. Rosenman recorded that

With all of them I repeated what President Roosevelt had said to me, namely that in order to establish documentary proof of all that the Nazis had done and to prevent the rise of a new Napoleonic myth, a trial should be held before an international tribunal. All of these individuals as well as the British War Cabinet itself, stated in no uncertain terms that they wanted to treat the top six or seven Nazi criminals in a political military manner, namely to execute them and to announce to the world the next morning that they had been shot.

In fact the very day that President Roosevelt died, the British War Cabinet held a special meeting and again decided formally that they favoured this kind of disposal of the top Nazis: there was always the precedent of the way Napoleon was treated after defeat except that he was not shot but exiled without any trial.

President Truman was not slow to endorse his predecessor's instructions that there must be a trial. He appointed Justice Jackson of the US Supreme Court, who had written about the scope and importance of such a trial as Chief of Counsel before an international tribunal. Jackson did not resign from the Supreme Court but in effect was suspended from active participation in its membership until his new task should be complete. There was a good deal of criticism of him on this account. Justice Stone thought it quite wrong that a Supreme Court Justice should go off on what he described as 'this lynching expedition'.

And so, at the beginning of May 1945, Jackson plunged into the great project, the nature of which had only been settled as a matter of principle by his own government and which had by no means been agreed to by Britain or the other Allies. Its implementation would present the most formidable difficulties. Indeed, the two tasks of research into the preparation of the case itself and the negotiations for an agreement as to the form and method of trial were the most difficult and the most important of Justice Jackson's contributions to the whole project.

The British still remained hostile to the idea of a trial. Only a week before Jackson had been brought into the matter, the British Government had submitted an *aide memoire* setting out their view, which was strongly against a judicial trial and in favour of 'executive action'. It is worth quoting:

1. HMG assume that it is beyond question that Hitler and a number of arch-criminals associated with him (including Mussolini) must, so far as they fall into Allied hands, suffer the penalty of death for their conduct leading up to the war and for the wickedness which they have either themselves perpetrated or have authorized in the conduct of the

war. It would be manifestly impossible to punish war criminals of a lower grade by a capital sentence pronounced by a Military Court unless the ringleaders are dealt with with equal severity. This is really involved in the concluding sentence of the Moscow Declaration on this subject, which reserves for the arch-criminals whose offences have no special localization treatment to be determined in due course by the Allies.

2. It being conceded that these leaders must suffer death, the question arises whether they should be tried by some form of tribunal claiming to exercise judicial functions, or whether the decision taken by the Allies should be reached and enforced without the machinery of a trial. HMG thoroughly appreciated the arguments which have been advanced in favour of some form of preliminary trial. But HMG are also deeply impressed with the dangers and difficulties of this course, and they wish to put before their principal Allies, in a connected form, the arguments which have led them to think that execution without trial is the preferable course.

3. The central consideration for deciding this difficult choice must, in HMG's view, be reached by asking – what is the real charge which the Allied people and the world as a whole makes against Hitler? It is the totality of his offences against the international standard which civilized countries try to observe which makes him the scoundrel that he is. If he were to be indicted for these offences in the manner that is necessary for reasons of justice in a criminal court, and if his fate is to be determined on the conclusion reached by the tribunal as to the truth of this bundle of charges and the adequacy of the proof, it seems impossible to conceive that the trial would not be exceedingly long and elaborate . . .

4. There is a further consideration which, in the view of HMG, needs to be very carefully weighed. If the method of public trial were adopted, the comment must be expected from the very start to be that the whole thing is a 'put-up-job' designed by the Allies to justify a punishment they have already resolved on. Hitler and his advisers – if they decide to take part and to challenge what is alleged – may be expected to be very much alive to any opportunity of turning the tables. Public opinion as the trial goes on is likely to weary at the length of the process. It is difficult to think that anybody would in

the course of time look on Hitler as an injured man, but it is by no means likely that a long trial will result in a change of public feeling as to the justification of trying Hitler at all. Will not some people begin to say, 'The man should be shot out of hand?' And if in the complicated and novel procedure which such a trial is bound to adopt – for Russian, American and British ideas must in some way be amalgamated – the defence secured some unexpected point, is there not a danger of the trial being denounced as a farce?

5. There is a further point. Reference has been made above to Hitler's conduct leading up to the war as one of the crimes on which the Allies would rely. There should be included in this the unprovoked attacks which, since the original declaration of war, he has made on various countries. These are not war crimes in the ordinary sense, nor is it at all clear that they can properly be described as crimes under international law . . . Under the procedure suggested this would be a matter for the tribunal, and would at any rate give the accused the opportunity of basing arguments on what has happened in the past and what has been done by various countries in declaring war which resulted in acquiring new territory, which certainly were not regarded at the time as crimes against international law. . . .

The President's overt reply to the above had been the appointment of Justice Jackson himself. The San Francisco Conference of the United Nations was imminent. A plan was drawn up by the US Departments which provided for an executive agreement between the Four Great Powers to implement the Yalta principles and establish a military tribunal. The memorandum accompanying the suggested agreement explicitly stated that the German leaders, to be charged additionally with specific atrocities, should be indicted for their joint participation in a broad criminal enterprise. This would permit full proof of the Nazi plan from its inception and would involve the organizations, like the SS, upon which the Nazi system rested. Some minor changes were made in the drafts at San Francisco and they were delivered to the foreign ministers of Russia, France, and Britain.

On 22 May Jackson went to Europe. He had innumerable and extended conferences with all concerned – General Eisenhower in Paris, the Lord Chancellor and Foreign Secretary Eden in London, and with representatives of the French Provisional Government. On 6 June he was able to report to the President that the British and French Governments accepted the United States' proposals in principle and that the Soviet Government, while not committed, was thought likely to unite in the prosecution. This was remarkable: within five weeks of his appointment, Justice Jackson had set up the administrative machinery required, had formulated the general principles on which the charges against the leading Nazis should be based, and had set out the manner in which he thought those charges could fairly and judicially be brought to trial. I cite just two passages from this notable report:

> The American case is being prepared on the assumption that an inescapable responsibility rests upon this country to conduct an inquiry, preferably in association with others, but alone if necessary, into the culpability of those whom there is probably cause to accuse of atrocities and other crimes . . . To free them without a trial would mock the dead and make cynics of the living. On the other hand, we could execute or otherwise punish them without a hearing.
>
> But undiscriminating executions or punishments without definite findings of guilt, fairly arrived at, would violate pledges repeatedly given, and would not sit easily on the American conscience or be remembered by our children with pride. The only other course is to determine the innocence or guilt of the accused after a hearing as dispassionate as the times and horrors we deal with will permit, and upon a record that will leave our reasons and motives clear.
>
> We must now sift and compress within a workable scope voluminous evidence relating to a multitude of crimes committed in several countries and participated in by thousands of actors over a decade of time.

By early June 1945 the matter had so far progressed that the British Government suggested that representatives of the four governments should meet in conference in London. The conference commenced on 26 June (about ten days before our general election), but in the meantime the Soviet Government had indicated that while they agreed in general with the American proposal for a joint trial of the 'leaders of the Hitlerite Government', they had very different ideas both as to the charges and to the procedure. It could in any event be no easy task. There were four different languages involved. Worse still, there was the problem of three, if not four, entirely different systems of law, each with its own technical vocabulary and each having its own principles and its distinct procedures. As the meetings of the London Conference dragged on, it became apparent that there were differences beyond those of detail.

Again I quote Justice Jackson:

I think we are in a philosophical difference that lies at the root of a great many technical differences and will continue to lie at the root of differences unless we can reconcile our basic view points. As the statement of our Soviet colleague said, they proceed on the assumption that the declarations of Crimea and Moscow already convict these parties and that the charges need not be tried before independent judges empowered to render an independent decision on guilt. Now that underlies a great deal of their position, and we don't make that assumption. In the first place, the President of the United States has no power to convict anybody. He can only accuse. He can not arrest in most cases without judicial authority. Therefore, the accusation made carries no weight in an American trial whatsoever. These declarations are an accusation and not a conviction. That requires a judicial finding. Now we could not be parties to setting up a more formal judicial body to ratify a political decision to convict. The judges will have to inquire into the evidence and reach an independent decision. There is a great deal of realism in Mr Nikitchenko's statement. [General Nikitchenko was the mouthpiece of the Soviet Government and later represented his country at the Nuremberg trial.] There could be but one decision in this case – that we are bound to concede. But the reason is the evidence and not the statements made by heads of state with reference to these cases. That is the reason why, at the very beginning, the position of the United States was that there must be trials rather than political executions. The United States feels we could not make political executions. I took that position publicly. I have no sympathy with these men, but, if we are going to have a trial, then it must be an actual trial. That is the position of the American Government, and it troubles me a bit

to think of trying to solve by a subcommittee so fundamental a disagreement as to trial. It raises the question of whether procedural
differences are not so great that the idea of separate tribunals for each
nation for the trial of its separate groups of prisoners may not be the
easiest and most satisfactory way of reconciling it. I do not know, but
just put that forward.

General Nikitchenko's philosophy was very different:

Perhaps I am mistaken, but I understand that our purpose is not to
discuss the philosophy of law but to try and work out an agreement,
the purpose of which would be the carrying on of justice in the name
of the war criminals . . .

Quite early, Justice Jackson had to make it clear — and this was no idle
threat — that if need be the United States would have to proceed without
the agreement of the Soviet Union. There were almost daily meetings,
but Jackson did not neglect the task of preparations: parallel with the
negotiations in London the work of preparing the case was gathering
momentum. The first weekend in July was seized by Jackson as an interval in the London talks and an opportunity to fly to Wiesbaden,
Frankfurt, Nuremberg, Salzburg, Munich, and then to Paris, where he
had set up an office in the rue de Presbourg for processing a large collection of documents. He reported back to the London Conference:

I think it is important for our preparation of the case that we know
how fast we can proceed. During the time the drafting committee was
at work, I went to the Continent. I may report that we have been
having most satisfactory results from the examination of captured
documents. We are getting proof tracing the responsibility for these
atrocities and war crimes back to the top authorities better than I ever
expected we would get it. I did not think men would ever be so foolish
as to put in writing some of the things the Germans did put in writing.
The stupidity of it and the brutality of it would simply appal you.

Jackson wanted to know whether the representatives of the other
three governments had been authorized to sign the agreements and

proceed with the preparation of the case for trial. It was not clear what powers the Soviet representatives had been given or even whether they would in fact be the prosecutors.

As the discussions went on, three matters in particular gave rise to difficulty. Did the guilt of the accused have to be established by evidence before the Tribunal, or were they to be regarded as already guilty men, the Tribunal being concerned only with meting out what the Soviet representatives called 'justice'. This was hardly a matter of subordinate importance but it was associated with another of even greater difficulty. The Soviet representatives were at last persuaded that the indictment should include a charge of waging a war of aggression. But they wanted to qualify or limit the charge to a 'Hitlerite' war of aggression. Were they possibly thinking that any general definition of aggression might give rise to painful memories in, for instance, the Baltic States? I do not know. General Nikitchenko maintained that the Axis policy had been defined as aggressive by the Allies and the United Nations, therefore the Tribunal would not need to examine that question. Mr Justice Jackson responded that if we were to proceed on that basis then there would be no need for a trial at all. General Nikitchenko kept to the Soviet line:

The fact that the Nazi leaders are criminals has already been established. The task of the Tribunal is only to determine the measure of guilt of each particular person and mete out the necessary punishment – the sentence.

Various compromises were suggested but Justice Jackson stood firm:

The draft before us submitted by the Soviet Delegation literally only confers jurisdiction to try persons; it does not, as I see it, define the substantive law which creates the crimes. Therefore, if this were adopted, it would be entirely open to the Tribunal if it thought the international law was such as to warrant it, to adjudge that, while these persons had committed the acts we charge, these acts were not crimes against international law and therefore to acquit them. That we think would make the trial a travesty.

Now let us take the Soviet proposal. If we look at it as defining a crime, it is one consisting of three elements: first, there must be

My parents and myself, soon after my
birth in 1902.

My mother in 1940, shortly before she
died.

With Alberta, my first wife

As a young lawyer

With Joan, my second wife, photographed by her cousin, Yevonde.

Outside Peckhams, our first house in Sussex.

Clement Attlee   Ernest Bevin

Herbert Morrison   Hugh Dalton

The British prosecution team at Nuremberg. Elwyn Jones
is on the left, David Maxwell-Fyfe is third from left.

Handing down the indictments of the War criminals. Mr Elwyn
Jones is on the author's right. Lt. Colonel Griffith-Jones is on his left.

The Nazi criminals in the dock. The front row includes
Goering, Hess, Ribbentrop and Keitel.

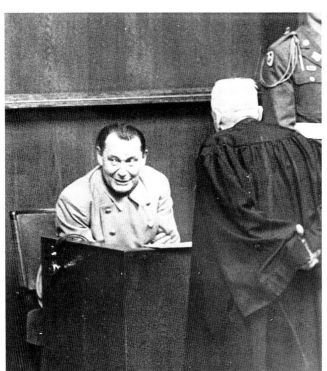

Hermann Goering at the Nuremberg Trial.

Rudolf Hess, eating from an American mess tin in the Palace of Justice.

'aggression against or domination over'; second, it must be carried out by Axis powers; third, it must be in violation of international law and treaties.

Then the second element contained in it – it must be carried out by Axis powers. We would like to think that had no place in any definition because it makes an entirely partisan declaration of law.

Two or three days later, Jackson spoke of his concern that the charter should remain relevant to any attack on the peace of the world.

Nikitchenko responded that if the document did not merely condemn specifically the Nazis' aggressions but included a condemnation of the initiation of war in general, then for the Soviets 'it would not be agreeable', a flat statement which is the more significant now that *glasnost* has revealed so much of Stalin's philosophy.

But these were not the only difficulties. There were also practical ones. Here the main problem was where the trial should take place. The Soviet representatives, for prestige or other reasons best known to them, wanted Berlin. They were keen that the whole proceeding should be very much under the aegis of the Allied Control Commission, in which, because it was in Berlin, the Soviets had a dominant position. While we agreed that the Control Commission might mitigate any sentences imposed, we were entirely unwilling that the Commission could review or in any way set aside the verdict and judgement. Berlin, moreover, was an entirely unsuitable place for a trial. It was a ruined city: there was no adequate courthouse, no prison, none of the facilities needed.

Nuremberg, which was of course a city of psychological significance to the Nazis, was in fact the only place in Germany where the necessary facilities remained. On 18 July Jackson proffered his aircraft so that the representatives of the three other nations could go there and see what was available. All accepted his offer. 'We would be glad', said General Nikitchenko, 'to take advantage of the kind invititation extended by Justice Jackson.' Arrangements were made to fly off on the following Saturday. But on Friday, the Soviet Delegation announced a lunch for the other delegations and said they could not go. Jackson offered to change the date to any other that was convenient to them. No, they said – obviously on instructions from Moscow – they could not go. It was suggested that while the first trial should be held in Nuremberg, the administrative seat of the tribunal might be in Berlin. Again the Russians would not agree. It had to be Berlin for all manner of reasons. It was by now 25 July. Time was getting on. Even General Nikitchenko felt impelled to say that 'if discussion went on he was afraid the war crim, inals would die of old age'.

The very next day, the result of the British general election was announced. The change in government meant that Maxwell Fyfe was replaced by Lord Chancellor Jowitt and myself on the Intergovernmental Conference and the British War Crimes Executive. All went on as before except that we were more decisive. The new team made decisions more quickly.

In the meantime, however, President Truman, Marshal Stalin, and Prime Minister Churchill (later to be replaced by Prime Minister Attlee) had arranged to meet in conference in Potsdam, and the British asked that the subject of the war criminals should be included on the agenda. Justice Jackson was apparently 'rather appalled' at the idea that the Big Three might get involved in this very difficult and highly tech, nical matter and he flew to Potsdam on 26 July to consult with Mr Secretary Byrnes. We had been afraid that Russian suspicions of our own and the American's intentions as to the trials might become an embarrassment, and we hoped to allay them. Eventually the subject was discussed both by the foreign ministers and the Big Three. The Russians put forward the proposal that the final communiqué of the conference should state that a four-power military tribunal was to be established with power to try, condemn, and execute the leading Nazis to be named by the conference. This greatly dismayed us: we felt that such a decision by the conference would confirm the Russians in their intransigence. Jackson said that he almost despaired of reaching agreement with the Russians and that the possibility of a three-power tribunal without the Russians could not be excluded, and so informed the President. On 1 August, the Big Three discussed the subject again; in the end a com- promise was reached on the basis of a British proposal. The three governments reaffirmed their intention to bring the war criminals to swift and sure justice, hoped that the London negotiations would lead to speedy agreement, and that the trials would begin at the earliest pos- sible date. The first list of defendants, they said, would be published on 1 September. There can be no doubt that Marshal Stalin, reassured, then sent instructions to London that the Soviet representatives must be more accommodating: the change in government in England also resulted in the chairmanship of the London Conference being taken over by Lord Chancellor Jowitt. Jowitt combined in high measure the qualities of *sauviter in modo* with *fortiter in re*. Business went through at the meeting on 2 August with commendable expedition. Telexes from Moscow led to an astonishing volte-face. The Russians no longer persisted in limiting the crime of aggression purely to Nazi acts, but instead of the crime of war it was to be called the crime against peace. Similarly, agreement was reached about the scene of the trial. General Nikitchenko made a welcome statement:

> We are prepared to agree to the first trial at Nuremberg, but we would like it considered that the administrative headquarters and the first meetings of the Tribunal and the prosecutors shall also take place in Berlin at a place to be designated by the Control Council. The first trial shall be held in Nuremberg and subsequent trials as we had it.

With the new Labour Government, I took Maxwell Fyfe's place as Attorney in the numerous government committees and activities, including the chairmanship of the War Crimes Executive. But Nuremberg presented a special difficulty. If and when the trial took place, it would obviously require continuous attendance abroad, and it would inevitably last a long time. My presence there would prevent my being available in London at all times to advise the Government and Parliament on legal problems. This duty was to be far heavier than ever before because of the great volume of legislation and complex legal problems arising from the war and the change of government. Furthermore, it would prevent my attending to the Attorney's normal court work in England, including the treason trials. The Nuremberg trial would, however, be the most important piece of international litigation that the Government was likely to be involved in, would affect the future development of international relations (in which I was particularly interested), and was of great historical interest. I did not want to be out of the matter altogether but did not see how I could take charge for the whole time. Having discussed the matter with the Lord Chancellor and the Prime Minister, I decided to appoint a deputy. Maxwell Fyfe was the obvious candidate. Although I did not have the highest opinion of him intellectually, he was obviously a capable criminal advocate and had been fully involved in the preparatory work. Moreover, I felt it would be a good thing to demonstrate that this trial had no party political implica/ tions. Why should he not, after all, have the opportunity of cross/exam/ ining Goering as he had said he would in his election speech? I made it clear to him that I would be the Chief British Prosecutor, would be in final charge both of policy and administration, that I should make the main speeches and come over to Nuremberg whenever occasion arose, and should receive progress reports each day. He would be in daily charge on the spot, while I would remain responsible, taking the blame for whatever went wrong, but probably without any of the praise for what was successful. Fyfe, having consulted Churchill, agreed, and it is certain that the brief greatly helped his subsequent professional career. He was paid 1,500 guineas on the brief with 75 guineas a day refresher. As I was only in court part of the time, I accepted a lower fee of £500 (incidentally the highest fee ever sanctioned for a Law Officer; Dalton reluctantly initialled his sanction with the comment 'These lawyers are all overpaid'!). The arrangement was well received politically, as it was by the Press, who represented it as a typically British solution.

Then there was the question of whom to appoint as the British judge. The Prime Minister, the Lord Chancellor and I discussed this and the Prime Minister – I think it was – suggested Norman Birkett. Norman was then a High Court judge. During the war he had regularly done 'morale' broadcasts on the BBC so he was well known. We all agreed and Attlee wrote him a personal letter inviting him to take on the job. I took this to Birkett who accepted without hesitation. But then came a very awkward difficulty. The Foreign Office – with more respect for peers than I had until I became one – insisted that the British judge should be a peer, so as to indicate internationally that he was indeed one of Britain's very top lawyers. We were persuaded. There was, however, no Lord of Appeal available. We had to go one level down. Lord Justice du Parcq refused, and so I conveyed the invitation to Lord Justice Lawrence, who accepted. Lord Justice Lawrence was much better known as a country squire with a good stable than as a great lawyer. But he was a gentleman, safe, even stolid, and likely to conduct the pro/ ceedings with firmness and dignity. A very unhappy situation arose, however, with Birkett. He agreed to become Lawrence's alternate or deputy, but was deeply upset and felt that his competence was in doubt; he was not one of those gifted with over-confidence and he suffered real distress.

II

On 8 August 1945 the Agreement and Charter of the International Tribunal was duly signed. Francis Biddle, the charming and cultured American member of the Tribunal, later wrote: 'Robert Jackson's tire-less energy and skill has finally brought the four nations together – a really extraordinary feat.'

In a sense the criminals chose themselves by the very notoriety of their conduct: it was not so much a question of who to include but of who could be left out. Originally, the American view had been that there should be fifty or sixty defendants. Jackson thought that apart from the obvious Nazi leaders, the first trial should include only the top men in the various organizations and departments whose effort had contributed to the whole conspiracy. Besides being individually and personally responsible for the crimes with which they were charged, they would be in a sense representatives of the different parts of the conspiracy. This presented difficulty only as to the industrialists. One of the obvious can-didates was Hjalmar Schacht, who had never withheld his services as a brilliant financier from the Nazis. Another was Gustav Krupp, the senior member of the great German armaments firm, which had made an enormous contribution to the Nazi war effort, and during the war had used slave labour. But Justice Jackson also wished to include Alfried Krupp and a number of other industrialists. Some of us felt that to have too many defendants, particularly of the same representative category, would detract from the impact of the trial, and would bog it down in too much detail; in the end, Jackson was outvoted.

The decision as to Gustav was, as it turned out, a mistake. Although nominally the head of the great Krupp firm he was now old and ill. He had probably not been very actively concerned with the running of the

Krupp installation in the latter years of the war. We should have selected the effective leader of the management. But the mistake – although it was a mistake – was not mine personally as Colonel Telford Taylor asserts in his book *The Anatomy of the Nuremberg Trials.* Taylor was put in charge of the so-called minor trials in the American zone after the main trial had been concluded. In the main trial he was merely an assistant in the large American team and did not know about everything that went on. In fact Gustav had been suggested by the French, but all the major prosecutors were parties to his inclusion. In the event Gustav Krupp was too ill to be tried and Jackson then pressed for the substitution of Alfried. He was supported by the French and by the Russians, who would have been prepared to try anybody, guilty or not. I recall it as the only occasion on which I had any real difference of view with Jackson. To have included Alfried at the stage we had by then reached would have involved postponing the opening of the trial, and I thought that this would have been a grave mistake. When the motion came before the Tribunal, I added that the trial was 'not a game of football in which we could field a substitute'. The tribunal accepted this view and the trial went on without any representative of Nazi industry in the dock, although Alfried was tried in later proceedings by the Americans – and dealt with surprisingly leniently.

The other defendant whose trial gave rise to controversy was Rudolf Hess. The question was not whether he was guilty but whether he was sane. He had flown to Britain in the middle of the war, landing in Scotland, and tried to make contact with the Duke of Hamilton in the apparent belief that with the assistance of the British aristocracy a peace might be negotiated. I mean no disrespect to a most distinguished peer when I say that this was in itself some evidence of insanity! But the Russians had, and perhaps still have, extraordinary suspicions about it. Possibly they did not understand why we had not shot Hess out of hand; possibly they imagined we had actually wanted to negotiate for a separate peace. At the Potsdam Conference, Stalin insisted that Hess must be tried as a war criminal, and we never dissented. Mr Ernest Bevin, the Foreign Secretary, assured the Soviet marshal that we would hand Hess over – and 'send along a bill for his keep as well'. But when the time came for trial, many thought that Hess was mentally unfit to stand trial, and his counsel entered a plea to that effect. A panel of distinguished doctors examined him, and although they found him to be affected by amnesia and not normal in other respects, they concluded that he was fit to stand his trial. Hess himself, in a very cogent and clear statement, asserted his right to be tried and his wish to stand beside his associates. As the trial proceeded and we had an opportunity of observing his appearance and behaviour, most of us felt doubtful about this decision, and concluded that he was mad.

The list of defendants decided, the next problem was settling the indictment itself, a document of 18,000 words. On the whole, Anglo-Saxon forms were followed. At one of the final meetings of the prose-cuting counsel before the presentation of the indictment, however, the Russians insisted that it should include a charge that the Germans were guilty of the massacre of thousands of Polish officers whose bodies had been found, many shackled together and shot through the back of the head, in the Katyn Forest. Jackson opposed this. I asked Maxwell Fyfe, as my deputy, to examine the evidence and report to me on the merits. He concluded, rather surprisingly at the time, that it was uncertain whether this horrible atrocity had been committed by the Russians or the Germans. I accordingly strongly supported Jackson and went privately to General Rudenko, the chief Russian prosecutor, to urge him, in the most tactful way, not to press the point. He insisted none the less, and rather than face a complete breakdown, the rest of us were forced to acquiesce. We informed General Rudenko explicitly, however, that we would ourselves not seek to establish this charge nor make any reference to it, and that the sole responsibility must rest upon the Soviet side of the prosecution. The evidence that the Russians eventually led upon the matter was unconvincing and the Tribunal completely ignored the whole charge. It is of course now known by the Russians' own admis-sion and much other evidence that this shocking massacre was commit-ted on Stalin's own instructions. Fortunately none of the defendants at Nuremberg was in any way punished for it, but it clearly demonstrated the hypocritical attitude of the Russians to the trial at that time. They insisted on prosecuting the matter, because to ignore it would have been taken as an admission of Soviet guilt.

The judges and the chief prosecutors, including me, had gone to Berlin early in October, and the programme was that the indictment would be formally and publicly presented to the tribunal there on 15

October. The day before, the Russians announced that they could not sign it. They were evidently under instruction from Moscow, but what the difficulty was we never understood. We opposed their application for postponement but in the end the Tribunal, I think wisely, agreed to a three-day adjournment which gave the Soviets time to fall into line and sign. The delay gave me an opportunity to see the devastation of Berlin. In spite of everything, they still managed to put on a very creditable opera performance which I went to see, though, alas, I cannot now recall which opera it was.

The final matter was the selection of a president. As it turned out this presented surprisingly little difficulty, for the Charter had left the matter open. The Russians wished to leave the presidency rotated between the four powers; the French had a nicely logical idea of a rotation by topics. Francis Biddle was an obvious choice. But during preliminary organizational meetings of the Tribunal in Berlin, the British judge, Lord Justice Lawrence, possibly because he was the only one of the four who was still acting as a judge in his own country, had somehow or other assumed the chair. Jackson later explained that to have had Biddle as president would have made the trial seem too predominantly an American exercise.

This was true. General Nikitchenko, the Russian member, proposed Biddle, but Biddle and the French agreed to nominate Lawrence, and he was elected. As a matter of courtesy, however, Nikitchenko was asked to preside at the first meeting in Berlin, to receive the indictment. And on 18 October, according to *The Times*, 'with fitting dignity but workmanlike despatch the Military Tribunal held its first open session.' I lodged the indictment on behalf of the prosecuting powers, rules of procedure were laid down, and the opening of the trial was fixed for a date thirty days after the service of the indictment upon the defendants.

The next day we went to Nuremberg. The old town, with its splendid medieval buildings, had been completely laid waste with only an occasional part of a building or wall left standing. Allied bombing had concentrated on the centre and, without the aids to precision available now, had certainly done its work, although not very efficiently from the point of view of the war effort, for the surrounding area and many factories had been left unscathed. After Berlin, it was the second city in which I was to witness the devastation caused by Allied mass raids. It was far worse than anything we had experienced in Britain. I had sometimes seen the mass flights of Allied planes – hundreds of planes – flying over my home in Sussex, but I had never fully visualized the destruction they would inflict.

When we arrived in Nuremberg it was clear that for our purposes much remained to be done. There was a large court building mainly undamaged, which the American Army was reconstructing for our use; apparatus was being put in for simultaneous translation, there were to be telephone and telegraph facilities for the newspaper reporters who were to come in hundreds, as well as accommodation and catering for all those concerned in the trials – 1,500 lunches were served in the court cafeteria each day. The expedition and efficiency of the American arrangements were extremely impressive.

The major task, however, was to be ready to open this greatest of all trials within a month, and here the burden lay more heavily upon Jackson than upon anyone else, for he was to open the case.

But we were ready. Less than seven months after the surrender of Germany and of Justice Jackson's own appointment as Chief Prosecutor, in spite of all the deaths and disruptions, the difficulties and dislocations of the most terrible war the world had known, and the manifold legal and technical problems involved, the trial opened on 20 November 1945 in solemn dignity. It was a remarkable achievement. And it was essentially an achievement dominated by the personality and dedication of Jackson himself.

I shall be referring to Justice Jackson a great deal, but I do not want either to appear over-eulogistic or to conceal his faults. Indeed, he had many. So have I. But his had more effect on the trial. He was a bad administrator. A brilliant legal stylist and orator, he was impatient of the details of organization and frequently was unduly belligerent, lacking the finer gifts of tact and diplomacy. At one point he aroused the antagonism of Judge Biddle, to whom he was openly hostile, as well as that of Lawrence, and was at constant loggerheads with his immediate deputy, General 'Bill' Donovan. He was vain and easily upset; sometimes, apparently in fits of pique, he would absent himself from the tribunal for quite long periods. Added to all this, he was reputed to have the comfort of a mistress in Nuremberg. Nevertheless, it has to be said that without Jackson there would have been no trial.

The vivid appearance of the courtroom was memorable. It was a large court and was packed with distinguished visitors and voyeurs; there had been a great demand for seats and these had been allocated well in advance to diplomats, politicians, and so forth. We, the prosecuting counsel, sat at four longish tables at right angles to the bench of judges which was on an elevated platform just to our right. Opposite us was a witness stand and boxes for the simultaneous translators. To our left was the prisoners' dock. Behind and above us was a large gallery for ticket-holders, and in the well of the court, tables for the Press. There were innumerable journalists. American soldiers, smartly dressed and drilled, took the place of police and warders.

It was rather more than just another case, but what struck me with some surprise was how very ordinary most of the prisoners appeared. In the street, or on the Clapham omnibus, apart from three figures – those of Goering, Schacht, and perhaps Keitel – they would hardly have attracted a second glance. One or two of them I had met before the war: certainly they appeared less spruce than in their peacetime days. In those days Ribbentrop, for example, had been a boaster and a braggart, but there was nothing of that about him now. Schacht, I think, one might have identified as some sort of businessman, but not a particularly distinguished one. The reason he was noticeable was due to the way in which he occupied his place in the dock. He sat at the end of the front row of prisoners, furthest from us, and should have appeared as just one of the row. He did not. He must have been a bit of an actor. Somehow he positioned himself with his back to the other prisoners and gave the impression of being completely detached from them. He rarely spoke to any of them and somehow appeared to be asking, 'Who are these awful people? Certainly no associates of mine.' As for the other prisoners, who were in truth his confederates, General Keitel was every inch a soldier: properly dressed, dignified and imperturbable in manner. When eventually he was sentenced to death, he asked whether, as a soldier, he might be shot rather than hanged, and when this request was rejected, he simply stood smartly to attention, turned and walked with dignity out of the dock. I understand that he faced the gallows with the same dignity.

Goering, however, was obviously the outstanding figure of the trial. He sat in the front row of the dock in the opposite corner to Schacht, immediately facing us. I had not seen him in person before, but here in court there was nothing of his renowned braggadocio. He had obviously lost a lot of weight (in fact while in custody he had been taken off drugs and put on a more healthy diet), and his simple uniform hung loosely around him. None the less, from the first, I think we all recog/ nized that this was the leader among these men.

I looked along the rows of defendants' counsel. I had not seen them before. In Britain, as Attorney General and Leader of the English Bar I had moved a resolution at a well-attended general meeting of the Bar to the effect that British lawyers should refrain from accepting briefs to defend at Nuremberg. The 'Cab Rank rule' did not apply. British bar/ risters did not normally hold themselves out to practise in Germany, and their appearance in defence of Nazi war criminals would be greatly mis/ understood. We should be regarded at the best as prostituting ourselves. This view was supported by many of the leading Silks and was endorsed by a large majority.*

All the defendants were represented by German lawyers, many of whom were distinguished, and they all put up an adequate defence. That is not to say that the German team was as good as those for the prosecution. The most eminent Nazi lawyers were conspicuous by their absence. Some of the German lawyers were ex/Nazis, some were not. They were severely handicapped by the lack of professional staff and assistants to help them in research and other work preparatory to the trial. And, I am afraid, the prosecuting team hardly treated them as pro/ fessional equals: the no/fraternization policy was strictly adhered to. They tended to become rather second/class citizens and their position was not enviable. Some were genuinely shocked by the terrible things brought out in evidence. Yet although some of the German advocates were better than others, I do not think any prisoner suffered through inadequacy of defence. I have met some of those advocates in happier circumstances since; one of them, Naval Judge Kranzbuehler, a most able man who would have reached distinction in any society, took part in a programme on German television with me in the 1980s: we met as equals and with courtesy.

The trial occupied 216 days. Thirty/three witnesses were called and examined for the prosecution. Sixty/one witnesses and nineteen

---

* Tom Bower, in his otherwise most careful and important book, *Blind Eye to Murder*, mistakenly says the opposite.

defendants testified for the defence; 143 additional witnesses gave testimony by interrogatories for the defence. The proceedings were conducted and recorded in four languages – English, German, French, and Russian – and daily transcripts in the language of one's choice were provided for each prosecuting staff and all counsel for defendants. The English transcript of the proceedings covers over 17,000 pages. All proceedings were sound-reported in the original language used. Over 30,000 photostats, 50,000,000 pages of typed matter, and more than 4,000 recorded discs were produced. It was a remarkable demonstration of organizational strategy.

The indictment was formally read out, pleas taken (all Not Guilty) and in due course the opening speech was made by Jackson. It had been arranged between the chief prosecutors that each would assume the main responsibility for presenting a particular part of the case. Jackson's responsibility was especially for the first and basic count of the indictment – the conspiracy to wage aggressive war. He built up an overwhelming case, based almost entirely on captured German documents, but welded together in a speech of great power. Early on, he came very much to what had been in my own mind, which was whether these men really mattered any more.

In the prisoners' dock sit twenty-odd broken men. Reproached by the humiliation of those they have led, almost as bitterly as by the desolation of those they have attacked, their personal capacity for evil is forever past. It is hard now to perceive in these miserable men as captives the power by which as Nazi leaders they once dominated much of the world and terrified most of it. Merely as individuals their fate is of little consequence to the world.

What makes this inquest significant is that these prisoners represent sinister influences that will lurk in the world long after their bodies have returned to dust. We will show them to be living symbols of racial hatreds, of terrorism and violence, and of the arrogance and cruelty of power . . . They have so identified themselves with the philosophies they conceived, and with the forces they have directed, that any tenderness to them is a victory and an encouragement to all the evils which are attached to their names. Civilization can afford no compromise with the social forces which would gain renewed strength if we deal ambiguously or indecisively with the men in whom those forces now precariously survive.

What these men stand for we will patiently and temperately disclose.

I am too well aware of the weakness of juridical action alone to contend that in itself your decision under this Charter can prevent future wars. Judicial action always comes after the event. Wars are started only on the theory and in the confidence that they can be won. Personal punishment to be suffered only in the event the war is lost will probably not be a sufficient deterrent to prevent a war while the war-makers feel the chances of defeat to be negligible. But the ultimate step in avoiding periodic wars which are inevitable in a system of international lawlessness, is to make statesmen responsible to law. And let me make clear that while this law is first applied against German aggressors, the law includes, and if it is to serve a useful purpose, it must condemn aggression by any other nations including those which sit here now in judgement. We are able to do away with domestic tyranny and violence and aggression by those in power against the rights of their own people only when we make all men answerable to law.

Civilization asks whether law is so laggard as to be utterly helpless to deal with crimes of this magnitude by criminals of this order of importance. It does not expect that you can make war impossible. It does expect that your juridical action will put the forces of International Law, its precepts, its prohibitions and, most of all, its sanctions, on the side of peace, so that men and women of good will, in all countries, may have 'leave to live by no man's leave, underneath the law.'

None of the arts of the actor was on view. This was no dramatic declamation, but, uttered calmly, in words of dignity and authority, the demand of a lawyer and statesman that law and justice should in the end prevail.

Owing to my increasing load of commitments at home, my own opening speech had unfortunately to be sandwiched into the American part of the case, the Tribunal and Jackson courteously agreeing to this in recognition of my difficulties. I do not think that this detracted from the purpose of my speech, which was largely to discuss the legal background of the whole proceeding, but it may have deprived it of some of its impact. Certainly by contrast with Jackson's, my own address was for the most part severely prosaic and legalistic, lacking any pretence at oratory or purple passages.

I sought to counter the idea, still quite widely held, that waging war had always been a legitimate form of state policy – 'after all, what is history about except wars?' – and that the whole Nuremberg procedure was in truth an *ex post facto* demonstration of vengeance cooked up retroactively by the victors but which had no respectable basis in International Law. This I think I did by showing that on the contrary, the Tribunal was administering rules of International Law which had been established, with the full outward concurrence of the Germans, many years before the war. What we had to concede and justify was not the rules that were being applied but the establishment of an International Tribunal to apply those rules to the individual leaders who had led their state into breaking them. And so I started my address by reminding the Tribunal that:

On an occasion to which reference has and will be made, Hitler, the Leader of the Nazi conspirators who are now on trial before you, is reported as having said in reference to their warlike plans:–

'I shall give a propagandist case for starting the war, never mind whether it be true or not. The victor shall not be asked later on whether we tell the truth or not. In starting and making a war, not the right is what matters but victory – the strongest has the right.' The British Empire with its Allies has twice, within the space of 25 years, been victorious in wars which have been forced upon it, but it is precisely because we realise that victory is not enough; that might is not necessarily right; that lasting peace and the rule of International law is not to be secured by the strong arm alone, that the British Nation is taking part in this trial. . . . From this record shall future generations know not only that our generation suffered but also that our suffering was the result of crimes, crimes against the laws of peoples which the peoples of the world upheld and will continue in the future to uphold; to uphold by international co⁄operation, not based merely on military alliances but grounded, and firmly grounded, in the rule of law.

Nor, though this procedure and this Indictment of individuals may be novel, is there anything new in the principles which in this prosecution we seek to enforce.

I then went on to set out the long history of international legal development which had constituted the waging of aggressive war as an international crime. And from that to establish the certainly more novel principle of personal liability on the part of those who planned and led their countries into its commission.

The trial proceeded. There were regular meetings of the chief prose-cutors. It would be idle to pretend that there were never difficulties, never vexatious incidents. That they were overcome was largely due to the great respect and friendship which in spite of personality problems we all developed for Jackson, upon whom the main responsibility fell, *primus inter pares*, with the chief prosecutors of the other countries. Jackson was not, as I have already said, immune from the human frail-ties we all possess. Birkett thought he was inclined to be pompous or even vain. But these were criticisms that were laid at times against us all. Indeed, there were singularly few personal difficulties, and they were for the most part quickly overcome. But one matter has been given promi-nence in many books and in some has quite wrongly been used to colour Jackson's whole part in the trial. This was only one incident in a very long case and cannot detract from his major achievement. I refer to his cross-examination of Goering. It was not a success. This was due, I think, to a combination of factors. Goering himself was a most remark-able man: a criminal no doubt, but a courageous one, and a man of great ability and of outstanding personality. Indeed, Birkett wrote in his diary:

Throughout this trial the dead Hitler has been present at every session . . . But Goering is the man who has dominated the proceedings and that, remarkably enough, without ever uttering a word . . . That in itself is a very remarkable achievement and illuminates much that was obscure in the history of the last few years.

It was curious that he asserted himself so little. Yet during his cross-examination his ability was left in no doubt – nor his agility. This was a man to be cross-examined in one way only – that first axiom of cross-examination in a criminal trial – by never asking a question without knowing that there is only one inescapable answer to be given to it, usually a 'Yes' or a 'No', and by that process to lead the witness up to the last fatal but inescapable response. Jackson would have been the last to pretend that he was an expert in this art: he had definite scruples about a criminal practice: 'I wouldn't want', he had once said, 'to cultivate a criminal practice . . . Pretty soon it is a hard thing to know which is the criminal and which the counsel.' Too true! His forte was, rather, advo-cacy and argument. I did not myself hear his cross-examination but one of the members of the British team, Elwyn Jones, wrote to me saying:

> Bob's error was to regard his confrontation with Goering as one between the personification of Nazi tyranny on the one hand and the quintessence of liberal democracy on the other – which of course in one way it was. This led him into a difficult cross-examination field where opinions were challenged instead of facts, always an unre-warding exercise.

In a sense Jackson's lack of success was due to his intellectual honesty. His whole case was to expose the evil philosophies with which the Nazis had sought to dominate the world: this inevitably involved him in putting forward matters of opinion and doing so in an argumentative rather than a factual exchange. But a third factor in the failure of his cross-examination was perhaps a weakness of the tribunal in allowing excess latitude to Goering, and Jackson, perhaps unwisely, protested against this in vain.

Birkett urged that the Tribunal should assert its authority and limit Goering to answering questions and not making speeches, but this the Tribunal did not do. As a consequence, Jackson's cross-examination did not demolish Goering. Faced with this situation the British team, in the words of one of its members, 'spent the night digging up documents signed by Goering personally, showing him to be a friend of Himmler, a bandit and a thug.' The result was an effective cross-examination by Maxwell Fyfe, who followed Jackson, which made his reputation. But Fyfe was, of course, essentially a criminal lawyer who had learnt how to cross-examine from the magistrates' courts up; he would not and probably could not engage in philosophical exercises (whether in court or elsewhere). Even so, his cross-examination did not satisfy Birkett's high standards. On 1 May he wrote in his diary:

Despite the flattering press notices of the cross-examination by the British it remains true that a true cross-examination has not yet been given. It is a cross-examination in name only which consists in putting incriminating documents to the witness. The true art of cross-examination is something in a different plane altogether and it has not yet been seen at Nuremberg in any shape or form.

Jackson's cross-examination of Schacht also failed: Biddle noted that the latter was 'far too clever for Jackson'. Birkett said it was a perfectly futile cross-examination.

It must be added that there are critical passages in Birkett's diaries about many of those engaged in the trial. Birkett was a man to whom I owe a great deal: a veritable guide, philosopher, and friend. He was also one of our greatest advocates. But at this period he was a disappointed and frustrated man. He had recorded 'a secret anguish' that he had not been appointed, as he had at first been asked, and by me as the Prime Minister's messenger, to be the senior British judge, and according to his biographer, not long after Nuremberg he was 'feeling personally depressed and dispirited'. I think that some of his impatient comments on the Nuremberg proceeding were due to these considerations.

The British part in the trial was not inconsiderable. I think I led a team that under critical foreign eyes was able to maintain the very high standards of our law. I can recall no gaffes like that of the junior American counsel who opened some minor speech to the tribunal with the words: 'The noise you hear is my knees knocking. They have never knocked so hard since the day I asked my lovely little wife to marry me.' To this observation, Biddle recorded in his notebook the simple comment: 'Christ!' Birkett was more harsh. Outside court, however, there was an occasional social contretemps in which the British were involved. Thus I was told that on one occasion at a party with the Russians, Geoffrey Dorling 'Khaki' Roberts, an English KC, took off his trousers to ape a Russian dance. The incident did not cause amusement.

There were some difficulties as to the general procedure. The problem with several different forms of procedure possible – Anglo-

Saxon, French, German, Russian – was to decide which should be adopted at the trial. This was discussed at the London conference and, inevitably, the other jurisdictions had to give way to the Anglo-Saxon procedure. This, then, was easy for the American and the British legal teams, but did undoubtedly make things difficult for the French. Their representatives were distinguished men – M. Donnedieu de Vabres and M. Falco – who had been brought up in the tradition of the *Code Napoléon* and the Inquisitorial system of procedure as distinct from our common law and adversarial method. Because of these and other procedural difficulties they tended to flounder about a bit during the course of the trial in what was very much an Anglo-Saxon scrap, although they were, as one would expect, always agreeable associates.

The Soviet representatives did not really pretend to understand the procedure – or care much about it. They doubted whether prisoners under cross-examination should be allowed to answer at all. As for giving evidence themselves, this should be very restricted and they should not be accorded the same tolerance or allowed to speak from the same witness box as witnesses for the prosecution! The prisoners were there simply to be sentenced. Indeed, at a dinner for all the judges and counsel held very early in the proceedings, Vyshinsky – an able lawyer, a Menshevik turned Communist prosecutor and the head of the Soviet legal system, a kind of Soviet Attorney General – offered a toast to the prisoners: 'May their path lead straight from the dock to the gallows.' He spoke so fast that the toast was drunk by all the judges before anyone seems to have realized what it was. Judge Parker, the US Deputy, was seriously upset and disturbed when he realized what he had done.

The German lawyers also found the procedure unfamiliar, but the tribunal took every care to ensure that the actual procedures followed were fair, and gave all parties a realistic opportunity of participating as they would wish.

One departure from normal Anglo-Saxon procedure was decided upon at a very early stage by the tribunal and that was that most evidence for the prosecution would be documentary, rather than oral. This was at first opposed by the tribunal and particularly by Lord Justice Lawrence. He was afraid that documentary depositions might be unreliable and unfairly biased against the defendants, without the safeguard of seeing the witnesses and being able to cross-examine them. We were, however, able to point out that for the most part the documents would not be ones specially prepared for the trial by the prosecution but would come from the Germans' own files and archives – an unbelievable mass of which had fallen into Allied hands on the surrender. They consisted almost entirely of directions by Hitler himself, memoranda and orders by the various leaders (including, I think, all those in the dock), departmental records, statistics on rearmaments and other matters, records of staff and top-level conferences, minutes relating to this and that, and even personal records. The Germans have always been obsessed with files and records but had not realized the importance of destroying them before the enemy could rifle through them. In the end, there was a superfluity of documents, and some trouble arose in the early stages due to the American team releasing documents to the Press which had not yet been introduced into evidence. The Tribunal stopped this by insisting that nothing must be used without being put through the IBM translating system, and this greatly cut down the flow.

The accuracy or significance of the documents has been criticized by various historians in the 50 years since, but although their relevance and weight differed greatly, there is no doubt that all were genuine and many had conclusive probative value. It must be conceded, however, that the use of documentary evidence put the defence at a disadvantage. Although they had access to all the evidence they did not have the facilities to process and analyse it, and they found very few documents that they could use in evidence. They had therefore to rely on calling oral evidence, including their clients from the dock.

The constant reading of documents in a language that most of those in court did not understand made the trial exceedingly tedious for long periods, especially the history of events leading to the invasion of Poland (which I had thought would be the most important part of the trial). It was especially slow because of the need for the interpreters to hear and understand, so much so that a French aide to the Tribunal once snored so loudly that the proceedings were interfered with and the Tribunal went briefly into closed session to administer a rebuke.

The evidence as to the actual war crimes was sometimes harrowing in the extreme and brought tears of grief even to my hardened eyes. During the recital of some of these grim stories I watched the defendants' actions in the dock. Some were visibly shocked. This was particularly the case with the showing of the British film of Belsen and the shovelling of hundreds of dead bodies by earth-moving equipment. The defendants had known of, even ordered, these things, but had not themselves carried them out, or perhaps visualized what they really involved.

The real difficulty of the defence was not the quality of their counsel in mastering the procedure of the trial, nor the language or the difficulty they had in finding witnesses to testify on their behalf, or even their general lack of resources to enable them to research particular matters. It was more fundamental. The defendants were not able to make common cause with each other on the basic issues, except in relation to those aspects that had been overstressed by the American prosecution, namely the charges against the SS and the SA. It was, from a collective point of view, an unco-ordinated defence in which particular defendants sometimes did more harm to their co-defendants than good for themselves in the conduct of their case. The position is summarized by Professor Bradley Smith in his book *Reaching Judgment at Nuremberg*.

> The twenty-two Defendants came from very diverse backgrounds and were sharply separated by class, and many of them hated each other: the old aristocrats treated the commoners with scarcely veiled condescension. The military looked down on the civilians and the rest of the defendants considered Streicher and Kaltenbrunner too unsavoury for their company.

As the defendants in the dock had been selected by the prosecution to represent the different parts of the Nazi system, their earlier political activities and the charges they faced varied greatly.

> . . . under the circumstances meaningful defence was impossible and agreement even on the approach to such fundamental charges as the conspiratorial plan to wage aggressive war could not be established.

One of the ill-considered moves by the defence was the calling as a witness of Rudolf Hoess,* who had been commandant of the notorious

---

* Rudolf Hoess was a camp commandant

Auschwitz concentration camp.† Hoess was called in a half-hearted attempt to counter the charge of conspiracy by showing that the defendants did not know what happened in the concentration camps. Hoess did testify that the killings had been carried out in secret and that they were not part of a general conspiracy. His evidence was given to a court that became hushed with horror, for he described coldly and unemotionally the mass suffering and deaths, but at the same time the efficiency with which he personally had supervised the deaths of a million and a half innocent human beings.

Jackson was amply justified in his closing speech when he said:

> Adolf Eichmann, the sinister figure who had charge of the extermination programme, has estimated that the anti-Jewish activities resulted in the killing of 6,000,000 Jews.
>
> Of those, 4,000,000 were killed in extermination institutions and 2,000,000 by Einsatzgruppen, mobile units of the Security police and SD.

But it was extraordinary that the Defence at Nuremberg actually called the commandant of one of the most evil of the extermination camps to prove that it was so.

After a few days' remission, we reached the closing speeches for the Prosecution. Jackson had put a great deal of work into his, and it was indeed a magnificent oration which did much to restore his standing and his own self-confidence, which had suffered badly from the failed cross-examination of Goering and Schacht and other unhappy incidents. In his opening paragraph he observed that

> It is impossible in summation to do more than outline with bold strokes the vitals of this trial's mad and melancholy record, which

† Its present relevance relates to the fact that recently some publicity has been given to statements coming in part from an anonymous source, in what seems clearly to be a co-ordinated campaign, the purpose of which is to suggest that there were no concentration camps, that no attempt was made to exterminate the Jews and that all the stories to the contrary were invented as part of the anti-Nazi propaganda. This campaign is associated with the name of an Englishman who calls himself an historian. Anyone who believes this rubbish should look a little at the Nuremberg evidence.

will live as the historical text of the twentieth century's shame and depravity.

It is common to think of our own time as standing at the apex of civilisation, from which the deficiencies of preceding ages may patronisingly be viewed in the light of what is assumed to be 'progress'. The reality is that in the long perspective of history the present century will not hold an admirable position, unless its second half is to redeem its first. These two-score years in this Twentieth Century will be recorded in the book of years as some of the most bloody of all annals. Two World Wars have left a legacy of dead which number more than all the armies engaged in any war that made ancient or medieval history. No half-century ever witnessed slaughter on such a scale, such cruelties and inhumanities, such wholesale deportations of peoples into slavery, such annihilations of minorities. The Terror of Torquemada pales before the Nazi Inquisition. These deeds are the overshadowing historical facts by which generations to come will remember the decade. If we cannot eliminate the causes and prevent the repetition of these barbaric events, it is not an irresponsible prophecy to say that this Twentieth Century may yet succeed in bringing the doom of civilisation.

Then came his peroration:

It is against such a background that these defendants now ask this Tribunal to say that they are not guilty of planning, executing, or conspiring to commit this long list of crimes and wrongs. They stand before the record of this trial as bloodstained Gloucester stood by the body of his slain king. He begged of the widow, as they beg of you: 'Say I slew them not.' And the Queen replied, 'Then say they were not slain. But dead they are . . .' If you were to say of these men that they are not guilty, it would be as true to say there has been no war, there are no slain, there has been no crime.

My own speech followed. The chief prosecutors had met to discuss the order and context of their speeches. At one point it had been thought that one of us only should make the final closing speech for the Prosecution. Eventually a compromise was agreed in that I was asked to speak on behalf of all prosecutors on the legal aspects and that the other three would each make shorter speeches, leaving me to make what was called an 'overview' of the whole case, which would be longer than the other three speeches. It certainly was!

A less than agreeable part of writing this memoir has been for me the realization that I lack the gift of being incisive. My speeches are all too long-winded. And this final speech at Nuremberg was far too long, occupying seventy-nine pages of the print as against Jackson's thirty-three. Alas, it is a lesson I have learned too late in life. I can at least spare my readers a repetition here of all the legal arguments I canvassed. It is enough to say that the German counsel, particularly Professor Exner and Professor Jahrreis, who represented all the defendants on the charges of aggressive war, put up scholarly and carefully reasoned defences, and argued that in spite of the Kellogg-Briand Pact of 1928, the right of self-defence remained. But was this such a case, I asked in my closing speech. I had in my opening quoted Von Blomberg, the then Reich Minister for War, as having said in 1937 that 'the general political position justified the supposition that Germany need not consider an attack from any side' and the evidence was overwhelming that each of the wars separately started by Germany from the attack on Poland in 1939 on was to pursue the German objective of securing *lebensraum* and domination without the slightest fear of attack from the country invaded. The only innovation of the Charter was, I stressed, to provide the long-overdue machinery to enforce already-existing law.*

After examining the position of each of the defendants, I answered the legal points raised by counsel for the defendants and also those put forward by academics outside in detail. Having read the speech again, I think that what I said at Nuremberg is still applicable to the views that

---

* This is still a grave defect in international law. The judgment at Nuremberg and subsequent resolutions of the United Nations adopting the Nuremberg principles have immensely strengthened and restated the rules against aggressive war as laid down in the Kellogg-Briand Pact. But, alas, we remain without a permanent international criminal court to enforce them. And this despite many efforts by the United Kingdom – at least in the period 1945–51 – to establish such a system. Had such a court been in existence in 1991 it is inconceivable that Saddam Hussein would not have been brought before it – not to mention the others such as Pol Pot who have violated international law. I continue to urge action on this important matter.

have been canvassed in recent years. I shall say something about the political implications of these criticisms, but so far as the legal aspects are concerned I am content to rest on the arguments that I put before the tribunal and which it accepted.

And so I come to the peroration of my speech:

In one way the fate of these men means little: their personal power for evil lies for ever broken; they have convicted and discredited each other and finally destroyed the legend they created round the figure of their leader. But on their fate great issues must still depend, for the ways of truth and righteousness between the nations of the world, the hope of future international co-operation in the administration of law and justice, are in your hands. This trial must form a milestone in the history of civilization, not only bringing retribution to these guilty men, not only marking that right shall in the end triumph over evil, but also that the ordinary people of the world (and I make no distinction now between friend or foe) are now determined that the individual must transcend the State. The State and the law are made for man, that through them he may achieve a fuller life, a higher purpose and a greater dignity. States may be great and powerful. Ultimately the rights of men, made as all men are made in the image of God, are fundamental. When the State, either because as here its leaders have lusted for power and place, or under some specious pretext that the end may justify the means, affronts these things, they may for a time become obscured and submerged. But they are immanent and ultimately they will assert themselves more strongly still, the immanence more manifest. And so, after this ordeal to which mankind has been submitted, mankind itself – struggling now to re-establish in all the countries of the world the common, simple things – liberty, love, understanding – comes to this Court and cries 'These are our laws – let them prevail.'

I was followed by Monsieur Champetier de Ribes, who made an able speech, his opening remarks setting out succinctly what, apart from establishing the guilt of the defendants, the trial had achieved.

In the course of the last nine months the events of more than fifteen years of history have been evoked at this bar.

For the chief concern of this trial is above all that of historical truth. Thanks to it, the historian of the future, as well as the chroni⁄ cler of today, will know the truth of the political, diplomatic and mil⁄ itary events of the most tragic period of our history. He will know the crimes of Nazism as well as the irresolution, the weaknesses, the omissions of the peace⁄loving democracies. He will know that the work of twenty centuries of a civilization, which believed itself eternal, was almost destroyed by the return of ancient barbarism in a new guise, all the more brutal because more scientific.

He will know that the progress of mechanical science, modern means of propaganda, and the most devilish practices of a police which defied the most elementary rules of humanity, enabled a small minority of criminals to distort within a few years the collective con⁄ science of a great people, and to transform the nation described by Dr Sauter at the conclusion of his speech in defence of von Schirach, as loyal, upright and full of virtue, into that of Hitler, Himmler and Goebbels – to mention only those of them who are dead. He will know that the real crime of these men was the conception of the gigantic plan of world domination, and the attempt to realise it by every possible means.

The French speeches were followed by a fairly long but well⁄con⁄ structed speech by General Rudenko, appearing as always in his smart military uniform. Knowing what we know now it is sad to realize that the Soviet Union was itself guilty of some of the crimes charged against the defendants at Nuremberg, beginning with the Nazi/Soviet Pact in July 1939 which led to the Soviet invasion of Eastern Poland. Here it is perhaps sufficient to say that none of the defendants was convicted by either the false evidence or the hypocritical arguments put forward by the Russians. The Western judges completely ignored the Katyn massacre. I cannot be sure whether General Rudenko himself knew the truth at that time. We all felt that the chief Soviet judge, Nikitchenko, did not, and that he was an honourable man. And General Rudenko's summary of the case against each of the defendants was effective, not less so because he naturally stressed the enormity of the crimes committed against the Russians in the course of Operation Barbarossa.

On 31 August 1946 the defendants made their own final statements from the dock. For the most part they did so with dignity and, as Birkett observed, with outward fortitude. Goering, in his loose-fitting field marshal's uniform, reminded the Tribunal of his oath of loyalty to Hitler.

It was then that he told the tribunal quietly 'I really meant it and I still do.' In his personal conduct during the trial he had remained true to his oath. Hess followed Goering. He was obviously mad and entered into a long, rambling speech. Goering and Ribbentrop tried vainly to stop him – 'Shut up' he said to them – but he was stopped in the end by Lawrence. Ribbentrop, on the contrary, behaved with dignity and warned the world against the Soviet Union. And so it went on. Schacht asked us to believe that he was 'shaken to the depths of his soul by the unspeakable misery he had tried to prevent'.

III

The tribunal adjourned until 23 September to consider its judgement, which was in fact delayed until 10 October. During this time all the four judges and their alternates worked hard and often until late into the night, continuing a process they had started in a private and informal way early in June. It took them over three months to reach their final decisions. There was no formal record of these deliberations, but drafts and notes prepared by assistants and the diaries of two of the judges have provided a good deal of information on how the discussions went. All the judges gave grave, prolonged and anxious thought to their eventual decisions. On some matters there was disagreement, as one would have expected, and sometimes the result was – I will not say a compromise – an agreed accommodation of previously differing views. The decisions were arrived at with the assistance of numerous alternative forms of words drafted by Birkett and without, in the case of the Western judges, any interference whatsoever by governments or the prosecutors. Alas, I cannot say the same of the Soviet judges. It was of course clear from the time of the London Conference on that Moscow was very much in control. This became a matter of acute personal embarrassment to

General Nikitchenko. He had eventually to accept his instructions but towards the end this so worried him that it was occasionally apparent that he was seeking relief in drink. After it was all over, at Christmas and other times, Birkett and others from England, including myself, wrote friendly letters to Nikitchenko and Rudenko. They did not reply. They had been forbidden to. This was a sad tightening of the Iron Curtain; we had frequently visited each others' homes in Nuremberg, and we had thought that in private life we could regard the Soviet repre-sentatives as almost family friends.

The cases of the individual defendants were difficult enough, but even more abstruse were the charges of conspiracy and the cases against the allegedly criminal organizations. When I became involved in the later stages of the London Conference I felt that they were somewhat esoteric for an International Tribunal concerned with the guilt of par-ticular individuals on some very concrete charges. By then, however, the principle of such charges, originated by the Americans, had been accepted, although it is fair to say that the French and the Soviet Union found them confusing and perhaps irrelevant. For my own part, I came to appreciate the significance of the charges in establishing for posterity the history of the Nazi movement. I had in my speeches to the Tribunal stressed the importance we attached to the conspiracy and aggressive war charges, but the Tribunal hardly directed its own serious discussions to these matters until it had received the first drafts of the judgement which the President had asked Birkett to prepare. This was in the late spring of 1946. The criticism of the drafts was led by the French judge, M. Donnedieu de Vabres, who maintained that such notions as conspiracy, crimes against peace and even crimes against humanity were not known to International Law. It was a courageous argument and as it developed the French judge laid emphasis on Hitler's all-powerful position as Fuhrer. This he said negated any voluntary agreement or conspiracy. Biddle gave some support to this view but Lawrence, Parker and the French Alternate Falco seem not to have gone along with it. Nikitchenko had no difficulty in agreeing with anything that involved the guilt of the defendants. Birkett, who had great influence with the Tribunal and who was, especially at this time, its unofficial draftsman, argued with great force that the very heart would be torn out of the case if the conspiracy and associated charges were abandoned. It would be a disaster. For the Western judges, this was a compelling argument. Nikitchenko told his fellow judges to abandon 'legal theorizing'; they should act like practical men and not like a debating society. And that in the end is what they did. They abandoned the idea of including crimes against humanity and war crimes as part of the general conspiracy charge, and limited this to a conspiracy to wage aggressive war, the starting date for which they put as the Hossbach Conference in November 1937, at which Hitler had set out his plans to seize Austria and Czechoslovakia by force. As for the alleged 'criminal organizations', the German general staff, although sternly condemned in general terms, was to be held not guilty, so also the Reich Cabinet and the SA. The Gestapo, the SD and the Corps of Political Leaders were guilty. These 'not guilty' decisions were not concurred in by the Soviet judges. Stalin was said to be furious about them and Nikitchenko, in obedience to orders, gave a dissenting judgement. These somewhat philosophical differences were only finally resolved in August.

The judges then turned their attention to the charges against the individual defendants. Here too there were disagreements. It was agreed without much discussion that Goering, Ribbentrop, Keitel, Frank, Streicher, Sauckel, Jodl, Kaltenbrunner, Rosenberg, Frick and Seyss-Inquart were guilty and should be sentenced to death. To my mind the surprising decisions were those relating to Speer, Von Schirach, Schacht, von Papen, Fritzsche and Hess.

In giving their evidence, many of the defendants had made significant admissions. Speer admitted that: 'Even in a totalitarian system there must be total responsibility . . . It is impossible after the catastrophe to evade this total responsibility. If the war had been won, the leaders would also have assumed total responsibility.' Von Schirach – 'the venomous vulgarian' as Jackson described him – was an evil man. He was one of Hitler's earliest and youngest recruits. He admitted, 'It is my fault that I educated the German Youth for a man who committed murders a millionfold', and his deputy said of the Hitler Jugend which they organized: 'In the course of years we want to ensure that a gun felt just as natural in the hands of a German boy as a pen.'

The Hitler Jugend, of which Schirach was the leader and head and which by 1939 numbered nearly 8 million, became under a special arrangement between him and Himmler the recruiting agency for the

SS, which was directly involved in the concentration camp system, in the killing of prisoners of war and in the atrocities in occupied territories. I had described this perversion of the youth of Germany – recruited by glamorous devices such as the right to a uniform and the right to be saluted by German officers, calculated to attract children quite innocent at the time of their enrolment – as perhaps the greatest crime of all. Yet the equally divided judges recorded a verdict of not guilty under Count 1 of the indictment (conspiracy) but guilty under Count 4 (crimes against humanity), basing this judgement on Schirach's conduct while gauleiter in Vienna and responsible for, among other things, the slave labour programme and the mass deportation of Jews to a fate of which he must have known. Two of the judges (Lawrence and Nikitchenko) thought he should be sentenced to death, and two (Biddle and Donnedieu de Vabres) supported Birkett's compromise view of 20 years in prison; Lawrence eventually agreed with this solution. Schirach was lucky.

And so, indeed, was Speer. He was a man of great ability, a technocrat without whose help the Nazi Government would not have become so efficient as it did. He had some culture and presence. Speer's case seems to have given the tribunal much difficulty. He was charged under all four counts of the indictment, but the gravamen of the case against him was the wholesale use of slave and POW labour, a crime under international laws. The case against him regarding the use of POW labour was not well developed, but Speer certainly knew about the crimes. In 1943 he was present at the Central Planning Board when General Erhardt Milch said:

We have made a request for an order that a certain percentage of men in the Ack Ack artillery must be Russian: 50,000 will be taken altogether. 30,000 are already employed as gunners. This is an amusing thing, that Russians must work the guns.

Whether Speer joined in the laughter is not recorded. This amusing thing was, of course, flagrantly illegal. That Speer was aware of the use of slave and concentration camp labour he did not deny, nor can there be much doubt that he was aware of the terrible conditions under which the slaves were recruited and worked. Sauckel, who worked under Speer and was designated the 'Plenipotentiary General for the Utilisation of Labour', stated that 'out of 5,000,000 foreign workers who arrived in Germany, not even 200,000 came voluntarily.' It was officially reported to defendant Rosenberg that 'recruiting methods were used which prob-ably had their origin in the blackest period of the slave trade.' Speer was Minister of Armaments and War Production and, as Jackson put it in his closing speech, he 'joined in planning and executing the programme to dragoon prisoners of war and foreign workers into German war industries which waxed in output whilst the labourers waned in starva-tion.' Speer was the king-pin of the German industrial organization at its most crucial time, and certainly one of the most able men in the Nazi hierarchy. He himself accepted total responsibility.

It is true that he was among the first to realize that the war was lost. After the bomb plot of 1944 he gradually became disillusioned with Hitler and in March 1945 he had an apparently furious altercation with the Fuhrer, telling him that he should withdraw his order for demolition in face of the enemy advance and that he had a responsibility to save the German people. There seems no doubt that he realized that the end was coming – how could a man of his intelligence have failed so to do? – but his very belated repentance, if repentance it was, hardly excused the vitally important part he had played before. None the less, the tribunal, after much anxious debate, acquitted him on Counts 1 and 2 and con-victed only on Counts 3 and 4. Not that conviction on these would not have justified a death sentence. Biddle was in favour of this. So of course was Nikitchenko. Lawrence and Donnedieu de Vabres felt 15 years was appropriate. In the end Birkett, not for the first time, proposed a com-promise of 20 years' imprisonment, and that was accepted with Nikitchenko's dissent.

What worried many of us about this sentence was its contrast with the death sentence passed on Sauckel. Sauckel was in effect Speer's deputy in the labour programme. Speer at one time called him merely his assistant. He was thought by some to be 'quite a decent fellow', and although he was a party to the whole slave labour programme he was not its originator or employer. Professor Bradley Smith suggests unhappily that there was some social prejudice in Speer's favour. Speer was a gentle-man, Sauckel an unpretentious proletarian. I also have an unhappy feeling that quite unconsciously Lawrence's thinking may have been

affected by such considerations. At all events, Sauckel was hanged, pro-
testing to the end that he could not understand it because he had never
been cruel to anyone in his life. And Speer, after his imprisonment, was
able to make a great deal of money by writing his memoir and justifying
himself.

As early as 1932 Schacht was writing to Hitler in the most adulatory
terms, and he was made General Plenipotentiary for War Economy in
May 1935. It is true, however, that from 1935 onwards, Schacht's attitude towards the Nazi Party became ambiguous and in some matters he
was openly critical. He did not hide his detestation of Goering and
from about that time he started advocating a reduction in the armament
programme because of its danger to the economy. In 1937 he had
resigned from his positions as Minister of Economics and
Plenipotentiary for War Economy. But Hitler made him a Minister
without Portfolio. He held this post until 1943 and thus continued to
lend his name and some weight to Hitler's campaign. The fact was that
Schacht was an extremely devious character. His support of Hitler was
cynical and self-serving. When Hitler came back from Paris in 1940
after his victory against France, Schacht joined in the tumultuous
welcome. A news film was exhibited to the tribunal that showed
Schacht giving Hitler what had every appearance of a warm and con-
gratulatory personal welcome. After the attempt on Hitler's life in July
1944, however, he was arrested by the Gestapo and spent the rest of the
war in concentration camps. The case against Schacht was well
summarized by Jackson in his closing speech in what seemed to me a
most damning indictment.

> Schacht says he steadily 'sabotaged' the Hitler government. Yet, the
> most relentless secret service in the world never detected him doing
> the regime any harm until long after he knew the war to be lost and
> the Nazis doomed. Schacht, who dealt in 'hedges' all his life, always
> kept himself in a position to claim that he was in either camp. The
> plea for him is as specious on analysis as it is persuasive on first sight.
> Schacht represents the most dangerous and reprehensible type of
> opportunism – that of the man of influential position who is ready
> to join a movement that he knows to be wrong because he thinks it is
> winning.

During the trial, as I have already mentioned, Schacht separated himself as ostentatiously as he could from his fellow defendants. When the film of the concentration camps was shown, he turned his back to the screen and ignored it; this is what we suspected he must have done when he was so successfully organizing the German economy. Goering loathed and despised him. I agreed with Goering. Schacht had all through his career sought to play both sides against the middle. In September 1934 he told the American Ambassador in Berlin that '. . . the Hitler party is absolutely committed to war and the people too are ready and willing. Only a few Government officials are aware of the danger and opposed.' Nonetheless, in May 1935 he was Minister of Economics and was made General Plenipotentiary for the War Economy in order 'to put all economic forces in the service of carrying on the war and to secure the life of the German people economically'. He wrote to Hitler, 'All expenditures which are not urgently needed in other matters must stop and the entire financial power of Germany must be concentrated towards the one goal – to win.'

It is true that before the invasion of Poland actually took place, Schacht had fallen out of favour. Goering secured control over the economic machinery for mobilization and Schacht resigned his ministerial position; in 1939 he was dismissed from the Presidency of the Reichsbank. The Tribunal had great difficulty in reaching a decision about him. Biddle was at first quite strongly in favour of conviction, so was Donnedieu de Vabres and, of course, Nikitchenko. But Lawrence, who thought Schacht a banker and a gentleman, quite different from most of the disagreeable men in the dock, was equally strongly for acquittal. And so, after quite bitter argument and a curious change of position by the French judge, Schacht was totally acquitted.

The acquittal astonished Goering as much as us. He snubbed Schacht and made his contempt very obvious. Nor was his acquittal received with rejoicing in Germany, where many felt he had been a fair-weather friend, profiting greatly from the earlier Nazi period and deserting the country when things started to go wrong. Indeed, it was deemed impolitic to let him leave the Nuremberg prison immediately in case he was lynched. Two days later he was taken away in great secrecy to some undisclosed 'safe house' and it was not very long before he obtained some lucrative consultancies. The last time I saw him myself was, I think, the following year when I was lunching with my wife in a smart restaurant in Rome and noticed at a table next to me a man whose face seemed familiar. I asked a waiter discreetly who it was and he replied 'Schacht'. The recognition must have been mutual, and in Schacht's case put him off his food, for he immediately got up and left, his lunch unfinished.

Schacht having been acquitted, the acquittal of von Papen was less of a surprise. He too professed old family and professional integrity; he too was a gentleman. But throughout the period he was a sycophant. Soon after he had co-operated in putting Hitler into power he realized that Hitler's Government meant oppression of opponents, pogroms of the Jews and persecution of the churches, including his own, yet he treated the concordat with the Vatican, which he himself had negotiated, as 'a scrap of paper'. He was acquitted, the judges being equally divided. Fritzsche was only included in the indictment because, being in Russian custody, the Soviets insisted on it. In the end, and after much argument, the three Western judges agreed to his acquittal. Goering agreed with this verdict. After it was announced and Schacht and Von Papen were freed, Goering snubbed them contemptuously and then deliberately crossed the floor and said to Fritzsche, 'You really did not belong to our set and I am sincerely happy you were acquitted.' Goering was probably right: he often was.

Hess, as I have said, was mad. He might have been given a short sentence and then released. That he was not was due to Soviet insistence and certainly not (as has been suggested) to any pressure by the British Government. As the trial proceeded and we had an opportunity of observing him (repeatedly), most of us felt doubtful about the decision that he should stand trial. Mr Justice Birkett recorded that in his final statement 'Hess betrayed the signs of a disordered mind in almost every word he spoke.' He was sentenced to imprisonment for life and he remained imprisoned, for many years the solitary inmate of the Spandau prison, until 1988 when he died, at a great age but in somewhat mysterious circumstances. I do not think any civilized country now regards imprisonment for life as involving just that. The Russians did and Hess could not be released without their permission. The US and UK Governments, supported by individuals like myself, made strong representations to the Soviet Government for his release. The Russians refused. I always thought the reason for their refusal was that Spandau prison was in the British Zone of Berlin but that under the Four Power arrangement the Soviet Military Government was entitled to take charge of it for every fourth month. This gave them the only opportunity to march their crack troops, equivalent to our Guards, through the British Zone. So far as Hess's position as a war criminal was concerned, the continued incarceration was an injustice and an irrelevance.*

No useful purpose would be served by examining in detail the other cases. Those sentenced to death appealed to the Control Commission but in every case the appeal was rejected. On 9 October 1946 the death sentences were carried out, except in Goering's case. Well informed as usual, an hour or two before the secret time he committed suicide, with a cyanide capsule that in some unknown way he had available. When I heard the news, I confess I laughed and said, 'Good luck to him.' Birkett, who was with me, was deeply shocked. Journalists who watched the executions say the American executioner was inefficient. The wretched men were choked to death. It must be said, however, that the prisoners met their fate with great dignity and courage. Their bodies were removed in the dead of night, taken to the concentration camp at Dachau, used for so many thousands of their victims, and there cre/ mated. The ashes were then secretly scattered. No memorial marks this spot.

As I have noted, I always opposed capital punishment, for I believe that in general it is not proved to have a deterrent effect and I doubt the infallibility of our systems of trial in avoiding an unjust result. I had, however, prosecuted or defended a good many murderers or traitors in the United Kingdom and avoided any personal feeling in a particular case, an attitude it is most important for an advocate to maintain. In those days the death penalty was the law. And my duty was to assist in the administration of the law. It was for Parliament to alter it. So far as the Nazi war criminals were concerned, however, I did feel that if ever the death sentence was deserved it was in most of the Nuremberg cases.

* Another irrelevance which I might dispose of now is the theory that the Rudolph Hess prosecuted at Nuremberg and imprisoned at Spandau was not the real Hess, Hitler's deputy, at all. This is just nonsense. Those who propound it must take a pretty poor view of his son's identification, the recognition of his co-defendants and the intelligence of the Allied lawyers and soldiers who had to deal with him.

Nor would any useful purpose be served now by my conducting a personal inquest here on the reasons why there were no further joint trials by the International Military Tribunal or why, at least so far as the United Kingdom was concerned, we eventually discontinued our own trials by military courts of so-called minor war criminals within our jurisdiction. At the time of the London Agreement in 1945, it was contemplated that there would be more than one trial before the IMT. Indeed, the matter arose in the course of the original trial at Nuremberg following the exclusion of Gustav Krupp from the defendants under trial there. When I addressed the court on the question of substituting Alfried for Gustav Krupp I expressly referred to the possibility of further trials:

> There is provision in the Charter for the holding of further trials and it may be that hereafter . . . other proceedings ought to be taken possibly against Alfried Krupp, possibly against other industrialists . . .
>
> I am certainly not less anxious than the representatives of any other state that the part played by industrialists in the preparation and conduct of the war should be fully exposed to the Tribunal and the world . . .

A few days later, on 20 November 1946, we agreed with the French delegation and filed with the tribunal a memorandum stating that we were engaged in examining the case of leading German industrialists 'as well as certain other major war criminals' with a view to their being indicted together with Alfried Krupp at a subsequent trial. We had several meetings between the chief prosecutors to discuss the matter. Among the individuals who we thought qualified for inclusion in a subsequent trial were Alfried Krupp, Schmitz, Schnitzler, Farben, Roechling, Schroeder, and Thyssen. The American State and War Departments thought that a further joint IMT trial was not desirable. Our Foreign Office officials were not enthusiastic about the idea of prosecuting industrialists. Lack of money and lack of staff were important considerations for us. It was common ground that any decision should await the end of the existing trial. In the meantime General Zorya, one of the Soviet deputy prosecutors, shot himself. We never discovered why. Perhaps the thought of a second trial was too much for him! Jackson took the view that the better course was for each of the occupying powers to assume responsibility for the trial of those criminals found within its own zone. And so it was in the end decided. This decision would have left Krupp in our hands for most of his properties were in our zone. But the Americans under Telford Taylor had assembled a very large staff which had done massive work on Krupp. They were anxious to take over his case and we agreed that they should do so. Krupp was not the only war criminal we transferred to them. In the event, Alfried Krupp was tried by an American military court along with eleven other officials charged with planning and preparing aggressive war and with what may broadly be described as organizing and using slave labour. They were found not guilty on the first charge but guilty on the second and received varying sentences of which the heaviest was 12 years' imprisonment for Krupp, who had been charged as a member of the directing body of his firm. Most of his sentence was later remitted. Looking back on it, I think it is regrettable that the British did not, in the end, try any of the industrialists at all. Curiously, the Americans seemed to have a much stronger view about slave labour and other so-called industrial crimes than we did, although we then had a Socialist government. More curious still, the Russians evinced no interest at all in such trials.

But most curious of all was the fact that having brought them to trial and sentenced them in their own tribunals, the United States very soon after started releasing the industrialists and other war criminals long before their sentences had expired. The matter was considered by HMG on 12 February 1951 when I took a very strong line against any remissions. I thought that the release of Krupp at the very moment when we were embarking on a policy of allowing Germany a limited degree of rearmament was most unfortunate. I corresponded with Biddle, who agreed with me, and Justice Jackson (who by then was again sitting as a Supreme Court judge) wrote to me on 20 February 1951:

. . . I do not think the United States could have handed the Kremlin a better propaganda issue, certainly in those countries which the Nazis occupied, than in the release of Krupp.

This is not a sudden change. The change here began when Mr

Stimson's influence left the Department of the Army and Secretary Kenneth Royall came in. It has proceeded rather insidiously ever since . . .

This country is so hooked up about communism at the present moment that the public temper identifies as friend of the United States any person who is a foe of Stalin. It figures that the Nazis were his foes, entirely forgetting that they did not hesitate to become her allies when they thought they would gain by it. General Eisenhower has pretty effectively stopped the movement which was in full swing to virtually rearm them. I hope a saner outlook will arrive here but at the moment the scene is rather depressing. . . . I hope to God we shall regain our senses.

In the United Kingdom we not only tried no industrialists, we ceased the trial of the so-called minor war criminals – minor only in the sense that they were not themselves members of the ruling hierarchy, heinous as some of their crimes were. We had compiled a list of around 10,000 such criminals within our zone of occupation. I had urged strongly that we should bring at least 500 to trial in our military courts by 1946. We did not succeed in approaching that figure. The military, whose task it was, were not keen on organizing such trials; they were dilatory in the extreme. On one occasion I told the Prime Minister that if instead of Montgomery I had been in charge of the matter, we would have got much nearer to our targets. But I was not. I had only a watching brief to advise the PM how things were going. All I could do was to write a series of forceful minutes to Mr Attlee which he immediately passed on to the military with firm indications of his own displeasure and instructions that these were to be conveyed to the commands. But a conspicuously weak War Secretary failed to get anything done. The trials became counter-productive; sometimes derisory sentences were imposed and public opinion turned against their continuance. We became more concerned with peace than punishment. In the end Parliament agreed without a single dissentient, Winston Churchill strongly supporting, that the trials should cease as from the end of 1947. All this is history and cannot be rewritten. But it must be admitted that in all zones of occupation, many thousands were left free who had committed often odious crimes which cried out for punishment.

During the fifty years since the trial took place many books have been written by many learned people and their verdict has been mixed.* The further we get away from the trial, the more adverse the verdict seems to become. But I would comment that the further we get away from the trial, the further also we get away from the reality of that terrible decade ending in 1946.

Professor Bradley Smith, in his book on the trial, was critical of the whole proceeding, both in its initiation and its conduct. He has made an exhaustive examination of the different policies pursued by the Allies, the errors made by the judges in individual cases, the fallibility of some of the arguments used. In much of this his observations are correct, but such as could be made of any very lengthy trial conducted before as many as eight judges.

Apart from his critical analysis of the details of the proceedings he does not, I think, believe that anyone was punished who did not deserve to be. He seems, however, to favour the view that if any action was to be taken against the Nazi leaders after the war it should have been of an executive or political nature. I have already discussed how the matter developed during the war. Although it was not finally agreed until early in 1945, I am sure that the decision to deal with the matter judicially was correct. Professor Smith naturally finds it difficult to recapture the atmosphere that existed in the closing months of the war, but I have no doubt that had we then proceeded to summary execution, history would have alleged, and ordinary people might have felt, that we had made martyrs of the people thus executed by their victors in revenge and without trial. The place of execution would eventually have become known and become something of a shrine. Unrest and division in Germany would have been exacerbated. Some would have seen the Nazis as martyrs and others, dismayed by the realization of what the

---

* Of the numerous books that have been written I commend in particular one by Professor Bradley F. Smith, *Reaching Judgment at Nuremberg*, and *Nuremberg* by Airey Neave, who was there. More recently Telford Taylor has published his very comprehensive account of the trial. He was a member of the American team and is inclined to be critical of others – particularly me! – and well satisfied with himself. It is, however, a detailed report of the whole proceedings. He dismisses Bradley Smith as 'less than temperate' but his own volume, although more detailed, involved no critical discussion of the philosophy of the trial.

Nazis had done and by the destruction of their country, would have sought themselves to take retribution against their former leaders. As it was, the knowledge that the Nuremberg trial was taking place undoubt-edly did much in those critical months after the Armstice to pacify the German population. The Allies did ensure that considerable publicity was given to the trial in the German media, which explained that the trial was exposing the criminality of the Third Reich. The German defence counsel seem to have accepted this view and to have agreed that on the whole the trial had been fair and the verdicts reasonable and acceptable.

More worrying, possibly, is Professor Smith's view that by their own conduct of the war, the Allies had lost the moral authority to conduct the trial. 'So' – he writes – 'the allies lost the moral triumph over Nazism with a double-edged quid pro quo of saturation bombing and a trial.' I have myself always felt that it was difficult to defend the saturation bombing of Dresden and Hamburg at a time when Germany was already collapsing. I have felt a similar difficulty about the atom bombing of Hiroshima and Nagasaki – especially if, as is now believed by some, this horrific demonstration was intended not so much to bring an early end to the war with Japan as to warn the Soviet Union of the reality of the power available to the West. But we did not pretend at Nuremberg that the Allies were entirely without fault. The trial was not of the Allies, but the Nazi Germans. And the *Tu Quoque* argument, even if it had been true, would have been no answer. Rebecca West, a brilliant and philosophical writer, put it well:

> Of course the trial was botched and imperfect. How could it be any-thing else? It took place within the same year as Germany's defeat. It had to deal with new crimes for which there was no provision in national law or international law, but which were obviously crimes, and no humbug, since they had left on the scene many corpses which would have preferred to be alive. But when it came to punishing these crimes there was need for very complicated thinking. The Nazi leaders could not have murdered or imprisoned the innocent had they not been upheld by the hosts of followers who had called them to power and acted as their assassins and their jailers, and it was neces-sary that the population should be deterred from forming such dark

loyalties ever again. The problem of how to do this had to be answered by recourse to the English and American concepts of conspiracy, which are not judged to be too convenient on their home grounds.

The difficulty of the task and the spirit in which it was performed are described by Mr Airey Neave as few other people could have done it. He was a much decorated soldier and his unique war service had given him an eyeball to eyeball view of Hitler's military organisations; he was a trained lawyer; also he possessed in abundance that quality which the Romans called *pietas*. My recollection of him made me smile when I read in Bradley Smith's book a passage relating to the letters of Colonel Bernays, one of the originators of the American trial plan:

> There is a breathtaking moment in the summer of 1945 when Colonel Bernays walked through the streets of a devastated Nuremberg as part of his job appraising the suitability of the Palace of Justice for the trial. In a letter to his wife, he chatted about his work and then gave a long and sensitive description of the mass destruction in the city and the helpless confusion and suffering of the German civilians. One waits almost breathlessly for Bernays to ask himself whether the Allies had not lost the right to sit in judgement because of the fact that they had used such patently inhumane methods of warfare. But the mood of the times created a moral tunnel vision that was too strong . . .

It might be Mr A. J. P. Taylor who was writing. Of course Colonel Bernays was not so stupid as Mr Bradley Smith supposes; and neither was Mr Neave. Nor were most of the other legal personages at Nuremberg. They wished not only that Germany might not do again what it had done, but they themselves need not do again what they had had to do against the Germans. If one has any imagination at all one sees that it really cannot have been easy for them; it occurs to one also the great pity that their pains were wasted when, before Vietnam, nobody troubled to remember Nuremberg.

For my part, while not excusing the imperfections and deficiencies of the trial, I still feel that it has laid down the law for the future, even if that law is imperfectly applied and still often disregarded.

The weakness of that contribution is not, I think, in the establishment of aggressive war and of genocide as State crimes of which State
leaders can now be found guilty. That surely is now clearly part of the
Law of Nations. The weakness is that we have since failed to establish
a tribunal to deal with such crimes if they occur. This could have been
done long ago either by establishing an International Court of Criminal
Justice akin to the existing civil Court of International Justice at The
Hague, or by giving a criminal jurisdiction to that court. So far –
although I have tried to persuade the UK Government and others – the
international community has failed to agree on such a policy. And here
I refer not to the United Nations as an institution but to its individual
member states. For the Assembly of the UN did indeed on my motion
in 1948 vote in favour of such a tribunal. At the time of the Gulf War
much lip service was given to International Law. I cannot help feeling,
however, that law or no law, the United States and ourselves would have
felt compelled by our political and economic interests in the Middle East
to go to the assistance of Kuwait. What is particularly to be regretted is
that Saddam Hussein's surrender for trial by an international tribunal
was not insisted upon as a term of the armistice with Iraq. And that no
effort has since been made to set up a permanent International Criminal
Jurisdiction. Mrs Thatcher had at an early stage expressly stated that
Saddam Hussein would be brought to trial 'as the Nazi leaders were at
Nuremberg'. But when the armistice became possible the Americans
were so anxious to get 'their boys' back home that they did not make the
further two days' march to Baghdad, with the result that Saddam saved
a large part of his crack regiment and still holds fast to the leadership.
Since the end of the Gulf War I have made several public statements
urging the establishment of an international court and have written
more than once to the Prime Minister – only to receive charming but
wholly non-committal replies. International law will never gain its full
impact until an international court is established. Nor would the
establishment of such a court present any great difficulty whether finan-
cially or politically.

CHAPTER 8

Politics, 1945–46

ON my return to Britain after the launch of the Nuremberg proceedings I was plunged into immediate work. There was certainly no lack of it either on the legal or on the governmental/parliamentary side. My maiden speech in Parliament was on 12 October 1945 from the front bench, and it was to move the second reading of the first bill of the new Parliament, validating the election of certain members whose eligibility was the subject of doubt. At the time of the general election they had held official appointments on tribunals and committees which, although in fact unpaid, fell within the definition of 'offices of profit under the Crown' and thus disqualified the holder from sitting in the Commons. I was able to tell the House that my own position would have been the same but for the fact that the Ministry of Labour had warned me that my chairmanship of the Catering Wages Commission might disqualify me and I had resigned from it just in time. I have very little recollection of this maiden speech, but the House was very kind to me. Political commentators were embarrassingly fulsome, 'Peterborough' of the *Daily Telegraph* said I impressed the House and William Barkley, another leading commentator, wrote in the *Daily Express* that I 'had no notes but spoke as a man who all his life had been speaking from the Front Bench.'

I mention this because speaking without notes marks an old practice now not often seen. In those days, most members prided themselves on speaking without notes. But nowadays hardly anyone fails to write out his speech beforehand, often because of the need to provide advance copies – 'check against delivery' – for the Press, and sometimes because of a personal lack of fluency or of self-confidence. Certainly, in the 1945

Parliament many fell into the habit of preparing a long note in advance. Such indeed was the practice of one who was perhaps the greatest orator of my period in Parliament, Winston Churchill himself. His speeches were carefully prepared and rehearsed, and although when delivered they had the sound of spontaneity, in fact Winston avoided *extempore* speaking because he knew he was bad at it. I myself soon got into the lazy habit of preparing a very full note. Indeed, for ministerial speeches the Department always wanted to know what I intended to say – perhaps hoping to persuade me not to!

In the winter of 1945 the UN Assembly met in London and I was appointed one of the principal UK delegates. This was my first participation in foreign affairs. It led to my being sent early in 1946 to Geneva to represent the UK at the formal dissolution of the old League of Nations. It was an occasion not without pathos, for some of the elder statesmen of the old world were there: Paul Boncour, Lord Cecil, Carton de Wiart, Carl Hambrow. We were not unmindful of the errors of the past which had culminated in the Second World War, but we were looking forward. It was a time of high hope.

It was spring in Geneva. In the Parc des Eaux-Vives, which I remembered well from my student days, the tulips made a blaze of colour and the sky was cloudless. I remember thinking of Wordsworth's lines:

> Spring and the light and sound of things on earth
> Requickening all within the green seas girth
> A time of passage – and a time of birth.

Were we not at the beginning of a new era of civilization in which all mankind, endowed with reason and conscience – so we claimed – would act towards each other in a spirit of brotherhood, co-operating together in developing the wonderful advances of science, the bountiful provision of nature, to bring a new fullness and dignity to the life of man?

Many brave speeches were made but we placed our hopes too high. I returned to more mundane things.

It had for a long time been an aim of the Labour Party to repeal the legislation affecting Trade Unions which had been passed after the short-lived but disruptive General Strike in 1926. In the postwar period the trade unions were still a very powerful element in the Labour Party, as indeed, although to a much lesser extent, they still are. It was not only that a large proportion of Labour Members of Parliament were super-annuated trade union officials, selected because local finances, includ-ing election expenses, came largely from trade unions. More compelling was that the central organization of the Party, like the constituency bodies, depended in the main on trade union funds. Those who pay the piper tend to call the tune, and the reform of trade union law had always been in the front of the programme, the 1927 Act being regarded as a vindictive and punitive measure imposed by the Tories.

The thing was more symbolic than realistic, but soon after I took office as Attorney General I was involved in consultations with the leaders of the Party, not least Ernest Bevin who, although his ministry was Foreign Affairs, remained, as a great trade union leader, deeply interested in the matter. By January the bill was drafted and a date for the second reading was fixed for 12 February.

Meanwhile I kept busy. On 7 January I was addressing the Tribunal in Nuremberg; two days later I was prosecuting Joyce at the Old Bailey; a little later I was moving resolutions at the United Nations Assembly.

On 12 February I opened the second reading of my bill. I began by suggesting that the Opposition would be wise to reserve its powder and shot 'for fundamental matters'. 'So this Bill was *not* fundamental,' I said. 'One of the most vulnerable points of the Government on this Bill is its irrelevance to the critical situation in which the country now finds itself.' I then illustrated one of the dangers of the 1927 legislation in regard to what was called intimidation. Thus, I said, if a political leader took to the wireless on the eve of a general election and told the public that the Gestapo would get them and there would be a State Police if they voted Socialist (the House did not need to be reminded that that was a para-phrase of Winston on the eve of the 1945 general election) he could be fined forty shillings under the 1927 Act if some timid housemaid could prove that his remarks had caused her a restless night.

Even Michael Foot permitted himself a doubt: 'And yet in the hearts of some of us there was a fear that we would be spending two days on an arid legal argument about a foregone conclusion. Was there not some-thing in the plea that other more urgent topics waited on the Agenda?' Of course there was. I now regret the bill which contained provisions enlarging the right of peaceful picketing and other industrial action, but at the time I assured the House that these would not lead to abuse. More recent experience of mass, and indeed, riotous picketing, however, shows that they could be and have been abused, for there is no doubt that our crowd behaviour was better in those days than it is now. At the time I was, I suppose, carried away by the impassioned enthusiasm of the Party, but I realized that the bill made no significant contribution to the improvement of the conditions of the working classes. Indeed, looking at the report now, I seem to have admitted as much when I said, 'The 1927 legislation had no effect whatever on the right to strike – not a scrap.' The justification for the bill lay, I think, in the widespread feeling that had been generated in the minds of the trade unionists that hard-won rights of theirs had been whittled away. Where such feelings exist they give rise to unrest and discontent and are better removed. I am afraid that I put it much more strongly at the time. The Second Reading was passed with what the Press described as 'loud and prolonged ministerial cheering.'

For my winding-up speech on the Third Reading I turned to one made by Winston Churchill at the end of the debate on the 1927 bill. He had then challenged the Labour Party to make it an issue at a general election. He repeated that challenge early in 1945 and said that the elec-torate's verdict would govern the way the matter was dealt with in Parliament. We had accepted the challenge in the 1945 election. It was a question of what his words actually meant. And so, I borrowed a quotation from *Through the Looking-Glass*.

'When I use a word,' Humpty-Dumpty said in rather a scornful tone, 'it means what I choose it to mean – neither more nor less.' 'The ques-tion is,' said Alice, 'whether you can make words mean so many different things.' 'The question is,' said Humpty Dumpty, 'which is to be the Master – that is all.'

I made a foolishly disparaging remark about Winston Churchill, saying that there were 'other respects in which he was like Humpty Dumpty. Humpty Dumpty had a great fall.' This was rightly rebuked by Opposition Members. And then I went on, 'We are the Masters at the moment. [Loud ministerial cheers.] And not only at the moment but for a very long time to come.' I swept on to my peroration and the bill passed into law. My 'We are the masters' attracted, I think, no instant comment, but it was a gaffe that has followed me when all else is forgotten. About twelve days later the *Evening Standard*, in a critical article by W. J. Brown, Independent MP for Rugby, charged me with having '. . . in an exultant voice, told the House that "We are the masters now."' The misquotation (by an MP who had heard the speech) was a trivial one: after all, 'at the moment' is 'now' and it cannot be said to have been intentionally inaccurate. But perhaps the 'now' gave our mastery a more permanent and frightening character than the words 'at the moment'. At all events the misquotation stuck and has followed me around all my life. If I had not been so politically naïve and so unsophisticated in the art of public relations I should have realized that the phrase could be used against me. At the time, I'm afraid it all seemed good fun, and it was fully shared on my side of the House – even by Hugh Dalton, who later hated me, who wrote in his diary that I had made a good speech.

In May I was prosecuting Dr Alan Nunn May for grave breaches of the Official Secrets Acts. Parts of this often-derided and criticized legislation are open to misinterpretation and attack – although I retain the old-fashioned view that it should be an offence for those who, in the course of their duty, have come into possession of secret information to publish it without authority.* In the Nunn May case there is no doubt that he had done something that the law of any civilized country would prohibit: he had given away to the Russians secrets about the production of atomic energy which saved the Russians years of research for them-selves and enabled them to produce an atom bomb probably four years earlier than they would otherwise have done. He pleaded guilty and he was sentenced to ten years' penal servitude, the judge at the Old Bailey saying that he had acted as a dishonourable man, not an honourable one. That Nunn May had to be severely punished as a deterrent to others I had no doubt. I confess, however, that I had a sneaking sympathy with his motivation which was well put by Gerald Gardiner who defended

* The growing tendency of employees to publish such information, for whatever motive, although usually it is money, seems to me a deplorable symptom of the decline in moral standards of behaviour, whether the employer is the State or a private one.

him. He compared him to the medical scientist who, discovering something of benefit to mankind, feels under obligation to communicate his
discovery to others. There was no question of gain for Nunn May, and
basically he was an honest man, but it was a crass conceit for him to
elevate his judgement above that of the State in deciding what was best
to be done with the knowledge the State had enabled and employed him
to acquire.

Early in May, Parliament considered the Bill for Nationalisation of
the Coal Industry, in the preparation and passage of which I took a very
active part. We sat until the early hours and Emanuel Shinwell, a
shrewd, amusing and patriotic man (Winston Churchill, I remember,
said 'he had his heart in the right place'), and I shared the main burden
of the work. In the following month, I led the legal team that was to
represent the Government before the tribunal to assess the amounts of
compensation payable.

Later, when disillusion was beginning to set in about the general
policy of socializing industry, I always felt that of all the nationalization measures in that parliament this bill was the most justified. At the
time of nationalization there were about 800 different firms in the
industry. Some – like Gresford, where the great disaster took place in
the thirties – were grossly inefficient, and the only matter on which the
owners were unanimous was in their opposition to the union. The
industry has, of course, now been welded into a single co-operative
whole, and although I am certainly very far from saying that the nationalization had been an unqualified success, it has to be said that the
industry was in a state of chronic deterioration when the bill went
through. In June I secured and announced government approval for the
scheme of Free Legal Aid which, as modified from time to time and in
spite of much mismanagement, is still in operation. It now needs drastic
modifications, as do the rules of legal procedure, in view of the extortionate cost of legal cases, which is quite beyond the capacity of the
middle classes.

Later that month, having been invited by the governments of Poland,
Czechoslovakia and France to visit their countries, I managed to link the
visits together and was flown with my Nuremberg Junior, who also
became my PPS, Elwyn Jones, first to Poland, and then on to
Czechoslovakia and France in a brand-new, gleaming RAF Dakota.

In Poland, I stayed as a guest at the newly re-established British Embassy. The Ambassador was the charming Bill Bentinck who subsequently became Duke of Portland, died only recently. My visit was regarded by the Polish Government, as indeed was intended, as an indication of our desire for closer relations and collaboration with the Poles, for at the time we had been the subject of some criticism, even attack there. It had been assumed that I would criticize the lack of freedom of speech and democracy in Poland, but on Bill's advice I took a different line, and emphasized our historical friendship.

In Cracow I went down a coal mine and spent an enjoyable day with the miners whose lives bore some resemblance to those I knew in North Wales. At the University of Cracow I reminded the Poles of something which at that time, and during the Cold War, many tended to forget.

> I hope that sometimes when you hear criticisms directed against Great Britain — some of it I dare say well-deserved for we do not pretend that our policy must always be right — you will cast your minds back to 1939, 1940 and 1941 and you will remember that had it not been for Britain declaring war on Germany when you were attacked and then fighting on alone when all seemed lost, while the world waited with bated breath from day to day expecting to hear of our final defeat, Poland might have been forever dismembered and Nazi–Fascist tyranny might have become permanently enthroned in Europe.

In Lodz I did what is called nowadays a 'walkabout' and met many ordinary citizens. Bill Bentinck told the Foreign Office that the visit had been very successful and it certainly increased my own deep interest in foreign affairs.

In Prague the visit followed a similar pattern, although we then had much higher hopes of Czechoslovakia developing both a thriving economy, such as it had before the Nazis took it over, and a more active democracy, in spite of the fact that the country was in the Eastern Zone. Indeed, it would have done both, had it not been for the eventual brutal military intervention by Stalin. The beauty of Prague's old city which, unlike Warsaw, had not been laid waste by the war is something I shall remember all my life. I had a long meeting there with Edward Beneš, a great democrat who was bitterly depressed and despondent at the growing autocracy of the Communists. Jan Masaryk, with whom I had already become friends in New York, was also there to greet me.

Then I moved on to France. No building of political bridges was called for with de Gaulle! In Paris, I stayed at the Embassy. Ernest Bevin was there for part of the time. I remember the Ambassador's wife, the beautiful Diana Cooper, dropping her handkerchief so that poor old Ernest would pick it up, which he did. The visit was essentially a legal one and its main occasion, although there was splendid entertainment at the Embassy, was to address the leading French judges and lawyers in the First Chamber of the Supreme Court of France. I had intended to speak in English but some kind lady in the Embassy persuaded me to talk in French, although by 1946 I had forgotten even the minimal amount of schoolboy French I had once known. We rehearsed the speech together in the vain hope of improving my execrable pronunciation. I approached the day with dread, but when I got into the magnificent salon in which I was to deliver my oration I was further dismayed to find the British Ambassador, Sir Alfred Duff Cooper, later Lord Norwich, sitting in a large armchair straight in front of me. He had not told me he would be present. He was, of course, a fluent linguist and I have wondered since whether he derived even more pain than I did from my murderous excursion into the French language. As for what I said, the central argument was simple enough, namely that no method of achieving order in the international field which is capable of preserving peace and liberty can be successful unless it is established on the firm basis of the rule of law in international affairs. It was not the law which had failed, I told my French lawyers, but international policemen to enforce the law against states and against individuals responsible for leading their states into breaches of the law. At Nuremberg at least we had gone some way in seeking to establish that law, but formal and institutional action was essential.

Early in July I was back in Parliament helping to shepherd the Civil Aviation Bill through the House and, more happily, arranging the christening of our first child, William, in the crypt chapel of the House of Commons, his godparents being the Lord Chancellor, Lord Jowitt, Mrs Clement Attlee and René Stockdale, a friend from Liverpool who proved a wonderful godparent and friend well into the 1990s.

In June 1946 in the Birthday Honours I was made a member of 'His Majesty's Most Honourable Privy Council'. Members of the Cabinet are automatically made members of the Council on their appointment, because it is in the nature of their work that they have to be privy to secret information. For ministers of lower rank, including the Law Officers, it is an honour awarded on the recommendation of the Prime Minister as a reward for merit, but it also implies that they are fit to be entrusted with high matters of State. By no means all ministers get it and usually it takes some time to earn. I was fortunate to be appointed at a very early stage in my political career. Privy Counsellors are entitled to the designa-tion 'The Right Honourable'. There has been a growing tendency recently for peers to arrogate to themselves the description Right Honourable, but strictly speaking they are not entitled to this designa-tion. The practice of non-members of the Council describing them-selves as such has, however, become accepted as a matter of courtesy, so one must be aware that the Privy Council, although large, is not by any means as large as the number of people styling themselves Right Honourable would suggest.

But I received the title as of right and I was certainly pleased about it – perhaps too pleased. Shortly after this, at a by-election in North Battersea, I made a bitter and biting attack on the Press, particularly the papers owned by Lord Kemsley and Lord Beaverbrook, which were placarding the constituency with posters bearing such slogans as 'Tell them we want more bread'.

My speech, as I was soon to be taught, was a crass example of lack of political *savoir faire*. The next day I happily set off for Cornwall on my sailing holiday, but I had not been long away when I received an intima-tion from Bill Mabane, with whom I had become friendly when I was a Regional Commissioner and who was working as an adviser to Lord Kemsley, that his Lordship was demanding an apology and, failing one, would sue me. I sent a note to the Prime Minister that I might be sued, but went on with my sailing. I decided to ignore the warning.

As we were entering Fowey harbour one fine morning, however, a coastguard vessel came to tell me that the PM wanted to see me. Joan and I motored back through the hot afternoon to Chequers, arriving about eight o'clock that evening. It was a typical Attlee occasion. I told him that if sued by Kemsley I intended to fight the case and justify what I had said. I could not do that as Attorney, so I would resign the office. 'No, you won't,' said Attlee. '. . . I want you to remain Attorney. You will apologize. It will all be over after a day or two's sensation. Now we will go into supper.' So it was that I had to make a humiliating apology, and Kemsley saw to it that all the Press covered the story thoroughly throughout the weekend. And that was it. Now, I realize only too well that my speeches were brashly and foolishly expressed, but in substance they were correct enough. Those organs of the Press that I attacked were grossly partisan and the news was, and still sometimes is, deliberately slanted so as to support or, at the least, not contradict a political stand-point. But this, after all, is probably something that one has to accept as the concomitant of Press freedom. Was it not Dr Johnson who said that in his parliamentary reporting he always ensured that the 'Whig Dogs' did not have the best of it? What I had said was, indeed, closely followed by Herbert Morrison in a speech of his own, and Michael Foot wrote an article supporting it. The *Manchester Guardian* in a reasoned leader said that my complaint of distortion and misrepresentation was not without some justification (I had paid express tribute to the *Guardian* as well as to the *Yorkshire Post* and *The Times*), but I had made my attack with a flamboyance that betrayed my lack of political sophistication at that time. Later, when I became – imagine it! – Chairman of the Press Council, I expressed similar views more soberly, although I fear not more effectively. Today, however, the evil some organs of the Press do is not so much political as social and moral. And here I fear the Press is exploiting if not promoting a grave lowering of public standards. Looking at most of the tabloids – particularly on Sundays of all days – I am appalled at the space devoted to sexual items and titillation, and this to the almost total exclusion of real news and opinions about current affairs. The only 'affairs' to which these papers are able to devote space are those with an obvious sexual innuendo. It is true that in all this the Press is apparently giving its readers what they want, and thereby build-ing up circulation and profit. But at what cost to the future of our society? Children seeing this sort of stuff day after day in the newspapers and on television will inevitably come to think that promiscuity, and sexual perversions are a normal part of everyday life. No doubt mine is a prudish and outdated point of view, but when one looks at the annually increasing number of so-called 'single parent families' and the

rising state of juvenile delinquency generally, I tremble at our decline
and fall. Are they proud of themselves – these newspaper-owners?

Lord Kemsley, at least, was not one of these. Eventually I got to know
him quite well. I liked him; he was not as intelligent as that other Press
lord, his brother, Lord Camrose, but his newspaper was largely controlled by his wife, Edith, and advance proofs of pages would be
brought into the dining room for her scrutiny. There was the famous
story of the picture on the front page of the *Daily Sketch* showing a prize
bull which had just won a championship. The animal was photographed 'full frontal', I believe the phrase now is, and her Ladyship was
outraged. Orders were given for the picture to be touched up – or rather
toned down – but I am not sure how much Lord Kemsley had to pay in
damages for libel on the bull. I used to enjoy dining with them occasionally in their home, Chandos House, but their social life was brought to
a sad and untimely end when, in the early days of plastic surgery, 'Aunt
Edith', as she was called, had a face-lift operation. Most unfortunately
the facial nerve was accidentally severed and her face was badly dis-
torted. Although Lord Kemsley took her to surgeons all over the world,
it was impossible to correct the accident and, as far as I know, she was
never seen in public again.

After my much-publicized apology I went back to complete the two
weeks of my sailing holiday. I did a little handicap racing with my yacht,
the 8-metre *Caryl*, a beautiful crack racing yacht which had won the
Seawanhaka Cup in America. Two events occurred at this time which
contributed to my education. One was at the annual regatta at Fowey
when we sailed up from Falmouth, and as I recall, easily won our race.
The boat was too small for Joan and me to sleep on so I left her (the boat,
I mean) with my skipper, Walter Paull, at anchor while we went to the
Fowey Hotel for the night. The hotel bedroom overlooked the anchorage, and at about 6 a.m. I got up, drew the curtains and tried to identify
my boat. There she lay, but to my horror someone had painted on her
pristine white and shining hull in large blue letters the words 'VOTE
LABOUR'. Joan and I dressed hurriedly, rushed down to the town,
woke up the paint shop, bought masses of paint remover and white
enamel, and rowed out to *Caryl*, where Walter Paull remained in bliss-
ful ignorance of the sacrilege that had been committed on his pride and
joy – and mine too – during the stillness of the night. The first race of

the day, back to Falmouth, was to start at 11 a.m. We all worked like slaves to eradicate the defacement, and thought we had succeeded. We duly entered the race and crossed the finishing line at Falmouth again, I think, first. Unknown to us, however, the flow of water over the hull during the 18-mile race had washed away our attempted cover-up and 'VOTE LABOUR' stood out clearly. The Tory bigwigs at the Yacht Club were, no doubt, amazed and may have thought that it was a deliberate piece of self-advertisement on my part, unless by then the true explanation had reached Falmouth.

The other incident turned out more happily. It was pointed out to Lord Beaverbrook that I had apologized for my attack on Lord Kemsley but, although I had used the same language to embrace (or demolish?) him, I had not apologized to Beaverbrook. I received an intimation that I should write him an apology. I swallowed what was left of my pride and did so. A few days later I received a personal letter thanking me, and saying that he would never inform anyone I had apol-ogized. We became good friends. I respected him greatly for this mag-nanimous – but also clever – attitude. He knew how to win friends and, unlike Kemsley, he was too big a man to need apologies. Nobody would have known that I had apologized to him had I not told Maxwell Fyfe that I had received this letter. A short time later, I was rather shocked to see that in a speech in the Commons in which he had criticized me, Fyfe said that he understood I had also apologized to Lord Beaverbrook. I consoled myself over this breach of confidence between friends by remembering the jingle 'There's nothing so like Death in Life as David Patrick Maxwell Fyfe'.

In the autumn of 1946 I was sent to New York as one of the UK's principal delegates to the Assembly of the United Nations, a post which I filled for four years. I travelled on the maiden passenger voyage of the *Queen Elizabeth* and, arriving in New York harbour at dawn, I saw the spectacular outline of the skyscrapers of Manhattan Island. As we dis-embarked there was no Customs examination for we had diplomatic status, and we were led by a motorcycle escort with sirens blaring to our hotel.

In the political (the main) committee I sat next to Senator Tom Connally of Texas on one side and Mr Molotov or Mr Vyshinsky on the other.

Senator Connally was a splendid fellow: I remember him principally for giving me a hearty pat on the back with the words 'Good morning, General.' He was a genial fellow who usually allowed complicated arguments to pass him by. His familiarity with postwar international affairs was perhaps illustrated by his greeting to a delegation from ECOSOC – one of the United Nations specialized agencies concerned with economic and social problems – which he received. 'I am very glad to welcome the representatives of your gallant little country,' said Tom effusively.

So there I was, in little over a year after entering politics, supported by Connally and sparring with the great Molotov and Vishinsky. I must have seemed a bumptious cad – and I'm sure I was – sporting a flowing red silk handkerchief out of my breast pocket and butting in, sometimes rudely, on every occasion. Towards the end of the Assembly there was a debate that began with a Soviet proposal for an international census of the troops of different countries stationed in occupied territories, but which quickly developed into a far-reaching discussion of disarmament generally. In this debate Mr Molotov, occasionally assisted by Mr Vyshinsky, and I dominated the scene with no significant interventions elsewhere. At one stage it appeared that the Russians were making undreamt-of concessions. My abiding recollection is the extent to which Mr Molotov appeared affected by the applause of the large audience before which our verbal duel was conducted. The discussion was confused and suffered from the fact that we were formulating vital issues of foreign relations *ex improviso*. Molotov and I sought to score debating points and, as I now recognize, possibly missed opportunities for more constructive and lasting commitments. I started by objecting to the Soviet proposal because it would have been subject, in its operation, to the use of the Soviet veto, which I said made it a humbug and delusion. (Loud applause.) I challenged the Soviet Union to agree to abandon its veto on this point. Molotov offered to agree provided that armaments were included as well as troops. I almost ran to the rostrum saying, 'I accept this challenge – this will make tonight [it was past midnight] an historic occasion.' But this proposal could have involved the Americans in an unacceptable disclosure of their atomic arsenal. Paul-Henri Spaak, the President, extricated us from this position by proposing that the whole matter should be placed in the hands of a new *ad hoc* commission, which with plenary powers could consider it in the light of general proposals for the reduction of armaments. By this time the Soviet Union had become uncertain about their own proposal for a damaging and one-sided census of troops and sought to withdraw it because we had insisted that it must include disclosure of home forces as well as those in occupied territories. I inserted in the disclosure provisions a reference to 'all weapons of mass destruction', and proposed that collective security and an international police force should be included in the purview of the proposed Commission. Mr Molotov, at one stage almost stuttering in his excitement, said he was prepared to accept my latest attempt to scrib-ble a compromise in principle but it must be referred back to the sub-committee. M. Spaak felt it was time to call it a day. He said that in view of the agreement in principle between the British and the Soviet ideas 'it should be possible to reach a reasonable disarmament solution within 24 hours. This will mark progress we could not have anticipated a few days ago.' The matter would be revived at the next meeting of the Assembly in 1947.

There was in fact no direct progress but that is not to say that the debate, dramatic and exciting as it had been, was entirely illusory. We had prevented the Russian proposal for an incomplete disclosure going forward. Hardline positions on the veto and on international control of armaments had at least been softened – and we had not lost a battle. The credit for this success – temporary although it turned out to be – was cer-tainly due to M. Spaak, a great international statesman. It was not his fault that the Russians eventually resiled from their more accommodat-ing position (Stalin was not influenced by what Mr Alistair Cooke called 'dazzling performances'.)

I recall a long and heated United Nations debate on Spain, then under Franco, in which the Security Council concluded, wisely enough, that whatever else was to be said that country then presented no threat to the peace of the world at that time. The whole matter was raised again at the General Assembly. Tom Connally used the then orthodox strong language about Franco and – unwisely – almost invited the Spanish people to rise in revolt against him. I took a slightly more con-ciliatory line by cautioning against any attempt by the UN to intervene in the domestic affairs of any State.

There was also the long debate on a resolution proposed by the

French and Mexican delegations asking the South African and Indian Governments to report to the next General Assembly what measures had been taken about the degrading treatment of Indians in South Africa. The United Kingdom at that time was anxious not to do anything too antagonistic to South Africa. General Smuts, still then the South African leader but in ill-health, had been a very wise counsellor of Winston Churchill during the war and we wished to retain his goodwill. Smuts in fact made a fighting speech in opening the debate, urging that the matter was one of domestic jurisdiction in which the UN could not intervene and asking that before further discussion an advisory opinion should be sought from the International Court of Justice. Smuts was supported in clear speeches by The Netherlands and Belgian representatives – who of course had their own colour problems – and I followed, Smuts calling me his 'great KC'. I took the line that I did not want to make any judgement on the substance of the Indian case but surely the Assembly would not ignore 'the reasonable request by a member state for an authoritative legal Opinion . . . would not a purely political decision by the Assembly exacerbate opinion in South Africa?' There was a memorable intervention by Mrs Pandit. I well recall her striding down the aisle to the rostrum, a striking figure, beautifully dressed and, in breach of precedent, applauded by delegates as she went. She made a brilliant speech in which she severely trounced me. She said I had shattered her 'hopes that the Commonwealth would at least remain neutral . . . he has spoken in a manner which I consider to be entirely partisan, however full of dialectical skill it may be . . . he referred to the differences in India with evident and unconcerned glee.' The motion was carried by thirty-two votes against fifteen. Smuts was upset. But there was not much tangible result. Later Mrs Pandit and I became good friends and I was able to assist her. She was much in the shadow of her brother, Pandit Nehru, but was a warmer person with whom one could have a frank relationship.

During the latter part of the Assembly, Ernest Bevin, the British Foreign Secretary, who had addressed the Assembly at an earlier stage, was still in New York attending a council of foreign ministers, but he was unwell, suffering from strain and tiredness, and was kept in his bed by his doctor, Lord Moran. We regularly reported to him, however, and if matters were urgent did so at once. Accordingly, we went to see him immediately after the disarmament debate, being a little unsure of whether he would endorse my action. He did, but with some cynical amusement, for while he approved of my manoeuvring he felt sure the Russians would find ways of overturning my 'historic occasion', as of course they did.

During the whole session of the Assembly the British delegation had included high Foreign Office officials, such as Sir Alexander Cadogan, who had been Permanent Secretary at the Foreign Office and who was now our permanent delegate to the United Nations, and Paul Gore-Booth. Cadogan was to me a somewhat dour and remote individual; apart from the opening session he rarely attended the meetings of the Assembly or its committees, but he represented us on the Security Council. Gore-Booth was a different character. Much younger, of course, he was already quite high in the Foreign Office hierarchy and a man of marked ability. He gave me the greatest assistance and advice at all times. I must often have been a great anxiety to him with my brash and rumbustious behaviour which he did his best to moderate. Thus I well remember an incident involving the Russian chairman of the Political Committee (Manuilsky, President of one of the Soviet republics), who had become a little notorious through the obvious partiality of his rulings. I noticed some procedural point on which the Chairman had made a ruling which I thought we could challenge. I turned to Tom Connally, who was sitting next to me, told him the point and remarked, 'We'll get the little monkey now!' Unfortunately I had not realized that the simultaneous translation system had already been switched on and my remark reverberated round the hall. That evening Gore-Booth said he would like to come back to my hotel and have a word with me. I had no idea, at that point, what about. But in my room he delivered a very firm and proper rebuke, emphasizing the etiquette of politeness and respect which was to be maintained at international gatherings and making it clear that my behaviour had not come up to the standard to be expected of me. I was grateful to him.

During my two months in New York I found many weekend occasions when I was able to accept invitations to speaking engagements; to the American Bar Association in Atlantic City, to a US Air Force Station in some remote part of the Mid-West, to Hyde Park (Mr Roosevelt's old home), to Chicago, even as far as Fort Worth and Texas.

And I had a successful meeting with the New York Bar Association (one of several) where I spoke about the work and policy of the British Labour Party, and I hope I relieved the often expressed anxiety that Britain under its Labour Government was moving towards Communism. And the friends I made – some of them for life – included many of the leading American politicians; Harry Truman, Jock McCloy and Bill Donovan; also Elsa Maxwell, and Bernard Baruch (an *eminence grise* and financier, he was a close friend of Winston and had the confidence of the American President; during a private dinner in his apartment he once showed me a letter he had received from Brendan Bracken warmly commending me). I also made friends with many foreign statesmen, such as Jan Masaryk whom I had met before when I made my official visit to Poland and Czechoslovakia. We shared good times in New York and I continued to see him until shortly before his death. Humorous, a good conversationalist and with wide and interesting knowledge of foreign affairs, he was pessimistic about the future of his country and saw its complete domination by the Communists as inevitable. I was not surprised when I heard he had died falling out of a window in his apartment in Prague. The authorities there said it was suicide but I felt sure he had been murdered. He had told me that he expected some such end. It was tragic.

The Assembly proceedings finished unexpectedly early. We had thought that they would continue over Christmas, and at Ernie Bevin's request I had reluctantly promised that I would stay on in New York to lead the UK delegation and forgo my holiday at home. Bevin was returning anyway on the *Queen Elizabeth*, sailing from New York on 14 December. As it turned out, things went differently. Andrei Gromyko failed to raise an issue he was expected to address. I got away in time to catch the boat, after asking Cunard to hold her till I arrived. I telephoned my secretary, fortunately still at our hotel, telling her to bundle all my things into a bag and bring them down to Pier 90 where the *Queen Elizabeth* was lying. Then I jumped into my car and, assisted by a police escort and with much siren music, dashed through New York streets. It was quite a drama.

The voyage home was uneventful. Bevin was on board but largely confined to his cabin. Molotov and Vyshinsky were also passengers. We saw little of them, but we did invite them to a drinks party, and I had one or two talks with them which were quite affable. However, that hour's delay in leaving the Hudson River had dire results. In spite of steaming as hard as we could, the boat just missed the tide going into the Solent to Southampton to berth, and I fear this caused inconvenience to a number of people, for there were complaints. The purser, however, who showed that admirable *savoir faire* and sang-froid for which in the old days Cunard officers were famous, dealt with these admirably. He said that the ship had been delayed in departing from New York by the late arrival of a passenger for whom they had had to wait. Which passenger? Why, Mr Molotov, of course. Cunard could not afford to offend the Soviet Union by not waiting for him.

There was one other dire result which Cunard could do nothing about. While in New York I had lived as economically as I could – I think we had a living allowance of about eight dollars a day – and had spent the savings on buying food to take home to my still heavily rationed household. I managed to make quite a contribution to our Sussex larder. I was aware that very few people were so lucky.

The months from August 1945 to the end of 1946 were to provide a somewhat typical pattern of work for the ensuing four years. When I consider those months of initiation and new experience now I can, of course, take a much more objective and critical view than I did when I attempted to review them in Christmas 1946. I think that in that Christmas vacation I was beginning to learn that in politics I was still very young and too much inclined to throw my weight about, when in fact I had little to throw. On many occasions I had been brash and sometimes arrogant. As for my work at the United Nations, it must have looked to some as if I was simply having fun, making debating points and trying to outbid Molotov. Indeed, that criticism was made at the time and there was some truth in it, for I did find the debates exciting and – yes – fun. But the fun was not entirely at the expense of achievement. It is true that because of the eventual development of the Cold War we did not succeed in implementing all that I had hoped for when I took over the leadership of the UK delegation. But as M. Spaak, to whose tact and wisdom the main credit is due, himself said, the Assembly adopted unanimously a resolution calling for progressive disarmament, the elimination of weapons of mass destruction, international inspection and control. 'Nobody could have imagined at the beginning of the session that such a difficult and delicate problem could have been considered and decided. . . . the Assembly had given the peoples of the world great hope.' At that stage we had made remarkable progress and I think that my advocacy, exuberant although it was, may perhaps have made a significant contribution and helped initiate the resolution. It was not my fault that the Cold War intervened. At that stage I had really believed that whatever their position had been in the past, Molotov and Stalin might see advantage for Russia in pursuing an internationally benevolent dictatorship. Alas, we had to wait for Gorbachev for that to happen.

In my sixteen months of office I had added to my experience immensely, I had met and talked with a great number of international statesmen and industrialists, and had far wider knowledge and appreciation of the problems confronting the United Kingdom and the world than when I started. Yet while I encouraged myself with the thought that I had not done too badly, I did realize with hindsight that I might have done much better. I think the experience of those sixteen months had – I will not say actually chastened me – but had at least modified the passionate conviction of the new convert with which I had started in Parliament. I was beginning to realize the importance of *festina lente* – hurrying slowly. It was not long before I came to accept that Socialism could not achieve all that I had expected of it; indeed, early in 1947, dismayed by the fuel crises in the bitter winter of that year, I was making impassioned speeches urging that much greater individual effort and hard work were essential to our salvation.

The end of 1946 brought me the possibility of a more formal excursion into wider fields outside the law. The Prime Minister sounded me out on the possibility of becoming Minister Resident in Germany, with a seat in the Cabinet. Things were not going well in the British Zone of Germany. The food situation was critical and there were constant complaints of muddle and inefficiency on the part of our administration. There was also the plan to unite the British and American Zones. Although this early promotion to the Cabinet was itself tempting, I took little time in rejecting the suggestion and here, I am afraid, I was more influenced by personal interests than by a due sense of service to the country. I did not want to detach myself any further from the profession of the law, in which I still saw my long-term future. And still more did I not want to detach myself from my family. I saw too little of him and of my wife and new son as things were. The proposed new job would have compelled me to live in Germany, with the chore of constant flights to and from London to attend Cabinet. Later I learned to subordinate these more selfish considerations a little, but at the end of 1946 I was still enjoying the Law Office, the scope of which I had greatly widened. To change the metaphor, the office was certainly now very much on the political map.

And so, after a few days of much-needed rest, I returned to my chambers at the Law Courts and my room at the Commons.

CHAPTER 9

Politics, 1947–48

ON the whole 1946 had been a good year for the Labour Government. Elected as we had been by an overwhelming majority, we were full of enthusiasms ourselves, while the public at large, relieved from the grim anxieties of war, but realizing that there were great difficulties in getting back to a peacetime régime, continued to support us. But there was little euphoria left by the end of 1947. The winter was quite exceptionally cold, railways and roads were dislocated by heavy snowfalls, and in March very severe flooding took place, causing great damage in some rural areas. The output of coal was much less than it ought to have been. There were power failures, lightning strikes and other interruptions of supply. Strict rationing of food, fuel and clothing continued in force. Deaths from hypothermia were significant. Altogether the people were having a bad time. And within the Government itself there were the personal antagonisms and intrigues which I suppose I was beginning to accept as inevitable in any form of popular democracy, but of which I had previously been naïvely unaware.

I was kept very busy in the courts and in Parliament but continued my usual round of weekend speeches. I found myself dashing round the country making impassioned pleas urging harder work, condemning unofficial strikes as disgraceful folly, and stressing that democracy could only survive through hard work and acceptance of controls during the critical period of reconstruction. According to the Press I was developing a less belligerent manner in Parliament. But I was still bitterly criticizing the Opposition for their attacks on the Government, for I could never bring myself to accept the doctrine that it is the duty of the

Opposition to oppose. And I was still incautious in my choice of language.

In the middle of 1947 an organization called the Housewives League was established. They wrote me a letter purporting to represent a group in my constituency and said they 'were writing as the Women of Britain'. Their complaint was the continued hardship and rationing from which they were suffering. I got into very hot water through my reply. Not only did I assert that general living standards were on the whole better than before the war – a doubtful but arguable proposition – but I said in public comment that their letter was 'an impertinence'. This is, as I soon learned, always a dangerous word to use in public controversy. In vain did I write to *The Times* explaining that it was their claim to be writing on behalf of organizations in my constituency, when in fact there were none, and on behalf of 'the Women of Britain', when in fact they only represented a small Tory organization, which I stigmatized as impertinent. The Press and other commentators insisted that I was saying that it was an impertinence for any protests to be made against Government policy. Thus I gave a tremendous boost to the Housewives League and for weeks the newspapers were full of publicity that it would probably never otherwise have achieved.

Nor was that all. In a speech in Aidan Crawley's Buckinghamshire constituency – he was later a Labour minister – I explained that I fully understood the privations with which the public had to put up – 'I have not had any butter or margarine myself for a long time; it went to my baby' – but added that I realized only too well how discouraging it was to come home week after week to find the only thing to eat was 'a shepherd's pie, full of carrots and gristle rather than meat'. Our cook in the country, who provided us with excellent meals and never a shepherd's pie, gave notice.

I did get a short break from adverse Press comment. One Saturday Joan and I went down to Burnham-on-Crouch where I was to speak for Tom Driberg (against whom I had not by that time been warned). We arrived early and went for a walk by the side of the river when we noticed a child floating face down in the middle of the stream and apparently drowning. Joan said I must go to the rescue. I hastily took off my shoes and all my clothes except a pair of short Aertex pants and dived in. I soon realized that a rather attractive young woman had done the same — dived in, I mean, not taken all her clothes off — and we were both swimming towards the child. I was severely handicapped, however. The waist elastic of my pants was loose and the pants kept falling down. The girl's proximity caused me to keep stopping to pull up my pants and so miss a stroke or two. In the event, she reached the child first, but we both took her ashore, none the worse for her experience. I went into the Royal Burnham Yacht Club where I had a hot bath and someone lent me dry pants, and Joan and I had dinner there. At the next table a group of members were talking about the rescue incident and a woman in the party, not recognizing me, remarked that she refused to believe it was 'that Sir Hartley Shawcross' who had dived in to the rescue. I did not disillusion her. The Press were kinder and I had very good coverage for my speech, the *Daily Mail* (I think it was) remarking that it had been one of the few weekends in which I had got into cold water.

I did include a good deal of serious speaking in my weekend meetings. One of the areas in which I was particularly interested was of course foreign policy, and because of my activities at the United Nations Assembly I made many speeches on the importance of that organization. I argued that the UNO should be strongly supported as an active World Parliament promoting general disarmament and conciliating differences so that eventually the rule of law might prevail internationally. As the only Nuremberg Chief Prosecutor who was a delegate to the UN, I somewhat naturally took a leading part in convincing the United Nations formally to declare genocide to be an international crime (as it is now generally recognized to be, although still committed), and to adopt the principles of international law laid down at Nuremberg. I was also concerned with the danger of economic nationalism, and I regarded the decision that had been made by the UN to set up an Economic Commission for Europe and another for Asia as a very important step. Equally important was the Marshall Plan, which was proposed almost casually by General Marshall, or so it seemed to us, and was immediately seized upon and developed by Ernest Bevin. It was a great misfortune that the Soviet Union refused to allow the plan to apply to the states in the Russian sphere of influence and that Poland, having initially accepted it, was forced to withdraw. The Soviet refusal marked the beginning of the Cold War. For the Western Powers this imagina

tive provision of material aid was of immense importance and high-
lighted the actualities of economic interdependence.

I stressed the importance of the UNO again when I went back to the
Assembly in New York in September 1947. I was there for about ten
weeks and again took a very active part. My activities under the auspices
of the British Publicity Agency were not confined to the Assembly and
its committees. I travelled widely in the United States where I carried on
my English habit of making weekend speeches. One occasion I remember in particular was at a meeting of the National Press Club in
Washington with a big audience of newspaper editors and representatives. In my speech I emphasized the British devotion to democracy
and freedom, particularly in relation to the Press. Although I admitted
I had had some keen verbal duels with the newspapers I said: 'Britain
has a very fine Press. It cannot be bought and it cannot be bullied. Its
professional journalists have a very high standard of honour. It is free,
courageous and, on the whole, responsible.' This was indeed a rather
different tune to the impetuous speeches at the Battersea by-election for
which I had had to apologize, and the British Press gave it very wide
coverage, taking it as coming from a repentant sinner.

I stayed on in New York until the end of November, when I travelled
back on the *Queen Mary*. It was an uneventful voyage. Vyshinsky, with
quite a retinue, was on board, and I had one or two friendly walks on
the sun deck with him, but he was very guarded in his conversation.
Once in London, I soon got into my usual swim. We were still in grave
economic difficulty. My first speech in 1948 – a long one in my constituency – emphasized this and stressed the possibility that we should
have to make further cuts, underlining the folly of unofficial strikes and
the necessity that 'prices should be reduced by greater productivity and
output per man. Any further increase in wages now, unaccompanied by
a corresponding increase in production, would defeat its own ends by
raising living costs and causing inflation here and reducing our sales
abroad.' I was coming to realize that Socialism was not the panacea for
all ills. But I continued to emphasize that we must stand on our own legs
despite the Marshall Plan. Success, I said, depended on the effort of the
common people. We must not rely on loans: only our own efforts could
pull us through. It is clear that by this time, partly influenced by what I
had seen of America and more by the disillusioning labour troubles at

home, my rose-coloured Socialist spectacles were getting misted over by doubts. It was, I think, these doubts which led to my increasing inclina-tion to move to a ministerial position with more scope for influencing policy. I was in something of a personal dilemma, for I still wanted to maintain my connection with the Bar – and all this time I had been doing Government court work – in case the moment came when I should need to return to practice, as indeed it did.

Looking back on 1947, I am happy with two achievements in the field of law to which, if I had had a more disciplined mind, I should have confined myself. These were the Crown Proceedings Act and the Legal Aid and Advice Act, which are both now taken for granted as part of our legal machinery. The first, which involved convincing a few legalistic bureaucrats in the Departments, but was welcomed by all parties, enabled the subject to sue the Crown – that is to say the Government and its services, not of course the monarch – by what was substantially the ordinary procedure. Up to that time it had been a complicated procedure involving a Petition of Right. It may seem now an obvious reform, and indeed it was, but it involved laying aside the traditional procedure dating from the Middle Ages, and it must be remembered that in many countries it is still difficult and often wholly impracticable to sue the Government. The Legal Aid and Advice Act was again an obvious and much-needed reform but it involved consid-erable negotiations with the legal profession whose earnings were likely to be affected. These were successful and so the bill was presented to Parliament with the approval of the Bar – of which, of course, as the Attorney General, I was the leader – and of the Law Society. It extended the rights of defence in criminal cases and made the very fundamental reform of making legal aid available to both plaintiffs and defendants, subject to a means test and provided that a locally consti-tuted committee of lawyers was satisfied that there was an arguable case.

A great deal of the litigation in our courts is now conducted with the help – to one side or the other and often both – of legal aid. It has been of immense benefit and has discouraged the activities of 'ambulance-chasing' solicitors who took on cases on a speculative basis. The two main grounds for criticism of the system are, I think, that it does not apply to actions for defamation and that the means test excludes many who deserve aid. As to the first, we thought at the time that actions for libel or slander were so often blackmailing 'try-ons' and of little merit that it would be contrary to the public interest to encourage them. This probably remains true, but with the growing tendency to invade privacy I am not sure, although as long ago as 1963 I was saying that libel actions should be tried by judges alone, at least as far as damages were concerned – a view justified by the ludicrous awards juries are still giving. As for the means test – although of course fixed at a much higher level than in 1947 – it does still exclude middle-class people with only very moderate incomes from being eligible for legal aid. Add to that the fact that legal fees of counsel and solicitors are much higher now in real terms than when the Act was introduced, and litigation for ordinary people has become truly prohibitive. In this context I must say that I feared that the new regulations introduced by Lord Chancellor Mackay in the early nineties would result in a further large section of the community being unable to use the courts. And the Courts of Justice are surely a form of social service that should be available to all? Justice is not to be the prerogative of the rich alone. The whole subject is one that certainly needs further consideration.

Those were – alas – the only permanent contributions I made to the British legal scene in spite of the large number of speeches I made both in Parliament and in the country.

In the field of foreign affairs, however, although I can point to no specific achievement, I think I did do some useful work. I was very active at the Assembly of the United Nations, and by the speeches I made about foreign affairs both in the United States and in Britain I did perhaps help to make the public more aware of the potentialities of the United Nations and of its great importance.

The United Nations has now, because of the Gulf War and the greater public appreciation that this has caused of the whole complex of Middle Eastern problems, come much more into the public consciousness as a part of the machinery of international relations. Now, more than at any time since the beginning of the Cold War in about 1948, the UN has the opportunity of being used as and becoming a real instrument of world organization. In the 1940s, particularly in the days of Paul-Henri Spaak's presidency, it appeared well on the way to becoming such an instrument – and with the terrible experiences of the Second

World War fresh in their minds, the public of most countries hoped that it could be so. But the Cold War destroyed the possibility of real co-operation and the two basically conflicting economic philosophies that divided the world between them seemed likely to perpetuate the situation. As a result, a series of lesser known presidents and weak secretaries-general put the organization very much on the back pages of the newspapers. It was the initiatives of President Bush and Margaret Thatcher which brought it back into the headlines when Iraq invaded Kuwait (the Secretary-General at that time had presented an image of pusillanimity). The organization should not again be allowed to slide into comparative insignificance, although here I am dismayed at the lack of support by Britain for an effective military intervention by the UN in the quite shocking and wholesale breaches of international law and ordinary human behaviour in my once-beloved but now strife-torn Yugoslavia.

Possibly, however, my speeches on domestic affairs generally may have had some positive effect. Although they were often expressed in rash and sometimes intemperate language, the substance of what I was saying in these speeches as to the gravity of our economic position, the folly and indeed wickedness of unofficial strikes, and the vital importance of everyone pulling his full weight in the short time we had for recovery, and as to the dangers internationally, may have made some impression. I naturally referred from time to time to Winston Churchill, and I recall that on one occasion he came up and spoke to me in a corridor at the House of Commons about a speech I had made at the weekend. In it, while attacking Churchill (cruelly, as I now think) for the peacetime policies of the Conservative Party, I paid tribute, as I always did, to his great leadership during the war without which I would not have been able to make speeches in freedom and fearlessness as I now could. On this occasion I had qualified the comment by saying that it was as a great overall leader then representing the British people that we owed so much to him, for he was not greatly involved in administration or day-by-day policy during the war. He told me that I was quite wrong: he was going to lend me a copy of the minutes he had addressed to various Department heads in one month of the war years, and he did so. It was indeed a remarkable document. What struck me very forcibly was the number of minutes on comparatively trivial matters as well as major ones. Thus there was one minute which, as far as I can remember, said, 'Pray inform me on half a sheet of writing paper by noon tomorrow why Mrs Bloggs of North Battersea was prosecuted in the South Western police court for having secured half a pound more than her weekly ration of potatoes' – or something to that effect, showing how meticulously he read the papers.

I do not recall a minute that in express terms said 'Pray inform me by noon tomorrow on half a sheet of writing paper how to reform the command of HM's Navy', but such a minute would not have been untypical. (Everything, however complex and difficult, had to be dealt with quickly and briefly and on half a sheet of writing paper.) The dis-appointing thing was that there was no record of the replies, although there was no doubt that Winston watched for details of public disquiet on the domestic as well as the military front and kept the Departments on their toes. I returned the minutes he had lent me and said I had been very much impressed by his interest in details affecting ordinary indi-viduals. That short talk, I think, initiated a new regard for him which ripened into friendship, particularly after he became Prime Minister again in 1951. The fact was that almost invariably, and usually as a first task, he read the newspapers with some care – and not only the political speeches. I saw examples of this many times when, years later, I would occasionally visit him at No. 10, at around 11 a.m., when he was still in bed and surrounded by newspapers.

At the beginning of 1948 the proceedings in the International Court of Justice against Albania in respect of the mining of British warships in the Corfu Straits began to take formal shape; they were concluded only in 1991. In October of 1946, two British destroyers were passing through the Straits of Corfu, a narrow channel at the southern end of the Adriatic which, although having its west side governed by the Albanians, was a recognized international waterway with the right of free passage for ships of any nationality including warships. Both ships struck mines and the lives of forty British sailors were lost. We had reason to believe that the mines were laid by or for the Albanians and promptly raised the matter in the Security Council. The Russians blocked its discussion there by using their veto, but eventually the Council agreed that the matter should be referred to the International

Court of Justice at the Hague. There were various procedural delays and in the end the Court had to meet on 20 April 1948 to hear and adjudicate on some Albanian technical objection. It was its first case since it was reconstituted in April 1946 under the United Nations. I was the first to address the sixteen judges and said:

> Your power is great, but you will not falter before political expediency nor be dismayed by military might. Your decisions are taken, not politically but in accordance with the settled principles of justice. This court is the pivotal point in the organization of peace. In a world still full of tumult, anxiety and misunderstanding the International Court must stand like a rock of confidence and impartiality.

The word was father to the thought. In the Corfu channel cases the Court did overrule the Albanian procedural objection and the case was set down for hearing on a later date which – as it turned out – unfortunately for me conflicted with a more pressing commitment in London.

Two days later I was moving the second reading in the Commons of a bill that *inter alia* abolished what I called 'the notorious and ill-favoured doctrine of common employment', which prevented an employee claiming damages against his employer when the injury had been caused by the negligence of a fellow employee. It was a wise bill and secured the support of the Opposition, improving the protection of large numbers of workers in industry. That evening I resumed my weekend speeches, first at Rochdale, home of my grandfather's cotton mill, and then in other towns, but I was back in Parliament as well as the courts by the beginning of the week.

At the end of April we had to face up to the evasions of the strict system of petrol rationing which were taking place on an increasing scale. A scheme was devised by which petrol used for commercial vehicles, which was more freely available but which on the black market sold at high prices to the private owner, would be coloured and thus be easily identified. The penalty was imposed on the car. If a private car was found by the court to be filled with red petrol the car would – subject to certain exceptions – be disqualified from use for six years. This was strongly opposed by the Opposition who believed the penalty should be a personal one and imposed entirely at the discretion of the court. I made a little speech explaining the reasoning behind the penalty clause. A Member, whose name of Prescott sticks in my memory for no other achievement, intervened and asked, 'Is not the Attorney General speak﹍ ing for himself and his Rolls Bentley in this case?' My colleagues on the Government benches almost visibly trembled: it was bad enough that a Socialist colleague should be known as the best﹍dressed man in the House; was it also the case that he had the effrontery to flaunt a Roller, that emblem of the idle rich? The Tories on the other hand preened themselves at this palpable hit. I decided to play them up. 'I wonder', I said, 'how the Honourable Member, as he is entitled to be called in this House, comes to make that reference to my possessing a Rolls Bentley?' (My colleagues were squirming even more). 'What assistance is it to the Committee to use personal arguments of that kind in order to influence the debate?' I paused for an answer. None came. Then I said, 'I do not and could not possibly own a Rolls Bentley. I own an eight﹍horsepower Ford and also a Wolseley but I have no Rolls: I wish I had.' There was a very audible sigh of relief on my side of the House. Prescott turned a little white and said, 'Is it not the fact that at one time the Right Honourable Gentleman did own a Rolls Bentley?' The Deputy Chairman intervened but I managed to say, 'I did not: I only wish I had.' The Tory front bench, who – as one of the newspapers com﹍ mented – know bad form when they see it, looked strictly ahead as if Prescott did not belong to them. My lot were delighted and shouted, 'Withdraw. Withdraw.'

One of the most troublesome personal problems I had during my period as Attorney General was in connection with the proposed aboli﹍ tion of the death penalty. We had introduced a Criminal Justice Amendment Bill into the House of Commons – a long﹍overdue and important measure for the passage of which the Law Officers were largely responsible. While it made many desirable amendments in the criminal law, as originally introduced it contained no provisions affect﹍ ing capital punishment. This was by a decision of the Cabinet reflect﹍ ing the undoubted opinion of the British public and supported by the Home Secretary, Chuter Ede. The matter was, however, left to a free vote of the House and the abolitionists secured the adoption of a new clause that did away with the death penalty for an experimental period of five years. The bill then went to the House of Lords where this clause was deleted. Lord Goddard, the Chief Justice, made a strong speech sup-porting hanging and most of the Law Lords at the time took a similar view. (This is an interesting contrast to the present controversy between the two Houses as to whether, the death penalty having now been long since replaced by mandatory life imprisonment, even that should go and judges be given full discretion on the length of sentence to be imposed in a particular case.) The bill came back to the Commons and I became involved in what for me was an unhappy conflict with the Prime Minister and Herbert Morrison. They and most of the Cabinet, mindful of the strong opinion in the country in favour of the death penalty, wished to accept the Lords' decision. I was deeply opposed to that course. For over twenty years I had been against the death penalty and this was well known in Parliament and by the public. I felt strongly that we should restore the clause abolishing the penalty for a trial period. A private meeting was arranged in the House of Commons between the Prime Minister, Morrison, one or two other ministers and myself, sup-ported by a junior minister, who said he would follow whatever course I took. We had a passionate discussion in which Attlee sought to impress on me the great damage that would be done to the Party if we split on an issue on which public opinion was so clear. In the end, having been pretty well brow-beaten by the Prime Minister and Morrison, I gave way and said I would vote with the Government but resign after-wards. I was very upset and on leaving the meeting was actually in tears. Morrison came out and tried to pacify me. Later, the Cabinet decided on an illogical compromise that created two classes of murder, the broad line of demarcation being premeditation, such murders only to remain subject to capital punishment. It did not work and soon led to complete abolition. It fell to me, however, to introduce this compromise proposal – I frankly called it that – into the Commons. I made a long speech which although ridiculed by many of the newspapers was the focus of a very good leader in *The Times*. Winston replied for the Opposition. He had great fun and put on what I thought was a splendid parliamentary performance which turned me inside out. He pointed out, as an example of the bill's lack of logic, that if he killed his wife because she was in great pain and had no chance of survival by administering poison over a period so that in the end she died, dreaming happily, he would be hanged by the neck until he was dead, whereas if 'you should decide to kill your wife because after cold, calculated and deliberate consideration you had come to the conclusion that you would live more agreeably with another woman or would benefit under the terms of her will, you will have a variety of methods available, none of them involving a death penalty.' I shook my head. Winston retorted, 'The Right Honourable Gentleman may shake his head until he shakes it off.' He could, he suggested, 'strangle her, hold her head in the gas oven, stab her, cut her throat or dash her brains out with a hammer.' I think he added that one could boil her alive in boiling oil or throw her out of the porthole of a ship. I interjected 'rubbish' – but of course it was not rubbish: the rubbish was the attempted division of murder into capital and non-capital categories.

I was still considering resignation. Attlee was anxious I should not do so and various pressures based on party loyalty were put upon me. It may be relevant to quote the letter Attlee wrote to me.

My dear Attorney,

I see that you voted with the government on the Lords Amendments. I am very grateful to you for this, as I know how strongly you feel on the subject. I did actually send the Chief Whip to tell you that, if you felt that you must abstain, you were at liberty to do so.

I am sorry that owing to the question not being specifically on the Cabinet Agenda, the Secretary did not call you to the meeting. This should, of course, have been done, though at this stage the matter had come to the break point as to whether or not we were to sacrifice the whole Bill on this one point which was not in the original measure. This was rather a matter of general policy than one involving any particular legal question.

You may, perhaps, have thought that I put my point of view too emphatically to you on a matter on which you hold strong views, whereas I am not a partisan on the question of the death penalty.

Long experience has, however, shown to me the danger of the good being lost through the devotion of some to what they think to be the best. I was, therefore, necessarily concerned to put the matter before you in what I consider to be its right perspective. This is the inevitable duty of a Prime Minister or Leader of a Party who wants to keep the team together, having regard to the major objection of the Party.

We shall now have to consider what is the best approach to the subject in the light of existing circumstances.

With all good wishes,

Yours sincerely,

CLEMENT ATTLEE

In the end I had to accept the position but there was, I think, no other occasion when I was so near to resigning.

That weekend I was invited to the Durham Miners' Gala — as I was on two later occasions. In those days this was a great occasion with the whole of Durham *en fête*, processions of miners from the then numerous collieries marching with their banners through the streets, past the saluting base at the Country Hotel where the special guests were on the balcony, and assembling in a vast field for speeches. It was a considerable honour to be invited as a special guest and here, on the first occasion, I was with Stafford Cripps and Hugh Dalton. In my speech I said that solidarity and resolution were the keynotes of the assembly. It was no part of the Socialist theory that the slowest or the least able should set the standard or pace for the whole. It was on this visit that I met the Durham miners' leader, Sam Watson. He was in every way a splendid man, a strong anti-Communist who had great influence with the leaders of the Party and encouraged moderation. We became good friends.

In July the Assembly of the United Nations met in Paris and I was again one of the principal delegates for the UK. I had a suite in the George V Hotel and used to sit in the lounge for an hour in the evenings drinking an Alexandrine and watching the young Parisiennes. Our subsistence allowance was very small and I was reported in a newspaper as having said I had to do my own washing — although I do not recall that particular chore. Back in London for some pressing business, I had to leave again for Paris on 20 September, the very day my wife was expecting our second child. Unhappily I could not wait for the birth and had to leave her, I think, playing bridge with friends. She took these occasions in a very matter-of-fact way. When I got on the Channel steamer I received a telephone message that all was well. She had given birth to a girl weighing 8lb 14oz, before the doctor had arrived. Fortunately we had a midwife staying in the house ready for just such an eventuality.

I was soon in the thick of battle at the UN Assembly, held in the Palais de Chaillot, and did not manage to get back to Sussex to see my new daughter, who was christened Joanna, until she was three weeks old. I was the leading speaker for Britain in a debate in the Political Committee on disarmament and, once again, the debate was almost confined to Vyshinsky and myself. Vyshinsky and I got on excellently in private and many photographs record our friendly relationship, but in public debate we went for each other hammer and tongs. I described the Soviet disarmament proposals as 'mere humbug' and Vyshinsky retorted that I had uttered 'a torrent of lies and slander'. *The Times* described my speech as having been made in true if studied moderation, although I had asked some pretty searching questions, and reported the Russian delegates as saying that they 'know that the British public wanted peace – but equally that men like Sir Hartley did not – a gibe which its victim received with a heavy smile'. In my closing speech, which delighted Mr Bevin, I suggested nine specific steps that the Soviet Union could take, and concluded:

> Mr Vyshinsky said that he and I speak different languages not because I speak English and he speaks Russian, but because our hearts are different. That made me sad. I hope and believe it is not true. For I know that my heart and the heart of my country wants peace. Not the peace of slavery. Not the still peace of death. But peace and honour and friendship amongst all mankind . . .

> And if in the end the Great Powers fail to reach agreement on proposals in this matter which are reasonable, practicable and effective the world will know and will not forgive the handful of men, despotic rulers of one State at whose door that failure will live.

This was on 13 October, and I am glad to say that the atmosphere did slowly get better. On 21 October a Mexican resolution called on the Great Powers to 'compose their differences in a spirit of solidarity and mutual understanding', and Vyshinsky and Dulles gave this a favourable reception. Spaak concluded the discussion by saying 'This is a wonderful day', much as he had done after the original disarmament debate at Flushing Meadow, but, alas, with equally little of the voice of prophecy.

In the latter part of September, an event had occurred which was to lead to the big sensation of the year in the United Kingdom. I was sud-denly and without warning visited in Paris by the Director of Public Prosecutions, Sir Theobald Mathew, a man for whom I had a great respect and regard. He told me that rumours were spreading all over London of gross corruption in high places in government, including a story that Frank Soskice, the Solicitor General, had accepted a bribe of £10,000 – a lot of money then – to stop some legal case. I was horri-fied, and although I could not believe that particular rumour, I realized that drastic measures would have to be taken to clear matters up. Mathew thought I should return immediately to London and I agreed to do so that very afternoon, giving Hector McNeil the text of the speech I had meant to deliver the following day. I spent the next day studying such particulars as there were and quickly consulted the Prime Minister.

The police were making enquiries over a wide field. They had not so far produced any clear evidence of offences that could be prosecuted but had disclosed a mixed bag of suspicious matters implicating a number of people in official positions, including a junior minister, in what appeared to be improper conduct. It all revolved round the remarkable character of one Sidney Stanley who lived in Park Lane but who, it turned out, was a man of straw. The Government decided to set up a judicial inquiry under the Tribunals of Enquiry (Evidence) Act 1921, which gave the Tribunal all the powers of the High Court in regard to the attendance of witnesses, taking evidence on oath, and so forth. The machinery had only been used twice since the Act was passed – once in 1928 to enquire into questionable police methods and once in connec-tion with a Budget leakage in 1936. I had assumed that I should be fully involved and in charge of the Prosecution or whatever judicial inquiry was established, but Lord Simonds, who had been a member of the 1936 Tribunal, explained to the House of Lords that in that inquiry the conduct of the then Attorney General had not always been helpful. He expressed the strong view that the Law Officers should not be left with the conduct of the proceedings since they might be placed in a position

where there was a conflict between their duty and their loyalty to parliamentary colleagues. I did not at all share this view and Lord Jowitt, the
Lord Chancellor, told the House of Lords that after consultation with
me he could assure them that every step would be taken to elucidate the
truth and test the evidence by cross-examination. At the same time, the
Lord Chancellor announced that Mr Justice Lynskey had been
appointed to preside over the Tribunal, assisted by two Senior Silks. The
Tribunal became known as the Lynskey Tribunal.

Lord Jowitt's statement by no means put the matter to rest and there
was much public discussion. Legal opinion consolidated in favour of
the view that it was the duty of the Law Officers to conduct the proceedings before such a Tribunal. The Cabinet did not agree and – in my
absence – they adopted a minute that said that while I might open the
proceedings in a general way, I should then withdraw and leave the
conduct of the case to other counsel. I told Attlee that I could not be dictated to in regard to my duties as Attorney. The *Law Journal* strongly
concurred. The general public took the same line – 'the Attorney
General will be expected by the public to do his duty . . . the public will
not be concerned with Cabinet pressure'. In the meantime I had had a
private intimation from Mr Justice Lynskey that the Tribunal would
support my position if I did not follow Lord Simonds's view. I decided
that that was clearly my duty even if it prejudiced my chances of a
Cabinet appointment. On 1 November the Tribunal met in the Law
Courts for a preliminary hearing to discuss procedure. I made a short
statement pledging 'every aid in reaching the truth' and promised 'a
relentless and ruthless probe'. The full inquiry was set for 15 November.
On Thursday 11th, I was addressing the International Court at the
Hague, opening our case against Albania for the mining of our ships in
the Corfu Channel. On the 12th, after attending a Cabinet in London,
I flew to Paris but was delayed by fog, arriving just in time to hear Hector
McNeil start to give a long and careful analysis of the Soviet disarmament proposals. It sounded very good to me. After all, it was what I had
drafted! That night I flew back to Sussex, but saw little of my newly
born daughter, for I had to prepare my speech for the Lynskey Tribunal.
And on Monday 15th I duly made it – nearly four hours of it. The
speech was given enormous publicity with the entire front pages of the
evening papers being devoted to it.

During that first week I had, of course, other duties as well: I introduced the Legal Aid Bill, to which I have referred earlier; I sat on the Front Bench each evening and spent six hours on the Thursday on the Bench as the main defender of the Wireless Telegraph Bill; on the Friday evening, I flew to The Hague to discuss the progress of the case against Albania which Frank Soskice had been looking after. It was going well. Certainly the Albanians had modified their earlier truculent attitude and were now seeking to represent themselves as the most peaceful of nations, quite incapable of laying mines. (The decision eventually went against them but they did not recognize it for over forty years.) In the meantime, however, we had been able to seize gold bullion belonging to Albania held in a foreign bank that recognized our rights. Eventually the matter was settled between the two governments.

I shall not write here about the details of the evidence given to the Lynskey Tribunal. The whole subject was reported from day to day more fully than anything I have known, either before or since. *The Times* and the *Manchester Guardian* carried daily verbatim accounts over several columns. 'THE TORCH OF JUSTICE', printed one paper in large capitals, and then below, 'SHINES OVER ENGLAND'. 'SHAWCROSS FOR THE PEOPLE', said others. Rebecca West published two excellent commentaries in *Harper's Bazaar* besides writing a daily article in the *Evening Standard*.

The highlight of the proceedings was when Sidney Stanley went into the box. Police had to be called to regulate the great crowds that were trying to get into Church House, said one of the reports. Hundreds of people were turned away and the Hall was packed almost to suffocation point. It was difficult at first to understand why so many public figures had decided to keep Mr Stanley's company, but he was a charmer and a tremendous storyteller. I must admit that, in quite a long experience, I have never had a witness with whom I could do so little. It was quite impossible to upset him, still more to tie him down. He knew everybody, and the first name to be dropped was that of Lord Woolton: 'I know him very, very well indeed.' A typical answer to me in my cross-examination was: 'Sir Hartley, you are trying to trick me with the truth.' Naturally everybody laughed, and my question was forgotten. 'Sir Hartley,' he said in another intervention, 'it is a pity you are not as ignor-

ant as you look.' The general effect of his evidence was, however, to disclose a considerable volume of intrigue and near-bribery by businessmen
of little quality, but sometimes much wealth, converging round the
Board of Trade. Attention mainly centred on the position of a Mr John
Belcher, who was Parliamentary Secretary to the Board of Trade, and a
Mr George Gibson, a trade union leader who had been appointed a
director of the Bank of England and Chairman of the new Board of the
(nationalized) electricity industry. They were in some sense the victims
of their own lack of sophistication. Both had been trade union officials.
Belcher was comparatively unknown; Gibson was highly respected in
his field – indeed, otherwise he would not have been a government
nominee to the Bank of England – but neither had any experience at all
of the slick businessmen who started to cultivate their close acquaintance. They were comparatively easy prey to the wiles of 'spivs' who
buzzed round their offices like bees swarming round a queen, and did
not receive any serious and authoritative advice from higher up on how
they should react. This is not to excuse them but to explain how it all
happened.

Typical of the people who sought the help of Mr Belcher and Mr
Gibson was a Mr Harry Sherman. He was the head of a company
engaged in operating football pools and was concerned with allocations
of paper. There was also at this time a Board of Trade prosecution
against Sherman for some offence against the regulations which Belcher
eventually discontinued after meeting him. Sherman had, as I recall,
started one of the first of these immensely popular pools and he was certainly a millionaire. A 'crafty and malevolent pools promoter', Belcher's
counsel later called him; he was certainly too crafty for Belcher. He
needed more paper for the purposes of advertisements and forms connected with his pools and he was apparently happy to use any method
of obtaining the necessary permits from the Board of Trade. I cross-
examined him at great length and we heard an astonishing story of
cheques here, dinners there, introductions over drinks at Grosvenor
House, prospects of 'guinea-pig' directorships, libatory benefactions,
and so on, all in the course of promoting his profit-making activities. It
was an illuminating picture of the sort of world that almost inevitably
accompanies a system where governmental regulations, controls and
permits are placed on commercial activities, such as we had in operation

then. One could see how malleable, inexperienced and unsophisticated men like Belcher and Gibson would be in the hands of so unscrupulous a manipulator.

Not that all the Members of the Government were unsophisticated. A very different witness was Hugh Dalton, who had shortly before been forced to resign his position as Chancellor of the Exchequer because of an indiscreet remark he had made to a journalist a few minutes before his Budget speech. His appearance at the inquiry was at his own request. As far as my information went, his only doubtful connections with the Stanley clique had been attendance at some party, a visit he had made to the Chairman of Great Universal Stores with Stanley, and a letter he had written to Stanley which suggested an odd degree of familiarity with such a man. We had concluded that it would be unnecessary to call and cross-examine him, since there was nothing significant involving him apart from these trivial matters. I spoke to Dalton about it and strongly advised him not to give evidence. He insisted on doing so and after giving an involved explanation of his relations with Stanley he said that he had been perplexed about the man, but after visiting him in the Park Lane flat he formed the view that 'he was a contact man of low repute with whom he would have no more to do'. He then came to a letter he had sent to Stanley addressed (in typescript) 'My dear Stan' but otherwise quite short and curt. He said that what he had dictated was 'My Dear Stanley' but his secretary had misheard the name. Even if that had been thought true, and I heard nobody who believed it, 'My dear Stanley' would have been a curious way to write to a man whom he considered a contact man of low repute. He also mentioned that Stanley offered him a place on the board of Great Universal Stores – pressing it by adding that he need only attend one meeting a month and there would be 'a substantial fee'. Dalton said he told Stanley he was not interested, but he had nonetheless accompanied Stanley to a long interview with Isaac Wolfson, the chairman of the company. His evidence did not impress and I believe he bitterly regretted having rejected my advice not to appear.

Eventually came the speeches of the leading counsel for those who had asked to be represented so as to answer allegations or innuendoes that had been made. A number of distinguished Silks appeared, including Edmund Davies, Derek Curtis-Bennett, Sir Walter Monckton, and

Dikes Watson, who was for Belcher, and who gave a brilliant four-hour speech. By 17 December – a Friday – those speeches were over and the Tribunal adjourned till the following Monday.

That did not mean, however, that I got a weekend off. During the inquiry I had twice flown to The Hague and Paris at the weekends. I had gone regularly to Parliament – usually straight from the Tribunal, although I am reported on one occasion to have arrived at 1 a.m. for a debate on a statutory order. In the week before my own final speech on the Monday I moved the second reading of the Legal Aid and Advice Bill.

This particular weekend I had long-standing engagements in the West Country and spoke at Torquay, Barnstaple and Exeter. In the meantime I had to prepare my closing speech for the Tribunal. This I did, I remember, in a hotel bedroom, probably in Exeter, where I had all the papers, including daily shorthand notes, laid out on the floor. How I got them there I cannot imagine. I suppose I came down by car; if so I must have driven myself, for my wife had just had the misfortune to break her leg in a riding accident. I am ashamed to realize that I cannot even have gone home to comfort her.

On the Monday, I began my closing speech which went on into the following day – nearly six hours in all – in which I attempted to review the whole proceedings. Of course, I did not press any particular conclusions upon the Tribunal. I ended up, a little dramatically perhaps – although it did not seem to be regarded as inapposite at the time – by quoting the famous lines from John Donne: 'Never send to know for whom the Bell tolls . . . it tolls for thee.'

The Tribunal then rose; there was an exchange of compliments between myself representing the Bar and Mr Justice Lynskey for the Tribunal. Everybody thanked everybody. And that included the still-irrepressible Sidney Stanley. He insisted on shaking hands with everybody, including the chief superintendent of police who had led the inquiries and to whom he said, 'You have done a good job.' Of the tribunal generally he is reported as saying

I am glad it is all over. My impression is chiefly of admiration for Sir Hartley Shawcross. He has been masterly. Although he was severe with me I bear him no malice. I am proud of him!

He was a man of infinite resilience. Photographs of him, in his flat, kept appearing in the newspapers. The most prominent feature was a grand piano on which stood a large portrait photograph in a silver frame. It was of me. During the course of the case I received a telegram congratulating me on the birth of my daughter, signed 'From your friend and enemy, Sidney Stanley.' I did not know my Stanley fully at that time and thought it must be a hoax. I asked the police to enquire and they came back with the report that he had indeed sent it. 'Why shouldn't I? It's a free country.'

After Christmas, the Tribunal produced its report which quickly became the best-selling White Paper (at £2 a time) since the end of the war. In a sense the report was an anti-climax. It completely exonerated the civil servants from any impropriety in the discharge of their duties while recognizing the difficulties in which some of them had been placed. It examined the evidence of Stanley and Sherman in some detail, and set out Stanley's method of operation which was to secure as many friends as possible in high places by lavish hospitality (including, in the case of Belcher, a holiday in a Margate Hotel for the family, something the wretched man had probably never been able to enjoy before); gifts such as tailor-made suits without payment or coupons; and occasionally cases of drink and the like. The Tribunal did not accept Sherman as a truthful witness. He was obviously prepared to use corrupt methods to influence ministerial decisions and he was one of those willing to use 'contact men' for ministers who allowed themselves to be so used. Stanley was his instrument. The Tribunal found that Belcher and Gibson had both improperly used their official positions to influence decisions in favour of Stanley's friends. A Scottish businessman who was also a Justice of the Peace, Sir Maurice Bloch, had also acted improperly, attempting to influence Belcher by gifts of wine. Hugh Dalton's lack of sophistication in his short acquaintance with Stanley was not commented upon. The Tribunal was satisfied that Stanley's offer of a directorship to Dalton was declined and had no influence on Dalton's mind. Significantly, the Tribunal made no reference at all to Dalton's explanation of 'My dear Stan' in the letter which he signed. The fact was they simply did not believe him; nor, I think, did anybody else.

In general, the Tribunal's report must have come as a relief to the

Labour Party, if only on the ground that 'it might have been worse'. But to the three men, Belcher, Gibson and Maurice Bloch, it meant public death. Bloch was removed from the Commission of the Peace, Gibson resigned from the Bank of England, and Belcher from his parliamentary secretaryship.

The report was debated in Parliament in February 1949. I made a fairly lengthy statement to the effect that the Director of Public Prosecutions had advised me that, on the information presently available, he did not consider that criminal proceedings should be taken and that I agreed. Everybody, I think, heaved rather a sigh of relief at this, and we then proceeded to listen in silence to a personal statement by Belcher which he concluded in a moving passage by saying that he proposed forthwith to apply for the stewardship of the Chiltern Hundreds, which is the formal way of retiring from Parliament.

The net result of it all was that the matter went to sleep – but not into oblivion. The Tribunal findings had cleared the air of very evil but rapidly multiplying and, if not corrected, most damaging falsehoods about probity in public life.

As for my own position, I feel rather ashamed to say that the Tribunal had done me a lot of good. Before it I was not the most popular member of the Treasury Bench – not that I became so later – but on the whole my standing in the House was improved. There were a few who felt that Belcher had been harshly dealt with, and were inclined to blame me for it. Indeed, I felt myself that in a sense he was more sinned against than sinning. And, of course, Hugh Dalton never forgave me for the fact that his evidence about 'My dear Stan' was disbelieved, his dislike no doubt being increased by newspaper headlines to the effect that I was a rival to him for a new Cabinet appointment. But Attlee came as near as he was able to giving me a pat on the back – he was really incapable of such gestures – when he congratulated me privately on having done a good job. And Churchill also was forming a more friendly and serious view of me. Quintin Hogg (then Member for Oxford, subsequently Lord Chancellor and still a robust character) said that 'the Attorney General had emerged from this business with a greatly enhanced reputation and had won for himself great gratitude from many sections of the community and from his profession.' This was very generous of him, for a few months later he was making sustained and strong attacks on me for my exposition (indeed a very flattering description) of the law on election expenses. Years later he proposed my health at a family party to celebrate my 90th birthday.

Immediately after Christmas I was back in my ordinary routine of court and parliamentary work, and the rounds of political meetings at weekends. Here, indeed, the demand for my attendance increased because of the extraordinarily wide publicity I had been receiving.

CHAPTER 10

Politics, 1949

THE legal work continued to stream in during 1949. But I became increasingly involved in parliamentary work, having to speak from the front bench in debates that were not strictly my concern as Attorney General. My outdoor speaking engagements also mounted up, not only at weekends but often on evenings during the week, after which I went back to the House.

One notable occasion in the Commons was the Married Women (Restraint on Anticipation) Bill which, in spite of my endeavours to the contrary, became known as 'the Mountbatten Bill'. Lady Mountbatten was the granddaughter of an immensely wealthy man, Sir Ernest Cassel, who on her marriage to Mountbatten made a big settlement upon her. This was, as usual in those days, made subject to a clause restraining 'anticipation', which meant that during matrimony she was not allowed to realize the capital and could only enjoy the income. A gross reduction in her income owing to taxation and other problems (to £4,500 from, Walter Monckton told me, about £80,000) made it quite impossible for the Mountbattens to live 'in the style to which they had become accustomed'! I could believe this, for living myself far more humbly I found it difficult to manage on my salary. In medieval times the effect of marriage was that the husband became entitled to all his wife's possessions. Although in the marriage service he said 'With all my worldly goods I thee endow', it was in fact the other way round. The law was gradually modified and by the end of the 18th century it was accepted that property could be settled on a woman, whether married or not, subject to restraint on anticipation. The sole purpose of this device was to protect the wife against the importunities of the husband: she was not to be 'kicked, or kissed' out of her capital. In 1935 the law was changed, but not retrospectively, with the result that such a clause could be set aside if contained in deeds made in future, but that in deeds already in existence with such a clause the restraint remained binding, as was the case with Edwina Mountbatten. In these circumstances the Mountbattens, advised by Walter Monckton, had introduced a private bill in the Lords to do away with the restraint in their particular case. The bill was passed in the Lords but it became apparent that, because of the Mountbattens' unpopularity with many Tory MPs, it would fail to get through the Commons.

Walter came to see me, pointing out that apart from, or because of, the Mountbattens' unpopularity, the view in the Commons was unfavour-able to altering the law for a single privileged person only. I told Walter that we would change the law so as to put all married women in an equal position, able to deal with their capital as they thought fit. It was a rash undertaking. The next thing was to get the Cabinet to agree. There was opposition and grumbling that we were showing favour to the rich. Attlee supported me; so did Stafford Cripps, and it was agreed that a Public Bill could be presented. I moved the second reading two or three days after getting back from the States. My speech was described as 'disingenuous' by so serious a statesman as Oliver Stanley, and so I fear it was. I did not deny that the bill was to some extent a consequence of the fact that the Lords had passed a Private Bill in relation to the Mountbatten case. There was, as one of the newspaper reports gleefully put it, 'much shuffling and muttering on the benches' behind me, but Oliver Stanley, making the first speech for the Opposition front bench after my opening, said that, speaking only for himself, he supported the principle of the bill. He doubted my claim that the bill was a response to 'long-standing pressure by women's organizations', which was fair enough. He also remarked that as one of the main objectives of the Mountbattens was to avoid surtax he was surprised that the Labour Government should facilitate this for them – a comment that increased the muttering behind me. Eventually the bill was passed, but although only forty-seven voted against, the number voting on the Labour side was much smaller than our usual majority.

Parliamentary work was increasingly involving me, but I continued to make speeches at meetings up and down the country. My speeches were becoming less extreme. I was realizing the practical difficulties of the full-blooded Socialism in which I had earlier believed. By the end of the decade, I was coming to believe in policies more akin to those that Mr Neil Kinnock, also a convert to moderation – although only after defeats in elections fought on traditional policies – later led the Labour Party to adopt. I was constantly urging that everyone should work harder: the economic battle was far from won and British export per-formance was most disappointing. We faced worsening austerity. I was worried about unofficial strikes and I said – and there was much evi-dence to support it – that labour disruption was part of the Communist conspiracy against social democracy organized from Moscow. Indeed, I went so far as to describe unofficial strikes as treason. I was becoming more worried about the abuse of the liberties we had created by the Trades Disputes Act in 1946. Press comment on such speeches was varied. One paper said that I was the blue-eyed boy, 'the Kiss boy Pin-up', but another excellent newspaper headlined me as a 'raving lunatic'. As for my speeches about the Press, they received excellent publicity when I praised it, as quite often I did, and abusive publicity when I crit-icized it. I made some speeches about the right to privacy, suggesting that editors, in publicizing what were *prima facie* comments or news about a man's personal affairs, should apply the test 'Is it true? Is it kind? Is it nec-essary?' On the other hand I stated firmly that it would be wholly wrong to take statutory steps to curb the freedom of the Press. Now I am forced to feel less certain.

Although I covered most of the political ground, my main interest remained foreign policy, and on this I largely concentrated on the work of the United Nations, sometimes strongly critical of its weakness in day-to-day matters but stressing always that it was, and must remain, the main instrument for avoiding war and resolving the more critical dis-putes.

In June/July 1949 I visited the United States at the invitation of the American Bar and in the course of a few days undertook a fairly wide tour that included Texas, speaking mainly about the economic problems – and I admitted we had many – of the United Kingdom and the work of the United Nations. When I flew back, the plane landed at Prestwick for refuelling, and there I faced a posse of pressmen who photographed me in the enormous Texan stetson I had been given by a Dallas millionaire and who asked me about a bag of food I was said to have; some newspapers reported 'dozens of steaks', one 'six', one 'three', and another '12 juicy steaks'. Of course, this received much publicity and caused John Strachey, then Minister of Food, a little embarrassment with a parliamentary inquisitor. I said I had been on a goodwill speak/ ing trip and the steak was evidence of Texan goodwill in return.

Foreign affairs being so often the subject of my outside speeches, my name was often spoken of as a possible candidate for the office of Secretary of State for Foreign Affairs. But 1949 was a year in which there was increasing speculation about ministerial changes. There were those who thought that Attlee had failed as Prime Minister. 'Ernie' Bevin was known to be in poor health and tired.

Some gossip columnists mentioned the possibility that I might get appointed Lord Chief Justice, and a few prophesied that I would succeed Ernie Bevin as Foreign Minister. In the House, the speculation was similar. I was myself far from certain what I wanted to do in politics. The question was not whether I would accept the Foreign Office if it were offered, but whether I wanted to go on in the House in any other position than that of Attorney. I realized that the Labour Party had lost a lot of popular support in the country. It was quite possible that we would lose the next election which, after all, had to be by the middle of 1950, in which case I would want to go back to the Bar. There was reason to remain well known as the Attorney General.

Meanwhile, I kept my hand in in the courts, and had the regular run of cases. Only one merits attention here: the Haigh case took place at the assizes at Lewes in the middle of July 1949. I had not done any cases as Attorney General in the criminal courts since the treason trials in the early days of my appointment. There was, however, a tradition that the Attorney would prosecute in any case of murder by poisoning. I waited for such a case. But there wasn't one. It was not because no one was mur/ dered by poisoning, but because no one was found out. Indeed, I under/ stand that the reason for the tradition that the Attorney should prosecute in such cases was the very reason that they were so difficult to prove. The characteristic of the Haigh murders was that the dead bodies were dis/ posed of in a vat of sulphuric acid; the resulting sludge was poured down the drain so that the fact of the death was unknown. I thought that this was sufficiently close to poisoning for me to justify reviving the old tradition that the Attorney would prosecute, and I had a public state-ment made that this was my intention. Thereupon a Sunday paper, having promised to pay him appropriate fees, announced that Maxwell Fyfe would appear for the defence featuring Shawcross v. Fyfe in 'the Battle for Haigh'. There were long articles about us both personally in the weekly papers. A proposal to hold the trial in London was opposed on my behalf: the proper venue was the assizes at Lewes, near where the alleged crime was committed. And so it was set down for trial there before Mr Justice Humphreys, the senior and most experienced criminal judge. Lewes was, of course, situated near to my country home, which was much photographed at the time, but it was not chosen for that reason; indeed, it was rather inconvenient for me as I had to go up to the House of Commons every evening of the trial.

The trial began on 18 July and I opened for the Crown. I told the court that in the early part of the year Mrs Durand-Deacon, a lady of some means, was living at a South Kensington hotel. Also living there was John George Haigh, a man who described himself as an engineer and a company director but who was apparently without any regular source of income; at the time he was in debt and being pressed for repay-ment. He struck up a friendship with her. In due time he 'inveigled her down to Crawley'; there he had access to a disused warehouse at which he had organized a large supply of sulphuric acid and other parapher-nalia, including rubber gloves to protect his hands. In a confession after his arrest he had stated that once inside he had killed the wretched lady by shooting her through the head and had drained some of her blood into a glass which he drank. He stripped the body and then disposed of it, he believed completely, in the tank of sulphuric acid. The next day he got rid of the valuables he had taken from her: a fur coat and jew-ellery. I told the jury that the law allowed a conviction for murder even if there was no body, but that in any event the body in this case had not been completely destroyed – there were some things which sulphuric acid did not dissolve. Mrs Durand-Deacon had suffered from gallstones and the remains of gallstones were found in the earth over which Haigh had poured the residue of the sludge.

Haigh made several elaborate and false statements about his associa-tion with Mrs Durand-Deacon but eventually made a statement to a police inspector admitting he had killed her and, curiously, asked what the judge might think about 'the chance of being released from Broadmoor'. I told the jury at the end of my speech that the case was a simple one of murder for financial gain.

Up to that time the defence had given no indication of their line save in the plea of not guilty, but after the police inspector had completed his evidence for the Crown, Maxwell Fyfe cross-examined and indicated that he was not disputing the facts and that the defence would ask for a verdict of guilty but insane. This he sought to establish by the fact that in his various statements to the police, Haigh had given details of five other murders which were authenticated and three cases which at that time we had not identified. I might have used these statements in my opening as evidence of system, but concluded that the Durand-Deacon case was so clear that it was simpler to let it stand on its own.

After Maxwell Fyfe's opening the defence called only one witness. He was Dr Henry Yellowlees, probably the leading psychiatrist of the day, a man with any number of distinguished degrees and diplomas. He stated in some detail in answer to Maxwell Fyfe that there was definite evidence of paranoia and said that the point he found unique about the case was 'the absolute callous, cheerful, bland, almost friendly indifference to the crimes he freely admitted he had committed'. I cross-examined — also at some length. Right at the beginning Yellowlees admitted that the evidence he had given in court about having examined Haigh in prison on five occasions was incorrect, and it might have been only three times, a mistake that did not impress the jury. He agreed that Haigh was a person 'on whose word it would be utterly useless to rely.' I asked him to state the objective signs of Haigh's insanity and he replied that to give those he would have to repeat all his evidence. My comment that I would be the last person to ask him to do that drew laughter which the judge rebuked. I pursued the question of what the symptoms were on which he relied. He said, 'His verbosity, his egocentricity, the fact that he has no shame or remorse for his deeds . . . his dreams and the fact that paranoia is of all mental disorders the most difficult to simulate.' I put to him that all the things mentioned arose from what Haigh had told him except the last, which was not a symptom at all. He had to agree. The legal definition of insanity in such cases — the McNaghton rule — is that the accused does not know the nature and quality of his act or does not know that it is wrong. Dr Yellowlees had not so far addressed his evidence at all to that. I cross-examined him strongly on these points. He agreed that there was no doubt that Haigh knew the nature and quality of his act. On the question of whether he knew it was wrong, he said he had 'no opinion on that'. In answer to the judge he said the prisoner believed he was acting under the guidance of a higher power. I pressed him to tell the jury whether he thought there was any doubt that Haigh knew that what he was doing was wrong according to English law. After a perceptible pause Dr Yellowlees replied that he thought Haigh had known it was wrong under English law. On that answer I sat down. Maxwell Fyfe in re-examination only elicited (was it by way of excuse?) that Dr Yellowlees had never before given evidence in a case of pure paranoia. The judge followed with his summing-up, short and to the point but clearly indicating a guilty verdict. After a retirement of only fifteen minutes the jury came back with a verdict of guilty and the then inevitable death sentence followed. So ended in two days this most sensationally publicized case, further immortalized by a number of characteristically brilliant cartoons by Feliks Topolski, one of which, large and in colour, still hangs at the Old Bailey.

Two days after the conclusion of the Lewes case I was back making political speeches on the seriousness of our economic situation in the Midlands.

Then I was back to my own profession. 'The Bar', I told its annual meeting over which as Attorney General I presided, 'must prepare its own defence.' (If that was not prophetic, what could be?) We would for the first time set up a permanent central organization with a proper secretariat.

And then – at last! – my sailing holiday. I still had a twelve-metre, *Vanity V*. I think that by this time I had had an auxiliary engine fitted, but otherwise she remained a fully rigged and very beautiful racing yacht. The engine was a concession to the fact that, unlike in the carefree days of the Bar's Long Vacation, I now had to stick to strict timetables and could not risk being becalmed out at sea.

Before the end of August, I was back at work, and busy. In October I went as usual to the Assembly of the United Nations in New York and had the usual verbal duels with Vyshinsky. For a month or so I was kept extremely busy travelling round the States on speaking engagements at weekends, but by the end of October the main work of that UN Assembly was over and I managed to travel home in the *Queen Mary*.

It was a very quiet voyage with hardly any passengers I knew. There was one elderly Russian professor, however, with whom I had had some casual acquaintance at the UN, where he was part of the Soviet delegation. He seemed alone and I sometimes sat with him and tried to talk, though he was extremely quiet and reticent. On our last night before disembarking at Southampton we sat together in the lounge, saying very little. Suddenly he got up to say goodbye. We shook hands and he then permitted himself one quiet remark. 'Never', he said, 'has anything more true been said than by your Lord Acton: "Power corrupts – absolute power corrupts absolutely." Goodbye.' I never saw him again.

We were getting near to the time for a general election and our opponents were quite rightly preparing for it. Industry, in particular, was engaging itself in increasing propaganda against threats of further nationalization. Packets of sugar being sold in the shops bore anti-nationalization slogans such as 'We have the best sugar. The State wants it'. 'Mr Cube' became a familiar anti-Labour image. Herbert Morrison made a speech suggesting that this expenditure by industry could be charged as an election expense of individual Tory candidates. This might have meant that their expenses would have exceeded the permitted level. A small panic ensued and the matter came to the House, Quintin Hogg (as he then was) putting down a motion for debate. I was the main speaker for the Government. The law was quite undefined. 'Unauthorized' expenditure by third parties with a view to promoting the election of a particular candidate was prohibited by law, but expenses on account of the conduct and management of the election were not. It would all have to be decided by the court – I said – on the facts of each particular case. This was no doubt vague and unsatisfactory but was the only answer that could properly be given.

I remember the autumn of 1949 mainly for the gossip among ministers in the corridors and the Tea Room (I hardly ever used the Smoking Room). At this stage there was an increasingly disagreeable amount of intrigue going on: Hugh Dalton was a prime intriguer, abetted by Stafford Cripps, although Stafford regarded himself as on a superior plane; Bevin hated Morrison and recognized Dalton for what he was; Morrison hated Attlee – and so on. I more or less kept out of all this, but Morrison and I had many talks about possible changes.

I made clear to him that I would like the Foreign Office if Ernie Bevin did resign but that I was in doubt whether I could continue at all in politics. At that early stage, Morrison strongly supported me as Foreign Secretary; his own position as Deputy Prime Minister and Leader of the House made him feel impregnable at that time. The Lord Chancellor strongly backed me, so did Lord Addison, then our Leader in the House of Lords. Dalton opposed me, which was to be expected. It was said that while Attlee thought well of me, he was opposed to the idea of having 'a middle-class lawyer' at the Foreign Office. In the event, Bevin did not resign as had been thought likely, and at the turn of the year it was announced that there would be a general election on 23 February 1950.

We went into that election with an optimism that was certainly not justified by experience or by the popularity of our programme. This included such unattractive issues as the nationalization of sugar, cement, water, coal storage, probably part of the chemical industry, with rather vague threats about the wholesale meat industry and agricultural land. The fact was that we had completely failed to appreciate the changed mood of the electorate; opinion polls were then in their infancy. In the event, our enormous majority of 145 in the 1945 election was reduced to one of eight overall, which made it obvious that the new parliament would be short-lived. The Cabinet changes were, for that reason, not numerous. Stafford Cripps had already resigned from the Chancellor-ship because of ill-health and Gaitskell had taken his place. (He and Wilson, at the Board of Trade at that time, hated each other.) Morrison remained in his predominantly influential position as Leader of the House and Bevin was still at the Foreign Office, although it was sus-pected that because of his seriously declining health he would not remain for long. Certainly he was very ill and, indeed, near to death when he retired in April 1951. Frank Soskice, the Solicitor General, unhappily lost his seat, but Attlee, having in mind that I would soon be moved and Soskice should take my place as Attorney, said he should remain Solicitor until another seat was found for him, a course with which I agreed. A little later, in preparation for the change, a newly elected Labour lawyer, Ungoed Thomas, was given Silk, so as to be available for promotion.

The results were mostly declared on Friday 24 February 1950. On the Monday I was back in court and on Wednesday I opened the prosecution case against Klaus Fuchs, who had betrayed our atom secrets to the Russians. I felt it was in many ways a tragic story and I did not altogether share the contempt for him expressed by Rebecca West in her comment upon the case. Fuchs was a Communist and he had started passing secret information to Russia in 1943 when the Russians were already our allies in the war. The Lord Chief Justice did not take a lenient view, however, and Fuchs went down for eighteen years – six years longer than Nunn May!

Parliament quickly reassembled and I was back in my old régime of legal work during the day, Parliament in the evenings till the House rose, and speeches round the country at the weekend. Unfortunately I had painful disc trouble, and for nearly six months had to live in a plaster jacket from shoulders to hips. This meant that my trousers had to be replaced hurriedly by Moss Bros for ones with a very big waist. I was extremely uncomfortable, and in my frustration one night I persuaded Joan to hack the cast off. Of course it had to be replaced the next day, but by then I had discovered the technique of puffing out the chest while the plaster was applied. By this time I had become something of a reformed character. The *Recorder*, admittedly not the finest of newspapers, put it, 'Sir Hartley gets wiser and wiser with every public utterance. In five years he has gone from the chirpy to the elder statesman. The House has forgiven him for his early brashness and acknowledges his proved ability.' In many papers I was, I think, regarded as the favourite to succeed Ernest Bevin, which was what I hoped.

But it was not to be. Before the election many people thought that Attlee wanted me to succeed Bevin. Indeed, while the election was actually in progress, I was informed that Attlee had decided on me as his successor at the Foreign Office. But after the election, as the gossip and the intrigues continued, it became clear that he and Morrison had both changed their minds. Morrison and I had further talks. Although Bevin was contemplating resignation, he was anxious for James Griffiths, Colonial Secretary, to succeed him, and on 21 February 1951 Jowitt wrote me in manuscript:

Dear A.G.

The only further thing I can do is through Christopher – and that I have done.

Left to himself I know that Clem would have given you the F.O. I can only guess that Ernie is pressing the claims of J.G. – either because he wants a 'pukka' Trades Unionist or because he thinks he can control J.G.

I think it's the unsound advice of a sick man – but the half dead Ernie counts for more than the advice of the wholly alive.

I like J.G. and admire his qualifications but I think they are wholly unsuited to the F.O.

I suppose 'the Party' speaks through the Chief Whip and I suppose the Foreign Affairs Committee (if there is one) is listened to.

It may be that these bodies will act. If they do not, and promptly, I would guess – 'tho' I know nothing, that J.G. will be offered the F.O. and you the Colonial Office.

If you are offered the Colonial Office I much hope you will take it. There is a great job to be done there and if you try it and succeed – the F.O. will almost certainly be yours in the future.

If you reject it, it will create a bad impression – they'll say, quite unfairly, that you are sulking.

I wish I could do more. I want you at the F.O. because I believe you'd do the job well and regain for us the initiative.

Yours,

J.

Morrison's attitude had changed. He had come round to the view that he ought to go to the Foreign Office. He realized that it was important to maintain his still very strong position in the Labour Party outside. He formed the view that if he did not accept the Foreign Office it would be thought in the Party that it was cowardly of him and would make his eventual election as Leader when Attlee resigned less likely. I felt that, on the contrary, going to the Foreign Office would kill him politically. Nobody knew the ordinary English working class, and particularly Londoners, better. But Herbert had never interested himself in foreign affairs, had only travelled abroad occasionally to conferences or as a tourist, had no languages and, to take a trivial but unhappy example, could not even pronounce foreign names. I recall him speaking of 'the Euphrates' in two syllables with the accent on the first, an occasion that provoked ill-mannered and cruel howls of laughter from the Opposition.

In the end he decided to take the Foreign Office, and I made it clear that for my part I would be content to remain in my present office and would help him where I could. This was early in 1951. That, too, was soon to alter. Gaitskell introduced a Budget including a charge on NHS spectacles. Bevan threatened to resign during this crisis. By an elaborate stratagem to mislead the Press, Herbert avoided coming to Peckhams, our country house which he had often visited with his wife, and asked us instead to arrange to go, after dinner, to some mutual friends, Leslie and Margaret Hunter, both distinguished journalists with whom he was staying the weekend in Surrey. Joan accordingly telephoned and we were invited on the following Sunday.

Morrison and I quickly completed our talk and returned to take our coffee. Our hosts were sworn to complete secrecy and were then told I had agreed to join the Cabinet in the office of Lord Privy Seal. This is often thought now to be something of a sinecure. Not then. I was to have wide powers as a co-ordinating minister with the chairmanship of various Cabinet committees so that I would join the top rank of Cabinet ministers. In the event, it did not, again, turn out quite like that. Bevan did resign, saying he would not go along with the more moderate policy of the Government, nor would he be a party to imposing charges in the NHS – although he had piloted a bill that gave power to impose a shilling charge on prescriptions. He was not interested in saving Britain; he wanted to save Socialism. Harold Wilson followed him together with John Freeman. This they did while Attlee was actually in hospital.

So two Cabinet positions became available: the Presidency of the Board of Trade and the Lord Privy Seal. The Board of Trade was the equivalent of the present Department of Trade and Industry. The office of Lord Privy Seal was to involve a lot of negotiating for supply from, *inter alia*, the United States. I went to visit Attlee in hospital. He also saw Dick Stokes, another 'right-winger', and offered us these two positions, saying we could choose between ourselves who should have which. Dick was a very close personal and political friend and he kindly gave me the first choice. I felt that the important thing in politics was to have a great Department of State behind me. Years later, Peter Carrington told me the same when, he having resigned the Foreign Secretaryship, I urged him to become a Member 'without portfolio'. I chose Trade, and am very glad I did. Dick at Supplies, Robens at Labour, George Brown at Works; these were all friends of mine and the right wing of the Party was greatly strengthened by the reconstituted Cabinet. These appoint/ments were made on 24 April 1951.

And so for the next nine months I was President of the Board of Trade (which was highly respectable and included the Archbishop of Canterbury but which actually never met, hence the taunt: 'There isn't any Board and now there isn't any Trade.')

The translation from the Law Officership (where Frank Soskice took my place very successfully) to the Board of Trade was, as I called it, 'an Irishman's rise' which cut my income by half.

I was installed in premises on Millbank which had been taken over from ICI and had the room normally used by the Chairman. It had a remarkable ceiling which rose or fell when a button was pressed. I never understood why. The first of many big industrial conferences I held was with the leaders of the tobacco industry. I had of course long been aware that we must get our balance of payments in better shape. Now I had the opportunity of trying to do something about it. I explained to the tobacco moguls that we must impose a heavier import duty. Naturally they demurred. I stood firm. In the event, the policy was not much help. The great British public grumbled, but paid the higher prices and large imports continued.

Although I was not so heavily burdened with official work as before, I travelled around the country making political speeches less, and con/centrated on talking more directly to industrialists and trade unionists about the urgency of modernizing industry and becoming really com/petitive in exports. Generally I got attentive audiences.

My real debut in Parliament as President of the Board of Trade was two weeks after my appointment on 7 May, although I felt I had hardly yet got to know the ropes. And I enjoyed myself! I had the most able and loyal civil servants. Hervey Rhodes, an immensely hard/working and able MP – who was brave both physically (he had a war wound in his thigh which still required daily dressing) and morally – was my

Parliamentary Secretary. He died as a peer and Knight of the Garter. Two Labour MPs, Richard Ewart (MP for Sunderland) and John Hudson (MP for Faley North), were my Parliamentary Private Secretaries. No minister could have been better or more loyally served. But I found myself presented by my new Department with a verbatim speech which I was supposed to make. After studying the material, I tore it up and prepared notes of my own. The debates had arisen because General MacArthur – still, I thought, feeling a little too grand after his victory in Japan – had suggested that we were helping Communist China in Korea, where the Chinese were at war with the United States and with Britain, by allowing unlimited exports of war munitions from Hong Kong. He made use of a secret list which we supplied to the United States Government each fortnight as part of the system of keeping a statistical check on exports to China. MacArthur referred to certain items on one such list, including petrol and various oils, but did not mention the quantity – which in each case was nil. He mentioned cameras; the quantity showed one only. Questions had naturally then been asked in the House about this export of strategic goods. So on Monday, 7 May, to a very full House, with the Prime Minister sitting on one side of me and Herbert Morrison on the other, and with Winston Churchill opposite, I set out the facts in some detail. Winston then rose and made a generous reference to me, saying that I had 'spoken in a manner not disagreeable to the House'. The Opposition decided to raise the matter in debate three days later. A general debate followed in which Shinwell made a rather unhappy speech. Churchill then wound up by concentrating an attack on the unhappy Shinwell.

I continued to be very busy. In June, I initiated the studies and discussion that led to Ted Heath's later and very successful legislation on retail price maintenance. I told the House that the Government would introduce legislation in the near future to prohibit the collective or individual enforcement of resale price maintenance going much further than a recent independent committee had reported, and that we also proposed to discuss with the Monopolies Commission methods of speeding up their work. Unfortunately Parliament was dissolved before we could legislate.

At about this time I had to take a week or so off, owing to a recurrence of duodenal trouble. Joan stepped brilliantly and courageously into the gap. She had, indeed, always and increasingly helped me, not only in keeping a very happy and charming home, but in accompany, ing me on many speaking engagements and in undertaking quasi-polit, ical engagements on her own. She had a great success — and scores of glamorous photographs — at the London Fashion Fortnight, an event sponsored by the Government with the objective of attracting overseas buyers. HRH Princess Elizabeth opened it at the beginning of June. Let the *Daily Express* take over! Under the bold headline 'London Fashion Fortnight gets a lead from Sir Hartley's wife', the story went:

> The mainly mink-clad guests commented on the Princess's dress . . . then they turned to admire her companion in the lemon corded silk dress and the lovely black hat. 'My, but that's smart,' they said — 'who is she?' That was the wife of the Board of Trade . . .
> The Princess remarked on the clothes . . . But it was the late stayers who saw the one-woman fashion show. Lady Shawcross made a second and a grander appearance. She made a quick change into a silver-beaded cyclamen ball gown. And as she came down the crimson carpeted marble staircase, managing her tricky train with the careless grace of a trained model, an American visitor paid tribute: 'Easily among the ten best-dressed women' she said.

Joan showed an astonishing adaptability. She was just as much at home sitting next to Prince Philip at dinner at Buckingham Palace, next to Queen Elizabeth at a country-house weekend listening to Noël Coward, as in the grim tenement of some unemployed miners in Lancashire. It was not an act; she was simply being her natural self, someone who had no side or affectation but liked people for their own sake, irrespective of what they were. And 'My love by her attire did show her wit, For every season she had dressings fit.'

While I was ill in bed in Sussex Joan took my place as the guest speaker at a dinner at the Dorchester of the Wholesale Clothing Manufacturers. Glamorously dressed, she made the main speech for the guests and according to the Press gave them an informal version of my notes. 'What a dreary speech,' she is reported to have said. 'No wonder he took to his bed.' Then she said of her husband that 'the only thing that makes life bearable for him at the Board of Trade is that he can go to dress shows. He's a good judge of women's dresses – but I always wonder whether the interest which sometimes leads him to spend money quite unexpectedly is in the dresses – or the lovely mannequins.'

Earlier that year Joan had been the guest of the furniture manufacturers. 'When', she was reported as asking, 'are you going to design a desk which a woman can put her legs under without getting her nylons laddered?'

On another white-tie occasion at which she again deputized for me, as I had an all-night sitting in the House, Joan had a special success. It was after 2 a.m. and the dinner she was attending at the Grand Hotel in Eastbourne was still going on and she evidently thought it time to return home to Peckhams, where we lived, and which was about 20 miles away. She got up, remarking that she had to go and 'shut the chickens up myself. I was hoping he would do it for me but he says he has an all-night sitting – and that sounds rather like hens.' The Chairman, a knight who shall be nameless, pressed her to let him drive her, but she had her own Jaguar and – wisely – preferred to go alone. The Chairman, evidently a determined man and a bit of a lecher, followed her alone in his own car. At Peckhams, he fell down on the newly tarred and gravelled drive. Fortunately he had been followed by a police car, whether because of his erratic driving or because the Sussex police were very kindly looking after my wife, I don't know. They accomplished both purposes – helping him to stand up and driving him and his car away – thus saving Joan from the awkwardness of shutting the front door in his face or offering him a bed – but not hers – for the night, which I suppose was the object of his exercise.

At Cardiff in July she opened the 1951 Welsh Industries Fair, easily the largest and most ambitious since the event was first staged in 1932. She made a long speech and had a good tale to tell, for unlike recent years, our policies in Wales had been outstandingly successful. She said the Fair would help to demonstrate the tremendous changes that had been brought about by co-operation between Government, industrialists and workforce since the dark days of the thirties when 39 per cent of the population were unemployed: in the Rhondda Valley the number was now down from 11,000 in 1939 to under 2,000 – and so on. But she had her quips too. The *Daily Mail* remarked that

Until recently Lady Shawcross has done little public speaking outside her husband's constituency. [But since he has been at the Board of Trade] he has been handing over his notes to her and she has put over his views on a variety of subjects with charm, confidence and some lively asides of her own. And if she has sometimes found her material to be on the dry side, she has not hesitated to warn her listeners.

Joan was a woman of remarkable loyalty, not only to friends but to causes. I well remember how, later in the 1950s when I was planning to give up my seat in Parliament and was being offered a life peerage by Harold Macmillan, I said, not very seriously, that I might join the Tories. Joan, who had been brought up in a traditionally Tory family, then said that if I did anything of the kind she would at once offer herself to the Labour Party as a candidate for St Helens. That was mainly because of the trust and affection she had formed for the ordinary people of the area – her first real contact with the lives of such people. I am sure she would have romped home with an overwhelming majority far exceeding anything I had won, but I never did cross over to the Tory benches. Of course her loyalty was much more significant than these social occasions indicate. No one will ever know the help and support Joan gave me during the whole of our marriage. Indeed, I did not fully know or appreciate it myself at the time. I owe everything to the three women in my life: my mother, my first wife, who gave up her life for me, and Joan. Joan made me, with whatever significance I ever obtained, and when she died I became again as I am now – nobody. Women have been kind to me throughout my life. After Joan's death I retained three faithful friends who have helped me a lot – one in particular being my regular companion in these declining years – but no one has, or ever could, take the place of Joan.

After a short absence with a virus infection I was back in full harness, visiting Bradford and Manchester for conferences with the wool and the cotton trades – 'The sky's the limit for cotton exports', I told my old family industry in Manchester, having said much the same to the wool trade in Bradford. 'The nation is looking to you!' Did I wear woollen vests and cotton shirts at this time? I hardly recall. In Manchester they made bitter complaints to me of the growing threat of imports from

Japan where girls worked hard in the mills for two and a half pence an hour. I had expressly said in the House that we would not extend 'most favoured nations' treatment to Japan and would retain our right to intro-duce protective legisation against unfair competition. But I had con-cluded by saying that I hoped we would work out policies and procedures on a live-and-let-live basis. I undertook to the trade that we would not set targets for textile exports but that we hoped that even at the expense of diminishing home supplies, exports would be increased.

At the beginning of August I agreed to give another £2 million to the National Film Finance Corporation and, with less popular approval, signed a trade pact with Cuba which was bitterly opposed by West Indian tobacco and sugar interests. No Havana cigars had been imported since the war and this would let about two million in, although many would be re-exported. This was a controversial measure, but what we got in return was an open door for our own exports to Cuba, since she cancelled the preferential tariff favouring the United States.

At long last, on 15 August, I commenced my holiday in Cornwall by giving an address at the opening of the Cornish Industries fair, appearing in a reefer jacket and flannel trousers to emphasize that I was on holiday. And so on to *Vanity* at Falmouth. Joan and I had earned a holiday. It has been a quite exceptionally busy summer for both of us and on the whole a successful one.

Our holidays were not to last long. On 18 August we had a mishap that all too easily could have been a tragedy. Joan and I were living on *Vanity* and were preparing her for a race in the local regatta. The boom, a very lengthy and heavy teak affair which it took at least two men to carry, was taken out of its crutch and suspended by a halyard 'topping lift' about five feet above the deck. Joan, who had been below, climbed up the companionway in the middle of the deck and, at the very moment when she got to the top step, the topping lift broke and the boom crashed down so heavily that, solid teak though it was, it cracked in half when it hit the deck. But before hitting the deck it struck Joan squarely in the middle of the top of the skull. She collapsed and a bump immediately came up the size of a whole egg. I was terrified. We carried her into a dinghy, rowed to the dockside, got into a car and rushed straight to the local hospital. There was no doctor there and no X-ray available. I rushed her on to the General Hospital in Truro and there, by contrast, the attention was immediate and efficient. She was X-rayed and put to bed. The X-rays did not disclose any fracture; I had been particularly frightened at this possibility for she had suffered a skull fracture and mild concussion in a riding accident earlier in the year. It was a miraculous escape. Of course, she was a little concussed, but after a few hours she insisted on leaving the hospital. I persuaded her not to return, as she wanted, to the boat, and she slept that night at my skipper's cottage in Flushing. But next day she insisted on rejoining *Vanity* and after a day or two seemed her normal self again. A week after the accident the *Standard* and other papers published some joyful pictures of Joan, our two children and me swabbing the decks! We got some good sailing.

Early in September I was back at the grindstone. I had agreed to address the Yugoslav lawyers at their annual conferences in Belgrade, my subject being 'Public and Private Legal Freedoms'. On the way to Yugoslavia we stopped in Vienna to attend the opening of Vienna's Trade Fair where the then President, a most charming man, escorted Joan and me around. We stayed most enjoyably at the Embassy for the weekend, and then went on to Belgrade where I gave my address to the lawyers before flying to Zagreb. There was the inevitable trade fair which I think I opened and Tito offered us the use of a large diesel yacht which had been – no doubt illegally – seized from British owners and was now part of the Yugoslav Navy. We joined her at Split accompanied by two or three young lawyers as guides, as well as a full crew and a lot of live chickens in the stern somewhere, to be killed for food. And we set sail. It was a wonderful trip. The Adriatic was practically deserted in those days; the weather was glorious, the sea warm for prolonged swimming. Nor did there seem to be any shortage of food. We picked up lobsters galore from the sea. The trip was memorable for many things. We called at charming villages typically Venetian in their style of architecture, and visited the lovely little islands. Everywhere we got a warm welcome from cheerful locals. There were no tourists; and on shore no food, and no consumer goods. It was pointless to give money, for the locals could buy nothing, but we had come prepared with packets of coffee, combs and other gifts which seemed to be welcome. We cruised as far down the coast as the border with Albania and right up the Gulf of Kotor to the medieval town, since alas destroyed in an earthquake. It is sad indeed to think of that once peaceful country, united under Tito, now rent and torn asunder by ruinous strife.

Back in Britain, the split in the Party had unfortunately become more obvious. Nye Bevan held a megaphone to the whole Party through *Tribune*, in which he wrote frequent and powerful articles. The rearma' ment programme which, under pressure from the United States but also because of our own needs to have credible defences, he had strongly sup' ported when in government, to the extent even of defending the hydro' gen bomb, now came under his attack. The 'Keep Left Group' revived activity in 1951 and became the Bevanite Group, a somewhat mixed bunch which nonetheless tended by its constant nagging to demoralize the Parliamentary party and increase the general scepticism in the country.

The Foreign Office had been a dismal failure for Herbert. He remained too preoccupied with his domestic interests, like the Festival of Britain; he spent too long abroad, including a holiday in Norway which he refused to cut short despite being asked by the Office to return; and his unfamiliarity with the possibilities of foreign policy was obvious. When he asked for Cabinet authority to send gunboats to Abadan fol' lowing Persia's illegal nationalization of the British oil interests, I had to remind him that he could not 'do a Palmerston'. More generally, our one'time American friends – and we had been good friends – were real' izing that Labour could do little and might soon have to go the country again. And so it was. Attlee informed the Cabinet of his intention, mis' taken, as it turned out, and the election was held on 25 October 1951.

The election campaign itself went well. Attlee asked me to make the first Labour election broadcast on television. Anthony Eden gave the first election broadcast ever and I followed the next evening, compèred by Chris Mayhew. The Party was anxious to appeal for votes from the middle and professional classes, and Mayhew's first questions to me were directed to this point. The fact was, of course, that although the Party had been in the main supported by the working class in its earlier days, as its name indicates, our support by this time came from all classes, and we had enjoyed a large measure of support from the middle and the so'called intellectual classes. Indeed, our worry had been that so much of the working'class vote went to the Tories. But the left'wingers had lost us a proportion of the middle'class voters who had flocked to us in 1945.

We had also been concerned at the large increase the Tories seemed to have made in their working-class vote in the earlier election in 1950: nearly two million, it was calculated. At all events, the broadcast was supposed to make a special appeal to the middle classes as their vote seemed likely to determine the result. Mayhew and I were brilliantly coached by a BBC official, Mrs Grace Wyndham-Goldie, who gave both Anthony Eden and ourselves the most expert advice in the use of this new and powerful medium. She eventually became Head of Current Affairs at the BBC.

Clem Attlee wrote to me the next day, saying that everyone was telling him that Chris and I 'had done brilliantly on the television. Congratulations and thanks. Meetings everywhere show great enthusi-asm.'

They did and I was encouraged by them. But the enthusiasm of the meetings was not reflected by the result. Labour was beaten, and so ended the first and most significant of the post-war Labour Governments.

The end of October 1951 thus saw me in Opposition in the Commons. I received another pleasant personal letter in his own hand from Attlee to thank me; I think that in spite of all my blobs and stupid-ities he had always looked kindly on me.

In Opposition I was expected, of course, to sit on the Front Bench and, as is customary, to 'shadow' (although I do not remember that we called it so then) the Government minister who had taken my place. I soon found this distasteful. More often than not I found I was expected to attack the Conservative President of the Board of Trade for action that had no doubt been advised by his permanent officials and which I knew was almost exactly the same as I would have taken myself if I had remained in office. Many of my colleagues enjoyed inventing opportu-nities, however spurious, for this sort of situation. And no doubt for some it can be a fascinating occupation. But I did not take to it. Indeed, it was the more difficult because the Tory Government was in fact often having to pursue much the same policy as we would have done. Rab Butler cut down on various imports, including some food; investment in building and other capital projects was reduced. It might well have been Stafford Cripps. I explained my difficulty to Attlee. After all, I had, in a speech in 1949, said that if a Tory Government were ever elected I would myself support them in any policy that I thought right – if they had any – and this had received much favourable publicity at the time. Attlee understood and, in spite of the fact that I was now a practising lawyer, wrote and asked me to be the Party's spokesman on foreign affairs. Possibly the experience with Herbert had made him think that lawyers could hardly be worse. This suited me much better and I did make occasional speeches in the House and sometimes in the country, but the occasions were getting fewer and fewer. The fact was that my practice at the Bar was mounting up at an extraordinary pace, a flood situation that every barrister who experiences it soon learns is dif-ficult to control. I do not recall that I made any contribution to parlia-mentary debate during this period which had any later significance. But I well recall my return to the Bar.

CHAPTER II

Opposition and Practice, 1951–52

ON the Monday morning after the poll on 25 October I paid a quick visit to the Board of Trade, said goodbye to my officials, and collected a few private papers. I then went straight to my chambers at 4 Paper Buildings and immediately committed my first lapse. As I walked up the steps to the chambers I noticed that there were one or two photographers waiting, but I did not give it a thought. I was so used to being followed by photographers that it did not occur to me on that first morning that I was no longer a minister but was back at my old profession. In those days, publicizing oneself was strictly forbidden, and when the *Evening Standard* published a photograph, with a paragraph stating that I had returned to practise at the Bar, my Chambers being at 4 Paper Buildings and my name being one of those under Sir Patrick Hastings' on the door, it looked like advertising. A complaint was duly made to the Bar Council which courteously accepted my explanation and assurance that it would not happen again. No sooner was I inside the door than another problem confronted me.

On the morning of the election the *Daily Mirror* published, for the second time, on its front page a picture of a large revolver over the caption 'Whose finger on the trigger' and carried an article implying that Winston Churchill was a warmonger and that war would be more likely if he were returned to power. I had hardly reached my desk when a retainer was brought to the Chambers. A retainer is a document which for a very modest fee reserves the barrister's services for a particular client either generally or in relation to some named matter, and which has to be accepted unless there is some professionally correct reason for refusing it. Retainers flooded in all that week, which was encouraging, but this first one that morning was not welcome. It was to represent the *Daily Mirror* in any proceedings that might be taken by Winston Churchill. I was not anxious to appear against Churchill and thought it would be somehow unseemly, but I had no excuse for refusing it and so it was accepted. About half an hour later a second retainer was delivered. This was to represent Winston against the *Daily Mirror*. Although it went against the grain I had no option but to refuse it. Winston then went to Gilbert Paull, who had been my Junior Silk in the Lynskey Tribunal proceedings.

I gave a good deal of thought to what should be done. The offending article was first published during the run-up to the election, a time when a good deal of 'fair comment' is allowed, however unfair some might think it. On the other hand, it might be easy to establish malice, and a jury would be likely to be very much prejudiced in favour of Winston. I thought the chances were that the *Daily Mirror* would lose the action and that we ought to settle. Moreover, I certainly felt that it would be unseemly for the Prime Minister to have to go into the witness box and be cross-examined by a former Opposition Cabinet minister and one-time Attorney General. Indeed, for the Prime Minister to be involved at all was unseemly.

I set about trying to settle the case. I had to persuade Paull to advise Winston to accept an apology, but no damages, and the *Daily Mirror* to make an apology rather than fight a spectacular action. It took some time, but in the end the newspaper very properly agreed to apologize, pay Winston costs and give a small sum to a charity. This was announced in April, and immediately afterwards *Punch*, under the heading 'A Good Man to Have on the Other Side', published an article that quite upset me. After setting out details of my career in a way to which, in itself, I could not object, the last three paragraphs coupled with the title carried – as I expressed it in a letter to Walter Monckton on 16 April – 'the innuendo that I am dishonest in my political and professional life and that I had betrayed my clients in the Churchill–*Daily Mirror* case in order to please my political opponents.' Walter replied that he thought the article offensive and unfunny, but that I could afford to ignore it and should not worry.

But I did worry. I consulted the Lord Chief Justice, the benchers of my Inn and the Bar Council. All gave the same advice, but Norman Birkett (I think it was) made a private approach to *Punch* and the magazine published an apology.

The briefs were continuing to roll in. One I particularly remember astonished my clerk, Matthew Robinson. Imperial Chemical Industries briefed me to defend them in an action for damages brought by a doctor whom they had dismissed from a job as personnel director. As far as I can recall the brief was marked £7,000 and the daily 'refresher' was £700. These were certainly good fees for those days, although mere chickenfeed by comparison with nowadays. My cross-examination of the plaintiff was described by ICI as 'a *tour de force*', so I assume they did not begrudge the fee. We won the case after a strong contest, in which Gerald Gardiner appeared against me.

Then there were the Dockers. Not the union, but the millionaire. Sir Bernard Docker was a harmless enough but rather stupid man, who had followed his more able father as Chairman of B.S.A. and director of the Midland Bank, and was extremely wealthy. He had married a remarkable woman whose two previous husbands, both deceased, had also been millionaires. The Dockers owned a large area of farming land near Salisbury, part of which had been let on an agricultural tenancy to a Mr Douglas Seligman, who had farmed it most successfully, as an integrated part of his much larger farm. Docker, however, had succeeded in getting leave from the Ministry of Agriculture to put an end to the lease. Mr Seligman appealed against this decision to an agricultural tribunal and I was briefed to appear for him and had to cross-examine both Sir Bernard and his Lady. This was quite amusing. In cross-examination, Sir Bernard made it clear that he knew very little about farming. The main product of his large farm seemed to have been butter and cream for his big houses (both of these products were still rationed to ordinary people), one nearby and the other at Hay Hill. At least Lady Docker had learned something practical about farming. She explained that she had been walking in a barn where there were some young pigs and she was bitten on the leg. 'I never knew pigs could bite,' she said. My strongest memory is of Lady Docker's clothes. On the first day she appeared in a designer suit, looking very smart, but nothing like a farmer's wife. The following day, a death occurred in the Royal Family. Now Lady Docker did not in any way – except in her own imagination – belong in court circles, but she appeared before the tribunal in the deepest mourning I have ever seen. The next day this was modified to a sort of semi-mourning, but on the last day, even though the court was still in mourning, she was back to wearing a fashionable suit. I invited the tribunal to conclude that the Dockers were not serious farmers and simply wanted the land back to add to their toys. In the event, the Dockers lost and Seligman kept his lease. I fear that Sir Bernard's personal flag, which, I elicited, was supposed to be raised whenever they entered their own county, did not wave so bravely that night.

I very soon heard from the Dockers again. Their solicitors served me with a general retainer on their behalf which meant that I could never appear against them. The first case came along soon. Sir Bernard was summoned under the exchange control legislation for conspiracy in obtaining foreign currency to cover the expenses of his 870-ton yacht *Shemara* in France. This was a very splendid boat with a crew of about thirty, berthed at Cannes during a large part of the winter with the Dockers on board. It was alleged that some of the expenses were met by each member of the crew purchasing French francs to the value of their maximum foreign exchange allowance, and handing them over to the captain, the sterling being repaid them by the Dockers. Lady Docker admitted that there were significant expenses for food, fuel and so forth which had to be disbursed in France and for which the franc pool was insufficient. 'And how did you pay for those?' asked Sir Laurence Dunne, who heard the case at Bow Street. 'Oh,' replied Lady Docker, 'I paid out of my earnings at the factory.' Sir Laurence, taken a little by surprise, enquired as to what kind of factory she worked in. 'Oh – the Casino,' she replied innocently. The case went on for three days. In the end, Sir Laurence decided that virtually all the money had been spent on food for the crew themselves, although a merely technical offence had been committed in not returning a small unspent balance to certain seamen. Sir Bernard was fined £50 and completely exonerated from any deception or conspiracy. The case, however, caused something of a sensation and did Sir Bernard's reputation no good. Indeed, he was asked to resign from the board of the Midland Bank even before the case was heard.

Lady Docker also sustained a temporary defeat at the time, but it was one she overcame. She had been put forward for presentation to the

Queen on the occasion of the Motor Show but for some reason it was decided that her name should be omitted from the final list. Daimler were exhibiting something that was the height of vulgarity – a gold-plated car. Her Majesty, in her tour of the show, was naturally invited to inspect the Daimler stand, for, next to Rolls-Royce, the company was then the most prestigious British car manufacturer. Refusing to be out-manoeuvred, Lady Docker stood herself at the door of the gold-plated limousine and so she had to be presented.

I recall another occasion when her association with the Royal Family was impressed on my mind. I had for some reason to call on Sir Bernard at Hay Hill and was kept waiting a few minutes in the drawing-room. I noticed what appeared to be an invitation card displayed on the mantelpiece. There was only one, and my curiosity forced me to look and see who it was from. It was an invitation to a garden party at Buckingham Palace, dated five years previously!

The Dockers, of course, are both dead now. He died before she did, of a long illness and old age, and I believe she looked after him well.

I was now earning a great deal more money than I had ever earned in government, but I had not entirely forgotten my political life. Somehow or other I still managed to attend weekend meetings up and down the country, and in Parliament I sat on the front Opposition bench in the evenings as often as I could, though I rarely spoke. When I did speak in the country, I took a pretty detached attitude: 'I do not really pretend to be a good politician,' I am reported as having said at a Labour meeting in Devizes late in 1952. 'I am interested in administration but I can work up no great enthusiasm for destructive criticism or opposition for opposition's sake. I have no political ambitions whatever. I shall continue to serve this Party, in whose basic ideals I deeply believe. But I can say what I think, whether others like it or not, for I have no personal ambitions save one, which it seems, politics or no, I shall not achieve – that of living my own life in peace and privacy in the bosom of my own family.'

From time to time I also made speeches stressing the view I held then that whatever might be thought about nationalization, one parliament ought not to reverse the legislation of its predecessor. On both sides we must avoid being too doctrinaire. My thinking was by this time more moderate and middle-of-the-road. On our side, I said, it would be folly to nationalize the industries on which our exports depended. Nationalization was not an end in itself. Nevertheless, I did lambast the Tories whenever I had the opportunity.

One great interest that I tried to promote was closer co-operation between the United States and Europe. In the summer of 1952 I was the main mover in forming a little organization called Friends of Atlantic Union, and a group of us wrote a long letter to *The Times* setting out our views. Broadly the aim of the group was to promote the expansion of the North Atlantic Treaty Organization into an Atlantic community, a comprehensive partnership with its own organs of consultation and eco-nomic co-operation embracing 'the democracies of free Europe, of the British Commonwealth of Nations and the United States of America'. This letter was published in *The Times* on 17 July 1952. It was signed by Lord Halifax, Ralph Assheton, Hugh Gaitskell, Arthur Deakin, Lincoln Evans, Joseph Grimond, Lord Robbins, Rebecca West, and others. I was the Chairman, Lord Tweedsmuir the Vice-Chairman, and Sigmund Warburg the Treasurer.

However, this was extra-parliamentary work, and although I did go to the House as frequently as I could, I was there far less often, and there was a good deal of criticism. Dalton was active in expressing his dis-approval. In his diary entry for 23 March 1953 he records a conversation with Gaitskell and Blenkinsop.

> Talk turned to Shawcross. H.G. praises him highly, thinks he has not only a very remarkable legal brain, easily best at the Bar but that he is also a national figure and as such of great value to the Party. I criticise him. His neglect of his Parliamentary duties has become an obvious scandal. He should not have rejected both the Lord Chief Justiceship and the Mastership of the Rolls when Attorney General. A Socialist Judge of high intelligence might have done things for the interpreta-tions of the law.

He nearly did me the kindness of crediting me with high intelligence! Gaitskell held to his views. It is true that I might have accepted the ten-tative offer (tentative in the sense that the PM made it in a way that sug-gested I should decline – 'I don't suppose you want it, do you? No. Good!') to become Lord Chief Justice in 1946 or Master of the Rolls in 1949. But even years later Attlee still thought I should remain in politics. On 3 April 1951 he had written to me concerning another possible appointment:

> . . . I am, selfishly, glad that you do not wish to go on the Bench as I am sure your continued activity in the Government is of great service to the Party. Thank you for your suggestion for the vacancy. I will discuss this with the Lord Chancellor. I hope your duodenum keeps quiet. I hope mine will settle down soon.

But other more significant things were taking place in my life while Dalton attacked me, which he had been doing ever since the Lynskey Tribunal.

On 19 March 1953 our third child was born. When Joanna had been born five years earlier, Joan had had to interrupt a bridge party to produce her. On this occasion it was a dinner party. But it was all over very quickly and before the doctor, hastily summoned, had arrived. The *Evening Standard* described it like this:

> The telephone rang in a flat at Dolphin Square. The time was 11.15 last night. Sir Hartley Shawcross QC MP picked up the receiver. He was in full evening dress having just returned from the Pilgrims dinner at the Savoy. Over the phone Sir Hartley heard the voice of his wife; speaking from their 14th century home in Sussex, Lady Shawcross told her husband she had given birth to a 7lb 6ozs boy 15 minutes ago. . . . Friends telephoning their home today had a surprise. She answered the calls herself. Sir Hartley (51) will not see his new son till tomorrow. He was in Court all today. Tonight he has a speaking engagement.

I seem to have taken it very casually. But it was a great joy to both of us. We called him Hume, after his maternal grandfather who, unhappily, had died a short time before.

Two days later something happened which I could not take casually. On the Sunday morning a Sussex friend telephoned and asked 'How is Superman today?' I did not understand and asked what he was talking about. He replied that I should read my *Sunday Express*. I turned to it at once. And there was the following column under a rather good photograph of me. (I quote it now only because of its repercussions.)

Man or Superman?
Look at this face. A face of many talents.
The face of a man at the height of his brilliant career.
The face of Sir Hartley Shawcross.
Admired by the Tories and Socialists alike, feared – and dismissed – as counsel in the courts. Hartley Shawcross has stepped into the stream of great lawyer-politicians.
In the steps of F. E. Smith, Carson, and Simon, he has risen in stature at the Bar and Westminster.
He prosecuted Goering, Ribbentrop, and Hess at Nuremberg.
He was for the Crown against the traitors William Joyce and Klaus Fuchs.
Haigh, the acid-bath murderer, faced his cross-examination – and went to the gallows.
And who can forget his cut-and-thrust with Sidney Stanley at the Lynskey Tribunal?
He has also appeared for (and against) Sir Bernard Docker, for J. Arthur Rank, for Anglo-Iranian in the Abadan oil suit.
Where is he going, this glittering, brilliant barrister, still only 51?
The *Sunday Express* is to publish the full, fascinating story of this extraordinary man. Written by Woodrow Wyatt, M.P., under the title of
Shawcross
Man or Superman?
It is frank, intimate and authoritative. And it begins NEXT WEEK.

I was embarrassed and ashamed. But at the time I do not think I appreciated that, apart from inviting ridicule because of its exaggerated terms, it might do me serious harm.

The following day I had a case in the Privy Council, my opponent being D. N. Pritt, QC. Pritt was then a Senior Silk and a formidable advocate; I was often pitted against him. He was, however, a leading Communist, a man at the very centre of an organized conspiracy of intellectuals engaged in political espionage and propaganda for the Russians.

In other respects, he was a genuinely kind and thoughtful man, although perhaps if the Communists had won, he would have had us all strung up on lamp-posts. But it would have been done with velvet ropes and the utmost of good fellowship. Pritt pointed out that the article would do me infinite harm professionally. It would be regarded as blatant advertising, earn the disapproval of the judges, and it would do me no good in politics. He said that if he had been in my shoes he would have abandoned the Privy Council case and gone out at once to move heaven and earth to stop the publication. And that is what I did, although Woodrow Wyatt and I were then and remain good friends. At this point I will let Dick Crossman, whose diaries, written while he was still an MP, attracted much discussion, take over the story, although his account is not entirely accurate.

(Extracts from *The Crossman Diaries*)
Harold Keeble (Editor of the paper) was away ill when somebody changed the proposed title to 'Man or Superman'. It was this title which caught the attention of Sir Walter Monckton (Note: Conservative MP for Bristol West 1951–7, he was Minister of Labour and National Service 1951–5, Minister of Defence 1955–6 and Paymaster General 1956–7. He became a Viscount in 1957. He died in 1965) who has never much liked Hartley's behaviour, who raised the matter at the Bar Council of which Hartley is Chairman. Hartley got cold feet, went to the *Sunday Express* and begged them not to publish, stating that he was a sick man and that his doctor had warned him that he might die if he had any shocks. The *Sunday Express* was going to publish until Max Aitken (Note: the son of Lord Beaverbrook . . . etc.) was rung up by Churchill who pleaded that the decorum of the Bar should be observed. Of course the unsolved problem is why should Churchill want to save Hartley from the predicament he has placed himself in? That's anybody's guess.

Walter Monckton had not, so far as I know, ever 'disliked my behaviour'. On the contrary, he was a close friend of Joan's and mine. Nor did he 'take the matter up at the Bar Council'. What in the end stopped the *Sunday*

Express was Winston's personal intervention with Lord Beaverbrook. What puzzled Crossman was why Winston should have intervened.

Since the *Sunday Express* agreed not to publish I did not mind what the other papers did, for by now it was clear to everybody that I was dead against any such publicity, although, because of the suppression, I received far more publicity than I would previously have had.

'Cassandra (William Connor), then a leading columnist in the *Daily Mirror*, wrote fairly enough that the suppression was preposterous, and said of me that:

> This is the very man who said 'On the whole I think we have a very fine Press. It cannot be bought and it cannot be bullied. Nobody contemplates for a moment any curtailment of the absolute freedom of opinion or the right of the Press to say exactly what it thinks.' Nobody but who? He also said that 'public men must put up with much harsh comment.'

Since the *Sunday Express* had, in announcing the article, already described him as 'brilliant' and as one who has followed 'in the steps of F. E. Smith, Carson and Simon' he would not have much score for complaint on this ground.

In 1946 Sir Hartley Shawcross condemned wildly and roundly parts of the Press and specifically singled out the Beaverbrook Press 'for distorting news, suppressing the evidence and the facts and giving importance to their own political opinions.'

Yet in 1951 we find him graciously commending the Beaverbrook Press for 'exhibiting a refreshing and stimulating independence which causes consternation to the Conservative Party.'

There you have it.

Praise and condemnation. Pats and clouts. Caresses and kicks. All mixed up with a brave stirring call for the Freedom of the Press that dies in his throat when a well-known writer in a well-known newspaper wishes to comment on the life of a well-known man.

Man or Superman?

Man – fallible, changeable man.

The publicity engendered by the affair went on for weeks. Little of it was unfair and most of it was flattering. I could not have objected to it and I came to wonder whether D. N. Pritt had not alarmed me too much about the original articles.

My practice went on. The cases varied greatly. I represented the Government of Ceylon before the Privy Council; the Income Tax Commissioners of Australia, again in the Privy Council; the trade unions and some Labour MPs for libel, including the lively Mrs Braddock who had organized the dockers' successful defence against the charges I had eventually felt forced to bring against them (she remained – in spite of her very left-wing vision – a good friend and always gave me a pot of raspberry jam when I went up to Liverpool). Naturally enough, I was attacked by some in the Labour Party for accepting briefs in cases antagonistic to Labour ideals; one Scottish group of local parties put down a resolution for the Party's annual conference condemning me for this.

A particular instance arose in the case of Jomo Kenyatta, the Mau Mau rebel leader from Kenya whom the then Government was prosecuting. I was asked if I would appear for the Government and said that although I had other engagements I would if the Government felt it necessary. For this I was bitterly attacked, and when I explained that I was simply adhering to an established and traditional role (the cab rank principle) I was ridiculed. *Tribune*, the Bevanite journal, said I had invented the rule myself!

What my dear friends in the Labour Party would have said had they known that I was occasionally actually acting very privately, informally and of course without payment for Winston Churchill at the time I cannot imagine. But they were not supposed to know, and I never said a word about it. Now that one such matter has been alluded to in a recently published biography, I feel I am free to refer to it myself.

The fact is that at some date after his return to office Winston spoke to me quite informally, but as one parliamentarian and Privy Councillor to another, about some little problems the details of which I do not recall. One thing can lead to another and, in the later part of 1952, a problem did arise which caused me a good deal of anxiety on Winston's behalf. It concerned Major-General Dorman-Smith who had been Deputy Chief of General Staff to Lieutenant-General Sir Claude (later Field Marshal) Auchinleck who, at the material time, was Commander-in-

Chief British Forces in Egypt. Popularly known in the army as Chink, Dorman-Smith was an Irishman with all the impetuosity, but also the brilliance, often associated with his countrymen. There is no doubt that he was largely responsible for the planning of the campaign against Rommel while Auchinleck was in command. But he was no respecter of persons and had somewhat advanced or unorthodox views on military matters. Consequently, he made enemies. Churchill was at the time of the Desert Campaign very much impressed with General Montgomery, whom he sent out to replace Auchinleck. Discussing this period in the fourth volume of his *History of the Second World War*, Churchill had written very critically of the Auchinleck command. Chink was greatly upset. He had been in effect compulsorily retired to the reserve, demoted in rank and taken out of the war. At the time he had attributed this to jealousy and ill-will in the military hierarchy led by Monty, but on reading Winston's book he found that he had been mentioned adversely in dispatches and that he had been sacked with Churchill's approval. Now let Chink's biographer take up the story:

'The Hinge of Fate', the fourth volume of Churchill's *History of the Second World War*, was published in July 1951. Flipping through to the pages that interested him, Chink learned that his name had been included in Cabinet despatches and that he had been sacked not by the military hierarchy, as he had always supposed, but on Churchill's recommendation. The personal revelation was less important, however, than the slur on Auchinleck's reputation, and an entry in a subsequent chapter steeled him to sue for libel. 'I am sure,' Churchill had written, 'we were heading for disaster under the former regime. The Army was reduced to bits and pieces and oppressed by a sense of bafflement and uncertainty. Apparently it was intended in the face of attack to retire eastwards to the Delta . . . Many were looking over their shoulders to make sure of their seat in the lorry and no plain plan of battle or dominating willpower had reached the units.'
. . .

On May 1953 a formal complaint was made on Chink's behalf that, unless amendments were forthcoming, proceedings for libel would be instituted. Any settlement would have to produce a public apology and the withdrawal of that volume in its present form.

Letters went out to Churchill as author, Cassells as publishers and Hodges Figgis as booksellers, claiming that readers would come to the conclusion that he was one of those primarily responsible for the disasters of Gazala and Tobruk, and had failed in his duties as Deputy Chief of Staff. Action was reserved against the American publishers and distributors.

It would be a sensational humiliation for England if the Prime Minister had to give evidence in a Dublin court, and damage to the British Army would also be unavoidable since the case could end with half the army in court on one side and half on the other. But there was a more humane reason for keeping the seventy-nine-year-old premier out of the witness box. Shawcross had been present at the dinner party earlier that month when Churchill suffered his second stroke and, through being in the confidence of Lord Moran, Churchill's doctor, he knew him to be on a knife-edge. The likelihood that the case could take as long as two years to reach court added to the health risk, and his predicament was exacerbated by the fact that news of the stroke had been kept secret from the public; even to the Cabinet. Churchill's absence had been attributed to severe overstrain, and it had been kept out of the press through the co-operation of the newspaper owners Beaverbrook, Camrose and Bracken. The plaintiff did not know it, and could not be informed.

The dignified Shawcross flew to Dublin in the first week of November 1953 to mediate, paying for his own fare. Over lunch with Chink and Sir John Esmonde at the Shelbourne it was agreed that a writ would not be issued if an acceptable footnote were inserted and Liddell Hart was agreed upon as a suitable interpreter of historical accuracy; drafts from Dublin would be submitted first. 'Sir Hartley Shawcross went to Dublin last week, and came back to find a fine crop of rumours about his visit', reported the *Daily Express*. 'Some said he had gone to see about the transfer of the remains of Sir Roger Casement, hanged for treason here in 1916, back to Ireland. Others said that he had an Irish grandmother. Sir Hartley has countered with the story that he went over to see if Irish girls are as beautiful and as charming as he had been led to believe.'

Behind the scenes, the first two drafts found no common ground. But Liddell Hart advised Chink to accept the third. 'The references to officers,' it ran, 'are factual only, and are not to be taken as imput/ing personal blame to any individual. . . . Major/General Dorman/Smith did not become Deputy Chief of Staff until after the fall of Tobruk and he had no responsibility there or at Gazala. He was sub/sequently appointed to a command in Italy.' Shawcross, too, advised that it was the most that could be expected. '[Winston] felt some doubt as to the last sentence . . . [about] Italy . . . in view of what hap/pened,' he soothed. 'I am afraid there is no prospect of the PM feeling able to go beyond the substance of the present note.' And by 12 March 1954 Chink had accepted it, after an amendment to the second last sentence, after his name, to read: 'only became Deputy Chief of Staff on 16 June 1942. He thus bears no responsibility for the fall of Tobruk or the defeat of Gazala. From 25 June–4 August he acted as General Auchinleck's principal operations officer at HQ Eighth Army'.

But a libel action still appeared unavoidable, because Chink was adamant about the need to rectify the 'retreat to the delta' slur, and here Liddell Hart, who had been translating Rommel's papers and knew the other side of the story, was wholeheartedly in agreement. 'The sentence *does* read like an imputation of funk,' he appealed to Shawcross. 'So his reaction is very natural and one that the PM of all men should be able to understand sympathetically.' The blandish/ment was wasted. On 29 March Churchill refused to alter a word, and Liddell Hart was prevailed upon to act as honest broker once more.

Again Shawcross judged that the moment was ripe for personal intervention, and to prevent the press tracking him as before he arranged a seat over on a freight plane, travelling incognito. Chink had agreed to a private meeting in the home of Churchill's solicitor on Howth Head outside Dublin, and when Shawcross landed at the private airfield of Baldonnel on 2 May he was driven straight there. The two men went into the dining room, and closed the door.

'It became clear that he was not acting because he had been slighted, but on principle on behalf of Auchinleck,' Shawcross said subsequently, emphasising that he had made no notes at the time. 'I was feeling very distressed myself – in fact I was near to tears. I was fighting quite a battle for the old man. But I felt I must go on until we'd reached either an agreement or a decision . . . I wasn't going to get very far playing on his heartstrings to win sympathy, and I thought he would insist on his pound of flesh whatever I said. I don't nor-mally pace around the room. But I did feel unhappy about it, and I did feel it was going to be extremely hard to justify the paragraph in the book.' Anxious to finish the case once and for all, Shawcross was prepared to settle, but the frailty of Churchill's health had now become public knowledge, which strengthened his hand.

Admitting from the start that Chink had a complaint, he coun-tered by asking if he was prepared to sully the reputation of the army and take the responsibility for Churchill having a fatal stroke in public. He had summed up his adversary well. Chink's code of chivalry won out, and after several hours he capitulated and they shook hands. Having given away his advantage, all he gained in correction of the insult to Auchinleck's generalship was one short sentence – 'My appreciation . . . of the handling of Eighth Army is supported by Rommel's remarkable tribute' – which was to appear beneath his other footnote, putting it out of context.

'We reached agreement on a form of words,' Shawcross informed Liddell Hart. 'I undertook to put this to the PM . . . I liked him [Chink] personally and had some sympathy with the position in which he found himself.' And grudgingly Churchill gave his consent, after consulting with Alexander. As he said in his letter of thanks to Liddell Hart, he had never wished to hurt Chink but nor had he considered him a factor of any importance in his narrative.

All this time I did shamefully little in the House of Commons and was regularly paired, but I managed to speak at a lot of meetings all over the country at weekends. My speeches were much disliked by the left wing. At the annual commemoration of the Tolpuddle Martyrs I was invited as the principal speaker, and Joan and I walked in the proces-sion through the then still-picturesque Dorset village. In my speech I condemned the proposal, part of Labour policy, to nationalize agricul-tural land, saying that the State would not be a good landlord and that nationalization would create an inefficient overstaffed bureaucracy. I said that nationalization would only be applied to those industries which, after careful enquiry, it was clear that the State could conduct more efficiently, not just as part of 'some woolly and doctrinaire theory'. I said on another occasion that 'soaking the rich was outmoded.' Again, when it was proposed to raise the pay of judges by £1,000 a year, I made a strong speech to the effect that the increase was not enough if we were to hope to recruit the best people to the Bench. All this was not palatable to the Left. But eventually it all became part of the official policy. Indeed, official and left-wing policy became increasingly discordant during this period.

At Christmas I was invited to accept an honorary degree at Columbia University and to give an address; I naturally accepted this flattering honour. I managed so to arrange my affairs that I would be away for about a month visiting a number of different places in various parts of the States to make speeches – mainly about foreign affairs and the United Nations – but also about British politics.

Joan came with me, and, as always, was a very great companion and help. On the day before we sailed – I think it was on the *Queen Mary* on New Year's Eve – I received a message from Lady (Nancy) Astor, saying that she was going to be on the boat accompanied by her grandson, Lord Willoughby de Eresby. He was only seventeen and Nancy asked whether we would sit at her table and 'look after him'. I had hoped that Joan and I would have been able to enjoy each other's company alone in the Verandah Grill; but naturally we had to agree to help with the boy. We all dined at a small table; Joan and I bravely (but silently) defied Nancy's teetotalism and had a bottle of claret for dinner each night, while Nancy and the boy drank nothing. After dinner Nancy went to her cabin and we took the boy up to the Grill. I remember saying to him the first time, 'I expect now you would like to have a drink with us.' He replied without hesitation, 'Oh, I arranged all that with my steward before I left my cabin,' and he produced a flask of whisky from his hip pocket. He drank a good deal but not to obvious excess, although what went on in his cabin I naturally did not know. I do not recall seeing Willoughby again, but we were deeply saddened years later to hear how in St Tropez, during extremely bad weather and having perhaps had too much to drink, he had taken himself out in his motor launch, left the harbour and was never heard of again. I always thought it was a fairly typical case of over-strict and rigid control during adolescent years having exactly the opposite effect to that intended. Nancy Astor was a truly remarkable woman, and although in some ways a crank, she played a very significant part as the first woman MP to sit in the British Parliament. Although we were on opposite sides politically, she was kind to me and I liked and admired her.

CHAPTER 12

Politics and After 1952–57

THIS trip to the United States was intended mainly as an interlude after a pretty hectic year, and for Joan as something of an adventure too, for she had never been to the States. For Joan, as for anyone imaginative seeing the States for the first time, it was an exciting experience, as was the discovery that although most American towns are very different from New York, all Americans are welcoming and friendly. On our departure from Southampton she was asked by the Press whether she intended to buy clothes in America. To this she is reported to have said 'No. I cannot afford the dollars and I am going to show the Americans we also can dress.' It was duly reported that she was wearing a dark grey costume, green hat, tweed coat and new black shoes. She had of course taken a suitable wardrobe – no doubt I thought too large – and she certainly got plenty of opportunity of showing that she could dress. According to Elsa Maxwell's famous column:

> Hamilton Fish Armstrong gave a dinner the other night for the Hartley Shawcrosses. 'Ham' Armstrong, who publishes 'Foreign Affairs', knows a lot about them. Sir Hartley's speech, which I heard the other night, was magnificent. The John Russells also gave a cocktail party in their honour; Sir Gladwyn Jebb gave them a dinner in Riverdale. I took them to dinner at the Pavilion, a theatre and then wound up for supper at El Morocco (which is the ambition of every visiting fireman).

The primary reason, however, for the visit was for me to receive the honorary LL.D. and deliver the promised address at the bicentennial celebration of Columbia University. The celebration included a two-day conference on the conflict between free thought and national security, a variant on the theme of the University's motto – 'Man's right to knowledge and the free use thereof'. It was the stated intention of the University that it should lead to discussion bearing upon the intemperate McCarthy campaign against Communism, a subject in which I was extremely interested.

In my speech I indirectly attacked the McCarthy campaign for the repression of Communism by contrasting it with British practice which sought to reconcile security with toleration. I said that the Communists were working in two ways to apply their techniques: within nations, by trying to destroy the sense of mutual confidence between citizens and breaking down acceptance of decency and fair play, which was the only basis on which democracy really works; and between nations, by trying to drive a wedge between Europe, especially Britain, and the United States. They did this not through avowed Communist organs but through those who, whether Communists or not, were playing the Party's game of undermining confidence and democracy. I then gave a fairly detailed presentation of our philosophy and method in regard to subversion. I emphasized that all parties in Britain agreed that repressive measures would make the danger to our way of life the greater, and that on the whole our community accepted the fact that if we claim the right to propagate the ideas with which we agree, we must accord to others a similar right to propagate ideas with which we disagree. 'The best way is to have a people with the light of knowledge in their eyes undivided by fear or suspicions of each other but united in their love of liberty, their "loins girt with truth".' While we did not deny a man's right to preach Communism, we did claim the right to choose whom we thought fit to be employed in sensitive positions by the State.

My other speeches both to organizations in New York and in some Mid-Western towns were about the British economy and our policy generally.

The last case of interest I had before leaving for America had concerned the Savoy Hotel. Mr Harold Samuel, a well-known West End property magnate, was seeking to take over the group (Savoy, Claridges, Berkeley, Simpson's, Stone's Chop House, and others). As part of the strategy to defeat the bid, the Savoy directors had apparently formed a new company called Worcester Buildings which acquired the Berkeley and Stone's Chop House from the Savoy in exchange for preference shares that were closely held and dominated by this company. The object of the manoeuvre was to put the Berkeley and Stone's beyond the reach of Mr Samuel and so destroy a vital part of his scheme for redevelopment. I had no interest in the case beyond hoping that the Samuel bid would not succeed, for I was a personal friend of the Savoy Group's Chairman, Hugh Wontner, later Sir Hugh, and was a regular user of the Savoy. One Friday before Christmas my clerk, Matthew Robinson, came in to tell me that Samuel's advisers wanted to retain me and that it was essential to have a consultation on the following day. I said, 'No – I don't want to be involved in the case – say I am too busy, not in town on Saturday, going away – any decent excuse.' After a few minutes Matthew came back and said that Samuel's people would not take no for an answer. I could not completely shut my mind to the 'cab rank' rule. But, on the other hand, I could perhaps say that there were no cabs on the rank on Saturdays. So I told Matthew to tell them that I could only see them in the country and, if they swallowed that, to quote a prohibitive fee. No good. They 'liked the country', and the size of the fee was irrelevant to Mr Samuel. So on the Saturday the advisers – I think three of them – duly arrived and when they explained the facts of the matter I was astonished to realize that the Savoy transaction was quite clearly illegal. Just then, Lord Goddard (who was spending the weekend at Peckhams as he often did) passed by the window for all to see. This – apart from boosting my prestige in the eyes of my clients – reminded me of the importance of being firmly in the right! And so I said, 'The Savoy Group's scheme is clearly invalid: you should at once inform the Savoy's people that you are going to the court to have it set aside.' I was afraid that this would at once be done and that they would come back to me with the brief as soon as I returned from New York. However, when I did return, I was informed that Mr Samuel had decided not to proceed with his bid. His reasons were not fully explained to me, but I think he did not want to be responsible for what would have been rather painful and disagreeable publicity for the Savoy which at that time was the most prestigious hotel group in the business.

I was very relieved at the outcome, but I think that the size of my fee must have got around. One of the Sunday papers had a ridiculous gossip paragraph which wildly exaggerated my earnings:

Over the Bar Counter:
  All hail, Sir Hartley. The Bar, like other institutions, is not what it was. The glamour, the causes célèbres, the special juries – all these have largely gone. But on the Shawcross level the old magic lingers. The other night he was talking at Oxford (to the Labour Club) – 'I suffer,' he said, 'from the usual defect of the lawyer in politics – I usually see two sides to each question.'
  But Sir Hartley – just back from America with an honorary LL.D. from Columbia University – makes his money and his reputation by arguing only one side of the question. In past months he has fought brilliant cases for the Anglo Iranian Oil Company and British Drug Houses Ltd. Two weeks ago he won a case for the Australian Government. How much has this brilliant man with his superb mind made during the past year?
  I believe he has surpassed the average earnings of the highest-paid advocate of our time, Lord Simon.
  Last year I estimate Sir Hartley's earnings at more than £60,000.

Sixty thousand pounds was worth many times what that sum represents in these inflationary days. It was a lot of money, and statements like this not only alerted the tax inspectors, but did me no good at all with the Labour Party. What most people then and now failed to understand was that I never managed to save a penny. Not only was there a marginal income tax rate at over 80 per cent, but the tax on any investment income, if I had found it possible to save, would have been at 98 per cent. Indeed, at one point, income of over £20,000 was taxed at £1.06 on each £1! This only encouraged one either to work too hard, or not to work at all. And when I had paid my taxes I had heavy expenses to meet. It is true that I was not living in a particularly modest way: an apartment in London, a country house, a yacht, two cars, two or more horses, nannies and staff. My dedicated Socialist friends still thought I should have given up such a way of life and gone to live modestly in Lewisham, letting Joan do the housework and nannying and sending the children to the local State schools. I dare say they were right, but I did not, and do not now, feel I could have developed the sort of practice I had if I had lived in that way. It would have meant a complete change in my whole philosophy and mode of life which I was too selfish to contemplate. And at that time, of course, I wanted to make comfortable provision for Joan, who I expected to long outlive me. So there it was, and such paragraphs in the Press did me much harm with my colleagues in the House.

My speeches did not help either. I tried to make up for my shocking silence in the House by continuing to make speeches all over the country, all arranged for me by Transport House, who were constantly urging me to do even more. I was increasingly taking a middle course, however, and two such moderate speeches of mine were given publicity in the Press, having been circulated in advance by the Labour Party. I returned to my old themes of falling standards. I referred to the old moral values, to the importance of marriage, working hard and responsibly at the work we were paid for, not keeping our eyes constantly on the clock. In Swansea I had spoken about shipyards, maintaining that the reason why our yards were doing so badly was that our costs made us uncompetitive. I commented: 'This is no political matter. We cannot say that the whole fault lies with the organization of industry or that nationalization would provide any solution. Largely it is a matter of individual responsibility on the part of all of us, management and men, in our particular job.'

At this time Attlee asked me personally to wind up a debate in the House on a motion on East–West trade. I was greeted with what a newspaper called a 'zephyr' of a cheer, but I made what all the newspapers seem to have considered was a good and thoughtful speech. Sir Walter Fletcher, a Tory MP for one of the Lancashire constituencies, who preceded me, remarked that

> The House would have the unusual pleasure of having the debate wound up by Sir Hartley Shawcross, the coelacanth of the Labour party. The coelacanth was a fish which was supposed to be extinct because it had never appeared for 10 millions years. Then it suddenly arrived large and important with a look of amazement and consternation on its face on finding where it was. Then it returned to the cavernous depths of the law again, never to be seen for many years.

William Joyce, 'Lord Haw Haw', arriving at a hospital near Lüneburg after his capture.

John George Haigh, manacled to a police detective, arriving at Horsham Crown Court to face a charge of murder.

With Joan and our children, William, Joanna and Hume in the early fifties.

Shaking hands with Winston Churchill at Bristol University, 1955.
The author has just received an Hon. Degree of Doctor of Law.

With Joan

Vanity V

Fun and games on Vanity V in the
early fifties.

Stephen Ward

Christine Keeler in 1963

On elephants in Cambodia with Tony and Christiane Besse.

With Joan and her horse at Friston, our second home in Sussex.

FELIX TOPOLSKI

Three cartoons

MARC

My ninetieth birthday

Still sailing.
At the tiller on my last boat, Talisker, in 1994.

The closing words from the Opposition side would be very important in this debate.

I tried to answer it in the same spirit:

The debate is now to be distinguished, if I understood Sir Walter
Fletcher aright, by the maiden swim of a political coelacanth. This is
a remarkable fish having long life and great endurance. It never
deserts its home: unlike the political minnows who drift and paddle
in more stagnant, if bluer waters, it never speaks unless it has something to say: and it has a sting in its tail which it uses, not with reckless prodigality but when occasion requires.

I added, however, that on this occasion the sting would not be needed
because there had been general agreement not bedevilled by party political considerations.

It was reported that Attlee and Morrison were delighted with the
speech and had welcomed me with open arms.

What effect this success had on my general standing in the Party I am
not sure. In the House itself I was not popular among the Labour back
benches for the very understandable reason that I left them to do all the
donkey work, labouring until late into the night for a miserable salary,
while I was attending to my own business and only turning up in the
House on prestigious occasions. I dare say that my success in extra-parliamentary political activities also caused some jealousy. Although I
could not understand my apparent popularity at Labour meetings I was
in increasing demand for weekend speeches and Transport House was
sending me up and down the country almost every weekend. I was
invited for a second time to the Durham Miners Gala in the summer,
which attracted on this occasion the enormous audience of 65,000.
Invitations to the Gala were greatly coveted. My speeches were increasingly serious and moderate, almost right-wing: I advocated systems of
payment by results and incentive taxation; I supported the retention of
the H-bomb while the Soviets had one and supported the entry of West
Germany into the European Defence Community with a right to rearm;
I consistently urged full political and economic co-operation with the
United States. I bitterly attacked Communism but advocated increased

trade with Russia. I urged the Party to seek to be less divisive: to abandon the cliques and clans in which they were dividing themselves and get back to the old spirit of Socialist unity on the basis of fair and practicable policies.

Towards the end of July there was a welcome break. I had been invited to give the inaugural address at the annual conference of the International Bar Association to be held in Monaco. I chose as my topic the role of international law in foreign affairs. Joan and I spent a very happy two or three days in Nice together on this occasion.

Soon after our return, the parliamentary session ended and the law courts adjourned for the Long Vacation. Off we went on the good ship *Vanity V*, still I think without rails, fully 'in class' as a twelve-metre. The children were on board, and our destination was Brittany.

The first stop was Guernsey, a lovely island but not very good as an anchorage for a deep-keeled yacht such as mine (we drew ten feet). We had previously had unfortunate experiences in Guernsey, having once been weather-bound for no less than three weeks. In the end I had to fly home leaving Joan in charge with my skipper, Walter Paull, two sea cadets and two young children. This summer all was well on our outward-bound voyage but on our return, after an agreeably placid visit to St Malo and the north Brittany coast, we were not so fortunate. Joanna, then aged six, got a virus infection. She was taken ashore in the ambulance launch, and wrapped up in a cocoon of blankets and hot-water bottles; 'I don't want to be tied up like a parcel!' she protested. She was at once admitted to the Queen Elizabeth Hospital in St Peter Port, where it was confirmed that she had pneumonia. Her condition became quite serious and for a time Joan slept in the hospital. As soon as the fever started to abate I had to go back to England to fill pressing engagements, leaving Joan in St Peter Port until Joanna was fit enough to fly back. I took *Vanity* back short-crewed, so I divided my time between the cockpit and the galley. It was an uneventful, if rather rough, trip. I made shepherd's pie for my son William; it was extremely good – I remain the acknowledged expert in my family on shepherd's pie.

By early September we were all back in our respective harnesses, then early in October I was off to the United States on another of my speaking trips for British Information Services. My cuttings book – which Joan kept up assiduously – reminds me of one occasion in particular.

This was at the Harvard Club where the theme was foreign affairs, with special reference to China whose Communist Government had been recently recognized by Britain. There was a danger of some difference of view as to China's right to a permanent seat on the Security Council. Since Britain had recognized China she had received little in return save increasing attempts to stir up trouble in Malaysia and elsewhere. Yet there was a growing opinion in most countries that if the Chinese Communist Government made some contribution in deeds rather than words to the easing of tensions in Asia, then she should be allowed a seat at the United Nations. The present position made nonsense of the facts, and in the meantime it would be better to leave the seat empty rather than have it occupied by those who did not have, and seemed never likely to have, any effective government over the whole of China. There were, of course, many in the United States who advocated seating the remnants of the Chiang Kai-shek regime, and my speech was intended as a response to their view. The UN was not a political club of like-minded people. On the contrary, it was the one place where people with very different minds might get together to talk about their differences. I developed this policy and finished on another of my favourite themes: namely, that the British and the other free democracies could hardly hope to survive save in association with the United States.

My main impression of this visit was the nervousness of the Americans about our attitude towards China. America, of course, is much nearer to China than we are. The Americans suffered heavy losses in Korea and they were suspicious of anything on our part which suggested appeasement.

On my return to England, I was involved in an important case concerning the Comet aircraft crashes. The Comet was a wonderful aircraft – the world's first scheduled jet airliner – and it gave Britain an immediate advance on America. The jet engine itself had, of course, been developed, largely by Britain, for military aircraft, but this was the first large passenger carrier flying international routes. Unfortunately, it met with a series of disasters. One aircraft crashed near Calcutta, another into the sea off Elba. These accidents, involving the deaths of all on board, seem to have occurred when the aeroplanes were reaching cruising altitude. After the Elba crash the Air Registration Board withdrew the Comet's licence to carry passengers while a careful investigation was made by

BOAC, De Havilland and the Board into the likely cause of the accident. The Board's minutes stated that everything humanly possible had been done to ensure the desired standards of safety, but in the end seven possible causes were identified as having been capable of causing the accident and modifications were introduced to remedy these. The Board then reissued the licence. But there was a third disaster when a Comet crashed into fairly shallow water off Naples. The Government decided to set up a formal public inquiry and appointed Lionel Cohen, a most able Lord of Appeal, to be the Commissioner with three distinguished experts as assessors. Many leaders of the Bar were there, about twenty in all, to represent the various interested parties. I appeared for De Havilland, the company that built the Comet. A remarkable feature of the inquiry was that it had been possible to salvage a very large part of the aircraft from the bottom of the sea. This had been done with great skill and care by the Navy, and the wings and numerous broken pieces of fuselage were stuck together on a moulding by the Royal Aircraft Establishment at Farnborough, thus permitting a minute and detailed examination. Sir Arnold Hall was then the Director of the Establishment, and he was the most significant witness at the inquiry. He was obviously a man of the very greatest ability. In addition to the reconstructed aircraft from the Naples crash, the Establishment had had and flown a prototype and it submitted another fuselage to tank tests at Farnborough to simulate the changes in pressure that would actually occur when the aircraft was climbing or descending. It was then carefully monitored for signs of fatigue. Sir Arnold's considered view was that the disasters were all due to metal fatigue developing in the fuselage, possibly becoming accelerated or aggravated by small cracks in the skin which had occurred in the course of manufacture. He was a most difficult witness to cross-examine, and although he tells me I asked him over a thousand questions, I obtained very little to damage his conclusions. He said he believed that the fatigue started 'as a fatigue fracture, not during manufacture at all but during the life of the aeroplane'. When the burst took place it had aggravated a manufacturing crack. He knew of no physical test that could be applied to metal to tell when it is fatigued or about to become fatigued. He agreed that, manufacturing cracks or not, metal fatigue was to be expected at this stage in the aeroplane's life. The lost aircraft had flown longer than the recommended fatigue safety period in light of the evidence that had been obtained from tank-testing. Sir Arnold agreed that if, in the light of those results, stronger materials were used in future, the presence of cracks such as those found would be of even less significance. The cracks had certainly not been the primary cause of the accidents. Provided a thicker skin were used and there was some strengthening of fuselage and wing, the Comet should go back into service and have a successful career. He agreed that the Comet was a safe aircraft, well designed and well made. He found many features 'quite excellent' and added, 'I have never had on my station an aircraft which flew so well and regularly as a test aeroplane: it was an admirable aircraft.' The inquiry went on for many weeks – it was the most thorough investigation of its kind that could be imagined, and the outcome was an acceptance of the fact that very little was known about the nature of fatigue, that every precaution should be taken against cracks or other defects in manufacture, but that with the thicker skin that was by this time being used the Comet would be one of the safest aircraft flying. Indeed, they were soon in operation again on passenger routes.

Lord Brabazon ('Brab', as he was affectionately called), who held the first pilot's licence ever granted in Britain, was Chairman of the Registration Board which had reissued the Comet's licence following the first two accidents. He was called to give evidence. Instead he gave a declamation that led the tribunal to complete silence. I quote:

> You and I know the cause of this accident. It is due to the adventurous pioneering spirit of our race. In this enquiry there is nothing to be ashamed of: there is much to be proud of. Here is a great imaginative project to build a machine with twice the speed and twice the height of any existing aircraft in the world. We all went into it with our eyes wide open. We were conscious of the dangers which were lurking in the unknown. Of course, we gave hostages to fate but I cannot believe that this court of our country will censure us because we ventured. You, my Lord, would not have the aeronautic people of the country travelling the world in craven fear lest they be censured in such a court as this for trying to lead the world.

I myself had travelled on Comets before the Naples accident (I recall one trip back from South Africa on which the Chairman of BOAC

was also a passenger) and I could scarce forbear to cheer. I then referred
to recent mysterious crashes in America. Lord Brabazon agreed that 'a
very famous American aircraft with a pressurised cabin' had had three
unexplained disasters and that in three other types of aircraft, twenty-
four had been found with cracks. There had been five unexplained disasters altogether but the aircraft was still flying. He therefore considered
British safety requirements to be in advance of those required in
America – or anywhere else.

Bristol University awarded me an Honorary LL.D. in November
1954. It was conferred by Sir Winston Churchill who was the
Chancellor, proudly attired in the robe his father had worn in 1886
when Chancellor of the Exchequer. The British Merchant
Adventurers, a famous dining club in Bristol, asked me to address them
and this I did the following day.

On the 29th of that month I was back in the High Court in an appeal
for some Polish seamen seeking political asylum. Lord Goddard dealt
with the case in his usual robust way and the seamen won.

On 2 December I flew off to Nairobi. The court in Aden had ruled
that a cargo of oil, sold by the Iranians to the Italians, in fact belonged
to BP, and the Italian shipowners had lodged an appeal, which was
before the East African Court of Appeal. We had been given special
authority to carry a revolver and ammunition against Mau Mau terror-
ists, and on 6 December the Shawcross 'posse' turned up in court in wigs
and gowns, but armed to the teeth, only to find the Italian appellants
barely represented at all and applying for an adjournment. After a
hearing that lasted less than thirty minutes, the court dismissed the
appeal and awarded costs to BP, though I doubt whether they ever got
them. It had been a long journey for such a quickly accomplished case,
but it meant that the judgement remained something of an authority in
British law for the very proposition I had always maintained, namely,
that the payment of fair, adequate and prompt compensation is the
condition of legality for expropriation by the Government of property
belonging to nationals of another state. The authority of the Aden
Court was not high, but so far it was the only court to have passed upon
the matter.

While I was in Nairobi I was asked to hold a Press conference. One
of the questions I was asked related to a matter that had started to blow

up before I had left England. Sir Winston had said that some time in 1945 he had sent a telegram to Field Marshal Montgomery, head of our force in Germany. The effect of the message was that if the Soviet Army continued to pose a threat by moving large forces further westward we might have to consider reissuing some arms to German contingents under British command. Years later, in 1954, the Opposition attempted to raise a scandal about this, and the situation was made worse when the telegram itself could not be found. Montgomery stated that he had received the message, agreed with it, but could not remember how it had been conveyed. Who would, after ten years? But the matter was made the subject of a violent attack on Winston. I was asked at the Nairobi Press conference what I thought about it and my answer – that I 'could not understand what all the fuss was about' – received wide publicity at home. I added that I agreed with Churchill's policy. The troops so enrolled would have been screened, would not have been Nazis, and would have been under British control. The fact was that some of my colleagues were trying to work up a campaign against Winston with a view to the forthcoming election which was expected the following year. In fact it took place in May 1955. The unhappy truth, as I saw it, was that we had no really plausible policy and were prepared to seize on any stick, however fragile, with which to hit Winston. Consequently, I was bitterly attacked for my Nairobi statement by the Bevanites and other left-wing elements in the Labour Party.

Keenly aware of the lack of a sensible programme, I had, in a speech just before Christmas, set out what I thought would be a suitable framework. I had started by saying that Socialism needed a new look! 'Slogans, shibboleths and doctrines are no good.' We would lose the next election if we did not get down to some responsible, clear-headed and quick thinking about policy. 'Nagging and nathering and blowing up frothy storms in little political teacups without putting before the public any broad principles of policy which would bring tangible and clear benefit to the mass of the people is not enough . . . It is no use turning back over our shoulders all the time to look at Karl Marx and applying all sorts of restrictions, curbs and freezes. We must deal with the very different world of today and go forward to the creation of an expanding, rising economy.' I then listed six points of principle in order to promote which I urged we should frame clear policies. There should be a deliberate economic policy of expansion to ensure higher earnings. We should promote greater efficiency and productivity in industry. 'Nationalization is as dead as the Dodo.' The real power which the state should hold in reserve was that of planning and control. Ownership was irrelevant. More flats rather than towns sprawling over good agricultural land, and houses to buy as well as rent. A system of marketing boards set up for agriculture. Site values should be rated to ensure that all suitable land was put to economic use. Break down the barriers and iron curtains that prevent peoples getting to know each other. Face the realities of the Cold War by changing the emphasis from expenditure on military armaments to expenditure on raising the standard of living in the backward areas. And finally education – which I had constantly stressed in my political speeches. Every child ought to have the opportunity of what in effect should be grammar-school education, and there should be no selective examination at 11-plus, which – because I could not, I suspect, have passed one when I was eleven – I regarded as a monstrosity. Teachers should be paid a wage likely to attract good people and more commensurate with their importance to the State.

I thought these vague headings better than the bickering that was taking place among the leading Labour politicians. Of course, it was easy to tear the various points into shreds and I would not adhere to them now, but they were better than our rather nebulous existing ideas. The speech received largely favourable publicity, but was bitterly attacked by the Communist *Daily Worker*, by *Tribune*, and by the left wing generally. To the critics, I simply said that I had not the least ambition to be leader; that I was a lawyer who saw both sides to most questions; and that I liked to say what I thought.

I had an agreeable Christmas present in 1954 in that I was elected Treasurer of Gray's Inn, which meant that for a year I was the leading Master of the Bench – a kind of chairman with some executive powers. It was a position I greatly enjoyed and valued. Gray's Inn was my professional – and beloved – domus. When I reached ninety they gave me a splendid house dinner in our beautiful hall, the seats for which were the subject of a ballot. It was a great occasion.

My political opinions became more mature and I did not make the extreme speeches of which I am afraid I was guilty in earlier years. On the other hand the description 'Sir Shortly Floorcross', which became applied to me and which delighted Winston, was not an accurate fore-cast. At no time did I contemplate cashing in on my apparent success as a speaker by crossing the floor to join the Conservatives. It is true, however, that in 1954 I had more friendly social contact with my polit-ical opponents. This was simple because, once out of office, Joan and I had more time and occasion to engage in ordinary social life. There was nothing new in cross-party friendships, although I regret that bitterness on both sides seems to make it less usual now. If some of my political associates looked askance at my friendship with, for example, Brendan Bracken, Walter Monckton, Rab Butler or Harold Macmillan, it was just too bad! The view that a difference in political beliefs should not affect personal friendships was, I think, generally accepted by all expe-rienced politicians in those days. Winston Churchill, who never shrank from crossing a floor, illustrated that. In 1911 he and F. E. Smith, later Lord Birkenhead, had founded the Other Club. The membership was designed to be equally representative of the two main parties, then of course the Conservatives and the Liberals. The original members were twelve from each side of the house. 'F.E.' was the head of the Conservatives. And who led the Liberals then? Why, Winston Churchill! Lloyd George came further down the Liberal list. It was never intended that the Other Club should be a forum for political con-troversy. It was explicitly stated in the rules that 'the object of the Other Club is to dine'. I felt highly honoured when Winston invited me to join the Other Club in 1953 and then personally proposed me.

In those days membership of the Other Club was small and more selective than it is now. I well remember an occasion when Winston remarked to me that while Mr Attlee was no doubt a very able and very honourable man, he was 'not the sort of man I would care to sit next to at dinner'. By this he meant no more or less than that Attlee did not enjoy conversation, true enough. The Club met at fairly frequent intervals at the Savoy, and members always wore black tie. I greatly enjoyed my membership, but to Winston the Other Club was something very special and he was absolutely devoted to it. At the time I joined the Club it was considered a special honour if one was asked to sit next to Winston. Later, as his physical and mental condition progressively declined, this attitude changed. Winston used to be brought in an

invalid wheelchair. As dinner was announced he would be put in position in his chair, usually opposite the Chairman at the long table. Most
members found that it became increasingly difficult to engage him in
conversation. His answers were hard to understand or were restricted to
one or two words, and he tended to forget what had been said immediately before. It sometimes happened that at least one of the two seats next
to him would be left empty. This distressed me greatly. If I could not find
a suitable volunteer I invariably occupied one of the seats myself. It was
often not enjoyable, but I never regretted doing it.

Nothing much happened in the early months of 1955. I spent a week
or two having an operation for a chronic appendix. Shortly afterwards,
I was briefed to make one of my infrequent excursions into the criminal
courts. This was to appear for the prosecution in a case alleging conspiracy to defraud involving at least £750,000 on the part of two Lloyd's
underwriters, a chartered accountant and his managing clerk. The
importance of the case was that such a fraudulent conspiracy could have
been conducted so successfully and have deceived the Lloyd's
Committee for a period of several years. The then enormous prestige of
Lloyd's was at stake.

The case started with a long opening speech by me on 28 February.
On 22 March the principal defendant, Alec Wilcox, who had been
something of a blue-eyed boy at Lloyd's, and who had not given evidence on his own behalf, withdrew his not guilty plea and pleaded guilty
to conspiracy and two charges of false pretences. This plea I accepted.
The case continued against the other defendants and eventually the
accountant's managing clerk was found not guilty and discharged, the
remaining two being found guilty. Wilcox was sentenced to eight years'
imprisonment; the others to four years and twelve months respectively.

I confess that I felt sorry for Wilcox. He had started his underwriting
business with no money of his own; he had struggled to keep it alive for
many years and to do so he had committed elaborate frauds. Of course
his offences were grave ones but he faced his 8-year sentence bravely and
pennilessly. The case gave me occasion to address an association of
accountants, and I stressed the view that accountants, while charging
larger and larger fees, had a duty to disclose the true situation to the committee of Lloyd's and must not conceal the facts. I wanted to emphasize
that auditors have a duty to the public and to the shareholders – not just

to the directors who employ them – to disclose anything wrong, for they are employed on behalf of the company. The duty is to the shareholders and, as shares are constantly changing hands in 'the market', this means, in effect, to the public. From that time on, I have interested myself in this point of view and have written and spoken on the subject often. In recent years I have felt that there have been too many cases in which this duty has not been fully recognized, and the ramification of the various Maxwell cases, and a number of other cases since, is a matter of very grave concern in which, I am afraid, the accountants have not been fulfilling what I regard as their duty to the public to act as watchdogs. I hope that such cases will lead the auditing and accounting professions to a greater appreciation of their public responsibilities.

In March, I was invited to speak at a Savoy Hotel dinner given by the Jewish Professional Association presided over by Victor Mishcon, now a colleague in the House of Lords. That speech, urging restraint on the part of Israel towards the Arabs, our traditional friends, although made over forty years ago, still represents my view about the seemingly insoluble Israeli–Arab situation.

In April, Joan and I had an opportunity for a short visit to Norway and Denmark. I met a number of ministers and had several speaking engagements when I spoke mainly on foreign affairs and the dangers of Communism.

We had a particularly enjoyable time in the brisk spring air. I had always claimed to be one-eighth Danish, an assertion I repeated a few years ago at a grand dinner party in London where I found myself on the right of a lady whose name I had not bothered to catch – it was enough for me that she was young and beautiful. On being told she had been born in Denmark, I asked casually, 'What does your father do?', to which she replied charmingly, 'Oh – he was the King.' The lady was in fact the Queen of Greece!

The visit gave me the opportunity to meet my Danish relatives. My Danish maternal grandmother had been a very remarkable woman and a fine linguist; my mother took after her in many ways. She lived with us (that is to say, my parents and me) in London till her death at a grand old age. I recall her telling me her experiences during the siege of Paris in 1870, when she had to subsist on a diet of stewed rat. Her father had been a leading judge in Copenhagen.

The most important political event in 1955 was the general election. It was a very hectic campaign and I travelled all over England and Wales making election speeches at meetings organized by Transport House. We travelled by car, Joan doing most of the driving and being through-out — as she always was — a tower of strength. I may not have enjoyed much popularity among the rank and file members of the House of Commons, but with Joan I had very successful meetings in the con-stituencies.

One of the controversial issues of the campaign was the problem of the hydrogen bomb. The Bevanites were making much play with the proposition that Britain should give an assurance that we would not use the H-bomb unless such a bomb had been first used against us by an aggressor. I said that such a policy would be folly, '. . . like a little man, about to be attacked by a giant bully with a bludgeon, throwing away the revolver with which he might have defended himself'.

My speeches certainly excited bitter criticism from the Bevanites. The fact was that in general I supported the foreign policy being pursued by the Foreign Secretary, Anthony Eden. It had been suggested that the four-power talks were being staged at that time for reasons connected with our election. I responded that

> It would be a great misfortune and augur ill for the negotiations if the Russians or any of our own people doubted the sincerity with which Britain is sponsoring and will go into these great talks . . . These matters are far too grave to be made the subject of mere party political exaggerations. The Russians should understand that in this country the people loyally accept the verdict which is given at free elections and that, whatever party is returned, Britain will stand solidly behind whoever it may be — Mr Attlee and Mr Morrison or Sir Anthony and Mr Butler — in desiring to reach a proper and lasting agreement for the avoidance of war and the easement of international tensions.

This view was of course anathema to the Labour left wing and the fact that I made it indicates that I was taking a much less partisan view than I had done in 1945, and perhaps also that I was psychologically unfit for the game of party politics.

It was, I think, my time as President of the Board of Trade, short as that had been, which had finally led me to a more realistic appreciation of the problems of our industrial economy. In the 1955 election I stressed that we were on 'a knife edge of uncertainty, between boom and bust. . . . this is a tripartite adventure – Government, employers and trades unions.' All this was no doubt very vague and indefinite but it indicated what I still think correct, namely that a completely free-for-all economy may result in recurrent booms and busts, with too much merely specu-lative investment and over-development, while on the other hand mere rigid governmental controls, nationalization and centralized planning will also not provide the answer either. In 1955, however, there was still some robust loyalty to the old Socialist ideas and the Bevanites were exploiting this to the full. In his constituency at Grantham, Woodrow Wyatt wisely stood up to them when he said

> I am continually asked at meetings about Mr Bevan and the leader-ship of the Labour Party. It is no good dodging this question. We have never shown the slightest sign of giving the leadership to Mr Bevan. The Parliamentary Labour Party have never given him more than about fifty votes for the deputy leadership and when Mr Bevan was censured for his conduct in the defence debate he said he did not want the leadership. Lord Beaverbrook and Sir Winston Churchill have been running a campaign for years to make Mr Bevan the leader. It is just a Tory stunt to try and scare the undecided voter, but Lord Beaverbrook does not decide the leadership. We do. Whether it is a good thing or not, there is no chance whatever of Mr Bevan control-ling the Labour Party or its policy. The great bulk of the Labour Party is solidly behind Mr Attlee.

Nonetheless, the Bevanite campaign did us great harm, and my realiza-tion of the extent to which this was so led me into what Mr Dalton would have called a little local difficulty.

One Friday night I travelled up by sleeper to Preston for a speaking engagement. On arrival, I met Godfrey Winn, a popular journalist, who was on the same train, and we exchanged a few words. He was a friend of mine and a neighbour in Sussex; his brother Roger was for some time a member of my chambers and became a judge. Next morning I was shocked to read in Godfrey Winn's column in the *Sunday Dispatch*:

Sir Hartley Shawcross emerges from the next sleeper. We are neigh-
bours in Sussex but have never met before at half past seven in the
morning. He is as debonair as ever in the morning but seemed
depressed about his party's prospects in the election though he himself
has a safe enough seat at St Helen's. 'Bevan has lost it for us,' Sir
Hartley prophesied sadly to me and was then whisked away in a
police car . . .

This was a grossly damaging remark to be published shortly before
an election, and although it was true, I was furious. But there was
nothing much I could do except to emphasize, as was largely true in his
personal case, that Bevan had now loyally come round to agree with the
Party's official policy. Bevan's political opinions were in fact largely
opportunistic and, having at one time bitterly attacked Attlee and later
Gaitskell, he eventually offered his support. He and I were personally on
good terms. I have sat up to the early hours with him – and a bottle or
two – listening to his racy stories. I recognized and, as I told him, envied
his great powers of extempory oratory, although an unguarded phrase
sometimes led him into trouble.

Largely because of the Bevanite scare, Labour lost the election, the
Tories winning twenty-four seats from Labour which, with other
changes, gave them a majority of fifty-nine in the new parliament. Attlee
was again elected leader of the Party and Herbert Morrison his deputy.

My normal routine continued and I was soon back in chambers.
Until the end of July, I was constantly in court, with no cases of any
specially enduring interest. But there were various public occasions, of
which the most remarkable was the Commonwealth and Empire Law
Conference, which was attended by over 1,000 delegates from all over
the Empire. The opening session took place in Westminster Hall.
Alongside the steps that lead down from the large stained-glass windows
were ranged the high commissioners and various legal notables from the
countries concerned. At a central table at the bottom was the Lord
Chancellor in his full-bottomed wig and black and gold robes, seated
between the President of the Law Society and myself as Chairman of
the Bar Council – both of us unrobed because the President has no
formal robes – then the Law Lords and the Lords Justice of Appeal in
their black and gold robes, while the delegates sat facing us in the body

of the hall. What rubbish it is to think that wigs and gowns and splendid robes do not add to the dignity and solemnity of formal occasions!
We all marched in procession in order of precedence and it must have
been quite a spectacle.

A number of self-governing colonies had abolished the right of
appeal to the Privy Council which they thought inconsistent with their
own complete sovereignty, and I canvassed the idea of a Supreme Court
which would meet from time to time in each Commonwealth country.
The proposal failed to salvage the unity that had been lost by the refusal
to allow appeals to the Privy Council; the centrifugal forces of nationalism were too strong to permit this strengthening of the Commonwealth
tie.

I also referred in my speech to the problem of fusion of the two
branches of the profession which was already the subject of much discussion and was indeed accepted in some, but by no means all,
Commonwealth countries. I said then that both the Bar and the solicitors here were firmly convinced that fusion would not promote the better
administration of justice from any point of view. There was no reason
whatever to think it would save expense to litigants. And there was no
doubt at all that in the circumstances of this country the mutual independence of both branches of the profession promoted the integrity and
efficiency of both and so helped to maintain the high standards of legal
administration which we enjoy. Today, of course, some degree of fusion
exists, but I still view the matter with misgiving.

In the meantime the Bar struggled on. I had been campaigning for
some time for the introduction of some form of tax relief on pension pre-
miums which would enable barristers to make provision for an endow-
ment pension on their retirement. The Government had indeed gone so
far as to appoint a committee under a distinguished Silk to enquire into
the problem of retirement for the self-employed, and this made favourable
recommendations which, however, did not go far enough in that they did
not allow an increased rate of relief for those already near retirement age.
So I continued the campaign, writing personally to Harold Macmillan,
then Chancellor, and making speeches. This greatly annoyed Harold
Wilson, who was opposed to such relief and indignantly stressed – as he
was fully entitled to – that I had been campaigning as Chairman of the
Bar, not as a Labour MP, and that it was simply a pressure group for the

rich. Eventually we met with a large measure of success, Harold Macmillan telling the House that he had been 'particularly struck' with some of the arguments I had put forward in a 'powerful case' and was sorry that he could not meet all the suggestions I had made.

In court I was briefed to appear at the Old Bailey for a youngish man who practised as an accountant. In those days there was nothing to prevent someone who had not passed any qualifying examination from calling himself an accountant. My client was hard-working and had built up some sort of practice in the course of which he had assisted in attempting to cover up a gross fraud by one of his clients. He and the client were both prosecuted and both pleaded guilty. The point was however established that the Inland Revenue, who were the prosecutors, had known of the offences for three years, before deciding to prosecute. Lord Goddard said that he regarded this as an unjustified delay. The men were 'left on tenterhooks: it was almost like torture', and he would certainly not pass anything like the sentence he would otherwise have done. I naturally made as much as I could of the delay in my plea in mitigation for the accountant, pointing out that he had repaid all the fees that he had received through his wrongdoing and was now left penniless. 'Well,' said Rayner Goddard, 'he does not seem to have exercised any notable economy in his defence.' Roars of laughter in court. I had to make some lame excuse that relatives and friends had come to his aid in paying my very modest fees. More laughter.

In August, aboard *Vanity V*, I had to cut short our sailing holiday in Brittany in order to undertake a case for HMG, involving a dispute between the British Government and that of Saudi Arabia as to the rights over a small area in the Gulf known as the Buraimi Oasis, bordered in part by Abu Dhabi and Muscat to the north and Saudi Arabia to the west.

Abu Dhabi was then a British protectorate. The inhabitants were poor and led a nomadic life, but the oasis was supposed to contain large resources of oil. If the territory belonged to Saudi Arabia, these would have been exploited under concessions granted to Aramco, the great US oil company. If, on the other hand, it belonged to Abu Dhabi and Muscat (for which sheikhdoms I appeared as well as for HMG), these resources would have been developed by the British Iraq Petroleum Company. The two rival oil companies were behind the case, and I have no doubt that the Iraq Petroleum Company had suggested employing me and were reimbursing the fee, which was more generous than those normally paid by the British Government. Similarly, although a distinguished Egyptian lawyer nominally led for the Saudi Arabians, the team was American and included Judge Manley Hudson, well known as an adviser to Aramco. There had been a flare-up between the competing states some years before which had been settled by an agreement to arbitrate on the boundaries at a hearing to have taken place in 1957. In the meantime, however, it was alleged that the Saudis had engaged in gun-running and in wholesale bribery. This was denied by the Saudis, and it was therefore agreed to bring forward the arbitration to consider these alleged breaches of the agreement.

The tribunal was high-powered, being presided over by Charles de Visscher, the Belgian judge on the International Court of Justice at the Hague, Sir Reader Bullard, who had been our Minister in Jeddah and Ambassador in Teheran, a Pakistani lawyer, a Cuban and, surprisingly, the Deputy Foreign Minister of Saudi Arabia itself, one Sheikh Yusuf Yasir. The tribunal met on 11 September 1955 in the old and rather shabby town hall in Geneva. We were nearly a week late because the Pakistani member of the tribunal failed to turn up. He had apparently been on pilgrimage to Mecca.

In my opening address, I strongly stressed the high value which HMG placed on our friendship of 100 years with Saudi Arabia, and our sincere hope that a stop would be put to the present malpractices and intrigues so that an amicable decision on the frontiers might be reached. We then called a number of witnesses to prove bribery on an enormous scale – running up to many millions of pounds – in order to induce Arab leaders to change their allegiance from the ruler of Muscat to Saudi Arabia. Secret gun-running, both by illegal flights of planes and on camels, was revealed, as were the activities of a certain Saudi political officer called Qureshi who had offered no less than 400 million rupees (about £31 million) to Sheikh Zaid, the brother of the ruler of Abu Dhabi, if he would ensure that Aramco and not the British company won the concession.

The Arab witnesses appeared in their traditional costumes, armed with daggers, and in the late afternoon the proceedings were suspended for a few minutes when they would turn towards Mecca and pray.

What, however, was less traditional in an international arbitration was the fact that Sheikh Yasir, although a judge on the tribunal, was himself briefing the Arab witnesses. Qureshi admitted to me in cross-examination that the night before he gave evidence he had, in effect, been briefed by Yasir, and we had evidence of similar meetings with other witnesses. Moreover, Yasir did not deny that he was himself the Saudi Arabian official in charge of affairs in Buraimi and that he had appointed Qureshi as the leading Saudi official in the territory. He could not possibly be expected to conduct himself with impartiality. There was also grave reason to doubt the impartiality of at least one other member of the tribunal.

Nonetheless, after four days of hearing I made my closing speech and was followed by the American, Dr Young, for the Saudis. Suddenly, to my surprise, we received a suggestion that Sir Reader and Sheikh Yasir should meet the heads of the two delegations and discuss certain issues with us in private. This I immediately refused to do, saying I would discuss anything openly before the whole tribunal. There was no response. I felt it proper to go to see Sir Reader in his hotel. I found him a greatly worried man, who was taking his duty of independence and impartiality most seriously, as one would expect, and who felt that the position of the tribunal had been hopelessly compromised. We concluded that there was no prospect of a satisfactory outcome to the arbitration. At that stage it seemed that nothing would persuade Sheikh Yasir to retire and be replaced by someone independent. Sir Reader's only course consistent with honour and dignity was to resign, and this he did.

We thought that Sir Reader's resignation might at least have led Sheikh Yasir to do the decent thing and himself resign. But Yasir held his ground. That was the end of the arbitration, for the British Government saw no point — nor was there any — in appointing a new arbitrator if Yasir remained a member. What happened after that my history does not relate. The oil companies got together in a businesslike way and the heat was taken out of the whole affair by the fact that there seemed to be, after all, no oil in the Buraimi Oasis. However, oil was found elsewhere in Abu Dhabi and the Sheikhdom became very rich.

In spite of Labour's defeat in 1951, and now again in 1955, Attlee had remained leader of the Party. Many thought he was waiting in hope that something would happen to eliminate Herbert Morrison as a possible successor. But nothing did and eventually, in November 1956, Attlee announced his resignation. Immediately the candidates for the succession started to line up, Morrison amongst them. At that time I had several close associates in the Parliamentary Party, particularly George Brown, Dick Stokes and some trade union friends, and we had many anxious discussions about the leadership, some of them over dinner in Dick's agreeable home in Palace Street. George, Dick and some others wanted me to stand myself, but I was completely opposed to doing so, at least while Morrison was a candidate. Nor was I particularly keen on becoming leader.

We carefully canvassed Morrison's chances of success, took straw polls, and were left in no doubt that he had no chance at all of being elected. This was mainly because of his performance as Foreign Secretary which, far from strengthening his claims, had led a great many Members to feel that he was not enough of an all-rounder to be leader of the Parliamentary Party. There were some who thought that since his remarriage about a year before, to a younger woman from a somewhat different background who had made him very happy, he had become rather detached and less interested in politics. I doubt whether that had any influence in the matter. In the elections for the Labour Party official positions, he had already been quite badly defeated in his attempt to become Treasurer. It was really a most undeserved defeat, but it happened, and it became very apparent that Herbert had no chance of winning the Parliamentary leadership. I, and several other friends, repeatedly spoke to him and urged him to withdraw, impressing upon him our conviction that he would lose. He simply could not believe it. He was convinced he would win. People continued to urge me to stand but I really did not give it a thought: Herbert was my friend.

Some time beforehand, Hugh Gaitskell had told Herbert that he proposed to stand. Herbert was in no way dismayed, so confident was he of his own success. Eventually Hugh Gaitskell did put his name down, though whether he would have done so had I already been a candidate I do not know. At all events, he won by a comfortable majority, Bevan coming second with Herbert collecting only a miserable number of votes.

It was a shattering blow to Herbert and in fact marked the effective end of his political life. After the initial shock, however, he publicly took it very well, and in his autobiography, a ghosted and somewhat inade, quate affair, he passed over it very lightly. In fact, he was deeply hurt, but his new marriage sustained him.

As for myself, there the matter ended. I thought Gaitskell would be a very good leader, and although his health was not perfect and he had some sort of heart problem it never occurred to anybody that this would become grave.

I did not give the matter another thought until some time in the 1970s, when a casual acquaintance whom I had encountered at the Savoy Grill remarked that he had just been talking to Harold Wilson who had told him that if Shawcross 'had played his cards correctly he, and not Wilson, would have been Prime Minister'. He had added – and this phrase struck in my mind – 'And nothing could have stopped him'. I was surprised by this simply because I felt it an unlikely remark for Wilson to have made. I have often been extremely critical of him and I felt certain that he disliked me and would have been unlikely to say any, thing complimentary about me. I continued to feel intrigued so I wrote to Wilson and asked him whether he had indeed said anything of the kind. He did not reply in writing but telephoned me very pleasantly, not answering the question but suggesting that we should have lunch together. I was again surprised but invited him to lunch at the Savoy Grill. We sat at my usual table near the door and continued our lunch till about four o'clock, much to the annoyance of the waiters, who wanted to get away. Wilson was extremely affable. He spoke very sympathetically about George Brown (who, for his part, loathed Wilson and did not hide it), and although he did not answer my question directly – he was a past master at parrying questions – he certainly did say that I could have been a, if not the, leading figure in the Party had I wished. He even said that he regretted I had not become such. And that was that. Only recently, as a guest on the BBC's *Desert Island Discs*, I was asked a question that led me to say casually that I had not stood for the leadership because of my friendship with Herbert Morrison. As a result of this remark, Bryan Magee, a philosophy don at Oxford, and a former Labour MP, wrote to Sue Lawley, who had interviewed me. The rest of the story can best be told by quoting part of the correspondence. His initial letter was as follows:

Dear Sue Lawley,
I much enjoyed your programme with Hartley Shawcross, and it prompted a question in my mind which perhaps you might pass on to Lord Shawcross.

When I was a Labour MP and Harold Wilson was Prime Minister, he said to me once in a private conversation that 'if he'd played his cards right' Shawcross would have been Attlee's successor, and therefore eventually Prime Minister – and 'that nothing could have stopped him.' Now Wilson was no slouch when it came to the tactics of polit-ical self-advancement, and I would as soon accept his judgement in such a matter as any other individual's – especially in view of the fact that he himself was a member of the Labour Cabinet in question.

My question is: Did Shawcross himself realize this? If so, does this mean he knowingly chose not to become Prime Minister? If so, why? Or did he himself not perceive the reality of his situation, a reality which the more cynically and perhaps more self-interestedly shrewd observer, Harold Wilson, did perceive? And if *that* is the case, how does he feel about it in retrospect? Is he kicking himself all over London? Or doesn't he really mind all that much?
Yours sincerely,
BRYAN MAGEE

Bryan Magee and I then exchanged a couple of letters and he sent me an interesting analysis of the matter as he saw it.

Dear Lord Shawcross,
I have just got back from the Bayreuth Festival to find your letter of 30 July. It reads as if, for some reason, you never really confronted the reality of the situation, even in your own mind. I say this for three reasons:
1. You say you knew that if you stood for election as Attlee's succes-sor you 'would have a good chance of winning that election. As far as I can remember I did not associate it very clearly in my mind with the possibility of becoming prime minister, although I must have known that that would be quite likely to have followed.' That reads very oddly: you know that B would possibly follow A, but did not associate the two in your mind.

2. You say you urged Morrison 'on a number of occasions' not to stand, and told him accurately what the result would be if he did. Since he knew this was your view, and events proved it to be correct, he would have had simply no ground for regarding you disloyal if you had stood yourself.

3. Your meeting with Wilson at the Savoy was expressly arranged so that you could find out from him what his views in the matter were, yet when it came to the point you never asked him, though you sat talking till teatime.

Perhaps somewhere deep down inside yourself it was an outcome you didn't want, and therefore didn't want to consider. Other parts of your letter give the impression that this may have been so. And you could well be right. Speaking for myself, I don't think being prime minister is worth making great sacrifices for; and it could well be that it would not have made you happy. But I suspect it is completely incomprehensible to Harold Wilson that a politician could have the leadership within his grasp and not take it, which is why he was still talking about it years later. His assessment of your chances would have had nothing to do with whether he liked you or not: he was far too calculating for that. Everything you say, and everything I know about him, makes me suppose that he was right on the central point: you could, had you chosen to, have become leader of the Labour Party and that would have meant that eventually you would proba' bly have become prime minister. But you held back and did not do so – and may have had a happier life in consequence.

These are fascinating matters, and they go very deep psycholog' ically. I hope you do not think it impertinent of me to have speculated to the extent I have. By all means make any use of my letters you wish. Good luck with your memoir.

Yours sincerely,

BRIAN MAGEE

I replied a few days later.

Thank you for your letter. It was good of you to write at length and I was very interested in your analysis of the circumstances.

I cannot disagree with your conclusion save on two matters.

Herbert would have resented my standing against him. He would have said – to himself, to me and to others – 'Now I understand why Hartley urged me not to stand: he wanted to stand himself and get me out of the way. Having failed in that he has now openly come in against me – this will split the vote and result in both of us losing.'

As for the Premiership, the fact is that I was never really ambitious – as is shown also by my refusing the Lord Chief Justiceship, or the eventual certainty of the Lord Chancellorship. My first marriage – although happy – had been childless and sexless and ended in tragedy. I was again very happily married and had three children and a charming home. I attached – I suppose – more importance to that than to politics. Although my second marriage, after 30 years, ended in tragedy too, I do not regret the course I took, although I cannot feel proud of it.

As far as I was concerned, Gaitskell's election was the end of the matter. I gave no further thought to the leadership of the Labour Party or the possibility of becoming Prime Minister. But I was not yet out of politics!

After a quiet Christmas spent at home with my family I was soon back in court early in 1956.

Among my retainers was one for Royal Dutch Shell, and this led to many briefs, including one to go out to Singapore to fight a claim against the Government. This concerned the ownership of oil in the large tank farms on the island when Singapore was recaptured from the Japanese by British forces under Mountbatten. Royal Dutch Shell had found that this oil had all come from wells outside the colony which had been owned by Shell before they were taken over by the Japanese when their troops overran the area. Shell argued through me that the oil belonged to them. Not so, said the British Government: it was the spoils of war captured by the forces of the Crown. In the Court of First Instance HMG won. We appealed to the Supreme Court of Singapore, composed of three British judges.

This was my first trip to the Far East and I took Joan with me, although we flew out separately – for the sake of the children in the event of one crash. In those days Singapore was a pretty seedy place with mean streets; one in particular, which has now been altogether eliminated, was full of prostitutes and transvestites. Housing for the local population – mixed Chinese and Malaysian – was in miserable-looking tenements, whereas the expatriate population usually had very good houses, large gardens and of course plenty of excellent servants whom they paid very little. We stayed with the local Shell Number One, 'Fish' Haddock, who had a delightful, airy house. While in Singapore, I met Lee Kuan Yew – then down from Cambridge with a brilliant record, though violently anti-British – and we drank coffee together in sleazy cafés and became friends. Later, he gained political power – indeed domination – and became a world figure. He still is – and he is now also a member of the J. P. Morgan International Council.

In Singapore the Shell case had for some reason aroused a great deal of interest and social activity. A lot of money turned on its result. I was elected to the local Bar, so as to be properly qualified to appear. The splendid courtroom was absolutely packed with expatriates: admirals in uniform, field officers, the local wives, and so on. The judges wore red robes and the Bar also wore wig and gown. I opened the appeal as dramatically as I could; a distinguished Silk, Geoffrey Cross, also brought out specially from London for HMG, replied. The argument went on for several days, the judges from time to time making pertinent interventions (I was rather impressed with them, particularly with one who later came to England to study and report on the ombudsman system for Justice, the law reform organization set up in the wake of the invasion of Hungary) and judgement was reserved. When it was given, we learned that justice had triumphed and Shell had won. There could have been an appeal but the Attorney General, Manningham-Buller, was so annoyed that he had not been consulted before the case started – as he should certainly have been – that he refused to authorize the case going further. So Shell got away with a great deal of money and I and my Juniors got away with our adequate fees.

From Singapore we flew to Hong Kong – the first of my many visits to this fascinating place. One of the excitements of the colony is that it seems to change its face with every visit, new buildings replacing old and reaching ever higher into the sky.

It was while staying with 'Fish' Haddock that I first met Run Run

Shaw, a man with whom I formed a friendship that has continued to the present time (he has encouraged his longevity by doing all the things I neglected to do; no alcohol, no smoking, very light diets, exercise in the fresh air, including the very graceful shadow boxing which he engages in regularly every day). He had started a film‑making and exhibiting business, first in Singapore and then in Hong Kong. Shaw Brothers expanded a little into Malaysia and their business made steady progress in Singapore, although they must have had a difficult time during the war and the Japanese occupation.

Run Run Shaw placed a charming villa in Hong Kong at our dis‑ posal. It had been designed by a French architect and was situated on the side of Repulse Bay, then about three‑quarters of an hour's drive from the centre of Hong Kong and near to what was then the still‑picturesque village of Aberdeen. Run Run also put a car (of course a Rolls, of which he has had many) at our disposal and entertained us royally in many excellent Chinese restaurants. It was a memorable visit and led to a closer association with Run Run's business activities, for I later became a director of Shaw Brothers and also of the Hong Kong Television Broadcasts company which he successfully established.

On leaving Hong Kong we broke the journey home – again in separ‑ ate aircraft – first at Bangkok, an exciting and fascinating city which we were later to get to know well, and then at Beirut.

The Lebanon was then an exceedingly attractive and peaceful country where you could bathe in the warm waters of the Mediterranean in the morning and drive up to ski in the mountains in the afternoon. Although the visit was a private one, it must have been notified in advance to the Government, for the Speaker (or his equivalent in the Majlis, the Lebanese legislature) organized a formal dinner of welcome for us. This was a very grand affair held in the St George's Hotel. During the dinner the chandeliers in the smart private room of the restaurant suddenly started to wobble backwards and forwards. This puzzled me at first, but it conveyed a very clear signal to the local guests who one by one excused themselves and left the room. It was explained to us that there was an earthquake beginning. Joan said she did not mind: it was the best French dinner she had had for a long time and she was going to finish it. This meant that the unfortunate Speaker had to overcome his obvious fear and stay; so did I, although I confess my taste for the food seemed to have diminished. There was some damage in Beirut, but the real impact of the earthquake was felt in more remote areas, where over one hundred people perished, we were later shocked to hear.

We subsequently paid several visits to Beirut and I became one of the trustees of that excellent institution, which still survives in spite of all the troubles, the American University of Beirut. I also formed a friendship with Mr Emile Bustani who was the owner of CAT, one of the largest contracting firms in the Middle East, who kept a wonderful cellar at his charming house. He was a man who took a realistic view of affairs: I recall his once telling me that he had just been appointed Minister of Works in a new government. I remarked that that must be awkward for him as he would have to resign from CAT. 'Resign?' he said. 'Of course not: it will be a great help to me!' No doubt it was.

Alas, in 1964 when Joan and I were again staying at the St George, he was killed in his aeroplane. He had flown to Damascus and was returning home to have lunch with us. I saw his plane approaching Beirut from over the mountain when quite suddenly it plunged straight down into the sea, for no apparent reason. It was never recovered.

Another sad event early in 1956 was the death of my clerk, Matthew Robinson. He was seventy-seven years old, but his death was, I was convinced, due to an operation going wrong. He had a stomach problem and consulted a very well-known surgeon whose name was more frequently mentioned for making distinctly risqué after-dinner speeches than for any achievements in surgery. This gentleman diagnosed cancer of such an advanced state that, he said, an immediate operation was vital. Matthew was rushed into hospital the next day and operated on without any time for the usual pre-operative preparations. In the event, the normal bodily functions did not resume, and a few days later he was dead. He had started his legal life over fifty years earlier in the Chambers of Horace Avery, who became a famous criminal judge. He was clerk to Patrick Hastings for some forty years, and when I took Silk in 1939, and eventually joined those Chambers, he became my Head Clerk. He knew the Temple intimately and was a great help to me, coming up as I did from the provinces. He was sadly missed in the Temple, and I shed real tears at his funeral service.

At its annual meeting in July the Bar cast aside the rule that limited the Chairman's term of office to four years and elected me, with only four dissentients, to a fifth year.

That summer two groups from the Soviet Union were making offi-cial visits to London. One was a group of sportsmen and women; the other was the Bolshoi Ballet. Unhappily, a member of the first group, one Nina Ponomareva, was tempted by the display in an Oxford Street store and stole some hats. She was seen, arrested and released on bail to appear at Marlborough Street Police Court. This she failed to do, taking refuge in the Soviet Embassy, thus giving rise to a good deal of awkward-ness in Anglo–Soviet relations. Eventually, the Foreign Office approached me and asked if I would go to the Russian Embassy and advise them. I called at the Embassy two or three times, being given moderate sustenance of vodka and caviar while I was there. I assured the Soviet diplomats that if Nina surrendered to her bail at Marlborough Street she would not be sent to prison but would be bound over and immediately set free to return to Russia. Their grim forebodings of a British version of the Lubyanka Prison eased, the Embassy were at last persuaded, and she duly presented herself at the Police Court. I had of course warned the Chief Magistrate. She was promptly dealt with and released, and later that day she boarded a Russian liner, appropriately named *Molotov*, to sail home (not I think sporting a stolen hat). I gather she subsequently became one of the first women to receive an Olympic medal for discus throwing.

A day or two later I received, with the compliments of the Ambassador, two tickets for the Bolshoi Ballet at Covent Garden. It did not occur to me to look at the date – not unnaturally, I assumed they were for the first night which was two or three days off. Joan and I duly turned up in full fig, white tie and the rest. We were admitted but the man at the door mildly observed that he assumed I had realized that the tickets were for three nights later. I had not. Fortunately we were found seats.

Joan and I flew to the United States – as usual, on separate planes – at the end of November, where I made one or two speeches on the inter-national situation following the Suez débâcle. We spent our last dollars on buying Christmas presents and – as always – caught the *Queen Elizabeth* by the skin of our teeth, less than five minutes before she pulled out of the dock.

Back in England I was very soon busy in the courts. Before Christmas, there came a case that was to result in a complete change in, if not the end of, my career and orientation. The Chairman of Royal Dutch Shell was at that time Sir Francis Hopwood, an able and highly cultured man. He had recently bought and restored a fourteenth-century manor house called Binghams Melcombe in about 800 acres of Dorset. The house was one of the most beautiful smaller manor houses in the country. He had furnished it impeccably with valuable sixteenth-century furniture, and was farming the land on each side of the beautiful valley in which the house stood. The problem was whether the cables of a 132,000-volt electricity grid should be erected down the valley to carry a trunk line from the east to a grid sub-station in Yeovil. When the scheme was first mooted, the Central Electricity Authority had agreed with the Dorset planning authority to a different line which avoided the valley. However, the planning authority suddenly revoked their consent and recommended the line through the Bingham valley. Sir Frank had lodged an appeal against this and I was briefed to appear on his behalf before the two senior officials appointed to hear the case. Never had there been as much of the atmosphere of a state trial in a planning enquiry. All the leading authorities, such as Sir Patrick Abercrombie, President of the CPRE (Council for the Protection of Rural England), Geoffrey Jellicoe, a famous landscape architect from the Institute of Landscape Architects and a member of the Royal Fine Arts Commission, Sir Albert Richardson, a past President of the Royal Academy, and various other notables, were arrayed as witnesses for us. I made what was no doubt an offensive attack on the Dorset County Council: 'One would have thought that as a county in which echoes of Crichel Down are still resounding, bureaucratic actions of this kind were not to be tolerated . . . the action of the planning authority was disingenuous, deplorable and even deceitful . . . the authority had obviously been content with the earlier route proposed until some curious and obscure and still hidden influence was brought to bear to make them revert to the valley route!' The authority called their main witness, Lady Digby, who was the county council chairman, coming as she did from a family who had almost traditionally ruled Dorset. I cross-examined her for nearly a day. She was, I recall, a most charming lady. I remember eliciting the curious (and probably irrelevant) fact that she did not seem to know the difference between local rate finance and national finance from taxation. The case lasted, I think, nearly a week. Soon after Christmas, ministers gave their decision. Justice triumphed – and the pylons were erected elsewhere.

Sir Francis was naturally delighted. For my part, I felt that in view of the kind hospitality I had received and of my long association as leading counsel for Shell, I would not charge a fee.

By now my personal uncertainties as to future plans were developing to a point where I had to make up my mind whether or not I should bring my legal career to a drastic and final conclusion. My recollection of my concerns has been much refreshed by the kindness of the Bodleian Library in making available to me a file of correspondence between myself and Walter Monckton. Walter and his wife Biddy had been for some years on terms of close friendship with Joan and me. Being a member of the Cabinet, he was at this time no longer in practice at the Bar. The alternatives he had in view for himself were the possibility of succeeding Rayner Goddard as Chief Justice, or going into the City. His situation was similar to my own. On 17 October 1956 he had written to me saying that he was very uncertain about his future and wanted to talk to me about it. As for my own position, he said that he saw 'Every advantage in you going to the "Morgue" [as Brendan Bracken described the Lords] except that it takes you out of the chance of the highest office in the political field. I should not have thought that the mere fact of your disagreements with your present colleagues need mean that your chances of the highest offices, and indeed of the highest office of all, have gone or are going. There are many of us, I suspect on both sides of the House and certainly on ours, who think of quite possible circumstances in which the lights would beckon you. Are you really decided to ignore them? Please let me know *at once* because . . . etc.'

I was, however, increasingly uncertain about my own prospects. As I have said, with the extortionate rates of tax and surtax, I was quite unable to save out of income. Joan and I had no capital to speak of, and there was much talk of the likelihood that the existing (but anomalous) rule that on retirement barristers could collect unpaid fees without liability to tax was going to be revoked. In the meantime, through the good offices of Brendan Bracken, Sir Patrick Hennessey, Chairman of the Ford Motor Company in Britain, had offered me a directorship at that company with a possible succession to the chairmanship. Brendan's own view at the time, however, was that I should stay at the Bar.

Walter and I exchanged considerable correspondence about our respective plans and met quite often. Early in 1957 Millard Tucker, a leading Silk specializing in tax cases, told me that he thought the exemption from tax on unpaid fees would go that year. Three factors then combined to force me to a decision. First, the risk that I could not collect my unpaid fees without tax would be realized by the threatened change in the law. Secondly, I had the firm offer of a directorship at Ford. And thirdly, I had now received a firm offer from Frank Hopwood to take a part-time job with Shell. I considered all this against the background of what I had long felt about politics, its drudgery and the complete absence of a private life.

And Brendan Bracken in one of his published letters to Lord Beaverbrook wrote:

> The newspaper reports that Hartley Shawcross contemplates retiring from politics are true. Hector McNeil tells me that great efforts are being made to persuade him to stay in his place but that Shawcross is not susceptible to blandishments. I had a talk with that eminent lawyer the other night and he told me that there was no such drudgery as politics. He declares that he has no private life and wonders how civilised members can stay in office. He may of course be forced to change his mind . . .

There was a further consideration in the background. Some time in the autumn of 1956, Gaitskell had told me at the Garrick Club that he wanted me to be his Lord Chancellor in the government that he was then confident that before long he would be forming. This was not a job I coveted at all, although I realized that if I were still in the Commons when Labour came back into office I should have to take it as being at least the most obvious candidate with the necessary standing at the Bar.

And so – reluctantly – I took the decision to leave the Bar. In February, Walter Monckton had become a director of the Midland Bank and was soon to be its chairman. He was happy. I also took the plunge.

I wrote to Walter on 4 March 1957:

My dear Walter:

Very many thanks for all your advice and help over so long a time. Having finally taken the decision I feel very gloomy about it; it is sad to leave the Bar. But it will be rather a relief to know that there will now be at least a pittance for Joan.

In January and February 1957 I had been very busy at the Bar and I had to time the date of my public announcement that I was giving up practice so as to avoid causing inconvenience to clients or difficulty with public engagements. Thus on 3 and 4 March I was in the Hague, presiding over a conference of lawyers which had been organized by the International Commission of Jurists to discuss the secret trials that had been taking place in Hungary. On the Monday I took the fateful plunge and told my constituents in St Helens of my decision.

There was much speculation that I would go back into more active politics and some papers implied that I was going to make a bid for the leadership of the Labour Party. There was no justification for their speculations. In my speech in St Helens announcing my decision I had said

... What my future employment will be is not a matter of national concern but I should make it clear to you that I have no intention of becoming a professional politician. As I have told you before, I have never thought I was the direct recipient of divine guidance to direct the lives of others or to push people around. As you know, the exaggerations of partisan politics have no attractions for me ...

The Times devoted nearly a column to this speech, but three days later, in a leading article of a very friendly kind, the newspaper pondered

If Sir Hartley comes back to front bench politics (and his decision to quit the Bar and 'to get to know more about the real world outside' points to that direction) he will make the Shadow Cabinet look a little more like an alternative Government ... his return would not leave undisturbed the balance of power in the Party.

The Daily Mirror columnist Cassandra remarked:

Take the case of Sir Hartley. I don't know the reasons why Sir Hartley is leaving the Bar but if I were Sir Hartley taxation would be my reason. He is the most famous barrister in Britain. In fact he is the only barrister whose name is a household word all over the country. He has reached the glittering summit of the legal career . . . and he is turning it in to take an appointment with Shell. Suppose that Sir Hartley makes £40,000 a year at the Bar and suppose that he makes much less than a quarter of that in his new post.

What difference will that make to his real income, the money he has to spend or save?

Nothing worth talking about.

On the other hand he will be relieved of the murderous pressure that the highest kind of legal work involves. Instead of sitting up to the small hours of the morning getting his work ready for next day he will be able to have some civilised leisure and will not be haunted with all the strains and tensions that the leading barrister of the land must suffer from.

He won't miss his imaginary thousands and scores of thousands because he never got them.

On the contrary he might be better off. When a barrister quits his practice he is entitled to get his outstanding fees free of tax.

The most brilliant forensic brain in the country is being withdrawn from the Bar because taxation makes it unprofitable to work and gives a bonus for stopping . . . We are strangling ourselves with taxes.

This was a pretty accurate assessment of the situation and some other journalists commented in the same way. It was true, as my correspondence with Walter Monckton showed, and as I have already mentioned, that the collection of unpaid fees was one of the factors that led to my withdrawal from the Bar at that time.

But much good it did me. Few will believe how naïve I was about City affairs then. I had told my clerk not to chase up solicitors who did not pay their fees promptly, but to let them accumulate. When I retired these unpaid fees were collected and amounted to around £50,000 – in 1995 terms about £500,000. I had to invest them. But at that time I had no broker and no financial adviser, for up till then I had not been able to save a penny. A close friend recommended a stockbroker who I assumed must be reliable and I handed over my capital nest-egg to him with instructions to invest it so as to secure capital gains. He invested it, however, in what must have been the most speculative adventures, such as oil companies on the north coast of Canada of which no one had ever heard. Within six months most of the £50,000 had evaporated. I remember recounting the circumstances to Sigmund Warburg as we were walking through the park together one afternoon. He had become a friend of mine in connection with the Friends of the Atlantic Union organization. He commented, 'I think we could do better than that. If you care to have whatever remains transferred to my firm we will look after it and not charge you any fees!' I gratefully accepted his offer and removed the remnants of the nest-egg to Warburg's who have ever since handled such money as I had to invest and – while Sigmund was in active management – I rather think without charging fees. I transferred such savings as I made to Joan's account.

By the middle of March 1957 I had become a non-executive director of the Ford Motor Company, run excellently and with the full involvement of the non-executive directors by Sir Patrick Hennessey.

At Shell I became nominally a legal adviser on a part-time basis, succeeding the famous Val Holmes, one-time senior Treasury Junior when I was Attorney General. The only restriction was that I should not accept any other directorships than Ford while working for Shell. As far as I can recall, I was only once asked for a legal opinion, which I gave carelessly and wrongly. I was nonetheless soon made a director of Shell Petroleum Ltd with an office, full-time secretary and the use of a car, but my duties were pretty vague; Shell had a very effective legal department which needed no help from me.

When I retired from the Bar I had also retired from the chairmanship of the Bar Council and from the Recordership of Kingston. I was however asked and I agreed to stay on as Chairman of the Bar Council, the Council being anxious that I should help in connection with the impending visit of the American Bar Association, which I did. Politically, in this transitional period of my life, I was more and more associated with Dick Stokes, and our speeches seemed largely concerned with the policy of nationalization. My remark that 'nationalization for the sake of nationalization is as dead as the Dodo' still had its reverberations, and the speeches Dick and I made attracted wide publicity and much criticism from the left wing. The leftwing union leaders described us as the 'Handmaidens of Monopoly Capitalism'.

My agreeable and friendly partnership with Dick Stokes was, alas, tragically broken. In July 1957 he was involved in a motor accident in which his car overturned and he sustained serious injuries. I used to go to see him in hospital, and I recall him saying that far from being afraid of death he would welcome it. I asked him why and he replied, 'Because then I should see God.'

I believed he was recovering from his injuries and went away on my usual sailing holiday, but while we were off St Mawes listening to the six o'clock news on the radio, I was shocked to hear that he had died. William, my eldest son, who had greatly enjoyed his company, was deeply affected too, and retired silently to his bunk. A funeral service was held in Westminster Cathedral, and sitting there on my own, not only did I shed tears but it was slowly borne in upon me that I had lost my main ally. Dick's death was to be a significant factor in my own eventual withdrawal from active political life.

I still had some useful work to do at the Bar Council. It came to our notice that a certain member of the Bar had been too closely engaged with a man said to be 'the Boss of London's Underworld', whom he had been briefed to defend. This information may have come to us in confidence from Scotland Yard. We also had reason to believe that the police had been tapping and recording telephone conversations between this notorious criminal and the barrister. I decided to ask the Home Secretary, Gwilym Lloyd George, to release the transcripts of these conversations to the Bar Council and he agreed to let me have them. I took the view that they disclosed an improper relationship and the Bar Council in accordance with its rules started a disciplinary inquiry. The barrister gave evidence and I crossexamined him, clearly indicating that I knew some details of his telephone conversations. In the event the Bar Council concluded that he had a case to answer why he should not be disbarred and we referred the matter to his Inn of Court, Lincoln's Inn. The barrister, however, complained to the Press, the television news and the police about what he professed to regard as a gross infringement of his private rights by telephone tapping. And this was the view many newspapers at first took of it. The barrister, with possibly some justification, said it was extremely embarrassing to him and his solicitor that the police, through tapping his telephone, should know how they were planning to defend three men whom they were representing at the Old Bailey. The Press went to town about it. So did the House of Commons, and nearly fifty questions were put down. There were allegations that MPs' lines might be tapped. On 26 June, the disciplinary proceedings against the barrister commenced before the benchers of Lincoln's Inn, including at least seven High Court judges. The hearing took three long days. Judgement was reserved. In the end, the unanimous decision was that although some of the many charges were not proved, the barrister had clearly been guilty of gross professional misconduct. He was disbarred and expelled.

I had not been involved at all with the hearing before the Inn of Court but the matter was by no means finished for me. The disbarred barrister threatened all sorts of proceedings against me personally, but these never materialized. At the annual meeting of the Bar, held shortly afterwards, Lord Chorley (who had been my Deputy Regional Commissioner in the NorthWest and was an old friend), proposed a resolution deploring the use by the Bar Council of the telephone intercepts. It was then announced that the barrister had appealed to the Lord Chancellor against his expulsion and that therefore any discussion by the Bar Council would have to be adjourned. Some members of the Bar resented this and said it was a device to stifle discussion. To this I replied with some vigour.

In due course – indeed with little delay – the man's appeal was dismissed and his expulsion from the Bar became final. But even this did not silence him. He continued to be given a great deal of publicity and sold his story to the Press, but although he threatened action against all and sundry until late in 1958, nothing happened. The Government did, however, after the expulsion of the barrister, set up an inquiry by Privy Councillors into the general problem of telephone tapping at which I gave evidence. In the event they found that the general system of telephone tapping, subject to strict safeguards, was justified.

Following the Privy Councillors' report the Bar Council resumed the meeting to consider the motion condemning the use of the intercepts.

The motion was withdrawn and to cheers the Bar Council passed a vote of confidence in me.

In my last year as Chairman of the Bar Council I presided over the visit to this country of no less than 5,000 members of the American Bar Association plus wives and families – the first since the Second World War. The main occasion of this visit was the dedication of a memorial – an obelisk enclosed by a circular temple structure designed by Sir Edward Maufe – placed in Runnymede Meadow as near as history could place it to the exact spot where some 750 years before King John has signed the Magna Carta. The sun smiled on us and a ceremony (solemn enough, although I took the opportunity of wearing my Texan stetson) was performed. There was also a great banquet at Guildhall and the visit was an outstanding success.

Meanwhile, no longer distracted by legal duties, I began to familiarize myself with the work of the two companies with which I was to be associated, and at the same time I joined Joan in looking for a slightly larger house. We had loved Peckhams and had been very happy there, but with the children beginning to grow up and wanting friends to stay and I myself looking forward to having much more time at home and needing a study, it had become rather small for us. After many searches and inspections we found Friston Place, a typical 13th-century 'hall house' in a valley of the Downs near to the Seven Sisters' cliffs. It is a Grade I listed building, with many attractive features, from which one can walk or ride straight on to the glorious Downs. It remains alive with Joan's memory and is – and I hope may remain – the family home.

My public life outside Parliament went on. I continued to make a good many speeches – rather 'Cross-bench' in tone because I was increasingly impressed with the unreality of purely partisan politics – and I continued to have the most loyal support from St Helens. By the end of 1957, however, I had made up my mind that politics was not for me and that I must resign my seat. Just before Christmas I went up to St Helens and held my periodical surgery after which I had a long meeting with the executive of the local Labour Party. It was a very friendly meeting. I warned them – not for the first time – that I thought it unlikely that I could stay much longer in Parliament. For their part they did their best to persuade me to stay. In the New Year I saw Gaitskell and told him I was going. He also did his best to change my mind, and repeated his promise to make me Lord Chancellor. I am not sure whether I ever told him that if it had been the Foreign Secretaryship he promised I might have been attracted to stay on. In my message to my constituents announcing the decision to resign, I said that it was a very sad one for me – my wife and I had a real affection for St Helens and deep gratitude for all the loyal support and generous confidence which its people had extended during the last 12 years. I went on:

My resignation at this time is not because of political disagreement with the Labour Party. It would no doubt be idle to pretend that I have not disagreed with certain proposals which have found some favour in the party while it has been in opposition, notably those involving further nationalisation of industry and certain aspects of foreign defence and educational policy on which I have favoured more bi-partisan consultation . . .

For whilst I think we must avoid being doctrinaire about methods, I still believe as strongly as before in the basic principles which led me to join the Party 40 years ago, in particular that there must be a reasonable minimum standard of life below which none should be allowed to fall, and above which everybody should have an equal opportunity and full encouragement to rise.

When I left the Bar a year ago, I had hoped that I should be able to discharge more adequately the duties of my membership of Parliament, but this has unfortunately not turned out to be the case. The immediate reasons for this are of a purely personal and private nature but a basic cause is that membership of the House of Commons is becoming more and more a whole time occupation.

The private Member can expect to have little individual influence unless he devotes substantially all his time, usually until late at night and to the exclusion of other and often even of family interests, to the various duties of a Member and to attendance at the House.

This I am not able to do and I have been forced to the conclusion that it is much better from all points of view that I should give way now to someone better able and prepared to plan this kind of part in the work of the House of Commons than I am myself.

There was the usual exchange of letters with Hugh Gaitskell. I think it is possible that if I had known that Hugh was dying the call of public duty would have sounded more loudly in my ears. But although Hugh and I had exchanged comments about our bodily ills – he and I had apparently similar symptoms in the diaphragm! – I had no idea then that he was gravely ill. However, on the day of my last visit I had made a speech at a Labour club in St Helens which outlined my disillusion with political life and earned a favorable leader in *The Times*.

Any industry run in the way we run our country would be bankrupt in a week.

How can it be thought that British foreign policy should influence events when foreign powers know that if a Government of a different political complexion were to come into power here, the policy might be reversed.

That is why it is so fatal to have what is merely a Tory foreign policy, or a Labour foreign policy; there ought to be a British foreign policy which will be pursued consistently and which foreign countries will know is supported by the mass of the British people. And that means there must be full consultation between the leaders of the Government and Opposition parties before great decisions on foreign policy are taken.

Or consider the way we govern ourselves at home. Parliament and Ministers are bogged down by detail and the trivial. A committee of ten sensible men of good will could accomplish in a couple of hours what may occupy the time of Parliament for a couple of days. And a great deal of Parliamentary time is occupied by sham fights on matters quite irrelevant to our real problems.

Mr Clement Davies, the former Liberal leader, said the other day that since 1945 nobody of real achievement or distinction in any outside activity had gone into the House of Commons. And that is true.

Parliament is becoming, if it has not already become, professionalized, composed of members compelled to devote their whole time to Parliamentary affairs and thus incapable of maintaining the same contact with or bringing the same experience from the outside world as used to be the case.

The *Daily Worker* was less favourable than *The Times*. They said the speech 'stank of Fascism'. I thought it hard that a slavishly Communist paper should use that expression when of course Communism is itself simply a different variety of Fascism.

Looking back at all this now I do of course wonder whether much of it was not unconsciously a kind of smokescreen to hide the abdica‑ tion of responsibilities that I ought to have been ready to accept. A higher power must judge.

Having resigned from Parliament I became increasingly active with a wide variety of outside interests. I was already a member of various com‑ mittees and chairman of some, such as Friends of Atlantic Union and of Justice, the law reform organization that had been set up by Peter Benenson (who also established Amnesty) following the invasion of Hungary. And I had of course my jobs with Shell and Ford. Pat Hennessey, Brendan Bracken and I continued to have our regular lunches together, always at the same table in the beautiful Grill Room at the Café Royal – still so well maintained by the Forte Group and for which I retain a sentimental affection.

The work at Ford and more particularly with Shell also kept me interested and busy. At Shell my responsibilities were undefined but included work of a social/goodwill nature. Joan and I hosted many parties which we gave in a private room at the Mirabelle restaurant to diplomats and influential visitors from foreign countries in which Shell had, or wished to acquire, interests. We made a series of visits to the out‑ posts of the Shell empire. These included Venezuela, Malaysia, Thailand, and the Gulf sheikhdoms of Oman and Brunei. Venezuela, of course, was a very large production field, but many of the other places we visited were small exploratory or production units, some of which had never seen a Shell director in the flesh before.

We used to be welcomed almost as royalty. We usually stayed with the Shell 'No. 1', who was extremely well housed and glad, because of the infrequency of such visits, to have the excuse of bestowing lavish hospitality. We visited Muscat and Oman, possibly the most pic‑ turesque of all the Arab countries and then a British protectorate, several times. When Joan and I made our first visit we were flown there from Aden in a Shell plane by Douglas Bader and we landed at Sallalah, the ruler's summer palace. The then ruler was a venerable and exquisitely courteous man. He apparently suspected his son, Qabus, of advanced ideas, such as doing things in his own good time rather than God's. Moreover, the father thought that the appropriate way to settle his son down was to marry him off to some lady he had never seen. In the meantime, Qabus was confined to quarters in the palace compound and was not even allowed to ride along the beach. It was in circum-stances of this kind that the son staged a palace coup. The father was wounded – but only in the leg – and he was banished to London, to a private suite at Claridge's, where he survived for some time in condi-tions significantly more agreeable than those on St Helena. We got to know Sultan Qabus quite well. Indeed, he stayed at Friston with us and we took him to Glyndebourne. He is a great lover of opera and classi-cal music.

Brunei was in some ways a rather similar experience. There the Shell No. 1 had a delightful house with a comfortable guest suite and swim-ming pool. The country was almost divided into two territories – the ruler's, and Shell's – and the No. 1 at the time of our first visit was a member of an advisory council that assisted the ruler, Sultan Sir Muda Omar. He was an elderly man who was extremely courteous and pas-sionately devoted to Her Majesty. I visited him from time to time, first to pay courtesy calls on behalf of Shell and later, when my Shell associa-tion had come to an end, as an old friend of his country and on behalf of the J. P. Morgan Bank.

The income flow from Shell was enormous – and still is. The old ruler saw to it that his people were very well provided for, with free housing, free schools and a very large and beautifully equipped hospital. But the oil revenue still accumulated. At a time of one of the periodic crises in sterling, the ruler had a very large holding of the currency which in view of the downturn in the exchange rate he was proposing to sell. I had from time to time given Sir Muda Omar very tentative and informal advice on the management of his funds and – to my surprise – somehow or other I persuaded him not to sell sterling. This resulted in a telex from the Chancellor of the Exchequer sent care of the UK High Commissioner in Singapore, warmly thanking me for my intervention. Later, in about 1967, Sir Muda abdicated in favour of his eldest son whom he hoped to assist to adjust to life in this high office. He died about nine years later. In the meantime, the country had been granted complete freedom from the United Kingdom, and in 1984 there was a great celebration of the country's independence to which my daughter and I were invited.

CHAPTER 13

Into 'The Morgue'

AFTER my departure from politics I continued to pick up odd jobs – some more odd than others. One was to become President of the British Hotels and Restaurants Association. Another appointment was as a member of the Court of London University, then chaired by Norman Birkett, a post I held for some 15 years. Whether I was of any help I doubt, but the University was good enough to give me an honorary degree conferred on me by Her Majesty the Queen, on termination of the appointment. I was for some years Chairman of the Board of Governors of Dulwich College, my old school, and in 1959 was appointed to the Council and Executive Committee of the new Sussex University. I was very interested in this project, the first of seven new ('chromium-plated', they came to be called, as distinct from the older 'red brick') universities, and was introduced into it by a local acquaintance, Mr Sydney Caffyn, an alderman of Eastbourne, head of a family firm of motor traders and a public-spirited philanthropist who, from the beginning, was one of the leading figures in the establishment of the University. His character was I think well illustrated by one incident which occurred when the main buildings of the University had been nearly completed. A model of the whole campus included a chapel, beautifully designed, along with the rest of the University, by Basil Spence. The cost was being underwritten by Sydney Caffyn. Up to this time no comment, apart from expressions of gratitude to Caffyn and admiration of the design, had been made. When, however, the actual building – which naturally had been delayed until the nucleus of the University itself had been completed – was commenced, a campaign suddenly started opposing the project. Some professor went so far as to say that from his study window he would be able to see the proposed chapel and the sight of it would make it quite impossible for him to work. The dispute went on for some time – to the discredit of the University – until Sydney Caffyn stated that he did not insist on the building being called a chapel. Let it be called a meeting house with – as the original design had always contemplated – the upper half, a large round auditorium beautifully lighted by slanting sunlight through coloured glass, being used for religious devotions by any denomination and the lower part for quiet concerts, meetings and the like. I confess that if I had been in Caffyn's position I would have been inclined to with-draw my support. As it was the meeting house has become a calm centre of university life and resident chaplains of the Protestant and of the Roman Catholic faiths regularly hold their services there, as do other denominations. I was at an early stage appointed chairman of the build-ing committee for the whole University, I think on the theory that it would involve one professional man – me – dealing with another pro-fessional man, the leading architect. This was not always easy but the redoubtable Basil Spence and I got on well together.

In 1960 I became Pro-Chancellor and in 1965 I was elected Chan-cellor in succession to Lord Monckton, a position I held for 20 years.

On 23 January 1959 I was made a life peer, and entered 'The Morgue'. This was on Harold Macmillan's nomination. The position was that in 1958 Parliament had authorized the creation of life peers, and Mr Macmillan made the usual consultations. My name was sug-gested by the Prime Minister but Hugh Gaitskell, then Leader of the Opposition, understandably did not want me to be included in the first list as by this time I had already detached myself from the Labour Party and he feared that the Labour Members in the House would resent it if I appeared on that list inferentially on his recommendation. Macmillan decided in view of this that he would introduce a second, non-political list, without too much delay. I remember Rab Butler telling me I would like the names of those with whom I was to appear in the second list. I did. They were Sir Eric James, High Master of Manchester Grammar School; Sir Edwin Plowden, a distinguished public servant, then Chairman of the Atomic Energy Authority; and Professor Lionel Robbins, a leading economist and Chairman of the National Gallery

Trustees, who was a friend. *The Economist* called the list 'a Brains Trust in ermine', the *Guardian* 'an excellent list', and the *Scotsman* 'Lords of Learning'. I was conscious of the fact that I really did not qualify under any of these titles but I bathed in their reflected glory.

It was expected that I would sit on the cross-benches. The *Daily Telegraph* said

> some may expect him to join the Conservatives as a further stage in his political pilgrimage. But though he left the Socialists because of their nationalisation policy he remains in other fields a radical. Hence a life and not a hereditary peerage. The Cross Benchers of the Lords will provide him with a delicately poised platform denied him altogether in the Lower House.

When earlier – while Eden was Prime Minister – there had been talk of a possible viscountcy for me, I had written to Walter Monckton, then in Eden's Cabinet, telling him to inform Eden clearly that there was no prospect of my joining the Tory Party in the Lords. So I did not get the viscountcy!

The expectation was that I would be moderately active in the Lords and so, at first, I was. I enjoyed the cross-bench position in which I did not have to speak unless I wanted to and did not need to worry about the effect of newspaper reports of what I said, or about constituents. But I did not speak often and still continued to make more speeches outside the House than in it. When Labour got back into power in 1964 I tended to be critical of their economic policy. I was soundly and indeed very offensively trounced by Lord Balogh and Lord Kaldor, that curious pair of economists from Eastern Europe ennobled on the recommendation of Harold Wilson, who verbally earned their keep. 'The odious pests from Budapest', we called them. Their attacks did not deter me but a few years later I was discouraged from further interventions. I received a longish letter from Lord (Frank) Beswick, who had been a PPS in the 1945–51 Parliament. We had become friendly when he accompanied the British delegation to one or two of the Assemblies of the UN. He was the son of a miner, deeply sincere as a Socialist of the Keir Hardie school. I recall an occasion when we both received formal invitations to a dinner party in Tom Watson's house off Fifth Avenue. The card had the usual 'black tie' note at its foot. Frank said, 'I am not going to be told what tie to wear.' At all events, years later, I think in 1970, he wrote to me more in sorrow than in anger to the effect that my speeches criticizing Labour policy had caused ill-feeling among his colleagues. After all, I had been a member of the Party and a friend of many of them, and they found it disagreeable that I should now be crit- icizing them. I understood his feelings very well. Dora Gaitskell also attacked me in a letter to the Press and evidently felt very bitterly about my criticisms. She was hardly naïve politically and had also once been a friend. Denis Healey ('make the pips squeak' will remain his epitaph) also lambasted me. Moreover, Gerald Gardiner, who was then Labour Lord Chancellor, refused to attend a meeting of Justice (the Law Reform Society) at which he had been booked to speak because I, the Chairman, had made speeches (not of course for Justice) warning that current Labour economic policy might lead to a further devaluation. (In fact, a Labour Government minister, as well as Lord Cromer and Lord Kearton and the National Institute of Economic and Social Research, had previously given similar warnings.)

I reflected that my speeches did no good and would not affect events in the slightest degree. I ceased almost entirely to intervene, and indeed explained the reasons for this in a speech I made later in the Lords.

I did not allow the announcement of the peerage to interrupt the plans I had already made for the New Year, and I was not introduced into the House until 6 May, my sponsors being Frank Pakenham (Lord Longford), an old colleague in the Labour Party and a personal friend, and Henry Cohen, the Professor of Medicine at Liverpool University, who was perhaps the closest of my lifelong friends. I made my maiden speech quite soon after, on 14 May, in a debate on the procedure followed by Tribunals – a subject on which, following the Lynskey affair, I was able to speak with some appearance of authority.

In the spring of 1959 my father published his complete rhyming translation of Goethe's *Faust*. One of the newspapers remarked:

There is a refreshing disdain for speed in the literary career of John Shawcross, 87-year-old father of Lord Shawcross. He published the first part of *Faust* 25 years ago in 1934 and he published his first major work, an edition of Coleridge's *Biographia Literaria*, 27 years before in 1907. It was because of his father's interest in Coleridge that Lord Shawcross was named Hartley – after the poet's son, Hartley. Mr Shawcross tells me he has now given up writing. 'I am getting on, you know,' he said. But he does a lot of reading and is very fond of walking. He lives at Friston, Sussex in the grounds of Lord Shawcross's home . . .

He continued to live there for another eight years, a dignified and gentle presence at Friston and a great friend to his grandchildren, who loved his poetry and his kindness. He died at the age of ninety-five. We buried him beside his beloved wife, my mother, at Fairwarp.

I was soon very fully occupied, not so much with Ford or Shell – both of which were after all part-time occupations – as with committees, newspaper articles on legal and other public matters that could be treated in a fairly non-partisan way, and speeches to various organiza-tions both in England and on the Continent. There would be no world war, I told the Civil Defence Staff College; the real danger, I said, was in the fields of economics and politics. 'The law of contempt of court is in a chaotic state,' I said in the report of a Justice Committee which I chaired; the law relating to domicile needed long-overdue reform. In both of these matters I did help in legislation in the Lords and I wrote lengthy articles in *The Times*. I see that, in a lighter tone in a speech to the Hotels and Restaurants Association, I condemned the British custom in the less-than-top hotels of having 'bottles of sauce on the tables, their proprietary labels often scruffy, suggesting to the customer either that his palate is jaded or that the cuisine is lacking in flavour'. The practice, alas, goes on and the implications of it are too true.

Around this time, in 1960, Justice was becoming more and more active, and we started a study of the Scandinavian ombudsman system under the chairmanship of Sir John Whyatt, QC. In the beginning there was much opposition and I was involved in a lot of work. It was worthwhile: the official adoption of the system in several branches of public activity in this country has been a notable success.

Life was by no means all work and no play. Early in the summer Joan performed the launching ceremony of *Aluco*, a new Shell tanker at one of the Newcastle yards. We had a special train full of guests, largely our own and our friends' children, to take us to Newcastle and back, and better than normal food. Joan made a graceful speech with suitable nautical allusions that I had provided, and cracked a bottle of champagne smartly, but regretfully wastefully, on the vessel's prow.

In 1959 Mr Macmillan's Government had decided to set up an advisory commission for the review of the constitution of the Federation of Rhodesia and Nyasaland. Lord Monckton accepted the chairmanship. The main body of members was quickly recruited. Three places had been left open for the Labour Opposition, but they refused to nominate on the ground that the terms of reference did not enable the Commission to recommend any other form of government than federation for the three territories, while much African opinion seemed to favour separation. This was a serious setback.

I received a message from Harold Macmillan and I went and spent about an hour with him at No. 10. He explained to me in some detail his general thinking about Africa, and in particular Rhodesia, and I was greatly impressed by his apparent knowledge and sincerity. He talked of the Labour Party's refusal to co-operate in the manning of the Commission and asked if I would join it. I did not particularly want to do so. It would mean a long absence from home in strange surroundings. And it would clash with an invitation I had just received from Rab Butler, then Home Secretary, to be chairman of a Royal Commission on the Police, a subject that was familiar to me. I felt, however, that as one who was still in public life but detached from party politics, it was my duty to accept any work that I felt competent to do and which the Prime Minister of the day asked me to undertake. So I accepted Macmillan's and declined Rab's invitation. Macmillan also secured Aidan Crawley, a friend of mine who had been a junior minister in the Attlee administration but had left the Labour Party because of disagreement over Suez, and Sir Charles Arden-Clarke, one-time Governor-General of Ghana.

Before my appointment was formally announced I had to get Shell's agreement. Macmillan accordingly wrote to John Loudon, the Chairman of Shell, in extraordinarily eulogistic terms, saying that there was no one in public life whom he so much admired as me. Loudon agreed to release me. He asked about Joan and when I said I would be going alone he said most generously that Shell would cover all Joan's and my expenses if I took her. Once the news broke in the second week in December 1959 there was of course a bit of a Press furore. The Labour Party were said to be grossly affronted. More trouble was, however, caused by an answer I gave to questions about the exclusion of any consideration of secession from the terms of reference of the Commission. It so happened that I had agreed to appear on the *Face to Face* programme conducted by John Freeman on the BBC, and he specifically asked me about the position. I admitted that I would regard it as a matter of conscience to recommend against federation and suggest secession if African opinion were universally opposed to it.

This remark landed me in grave trouble. Sir Roy Welensky, the Federal Rhodesian Prime Minister, said my answer was 'deplorable', that Sir Edgar Whitehead, Prime Minister of Southern Rhodesia, held the same view, and that my position was 'completely at variance with the terms of reference.' 'Shawcross must go' was the policy. The matter was raised in the Commons, Hugh Gaitskell saying that it was an extraordinary situation. But the Government refused to comment on this and Macmillan himself took a tough line on African policy generally. Terms of reference had never over-worried me and the argument blew over. And later Sir Roy, a most remarkable man who had risen from a modest beginning on the railways and had taught himself Greek on the footplate of a railway engine, became reconciled to me.

I had many irons in the fire which had to be dealt with before I could leave for Rhodesia. There was discussion on the idea of a multilateral foreign investment treaty, the possibility of my introducing a bill in the Lords to reform the law relating to contempt of court, the Justice study on the ombudsman, and other matters on which I was either speaking or writing Press articles. In due time these irons were set and John Loudon asked me to join him on a tour of the Gulf and the East African outposts of the Shell empire, the plan being to end the tour in Nairobi where I would join the Monckton Commission.

At Aden the colony's oil supplies were handled by a Shell employee, resident there with his wife, and Loudon stayed with them. I was told I was to stay with the Besses, a much-Anglicized French couple. Tony Besse ran the largest merchanting and entrepreneurial business in the area. Christiane Besse was a most vivacious and striking young woman and she and her husband, fairly recently married, kept a quite luxurious home, including a resident French masseur of whose attentions I was very glad. It turned out that we shared a common interest in sailing. I had just, in a moment of folly, sold my beloved boat, *Vanity V*. So Christiane, I suspect to Tony's horror, but with her characteristic generosity immediately offered to lend us their yacht *Ariel* for a family holiday. Tony agreed at once. I found them both enchanting, and when Joan met them, so did she. They became our closest friends, and remain so to this day.

Shell arranged a trip across the nature reserve between Kenya and Tanganyika. We travelled in Land Rovers, camping for the night, but the going was very rough and I was suffering from a recurring spinal disc problem. This was an old complaint, caused when I was in my twenties by a climbing accident. The pain grew worse and I had to go into hospital in Lusaka where, after X-rays, an excellent local surgeon gave me a spinal injection of some anaesthetic which brought immediate and complete relief. But, alas, it only lasted a few days and the pain, now crippling, returned. I was flown to Salisbury, crawling out of the aircraft, there being no stretcher, and went into an admirable nursing home run by nuns. There a surgeon who said he had done 5,000 disc operations wanted to operate at once. After cabling my neuro-surgeon I decided, however, that it was better to return to England. I was flown home on a DC-7C aeroplane fitted out with twin berths and it was arranged for a Shell doctor to meet the plane at every stop on the way back to London to give me an injection of morphia. At London Airport I was taken out of the aircraft on a fork-lift truck and met by a doctor, a nurse and an ambulance. I was also greeted by Lord Home – one of the great gentlemen in politics – then Secretary for Commonwealth Relations. I was operated on at the London Clinic within two or three days and was able to leave about a month later. But the doctors would not agree to my going back to Africa and I was forced, very reluctantly, to resign from the Commission early in June.

By the summer I was sufficiently recovered to take advantage of the generous Besse offer and we had a most enjoyable cruise with all our three children on the yacht *Ariel* in the Mediterranean. Thus encouraged, I bought myself another boat, a 12-metre called *Stiarna*, thought to have been one of C. E. Nicholson's most beautiful designs. She was a much more comfortable boat than *Vanity*, built entirely of teak, and she gave us very much pleasure until, like all my boats, I sold her because I felt I could not afford yachting. I have reached this conclusion often. But it has invariably been followed a month or two later by a realization that there are some things in life I could not afford to do without, and so I have persuaded myself to buy another boat.

In 1961 my relationship with Shell and Ford changed. Ford was taken over as a wholly owned subsidiary of its American parents, and in anticipation of this I resigned my non-executive directorship in the company. It had been an interesting and useful initiation into the running of a great industrial concern and I had been much impressed with the quality of its management, later on drawing odious compari-sons between it and other companies with which I became associated. This change in my relationship with Ford enabled me to become a full-time director of the Shell Petroleum Company, although without any executive responsibility.

At that time the Secretary for State for Science was Quintin Hogg – Lord Hailsham. I had always admired and liked him; we were neigh-bours in Sussex. He appointed me Chairman of the Medical Research Council, for a four-year term. It was a fascinating position, though, of course, I was hopelessly out of my depth. The members of the Council were without exception men of the highest intellectual attainment, most Fellows of the Royal Society and with strings of letters after their names which indicated real achievement among the élite of world scientists. Possibly because of my earlier intention to be a doctor myself, but more because I had had personal reason to understand the immense impor-tance of medical research, I found the work of the Council intensely interesting and I was disappointed when at the end of the four years my appointment as Chairman was not renewed. But by this time a Labour minister, Tony Crosland, was the Secretary of State for Science.

At about the same time as I was forced to retire from the Monckton Commission, Harold Macmillan asked me to be Chairman of a new Royal Commission to study the Press. The Commission was set up to examine the financial factors affecting the production and sale of news-papers and to consider whether they affected diversity of ownership or the number and variety of publications. I insisted that the membership should be small. No doubt I thought that the smaller the number the easier it would be for me to get my own way. In the end we secured four members: Sir Graham Cunningham, Chairman of Triplex Glass, who became my deputy chairman; Professor Robert Browning, an accountancy don at Glasgow University; W. B. Reddaway, a somewhat left-wing and distinctly independent economist who was head of the Department of Applied Economics at Cambridge; and W. J. Webber, the shrewd and down-to-earth General Secretary of the Transport Salaried Staffs Association. I doubt whether any Royal Commission was more expeditious. Having started our inquiry on 6 April 1961 our report was published on 19 September 1962 – all ten volumes of it, recording nearly 14,000 questions put to witnesses, the overwhelming majority by me! And it was a pretty forthright report. We concluded that the production of national newspapers in London was 'grossly inef-ficient', that a 34 per cent saving in labour in production and distribu-tion could be made by proper organization, but that the employers were weak and disunited and the unions demanding and dishonest.

Our report was widely discussed and approved by almost everybody except the trade unions. They came out quickly with a statement that 'charges of wholesale overstaffing are a gross exaggeration and could only have been made after an inadequate study of the problems of national newspaper production.' They would, wouldn't they. But the newspapers also had fun with the Commission and one parody that I liked ran as follows:

Lord Certainly: Now, Mr Pink, I want to warn you that everything you say will be taken down in writing and used in evidence against you. A copy will be sent to you in about six months' time when you will have forgotten what you have said. You may cut it all out if you like, because no-one will read it so it doesn't matter really, but leave it all in if you can because it does show that we have been doing some-thing – and that's something, isn't it? Now shall we ask you questions or would you rather ask us questions?

Mr Pink:	Neither, thank you.
Lord Certainly:	Well now, that's splendid, because I can't think of anything to ask you.
Prof. Greening:	Er – er – Mr Pink – I have been looking at the figures you have given us on – er – now let me see – oh yes – here it is on page 5 – eh – er – on comparing your profit on capital employed in the business with your profit on your capital based on insured values – and – er – the former is 5.5% against only 5.4% in the latter – now how do you account for the vast difference in these percentages?
Mr Pink:	I don't.
Prof. Greening:	Yes, but I think . . .
Mr Pink:	Ask the donkey.
Sir Blackham Slybacon:	Mr. Pink can you tell me . . .

But although the report got a very good general reception, it took a long time for anything to be done. The Government was shy about setting up a court to deal with amalgamations, but eventually this jurisdiction was established, under a different name (the Monopolies and Mergers Commission), and the Press Council was reorganized under an independent chairman. Indeed, I later became chairman myself. On the question of the more efficient organization of production, the unions put up a long and discreditable fight. In the end, after 25 years, it was Rupert Murdoch's decision to leave Fleet Street, re-establish in Docklands and break the unions, that finally implemented the recommendations of our commission.

There were suggestions early in 1961 that I might go either to Canada as the UK High Commissioner or to Washington as our Ambassador. I was not attracted by Canada. Much as I like and admire the country, it hardly compares with Washington as the hub of the universe. I was certainly interested in the possibility of succeeding Sir Harold Caccia in Washington; Joan and I both liked the United States very much. It was, however, too much of an upheaval in our lives. Not only would it have meant giving up many of the jobs I had recently taken on, it would have caused very difficult problems in regard to the education of our three children and other domestic affairs. Regretfully, I had to tell the Prime Minister that he must rule me out of consideration.

In 1963 a scandal arose concerning Dr Stephen Ward, Miss Christine Keeler and Mr John Profumo, a Cabinet minister, and I was consulted by one of the Astors and some other very well-known people. Dr Ward's case was indeed a tragic one. He was a good osteopath (he had qualified as a doctor in the United States) and a successful portrait artist. Indeed, he made two excellent large drawings of me which were shown at an exhibition of his work held in Hugh Leggatt's gallery in St James's. I do not believe he was a professional procurer in the sense of making a business of organizing the services of prostitutes in return for payments to himself, but he enjoyed café society and he found the entrée to it made easier by his ability to introduce certain members of it to the beautiful Christine Keeler. (My complaint against him at the time was that he never introduced me to her – but then I was hardly in café society!) Ward, because of the prosecution and the social pressures upon him, which might have led to the disclosure of names other than Profumo's, was driven to suicide. Many people must have felt rather hypocritical about what happened.

Profumo was informally advised by the Attorney General of the day. I would have advised him from the beginning not to admit or deny to the House of Commons any adulterous relationship with Miss Keeler, but to maintain that his relationship with her was a matter between him and his wife which he did not propose to discuss before the House beyond saying that there was not the slightest truth in any suggestion that he had discussed any State secrets with her or her friends. He would no doubt have resigned from Parliament but he would not have been guilty of lying to the Prime Minister and to the House. It must be added that after the truth became known, John Profumo, with the loyal support of his wife, Valerie Hobson, pursued a most honourable course in life and has clearly been forgiven by society. At the time, however, newspaper discussion and gossip about the case dragged on and Professor H. W. R. Wade, the leading expert on constitutional law, wrote a letter to *The Times* suggesting that the publication of indecent matters in the Press should be restricted by law. I rarely disagreed with Professor Wade, but I did not agree with this suggestion and I wrote a letter to *The Times*:

. . . Press freedom should be interfered with only in the last resort: for the reason suggested in the last paragraph of this letter, if for no other, its limitation in the existing context would not command public support. Moreover, any such censorship would be highly uncertain in its operation depending, as it would, upon the view of each particular Court of the particular publication before it.

Yet it remains true that increasing anxiety is felt by all thoughtful people and especially by those concerned with delinquency, about the effect which the present news coverage given to these matters is likely to have upon the morals and manners of the country. It seems to me essentially a matter in which newspaper proprietors, editors and journalists who, apart from an understandable financial interest, may as citizens and parents be assumed to be as much concerned as the rest of us in preserving a healthy community, should earnestly reconsider whether their present policies are likely in the long term to contribute to its health. To this process of reconsideration the about to be reconstituted Press Council might make a valuable contribution.

The matter is, however, by no means confined to the press. Similar coverage has been given by the BBC over which the Press Council has no jurisdiction. That immensely influential organization sought, in its '10 o'clock' feature on July 1, to meet the criticisms which had been made in the New Daily, and the Editor of that paper was interviewed by a Mr G. Scott. In justification of the BBC's elaborate reporting of the Ward case, Mr Scott saw fit to say (and to say more than once in the course of the five minutes spared for the discussion) that the case was one 'in which the Prime Minister has come to the point of resignation, in which a Cabinet Minister has been forced to resign and in which rumour involved many other Cabinet Ministers'.

This statement was of course untrue; no one has ever suggested that the Prime Minister or any other Cabinet Minister apart from Mr Profumo (himself not a member of the Cabinet) was in any way involved in the unsavoury details of the Court case nor does the name of any politician on either side of the House, still less of any Cabinet Minister, apart from Mr Profumo, appear ever to have been mentioned in the evidence. These are no party matters and the technique of smearing by association made familiar by the late Senator McCarthy is hardly expected from the BBC. The details of the

Court case were in no respect necessary to the proper information of the public about the real problems of ministerial responsibility and political concern arising from Mr Profumo's conduct.

Nor is the general problem limited to the so called news coverage. The subsequent advertisement, photographs, and general glamoriza' tion of the women involved (without which they would be less likely to reap a rich financial harvest) must cause the millions of good and honest, and one may add, often more beautiful young women who daily work for modest wages in our offices, shops, and factories, to wonder what sort of moral values it is that all this publicity is intended to support.

The true justification which the press and the BBC might advance for all this squalid stuff is, I am afraid, that they publish it because we, the ordinary readers and listeners, like to wallow in it. Any pros' titute can say the same. But the real fault is in ourselves. We need some stronger leadership in the 'old' morality to rid us of this morbid appetite.

Yours faithfully,

SHAWCROSS

House of Lords, July 5

At around this time I began to speak and write more about what I saw as the malaise in our society. I had some support from Cecil King, then the Chairman of the Mirror Group, and from serious publications such as *The Economist*, the *Guardian*, and the *Spectator*, but my efforts had minimal (if indeed any) effect. On 15 December 1963 the *Daily Telegraph* reported:

Lord Shawcross said that listening to 'these miserable little men without a constructive idea, who for money tear down and destroy accepted values and ridicule those who seek to serve their country, you might think there was nothing noble, nothing worthy in our society.'

For some films, theatres, television, paperbacks and newspapers it might be thought that crime, greed, lust and sex were the accepted commonplaces of society.

'You may be as puzzled as I am about these exhibitionist intellec' tuals, these psychiatrists in a small way of business, these publicity' seeking clerics who talk about the new morality. There is no such thing: this so called morality is too often the old immorality condoned.

'The great principles of good or evil, kindness or cruelty, generosity or selfishness, love or lust, do not change because some confused bishop writes a book about it.' The causes of sorrow, evil and crime to-day remain as one thousand years ago, lust cruelty and greed.

'Discard, by all means, the out-worn traditions and sometimes the hypocrisies of the old days. But not all the traditions are outworn, nor all the old virtues hypocrisies.'

Morality is neither ancient or modern. It is surely what one knows instinctively to be right and good when one looks into one's heart and conscience. The trouble is that we do not ask ourselves such questions sufficiently nowadays, or, if we do, we do not speak out bravely with the answers. Looking at the newspapers, the paperbacks, the television, the films and the theatre, one might be excused for thinking that sex, lust, greed and crime were the normal, the accepted commonplace of our society. But it is not so. Not yet. The mass of the population still pursue, as I believe, honest and decent lives. But we acquiesce through weakness and fear of being thought old-fashioned in the activities of those who, for gain or sensationalism, engage in such evil communications.

But although my campaign – for it was almost that – achieved little it did achieve something. The Press Council was reformed on the lines recommended by my Royal Commission. After Cecil King invited me to be its first Chairman, Lord Devlin took over on my private recommendation.

And it did set people talking. The BBC put on a debate over which I presided at Gray's Inn, which the *Guardian* reviewed favourably:

Over the years there have been all sorts of television debates and conversations following many different methods, but none, so far as I can remember, that was so natural and so brilliant as last night's debate 'A Nation in Doubt' held in the Inns of Court, with Lord Shawcross in the chair.

This was an ATV production and it was remarkable for its straightforwardness. There were no pompous introductions, no questioner or interviewer to ask silly questions or confuse the issues, and no interruption (barring the inevitable advertisements) in an hour of continuous and stimulating discussion held before an audience, although the audience took no part in it. The other speakers were Professor Hugh Trevor Roper (Lord Dacre), Lord Boothby, Paul Chambers, Frank Cousins, Angus Wilson, and Gerald Gardiner, QC. The last was the most clear and incisive speaker whom I have ever seen on television and indeed the whole of this long debate made one wish that a lot of the wool and the wind could be taken out of normal television talk. The discussion was steered by Lord Shawcross so deftly that it was not apparently steered at all. Lord Shawcross himself disagreed with the proposition he was required to put that the Nation 'is slipping morally, socially, and intellectually.'

The other speakers generally did not agree with this either. Gerald Gardiner said that our trouble was inefficiency, that good government was needed to put things right, that Parliament had lost control of the Executive, and that the Civil Service was a closed shop. Lord Shawcross suggested that instead of calling for moral leadership from the Government and the trade unions and the churches, the writers, and playwrights, television, radio and the press might try to give some themselves.

CHAPTER 14

Other Business

IN the autumn of 1965, to my surprise, I was summoned by the Shell Chairman, David Barran. He was an experienced and able manager who succeeded in never hitting the headlines. He had what turned out to be very good news for me. I was to be retired at the end of the year. I would remain a member of the top holding company, Shell Transport & Trading Co. Ltd, until I reached the mandatory retiring age of seventy, but my full-time executive directorship of Shell Petroleum Co. Ltd was to end. The reason why the termination of my employment with Shell Petroleum turned out to be a good thing for me was, of course, that it meant I became free to take up formal associations in other fields.

Soon after this, Oliver Lyttelton (Lord Chandos) invited me to join the board of AEI. It had a distinguished board which included Reggie Maudling, who I do not think ever opened his mouth at any board meet-ings. He certainly opened it wide for the expensive wines that accompa-nied the excellent lunches following the boards. So did I. But I had also opened it often and anxiously at our board discussions, for I was increas-ingly anxious about the company's viability. About a year later, halfway through a board meeting, we received news that GEC, under Arnold Weinstock, was to announce a takeover bid for us at midday. This created consternation, although for my own part I thought and said that, sad as the demise of our once great and successful company could be, from the shareholders' point of view amalgamation with GEC would be an acceptable way out of our difficulties. The board, however, thought otherwise. Barings were employed, at great expense, to resist the bid. But in the end GEC succeeded in its takeover. Following the acquisition there was, of course, a great reconstruction and the amalgamated company succeeded in going from strength to strength. Arnold Weinstock offered me a directorship in GEC. I was greatly tempted, but as I was the only one of the old AEI board to receive such an offer I felt that it would be unfair and discourteous to my old colleagues to accept.

In August 1965 I had travelled to San Francisco (without Joan this time) in order to participate in an international conference organized by the National Industrial Conference Board at Stanford University. How or why I got invited I have never been able to guess. *The Times* called it 'The Tycoons' Summit: certainly the most starstudded event of its kind.' It was attended by around five hundred industrialists and financiers. I felt alone and quite out of place. I had been asked to speak on the protection of foreign investment and I duly said my little piece without, as far as I could see, arousing much excitement. I went back to my hotel at the top of Nob Hill for lunch. As I was looking for an empty table a man got up and asked, 'Why not join us?' I had no idea who 'us' were but they looked agreeable enough and I joined them. It turned out that they were top people in the Morgan Guaranty Trust: Tom Gates, the Chairman, Henry Alexander, his deputy, John Meyer and Walter Page. We had a very friendly general talk. I told them that I was returning to London almost at once via New York. I was then invited to go and lunch with them and see what Wall Street was like. We had an agreeable lunch together in New York at the end of which I was told that Morgan would like to offer me a consultancy. I was completely surprised. I protested that I did not know the least thing about banking except that my overdraft always seemed too large, that a balance sheet was like a piece of modern art to me – it looked the same whether it was the right way up or upside down – and that I could not be of the slightest use to them. 'You must let us be the judges of that,' said John Meyer.

Since my directorship with Shell was soon ending, the Morgan offer was very exciting. In November 1965 Joan and I went back to the States, nominally to address the Chicago Crimes Commission, but the visit gave me the further opportunity of discussing plans with Morgan. At the beginning of December it was announced that I was to be a special adviser and consultant to the bank on foreign business. Thus began one of the happiest associations that Joan and I ever had in the international business world, though whether I have been of much value to Morgan is much more doubtful.

One thing, perhaps, that I did do for them was to help to establish the bank's first International Advisory Council. John Meyer and I travelled around persuading eminent businessmen and others to join. Robert Menzies agreed, and so too did Akio Morita, Maersk Møller and other well-known international figures; Lord O'Brien also joined on his retirement from ther governorship of the Bank of England. I remained Chairman for about eight years. Lord O'Brien and Lord Cromer were among my successors.

Morgan Guaranty was not the only affiliation I formed around this time, Joan and I travelled widely. Early in 1966 we visited Australia and New Zealand; we went to the Far East and Hong Kong on several occasions; Denmark again; Sweden; and of course, we frequently travelled to the United States. Leafing through the cuttings, I see that in February 1967 *The Times* published a letter sent by me from Saigon. It represented a view that I still hold about our membership of the European Community. I quote part of that letter.

I write as one who is convinced that British entry into the Common Market would be good for Britain. And good for Europe. But the European Community in which I hope Britain will come in to play her part must not develop into an inward-looking association of nations seeking to establish some sort of economic autarchy or to constitute themselves into a so-called 'third force' in world politics.

Such a course would be economically impossible and politically stultifying. The Common Market has already done much for Europe. And with Britain in, it could do more. But the new Europe must be outward looking, seeking to develop the natural associations which link Britain and the United States into the wider but non-institutionalized concept of the Atlantic community embracing those like-minded nations which share a belief in the same political philosophies and principles of law as those to which the letter from your American correspondents refers.

But it is, of course, by no means such beliefs alone which would contribute to the strength of the Atlantic community. Practical co-operation and joint ventures in the industrial and general economic field, the interchange of technological and scientific experience and the cross-fertilization of investment are all matters of immense importance.

It is, of course, a much more difficult problem now than I had realized at that early stage. I had been in favour of going into Europe and joining the Treaty of Rome from the beginning. When the original 1975 refer-endum, which the then Labour leaders hoped would go against Europe, was held, I spoke strongly in favour, though I believe that in our parlia-mentary democracy referenda are inappropriate and unwise. I was pleased when the great British people voted as it did, in favour of Europe. I now feel instinctively that the British people, if asked, would be opposed to full-blown federalism and the domination of civil servants in Brussels. But then, it is asked, is that a safe test? The electorate would, for instance, be massively in favour of a return to hanging which I am equally convinced would be wrong. Fundamentally, however, I con-tinue to believe that our natural allies are the Americans, the Canadians and the Australians, and that a too tightly knit European Federation might become inimical to that association.

In 1966, the Monopolies Commission approved a takeover of *The Times* newspaper by Roy Thomson (later Lord Thomson of Fleet), the Canadian Press magnate, from Gavin Astor, whose family had pre-viously owned it. The Astors had jealously guarded the reputation of *The Times* and, when they reluctantly sold to the Thomson company, Gavin Astor suggested an arrangement that was intended to ensure the continued standing of the paper. Four so-called national and inde-pendent directors should be appointed to serve as protectors of the public interest, two to be appointed by Thomson and two by the Astors. This proposal certainly influenced the Monopolies Commission in approv-ing the merger. Gavin Astor nominated Sir Eric Roll and myself. It was a most interesting assignment which continued for several years and only came to an end when I was persuaded that I could more usefully take over the chairmanship of the by then reconstructed Press Council – alas a forlorn hope.

Many years later, when Lonrho sought control of the *Observer*, I gave evidence to the Monopolies Commission suggesting the appointment of independent directors for that paper and the Commission agreed. I greatly enjoyed my experience on the board of *The Times* and valued the friendship both of Gavin Astor and Roy Thomson, but I do not seem to have allowed it to interrupt my frequent interventions by articles in other newspapers on the freedom and responsibility of the Press. I fear there was hardly any subject on which I did not write, from excessive taxation to foreign policy, law reform to government ineptitude, civil defence and the international law of trade.

In 1967 I also joined the board of the Hawker Siddeley Group. This famous company had a record of great achievement behind it: the famous Sopwith aeroplanes, the Comet, the first passenger jet, the Harrier jump jet, and not least the short-take-off-and-landing aircraft, the Dash-7 and Dash-8, the aircraft that made possible the use of the increasingly important City Airport with its short runway. I have long since retired from Hawker Siddeley and should not express any view on the matter, but it is sad to see a company with such a name and such a distinguished lineage merged in a conglomerate, its name and identity lost.

Joan was as active as I was: I recall an occasion when she wrote 500 letters in her own hand, inviting people to come to a 'lunch by lottery' to help the Professional Classes Aid Society. The guests drew lots not as to what they should eat, but, even more riskily, at what celebrity's table they should sit. There were fifty celebrities scattered around on separate tables at the Savoy. It was a great success.

Joan and I travelled for fun as well as for work. One of the many foreign journeys I remember with affection was when we visited Cambodia with our French friends, Tony and Christiane Besse for the first time in 1967. We travelled in one of the Shell private aircraft to Kep, where we had been lent a charming villa, belonging to a princess, on the beach, and from there to Siem Reap and Angkor Wat, where we stayed at a little French hotel, the Auberge des Temples, which I fear no longer survives. Angkor, with its multitude of ancient temples long lost in the forest but recovered by the French who were still carefully restoring and tending them, is truly one of the wonders of the world. To a surprising extent it escaped destruction and serious looting during the long period of war in Cambodia, but, alas, it is being badly ravaged by thieves and looters now.

We rode around Angkor on elephants, for the area covered by the temples is very considerable. And we met a lady who later became a very valued friend and travelling companion. This was Pamela Egremont. I well remember the first time I saw Pamela – then Pamela Wyndham, the wife of John Wyndham, Harold Macmillan's political secretary and confidant, whom I had known quite well as a fellow MP – and mention it now as an example of how bad and prejudiced my personal judge- ments have sometimes been. It was at a royal reception in Buckingham Palace – I think the first given by the monarch to members of the Attlee Government. It was a black-tie occasion at which Aneurin Bevan insisted on vulgarly demonstrating his independence by going in a lounge suit. Walking through a room in the palace, I noticed sitting on a chair a lady of striking beauty, dark-haired and dressed in a beautiful gown and some lovely jewellery. I glanced at her as I walked past and while admiring her beauty thought to myself, 'That's obviously one of the idle rich.' I must have noticed her casually on many intervening occasions, but that was the image that remained firmly in my mind twenty years later when I met her in Angkor Wat. I could not have been more wrong. She was a woman of extraordinary versatility, not only a great beauty – as she still is – but a person of great charm, with a wide knowledge and experience of current affairs, and close involvement in personal service and charitable work. For many years she had been spending several months each year working in a hospital operated by nuns near Saigon, and she had continued this work during the Vietnam War, remaining at her job until the Communists took over. She endured the most primitive conditions, the legs of her bed standing in tins of water to discourage cockroaches from infesting it. There was no act of kindness or charity which she would not unobtrusively perform. Rich certainly – her home then was Petworth House, one of England's most beautiful stately homes – but 'idle' never.

Joan and I also went to Phnom Penh which in those days, before the Khmer Rouge and the odious atrocities of Pol Pot, was a charming, peaceful little town such as one might have found in provincial France. Later my son William became deeply involved in writing about Cambodia and its travails.

CHAPTER 15

Disaster

EARLY in 1968 Joan and I were in Canada once more and I found myself giving evidence to the Commission of Enquiry that had been set up in Quebec to study the administration of law. During evidence that extended over two days I told the Commission that I favoured the French procedure of the *juge d'instruction* who conducts a preliminary examination of witnesses, including the accused, whose answers then form part of the evidence in the case. In 1968 the crime figures in England were already alarming enough. I said then that we were losing the war against crime. I urged strongly, as I continue to urge, that a defendant's right not to testify at his trial should be abolished. 'Silence', I remarked, 'is the refuge of the guilty . . . the innocent man will speak out as soon as he has the opportunity.' Meanwhile it is inevitable, however reprehensible, that some police officers will try to bolster the evidence against men who they believe and often know for certain are guilty, but against whom the evidence admissible under our rules is insufficient. It is a peculiarly Anglo-Saxon doctrine — the English philosophy seems to fall over backwards to protect the accused. In England judges are more or less umpires enforcing the rules of the game after which they throw it to the jury and ask 'Howzat?' The French *juge d'instruction* on the other hand is more like a scientist, probing for the real truth.

Back in England, in between my various board activities, I still engaged in newspaper articles and occasional speeches. My weekend political speech-making period was of course long since over. Yet there remained occasions for speeches which now and again took on a political flavour. This was indeed a gloomy period in our political history.

Harold Wilson was Prime Minister and there had never been in my time a less respected government. In January 1968, I was reported as saying, 'Almost every pledge Mr Wilson has made has been broken. The feeling of distrust which existed from the beginning inside the government is now felt throughout the country and abroad. The best service the Prime Minister could render the country would be to leave it.' I was not alone. Edward Heath and Sir Alec Douglas-Home on the Conservative side, and Woodrow Wyatt, Reggie Paget, Sydney Silverman, old colleagues of mine still in the Labour Party, were saying that 'no one any more believes anything the Prime Minister says'. Yet his government retained office until 1970 and, after a brief Conservative period, regained it in 1974 when Wilson again became Prime Minister till he resigned, in 1976. Frustration at the situation under Harold Wilson led to a good deal of discussion in political circles about the possibility of some form of coalition government. During this period I did think a government of all the talents might become necessary to drag us out of the stagnation into which we were sinking. Many more powerful voices were expressing the same view. One of these was Cecil King, the head of the Mirror Group, a man of much ability and strong progressive views. It was said by his critics that he was intriguing with other public figures to set up such a government, although I did not believe there was any kind of conspiracy or intrigue.

The *New Statesman* published an amusing cartoon by Horner entitled 'Shadowy Cabinet' which caricatured the various members. Alfred Robens was Prime Minister; Cecil King, Chancellor of the Exchequer; Hugh Cudlipp, Minister for Propaganda; Enoch Powell, Minister for Repatriation; Rees-Mogg, 'Leader-maker of the House'; Lord Goodman, Solicitor General; Malcolm Muggeridge, Ambassador to God – and so on. I was also there, unsuitably, as Lord Chancellor! We British remain, however, reluctant to abandon our system of parliamentary democracy except in case of dire emergency. The Ramsay Macdonald/Baldwin precedent had not been a notable success and was never accepted as representing the whole country. I became personally friendly with Cecil King, and used occasionally to lunch privately with him at the Mirror building in Holborn. I say 'privately', although much of what we said in conversation was recorded in the diaries that Cecil kept and sometimes published.

Towards the end of 1968, I was awarded an honorary degree at the University of New Brunswick, where Lord Beaverbrook had been the Chancellor, succeeded by his son Max, who was no doubt responsible for the fact that the University offered me an LL.D. and asked me to deliver the address at the convocation. Joan and I flew to Canada with Max Aitken's wife, Max being prevented by government business from attending himself.

At home, another invitation awaited me, to receive an honorary LL.D. at Liverpool University where I had once been a senior law lecturer and where I had in effect established my career as a junior barrister. To clothe my complete lack of academic qualifications they had in fact given me an '*ex officio*' LL.M. at the beginning of the 1930s.

In my address at the ceremony I took the opportunity to attack the commercial exploitation of sex and complained again of the constant publicity given – as it still is – to the activities of 'pimps, prostitutes and perverts' in my favourite alliterative phrase.

In 1968, much disturbed by a number of cases – I will not say scandals – relating to takeovers in the City, the authorities had set up an organization called the City Panel, chaired at the beginning by Sir Humphrey Mynors, a Deputy Governor of the Bank of England. The object of the panel was to introduce some degree of regulation and control in takeover procedures.

One fine day I received a summons to go and see the Governor of the Bank of England, a man whom I knew only through a slight social acquaintance but whose authority, as it used to be said, could be exercised by the mere raising of an eyebrow. I was received by Sir Leslie O'Brien, who told me that he wanted me to become Chairman of the City Panel and explained the importance he attached to it. I was flabbergasted, but did not have the courage to refuse outright. I prevaricated and said that I would have to consider the offer and consult Morgan's. I immediately wrote to Walter Page at Morgan's and made it clear I wanted them to say I should not do it, but instead they rather encouraged me to accept. Meanwhile the matter had leaked to the Press, my name being coupled with that of Ian (later Sir Ian) Fraser, then a director of Warburg's and a man with immense experience in takeovers, as its Chief Executive. Most papers said that Fraser and I had not yet accepted but some took it for granted that we were already in place. 'The City gets a

Policeman,' said a large headline in the *Evening News*, accompanied by a photograph of me. Fraser and I both accepted, and Wilfred Wareham, Secretary of the Stock Exchange's prestigious Quotation Committee, became Deputy Director General.

Before accepting the task, however, I had naturally given some thought to the question of whether such a voluntary, self-regulatory mechanism could discharge its task effectively. The whole subject was entirely new to me: I had never been involved or interested in it before. At that time my conclusion was that for us a voluntary system with suitable sanctions was to be preferred. Subsequent experience during the eight years that I served as Chairman confirmed that view, although whether I should still hold it now I am not at all sure.

It is curious to note that the City Panel's first big case concerned Robert Maxwell. An American company called Leasco had announced a bid for a British public company, Pergamon, of which Maxwell was Chairman and Managing Director. Maxwell accepted the bid as far as his own and family holdings, amounting to about 31 per cent of the equity, were concerned. There were then long negotiations between Leasco and Pergamon in order to settle a formal offer document of which there were no fewer than nineteen drafts! In the end the American company found these discussions so unsatisfactory that they withdrew the bid. Withdrawing a public offer was a course discouraged by the City Code, as in the meantime market transactions would have taken place on the basis that the offer existed. It was required that on such a withdrawal the offeror must be prepared to justify his action to the Panel. Maxwell lodged a complaint with the Panel and a hearing was set up for consideration of the matter. This was in the middle of August, and I was with my family on our boat in the Adriatic. Fraser, however, managed to contact me by radio telephone and – with great difficulty because all flights were booked up – I managed to get back via Paris. We sat all day on a Wednesday and till two o'clock on the Friday morning after a full day sitting on the Thursday. The matter was complicated by the holdings of what were called Maxwell family interests and by Robert Maxwell himself, who made blatantly unfounded allegations against Leasco, and spoke at great length. It became very apparent to us all on the Panel that he was operating his companies without due regard for the interest of outside shareholders and as if they were his own private businesses. I felt that the most important consideration in dealing with the Leasco bid was the protection of the outside shareholders. We so conducted the proceedings that Leasco renewed a takeover offer and Pergamon accepted it. We consulted Maxwell and Saul Steinberg, the head of Leasco, and drafted the Press notice, settling it at two o'clock on the Friday morning. Maxwell became very emotional and actually wept. Whether this was an act I do not know. But I was affected by it and was actually moved to make our statement less critical of him. One of the conditions of the bid was that Maxwell should resign as Managing Director and that his place should be taken by a Leasco representative, Maxwell remaining Chairman in what was intended to be no more than a face-saving position. Maxwell agreed verbally to this, and Mr Steinberg actually suggested that this undertaking should be put in writing. I unwisely and (according to the report in the *New York Times*) coldly said that that was unnecessary since verbal undertakings were accepted in England and it was inconceivable that Maxwell would depart from the custom. I did not yet fully know my Maxwell. He did most impudently renege. I had to fly back again from the Adriatic and read him the Riot Act. No good. He appealed to our committee, presided over by Lord Pearce. He was particularly incensed at our having publicly drawn attention to his failure in disclosure and that we had asked the Board of Trade to set up a full-scale inquiry. Maxwell addressed the appeal committee for nineteen hours, but the committee had no difficulty in dismissing the appeal. The Board of Trade inquiry took several months to conduct a thorough investigation and reported that Maxwell was unfit to be a director of a public company, that he was reckless and would not listen to others — views that entirely confirmed the opinions of my colleagues and myself on the Panel.

One cannot ignore the fact that a number of people of some experience and rank, presumably with thoughts of gain, associated themselves with Maxwell despite the fact that he had been thus publicly branded. There were extraordinary eulogies paid to him by the Prime Minister of Israel, and other important people in Britain too, on his death. Perhaps they were all overcome by his charm, for like all bullies he could also appear charming when he wanted. After the Panel case I made a point of trying to avoid any encounter with Maxwell on social occasions, but at the end of the eighties, at the United Newspapers annual luncheon at the Savoy, I saw that he was on the guest list. I took myself to a remote corner of the room in which we were having pre-lunch drinks and told my friends there I was hiding from Maxwell. A few minutes later they warned me that he was approaching and apparently looking for me. Up he came, beaming all over and full of bonhomie. 'Hallo, Hartley, old boy,' he said (never before had he permitted himself to address me by my Christian name). 'How good to see you looking so well.' I had to smile and accept his handshake. Since his death – suicide, I suspect – his widow and sons seem to have remained aloof from any notion of atonement, and those eminent persons who supported and lauded him in his lifetime have been curiously impenitent and self-righteous.

I continued as Chairman of the Panel for some eight years, and it was a period which, together with my other activities, kept me very busy. We had a large number of cases because attempts at takeovers were becom-ing more numerous and many received a lot of publicity. I subsequently had as a deputy Sir Alexander Johnston, one-time Chairman of the Board of Inland Revenue, who worked very hard and with great ability in briefing me and backing me up. There is no doubt that at that time the Panel, enjoyed high prestige and standing.

Later, in 1979, I was made GBE (Knight Grand Cross of the Order of the British Empire) on the recommendation of the Governor of the Bank, Leslie O'Brien. It was good of him, but hardly deserved. I would have preferred (but still less deserved) to have been made a Companion of Honour, which seems to have become the normal honour for retiring Cabinet ministers but which, although one down from GBE in the hierarchy of these things, was, I thought, a very high distinction. However, GBE is the familiar reward for people in the City, and I suppose that by this time I was a City figure of some sort.

Indeed, around the time I was appointed to the Panel, I was given two other City appointments. One was to be the first Chairman of Thames Television, the other was to join the Board of BSA, a famous firm estab-lished in 1861 and one of the leading industrial concerns in the Midlands.

From time to time I had occasion to visit Tehran. On one occasion my good friend Ardeshir Zahedi (at one time Iranian Ambassador to Britain) was kind enough to arrange for me to be presented to the Shah of Iran. Ardeshir Zahedi had had a varied career in the Shah's service and had, indeed, married the Shah's sister, Princess Shahnaz, the marriage being subsequently dissolved without, as far as an outsider like myself could see, affecting Ardeshir's career. As well as being Iranian Ambassador to the USA and to Britain, he had been Prime Minister and Foreign Minister. He had a wide circle of friends in this country and entertained often at his embassy, where caviare was always in plentiful supply along with much other delicious Iranian food, including the very special rice, baked with a crisp golden crust, which we never seem able to equal in our English kitchens. Our friendship was so agreeable that Joan found Ardeshir a small country house in Sussex which he used at weekends and where he often gave parties. He now lives in exile in Switzerland, and remains a close and valued personal friend.

Subsequently I had audience with the Shah on three or four occasions. These meetings were formal and correct although not so formal as those with Haile Selassie, where one had to walk backwards down a long reception room, past the live but not lively lion at the entrance, though in greatest danger of tripping over one's tail-coat.

In the autumn of 1971 the Shah gave a fantastic party at Persepolis to celebrate the 2,500th anniversary of the Persian monarchy. The founder of the Persian Empire was Cyrus, a man far in advance of his time. It was he who ended the Babylonian captivity of the Jews and ordered the rebuilding of the Temple of Solomon. He was a man of astonishing tolerance who treated the nations and tribes he had conquered with comparative patience and leniency. Indeed, he was famous for the promulgation of a statement of liberties, a kind of primitive Bill of Rights partly engraved on a seal which — perhaps as inappropriately as the Elgin Marbles — is kept in the British Museum, and which had been lent to the Shah for this commemoration.

The first ceremony was a solemn requiem at the tomb of what was said to have been his body, situated in a lonely and windswept valley some way from Persepolis itself. The Shah was there with his Empress Farah, surrounded by his court bedecked in all their glory and jewels. It was a moving occasion. Persepolis itself consists of the ruins of a palace built by Darius, long buried in the sands of the desert, thus preserving some of the remarkable stone carvings. Around these ruins a village of tents had been constructed by French contractors with great skill out of some red silk-like material, as well as a great banqueting marquee, and private tents for the most important of the guests, fitted with bathrooms and all mod cons. There was red and gold carpeting and the insides of the tents were decorated in red damask. The banqueting marquee was fitted out with blue tapestries and splendid crystal chandeliers which swayed slightly with the strong wind outside. There was a great, cleverly zig-zagging table 225 feet long to seat ninety guests, and small tables for eight or ten for about 500 lesser mortals, including Joan and me.

From Britain came Prince Philip and Princess Anne. Altogether there were one emperor, eight kings, five queens, three ruling princes, thirteen presidents, two sultans, and ten sheikhs at the top table – or so the newspapers said; I did not count them! At the top table they had gold plates and cutlery. At ours, silver with gold borders. Women wore their most beautiful gowns and tiaras and the whole affair was a blaze of colour. After the banquet the Shah proposed a toast to the Founders of the Persian Empire. He appealed to his guests to 'turn the world into one of love, peace and co-operation for all mankind. All the people of the world, irrespective of race, nationality and social condition share the desire for a world free from fear, anxiety and the constant threat of annihilation.' The Emperor Haile Selassie, being the oldest ruler there, responded.

After the dinner we were all shepherded out to the ruins for a *son et lumière* – a historical march-past of events 2,500 years ago ended by a contingent of the very modern Iranian army.

It was certainly a long way from the Miners' Club in St Helens.

It would be easy to write the whole thing off as a vulgar display of ostentatious wealth and power – a terrible waste of the money of a not-wealthy nation. In fact it was a carefully calculated act of State, as one distinguished journalist put it, but it failed, and only a few years later the Shah's empire collapsed.

To me, the Shah seemed to be a man of sincerity, deeply devoted to bringing his country forward in the modern industrialized world. However, as so often happens in the case of an absolute monarch, there were many in his entourage who were sneaks, sycophants and cowards, who were responsible for widespread corruption and all manner of intrigues. His ministers seldom remained in office very long and were sometimes unjustly treated. He incurred the enmity of the religious leaders by breaking up the large estates owned by the mullahs and other rich Iranians, and he promoted the unveiling and emancipation of women far too quickly. Surrounded as he was by 'yes men', he was not properly warned by his advisers of the dangers into which he was running.

Some British people were also party to the disinformation, and when the unrest became very manifest, even individuals like George Brown advised the Shah that if he would leave the country quietly, ostensibly for a holiday, the military would act strongly in his absence and he would be able to return to a stabilized situation within a few months. In fact, he did follow such advice and left the country, fully believing that he would return, but by then he was already a very ill man. And so began what my son William called his book on the subject, 'the Shah's last ride'.

A revolutionary government was set up in Teheran and the Shah, once so lauded and praised, was shamefully banned from almost every country in the world, even from Britain, where he owned a large estate. At this time there was actually talk of putting him on trial, although for what offences it was not clear. The Shah took the threat seriously and employed a reputable American lawyer – in fact the son of my friend Justice Jackson, the Chief Prosecutor at Nuremberg – to represent him. Jackson got in touch with me on the Shah's direction, and asked me if in the event of a trial I would appear for His Majesty. I at once replied that I would certainly do so provided that the trial was before a properly constituted international tribunal composed of men of integrity – and not simply stooges of the then revolutionary Iranian Government. I thought, however, that I ought as a Privy Councillor to keep the Government informed, and I wrote to the Prime Minister explaining what had happened and that I had accepted a retainer. To my surprise, and indeed consternation, I quickly received a reply begging me not to do anything of the kind and saying that because I was a Privy Councillor, an ex-minister, and a QC my appearance for the Shah would be gravely misunderstood and would be most embar-rassing for Britain. The Prime Minister, however, added a short post-script in her own handwriting. It said, 'I am very ashamed of this letter. He was a good friend of ours.' I shared the shame. Fortunately, in the event, the problem did not arise. I do not know how I should have resolved it if it had, but I hope I would have had the guts to represent the Shah.

In 1972, having reached the normal statutory retiring age I did resign most of my non-executive directorships. Two years later, suddenly, disaster struck. The year 1974 had seemed to begin with reasonably happy auguries, but on 26 January all that was shattered. Joan had set out that bright Saturday morning for a ride across the downs with our daughter, Joanna, to whom she had lent a newly purchased thoroughbred horse, fresh with oats, and she was killed by a kick from that horse. Nobody could understand how much Joan had meant to me in her lifetime nor how utterly bereft I have felt ever since. I simply cannot write about it, save to acknowledge how much I owe to the succour of my three loving children and those friends who have rallied round and supported me, such as Monique Huiskamp, Mary Brabin, widow of my first pupil, Zara Cazalet, Pamela Egremont, Tony and Christiane Besse, Joan's devoted cousin, Gerald Bowser, Ardeshir Zahedi and others. Meanwhile, I await the day when, as Henry Scott Holland expressed it, I shall find Joan 'waiting for me, after an interval, somewhere very near, just around the corner'. I lack the conviction of those with deep religious beliefs but I try to fortify myself with the hope that God may make it so.

> Yet O stricken heart remember, O remember,
> How of human days she lived the better part.
> April came to bloom – and never dim December
> Breathed its killing chills upon the head or heart.

CHAPTER 16

Picking up the Pieces

LIFE had to go on — although very differently. I had always told Joan that in the (as I had imagined) very unlikely event of her dying before me I should follow immediately. But I realized that my immediate death would only increase the tragedy and would be a cowardly act. One's life was not one's own to deal with in that way.

And so life did go on. I never resumed the active and gregarious social life that I had enjoyed with Joan. I largely gave up attending in the Lords. I fear that I isolated myself at first in a way that offended some. People do not realize that I happen always to have been and remain an intensely shy person and enjoy social life only with those whom I really know well and like.

The first fortnight was fully occupied in writing personal replies to over 1,000 wonderful tributes which had been sent to me about Joan. People were extraordinarily kind.

Gradually other activities seemed to develop. One of the earliest diversions was a series of visits to China.

I had of course been a frequent visitor to Hong Kong but had never been on the mainland. In London, however, on the diplomatic circuit, I had come to know the then Chinese Ambassador and in 1973 he suggested that we should visit China. This was an exciting prospect and we planned to go early in the New Year. Alas, it was not to be. On hearing of Joan's death, the Chinese Ambassador to London got in touch with me in a very understanding way and said that while of course I must postpone the visit, I might consider undertaking one a month or two later accompanied by my children. William and Joanna both thought that it would be wise to get away from the now silent and cheerless Friston on a visit that would at least occupy our time and some part of our minds with something quite new.

So, early in March 1974, William, Joanna and I set out together. It was indeed a great consolation to have my two elder children as close companions at this time. We had planned to go as ordinary tourists but, as it turned out, we did receive very special treatment. We had a very agreeable English-speaking guide allotted to us for the whole of the trip, and the head of the Chinese Travel Service in Peking and the provincial heads in Shanghai and Canton entertained us to dinner – or 'banquets', as they call any such occasion involving foreigners – together with members of the 'revolutionary committees' of the respective areas. We were afforded complete freedom of movement without guides or surveillance when we wanted to explore alone and we were shown everything we wanted to see, as well as those famous monuments such as the Forbidden City, the Summer Palace, the Great Wall, and the Ming Tombs.

This was my first exploration of the Communist world. I had of course bitterly criticized Communism during my political activities in Britain, but my attacks were directed against the Communist régimes in the Soviet Union and Eastern Europe and against the attempts to get control of the British trade union movement. I had not concerned myself with China or with the theory of Communism. And I must admit that on seeing the Communist régime as it existed in China in 1974, I was in some ways agreeably surprised.

If one accepts (with whatever misgiving) the quite obvious fact that everyone in China was brainwashed from birth, the material conditions were much better than I had anticipated. In the nursery schools to which children are admitted after the age of two, they all sang in depressing unison songs dedicated to Communism with such themes as 'I had a wonderful dream last night – I dreamt Chairman Mao came to see me.' But children and adults generally appeared well nourished, adequately, if drably, clothed in unisex pattern, and all had roofs over their heads; we did not see in China what is common enough in the rest of Asia – barefoot and ragged children, beggars, or people sleeping or dying in the street. The standard of living was, however, modest to the point of being elementary.

The visit had so much intrigued and surprised us that in November 1975 I made a second visit.

On this one I was accompanied by William, my elder son, and his then wife, Marina Warner, and by Christiane Besse. We were again warmly welcomed everywhere we went and we were allowed to have the same guide as on the previous visit. Compared with the visit eighteen months before, there appeared little obvious change in the political situation, but changes were imminent: Chou En-lai was understood to be dying, and Mao Tse-tung was eighty-two and suffering from Parkinson's disease and the speech defect that often goes with it.

My guess was that on the death of Mao there would be an orderly takeover by a collective leadership in the Standing Committee and that in this Teng Hsiao-ping would, on present form, emerge as the most powerful figure.

We travelled extensively and saw much that was beautiful and also politically interesting. I well remember our visit to Yenan, a small town in north-west China which we reached in an antiquated aircraft, landing on a runway made of old bricks. Yenan is off the beaten track but it is of historical interest because Chairman Mao and the Red Army lived here from the end of the Long March for nearly fifteen years until Mao entered Peking. He lived here in a cave in the rocky hills.

In the course of the following years I paid no fewer than ten further visits to China, partly to see more of this fascinating country, and partly to improve business and political relations. During most of them I was the guest of the Chinese People's Institute of Foreign Affairs, an active body corresponding to our Royal Institute of International Affairs. It was part of the routine of these later visits that a meeting would be organized by the Institute at which I would give a wide-ranging talk on the international situation, followed by a general and usually well-informed discussion. In Peking I would normally call on leading government officials, the Chairman of the Bank of China, and friendly ambassadors. A similar pattern was followed in the great provincial cities, and there were always 'banquets' in venues ranging from the Great Hall of the People in Peking down to modest restaurants in the smaller provincial cities.

I was especially fortunate in that on a number of my later visits to China I was accompanied by Pamela, Lady Egremont. Some years after

Joan's death, I mentioned to her that I was about to make another visit to China and she told me that she also was planning a trip, so we agreed to make the visit together. I fear that my gaucheries must have been a source of some embarrassment, not to say amusement, to her. I remember that on our first visit we travelled from Hong Kong by air to Peking and were driven to the Peking Hotel – a great government caravanserai, then the only hotel in Peking. We arrived with a group of others from Hong Kong and were met by the hotel management, who allotted us our rooms. When it came to our turn they said, 'Lady Egremont and Lord Shawcross – Room No. 144.' I was somewhat nonplussed and said that would not do. 'We are not married,' I exclaimed loudly – no doubt blushing. It was then the management's turn to be nonplussed, for they said there were no other rooms. Silence – until a male member of the group spoke up and said, 'I don't mind sharing my room with Miss Smith – and this will solve the problem.' Miss Smith did not mind either, and so our problem was solved. I hoped that Miss Smith had a happy night and was duly grateful to me.

Altogether, in the course of several trips Pamela and I travelled through most of China, venturing right up to the north-west boundary with the Soviet Union, and including Tibet. We were, indeed, among the first Europeans to visit Tibet after the Chinese occupation. Lhasa, the capital, is, at a very high altitude, and we were met at the landing ground by a car containing a lady doctor and an oxygen cylinder.

Tibet's beauty is disfigured by political and religious division. It is, I fear, no longer a matter of practical politics to urge that China should renounce its sovereignty over this conquered territory. But it should be pressured to observe human rights and some religious modus vivendi must be reached. Not that this will be easy. Since taking over the administration of the country, China has used the school system to bring up the young in the belief that the religion of their fathers is no more than a superstition that has no real basis.

Unless the Dalai Lama were to abandon any temporal powers and restrict himself to a purely religious role, it may be difficult to find any solution. Although we were assured that religious worship was not forbidden and that specified monasteries were left open for this purpose, we never saw any kind of organized service and the particular monastery in Lhasa that was designated was, on the two occasions we visited it, empty

of worshippers. I was left with the impression that the religious believ-
ers were reluctant to pursue their beliefs publicly, and that because of the
scepticism of more of the young, and the anti-religious attitude of the
significant Han Chinese immigrant population, they are an inevitably
diminishing section of the population.

But I hope this is a fallacious view. The same thing could have been
said of Russia before Gorbachev, yet today the Orthodox churches are
full – and with many young people.

When the final survivors of Mao's Long March follow Mao, younger
men with new ideas will no doubt rise to power in China. I say younger,
for it is not likely that they will be by our standards young or even middle-
aged: China has a traditional respect for old age, and those who succeed
to power are not likely to be young demagogues but rather men already
highly regarded for their experience. That they will be reformers may
well be true, but their reforms are likely to progress on line already laid
down in the sphere of economics and social conditions, rather than
mirror the abrupt changes seen in Eastern Europe. The Chinese
economy has grown with remarkable and consistent success and will
continue to do so, until perhaps it becomes the most powerful in the
world. The Chinese approach both to their certainly very numerous
internal problems and those of their foreign relations is likely to remain
pragmatic. In time the practical theories of Communism will give way
to the more convincing realities of private enterprise, as indeed they are
already doing in a most remarkable way in South China and in that part
of China which is agricultural. And not only in agriculture. One of the
very significant factors is the development of a rapidly increasing
private-enterprise industrialization in the south of China directly linked
with Hong Kong, and in part owned by capitalists from Hong Kong.
This seems to be accompanied by some degree of popular local government. This development cannot be overthrown by Communism. It
marks the beginning of 'privatization', which will displace the
Communist organisation. Nothing, I think, can hold this movement
back, and it behoves us in the United Kingdom to maintain the closest
and most understanding relationship with those in power in Peking so
that we may ourselves benefit from the enormous growth that will take
place in that vast country. Some day there will come a demand for direct
elections to a real national parliament. In the meantime, Peking will

continue to concentrate on economic and social reform, and I would think it unlikely that the establishment of democratic institutions on Western lines will be seen until well into the first quarter of the next century. The factors that led to the disintegration of Communism in Europe and elsewhere – widespread unemployment, the high cost of living, the collapse of supplies, the abuse of power by officials, and so on – are not experienced in the same way in China as they were in the countries of Eastern Europe, although the fact remains that few of us expected the rapid disintegration of the Soviet Union.

CHAPTER 17

Aftermath

THESE long years following Joan's death have largely been ones of gradually fading out of public life, partly because of my increasing age – although for the most part I remain remarkably fit – and partly because of my own inclination. I have lacked much enthusiasm for anything. But occasionally things would turn up which I felt constrained to do, for I did not want to become more of a burden to my family and friends than I already was. Warburg's asked me to accept the chairmanship of a new bank – London & Continental Bankers – which the European co-operative banks wished to establish in London, and the chairmanship of the City Panel continued to occupy a good deal of my time. I had, of course, in the years up to then several times told the Governor of the Bank of England that, in view of my age, my resignation was entirely in his hands. But I was surprised when he eventually accepted it. Early in 1980 I was summoned to see the then Governor, Sir Gordon Richardson, who at once told me he thought the time had come when I should resign. I did not demur, and asked him whether he had anyone in mind to succeed me. He replied affirmatively that he thought Sir Jasper Hollom would be the man. I was amazed and fear I looked it.

Sir Jasper was, and had been since 1970, a deputy governor of the Bank of England. He was an established figure in the City, a man of complete integrity and goodwill. In the Bank he had long had a reputation for 'sitting on things', and in the newspapers he was referred to as 'the Silent Man' who was never known to say anything. I am bound to say that, although he was a member, he had been of little assistance to the City Panel. I murmured my doubts to the Governor, but seeing that he seemed strongly in favour of it, I suggested that he would want to consult with some of my senior City colleagues on the Panel. However, Gordon, to my further astonishment, said he had already asked Sir Jasper to accept the job and he had agreed.

The newspaper comment was not encouraging. *The Times* remarked that

> the choice of successor (to Lord Shawcross) seems to have caused surprise amongst members of the Panel . . . most City opinion was that Lord Shawcross's successor in this key position in the City's system of non-statutory self-regulation would be either a lawyer like Lord Shawcross or someone with detailed experience of the security markets . . . until the decision the most likely candidate appeared to be Sir Patrick Neill . . . or Sir Alexander Johnston . . . Sir Jasper Hollom's whole career has been with the Bank of England.

I duly resigned, having been Chairman since 1969 – a good ten years of most interesting and sometimes exacting work. Thanks to the assistance of my most able and diligent deputy, Alec Johnston, and a succession of highly experienced merchant bankers such as Ian Fraser and John Hull, we had performed a useful service in putting some order, openness and discipline into the takeover field, and helping to establish the Council for the Securities Industry with overall power over the whole securities field in the City, first under the chairmanship of Patrick Neill, QC (whom I also secured later as Chairman of the Press Council).

Alec Johnston and I were members of the Securities Council. We had initiated measures to curb the so-called dawn raids – a very unfair abuse of the market by powerful bidders – and we had persuaded Parliament to legislate (although too mildly) against insider dealing. The courts have been curiously weak in enforcing the power thus given to them. For a few years under its new chairman (who also, on the Governor's nomination, became Chairman of the Securities Industry Council) the Panel at the best marked time and did little but lose standing, but its prestige revived when, following Sir Jasper's retirement in 1987, the chairmanship reverted to two distinguished lawyers – first Robert Alexander, QC, and then David Calcutt, QC.

Since then the Panel has been seeking to recover its influence, and I am sure that the experience of the legally qualified chairmen has greatly assisted this process. I fear however that before long we may have to have a statutory system. It is a pity. The City today is a very different place from what it was in the twenty years leading up to my acceptance of the Panel chairmanship. In those years the traditional City motto of 'My word is my bond' was almost universally accepted. But not since the Maxwells of this world.

It may sound snobbish to say so, but I find the classless society of the City today much more motivated by a get-rich-quick devil-take-the-hindmost philosophy than was the case 30 or 40 years ago. One has only to look at recent cases in the City – and there should have been more – where practitioners have been found guilty of various criminal offences in connection with takeovers, insider dealing and so on. Yet such offences seem to carry little opprobrium. I very much fear that sterner and statutory measures are becoming necessary now. And social repudiation should follow disgraceful behaviour in the City – such as the award of enormous salary increases – even if no actual crime is established.

The Labour Party (although it may have deserted many Socialist principles) still has more confidence in rules and regulations than the present Government, and in this instance they could be right.

Another interest that my involvement with Shell led me to develop as long ago as the late 1950s, and one I have maintained, is in the position of foreign investments made by the industrial countries in those that are less developed.

While governmental financial aid has done a great deal and can still do much more to build up the economies of the developing countries, particularly in regard to their so-called infrastructure, it is equally certain that industrial and general economic growth must continue to depend mainly upon the provision of risk capital from private sources. If capital is not made available from the free world in sufficient quantities, the developing countries are bound to sink into revolution, instability or stagnation and widespread starvation. For many years now, an appall-ingly large part of the world's population has been contending with conditions of actual or near starvation that inter-governmental aid has failed adequately to alleviate. The problem has been how to promote the flow of private capital investment and ensure that it goes to those countries where it could do most good. This means that investors must be given some guarantees against arbitrary expropriation and for compensation.

The accepted rules (accepted at least by the developed countries!) of international law did indeed provide that while it was legitimate for a government to take over the property of foreigners, compensation must be paid which was prompt, effective and adequate. The difficulty has been that there were no formal means of enforcing the rules of international law in this field. None of the states making such expropriations was likely to have accepted the jurisdiction of the International Court of Justice in the Hague. Aden comes to mind. In 1969, after the British had ignominiously abandoned the colony without first securing protection for foreign interests there, the Communist Government that took over, at once expropriated the property of foreigners, and failed to pay compensation.

In March 1958 an initiative that the celebrated German banker Herman Abs had taken in San Francisco two years before was given added impetus by a most significant speech at the Conference of the Economic Commission for Asia and the Far East made by the Prime Minister of Malaya, the Tunku Abdul Rahman, to whom I have already referred as one of the outstanding statesmen in the British Commonwealth. He specifically suggested that an Investment Charter should be drawn up in order to establish some system of legal security for international investment in the form of a Multilateral Investment Convention. It was, I think, shortly after this speech that I met Herman Abs, for the first time and we became good friends.

Later in 1958 an opportunity of close collaboration between us arose when an important step forward was taken by the French Association de Droit Minier et Petrolier in association with the University of Aix-en-Provence to discuss the problem of securing better protection for foreign investment. The result of the conference and of my own discussions with Herr Abs was that towards the end of the year there was established, with headquarters in Geneva, a small international study group calling itself the Association for the Promotion and Protection of Private Foreign Investment (APPI). This body, which is supported by voluntary contributions from banking and industrial concerns interested in the problem, has ever since been doing important co-ordinating work in this field. In 1959, we were able to present a draft of a model multilateral treaty to APPI which had been drawn up at a series of meetings between Herr Abs and his colleagues on the one hand and my friends and myself on the other. Lawyers, diplomats and businessmen from five countries had contributed to these discussions and the draft treaty that emerged from them represented a certain compromise between the views of those who would have preferred ideally a comprehensive and fully embracing code and those who thought that it would hardly be possible to negotiate more than a submission to some form of arbitration, with perhaps one or two guiding principles. This draft was adopted by APPI as a basis on which to attract public discussion of what it might be practicable to achieve.

As a result of the activities of APPI, of Dr Abs' group and of my own, the proposal did, indeed, attract attention. It became known as the Abs/Shawcross draft, and was recommended as a model by the European Commission.

What is really needed, however, is some international arbitral tribunal accepted by states party to the convention, to which private nationals might have recourse in direct proceedings against states. Such a system would have manifest advantages in expedition, economy and, perhaps more importantly still, in tending to keep disputes out of the arena of international politics and prestige. States willing to do so could submit to arbitration proceedings at the direct instance of foreign nationals. The idea of proceedings of this kind is a matter of great importance.

My background as a lawyer and my continued association with Justice and other organizations has led to my frequently chairing committees, giving evidence or writing articles or letters relating to legal or quasi-legal matters. I was asked in 1975 by the International Chamber of Commerce to chair a committee of so-called 'Eminent Persons' on the subject of corruption in international business. It did contain some very eminent persons, such as Jean Rey, former President of the European Economic Commission, William Simon, previously US Secretary of the Treasury, Sheikh Yamani, the Saudi Arabian Petroleum Minister, Gascon Kheradjon, a distinguished Iranian banker, Georges Picot, one-time director of the French Suez Company, and a number of other experienced and distinguished international businessmen. I was indeed honoured to be accepted as their chairman.

We usually met in Paris, and after two years' serious work we produced both a code of rules and a procedure for enforcement. It was agreed that our report should not be released for general publication before being considered by the 54-member council of the International Chamber of Commerce. Nonetheless, it was leaked to the Press whose first reaction was favourable. The main recommendations were fully reported in the *Financial Times* for 17 November 1977, the report concluding (and I set this out in full because of the continuing importance of the matter):

Public opinion has sometimes tended to assume that corruption is generally initiated by enterprises. This is not so, and it ignores the often subtle but effective pressure by recipients of bribes or agents acting on their behalf. The truth is that much bribery is in fact the response to extortion. Enterprises have too often had the experience, in many countries, of having to choose between giving in to extortion or not doing business. What then is the solution. Neither governments nor business can alone deal effectively with this problem. Therefore, complementary and mutually reinforcing action by both governments and the business community is essential. This action should be on the following lines:

(a) All governments should enact stringent and, as far as possible, comparable laws, where they do not already exist, prohibiting and punishing all forms of corruption, whether commercial or political. But this alone is not enough. There must be both the political will and the administrative machinery to enforce such laws.

(b) By the business community:

The ICC considers that the international business community has a corresponding responsibility to make its own contribution toward the effective elimination of extortion and bribery.

In this connection, it should be stressed that the promotion of self-regulation in international trade has always been one of the major objectives of the ICC as reflected over the years in the publication of its Codes of Fair Practices in marketing, its guidelines for international investment, and its environmental guidelines for industry.

In its recommendations to governments, the report calls for States to review their laws to ensure these effectively prohibit the giving and taking and solicitation of bribes, as well as so-called facilitating payments to expedite performance of functions by government officials.

By way of preventive measures it recommends certain disclosure provisions:

(a) For government officials involved directly or indirectly in business transactions with enterprises, and within the limits defined in national legislation procedures should provide for periodic reports to an appropriate government body of —

(1) Financial interests held by, and total wealth of, such officials and their immediate families; and

(2) All payments or gifts received by government officials and their immediate families directly or indirectly, from enterprises engaged in any transaction with the government or from any agents acting on behalf of such enterprises.

(b) For enterprises engaged in transactions with any government or with any enterprise owned or controlled by government, disclosure procedures should provide for access, upon specific request, by the appropriate government authorities to information as to agents dealing directly with public bodies or officials and as to the payments to which such agents are entitled.

In relation to transactions with governments and inter-governmental organisations, the Commission says such transactions should be subject to special safeguards to minimise the opportunities for their being influenced by extortion or bribery.

As to political contributions, it is proposed that the ICC should say that, while it recognises that political contributions are usually legitimate and proper, undisclosed political contributions may on occasion serve as a vehicle for extortion and bribery. Therefore, governments should consider, having regard to all the circumstances prevailing within each country, enacting legislation which ensures that such payments are publicly recorded by the payers and accounted for by the recipients.

The panel undertook to keep under constant review and publicly report from time to time on the extent to which the evil practices of corruption continue to prevail and laid down the basic rules of a rec-ommended code which were:

1 – No one may demand or accept a bribe.

2 – No enterprise may directly or indirectly offer or give a bribe in order to obtain or retain business, and any demands for such a bribe must be rejected.

3 – 'Kickbacks'. Enterprises should take measures reasonably within their power to ensure that no part of any payment made by them in connection with any commercial transaction is paid back to their employees or to any other person not legally entitled to the same.

4 – Agents. Enterprises should take measures reasonably within their power to ensure (a) that any payment made to any agent represents no more than an appropriate remuneration for the services rendered by him, and (b) that no part of any such payment is passed on by the agent as a bribe or otherwise in contravention of this Code.

5 – Financial Recordings. (1) All financial transactions must be properly and fairly recorded in appropriate books of account avail-able for inspection by boards and auditors. (2) There must be no 'off the book' or secret accounts, nor may any documents be issued which do not properly and fairly record the transactions to which they relate.

Alas, as soon as the report had been circulated to the members of the ICC, clandestine intrigues were started to suppress or emasculate it and the 'do nothing effective' advocates on the ICC were successful. In an address to the Royal Institute of International Affairs at Chatham House on 19 December 1977, I said that what had emerged from the Council's discussions was not ratification of the Commissions's pro-posals but an ICC code that was even more diluted than the Commission had felt it possible to make it, and with the minimal enforce-ment provisions taken out altogether. I added in a widely reported passage that 'There are times to take a stand. I feel bound to say that the emasculated animal, with its tongue cut out and its teeth extracted, is not likely to make a major impact . . . this was the result of a very odd undercover intrigue taking place between a few individuals in France, West Germany and Belgium to wreck the project.' And wrecked it was.

I have thought it worthwhile to set all this out at length because bribery, corruption and extortion are increasing both nationally and internationally. Some valiant attempts are being made by some states to suppress these evils, but they cannot be successfully suppressed by police action alone. The State must be assisted by the full weight of the orga‑nized business community and public opinion. The ICC felt impelled to move in a weak spirit of compromise. It did not increase its public credibility or influence.

Another aspect of international law in which I had long been involved was that of human rights and breaches of the international criminal law.

I have already written on the subject of international law. I have done what I could by articles and letters to the Press, occasional speeches – and a still‑continuing but fruitless correspondence with the Prime Minister to reiterate the view I first expressed to (and on which I obtained approval from) the United Nations in the 1940s, that an International Criminal Court should be set up, perhaps as a second chamber of the existing and very successful court at the Hague. But far too little has been done. Meantime there have been shocking violations of the most obvious human rights in many different parts of the world. The Soviet treatment of the Hungarian people after the 1956 revolution, and the suppression of Dubcek's 'Socialism with a human face' in 1968, which my son William wrote about in his first book, were great blots on Europe. The position of black people in the United States and indeed nearer home has still discredited otherwise creditable records. Asia Minor and the Arab countries have been disfigured by wars with ethnic overtones involving a ruthless trampling on human rights. And now there are the cares of the once‑lovely Yugoslavia, and of Rwanda.

It is true that the problem of human rights has been a good deal better publicized in recent years. But the firm establishment of basic human rights requires more than speeches or brave declarations in constitutional documents. It needs active aid in food and humanitarian assistance. And it needs enforceable laws – and by enforceable I mean laws that can be enforced by international means if the country in which the rights are violated is unable or unwilling to enforce the law itself. Indeed, the 'New World Order' must – if it is to be more than an eloquent pre-election oration – depend upon the rules of international law and the enforce-ability of such rules before international tribunals. This has indeed been made very plain by the inability to enforce not mere declarations of human rights but the clearest and most solemn enactments to which most nations had agreed. I think in particular, of course, of the grave breaches by Iraq of the rules of international law as to waging aggres-sive war, as to genocide and to crimes against humanity generally as embodied in the international conventions of 1946 and 1949. It is true that Kuwait was subsequently liberated, but it should not be thought that going to war is always or necessarily a vindication of international law. The rules of international law since 1945 at least are clearly laid down as binding on individuals as well as states. So far, since Nuremberg, no leader of a state has been punished – or even proceeded against. On the contrary, Saddam Hussein seems to go from strength to strength, and unless deposed in one way or another he constitutes a grave danger. One of the reasons, or at least excuses, for the failure to require the surrender of Saddam at the time of the – as it now seems – premature armistice following the Gulf War was the absence of any formal machinery for his trial. His surrender could no doubt have been insisted upon and – if at first refused – have been secured by a two-day march against little resistance into Baghdad. But once he had surrendered, he would probably have had to be brought before an *ad hoc* tribunal set up by the Allies much in the pattern of the Nuremberg tribunal after the Second World War. That tribunal attracted some criticism – not unnat-urally, although quite wrongly – by Goering and others as 'victors' justice', and much the same criticisms would have arisen, especially in the Islamic countries, if Saddam had been put on trial before such a tri-bunal. I say that course would 'probably' have been necessary, for consideration would have had to be given to a clause in the Genocide Convention which has hitherto been conveniently ignored – namely that it is the duty of the states signatory to the Convention, including of course ourselves and the United States, 'to search for persons alleged to have committed grave breaches . . . and bring them to trial before the courts' – that is to say our own courts. We have, unhappily, chosen to regard much of this convention as a dead letter.

The difficulties in regard to the Allies' often-stated intention (in the words of Mrs Thatcher) to 'bring Saddam to trial for perpetrating brutal cruelties, just as happened after the Second World War' would hardly have arisen had there already been in existence an appropriate international tribunal set up under international convention with jurisdiction to try criminal cases. It was precisely because the Nuremberg process had attracted misguided criticism as 'victors' justice' that long ago the United Nations discussed the proposal to set up such an international criminal court. In 1948 it was the Government's strong policy – I know, because it fell to me to expound it at the UN – that such a court should be set up. In that year the International Law Commission was instructed by the UN to examine the proposal. In the early 1950s the UN itself decided that such a court should be set up and a statute was drafted. The Cold War intervened. What is British policy today? Negative and discouraging. The Government seems now to regard war itself as being a sufficient vindication of international law. The fact is, however, that before the Gulf War there had been only one occasion, that of the concerted action in Korea under UN auspices, in which international law had been invoked. Apart from that case there have been innumerable instances – from Cambodia and Pol Pot on – which were undoubtedly breaches of the rule of law but which attracted no international action.

Nor can one regard the more recent cases of the Falkland Islands or the Gulf as 'vindications' of the rule of law. Both were instances of the inalienable right of self-defence. As for the Gulf War itself, the UK – and still more the US – could hardly have allowed our interests in Kuwait and Saudi Arabia (for that country would have been next) to be completely subordinated to the Iraqis. Had these incidents taken place in the African sub-continent, or Asia or Latin America, and without any economic or political interest on our part, the history of the last forty years suggests that we would have done nothing. Current events in what was Yugoslavia have led to much talk, but so far little action. The International Law Commission has been working on a code of 'Crimes against the peace and security of mankind' for very many years. And in its accustomed and leisurely way will surely do so for many years to come. But the fact that, as HMG no doubt rightly consider, many of the proposals for this code are 'vague or even nonsensical' is no reason for not proceeding at once to the establishment of an International

Criminal Court. International law has grown up gradually, rather in the way of Anglo-Saxon law, and not as the result of embodiment in one single code. If the fear that some proposed laws might be vague or unwise had obstructed the establishment of our English system of courts we would never have had any courts at all. An International Criminal Court should and, given goodwill between the great powers, could be established now to deal with such crimes as are well established, includ-ing waging aggressive war, genocide, the grave crimes listed in the 1949 Geneva Convention, and so on. Without such a court – and eventually, one hopes, also an international police force – the new world order and the rule of law cannot be more than illusory.

This view, which I had been urging during all the years since I had left party politics, I continued to promote on occasion since, particularly after the Gulf War, and I shall continue as opportunity arises to urge it now.

But human rights under international law are one thing; the private right of the individual citizen under his domestic law is quite another – though far easier to deal with in our domestic political system. Do we need a Bill of Human Rights in this country? The whole problem has to be looked at not only against the background of an increasing and irresponsible use of power, whether by governmental agencies or sectar-ian ones, but also against the very significant changes in public attitudes, outlooks and beliefs – as for instance in the field of personal morality.

We must accept that the growth of a modern civilization cannot evolve into an endless extension of the boundaries of liberty; if it did, civilization itself would degenerate into anarchy, the seeds of which are indeed present in every liberal society that concerns itself more with rights than with their corresponding responsibilities. It is the limitations that are either imposed by law or by self-discipline (if the notion of such a thing is not old-fashioned) which enable liberty to thrive. When one is weighing up the loss of one liberty against the gain of another, one should use scales that register in terms of the welfare of the community. But do such scales exist? Is there now such a thing as a national philos-ophy or faith or culture – any corpus of ideals to which we have a loyalty? In the last century, the family, the Church, the schools, the universities, all combined to instil or inspire in us a certain body of common belief, of decent feeling, of manners, even of duty, which gave cohesion and, under the monarchy, even unity to our nation. Now these institutions have largely lost their influence. Their place has to an extent been taken by a congeries of publicists using the mass media. The religious ethic has largely disappeared and no other ethic has taken its place to tie us together. The cohesion has diminished; the unity is gone. If all this is the consequence of an extension of liberty, is the price too high? In a world in which it is increasingly difficult to know what to believe, one fact still does remain even more obvious today than when John Donne wrote it: 'No man is an island'.

But this is the sort of philosophical ground upon which I fear to tread.

Overall, I believe we should have a 'Bill of Rights'. After all, we did have a Magna Carta, and in the seventeenth century, the Petition and the Bill of Rights. We are already legally bound by the 1944 Universal Declaration of Human Rights by the United Nations – I had some part in it – and by the more recent European Convention. We have insisted on the adoption of entrenched clauses or a Declaration of Human Rights in the constitutions of every colony to which we have given freedom and independence – although much good it did them! Can we any longer take our own rights for granted? Why should we not, and with much greater hope of observance, give to our people that which we have insisted upon for others – the great charter for the little man, ensuring his right not to be pushed around?

I do not think we need a Royal Commission to decide. Such a bill should primarily declare the more elementary rights of the individual. What perhaps we need even more than a Bill of Rights, but what we shall certainly not get, is a Bill of Duties, for there is far too much disregard of the individual's duty towards his neighbour, even though we are, I think, a more caring society than we were. For the corollary to fundamental rights is that their existence depends on the observance of duties.

Of much more practical importance, is the problem of administering the law of the land. No constitutional safeguards, no other legal provisions or declarations in any Bill of Rights, can provide adequate protection for the individual unless the courts of justice are functioning efficiently and available to all. They are not.

The present state of our law, with the innumerable statutory provisions, the judicial precedents and their 'wilderness of single instances', the obsolete and complicated procedures, have made our legal system, once our great pride, totally inadequate to the needs of a modern and progressive society. Lord Gardiner, a distinguished Lord Chancellor, dedicated not so much to politics, of which he knew little, as to the law, of which he knew much, set up the Law Commission which has promoted important reforms in our substantive law. The problems have, however, become urgent, especially in regard to litigation.

Right through our courts the delays are intolerable, the costs extortionate. Nothing less than revolutionary changes in our procedures will meet the case. And I am not thinking of the foolish and irrelevant talk of abandoning wigs and so destroying the solemnity of court proceedings. Far more important are cheaper and quicker procedures in the ordinary Courts of Law and, with them, a completely different philosophical approach to law and procedure. The law is in an appalling mess. In one sense, it always has been. We have never had codified systems like the Romans or the French Code Napoléon. Nor, fortunately, do we have a constitutional straitjacket like the United States. Our law has grown up like Topsy in *Uncle Tom's Cabin*, following rather slowly our social and economic development. On the whole it has served us well. But where we are now gravely deficient is in the administration of the law. Among the population there has been an enormous increase in litigation. This is no doubt partly because of the fact that there is – for some – a legal aid system. As a result, there has been a great multiplication of legal claims, resulting in intolerable delays. And on the criminal side the alarming increase in crime has resulted in the criminal courts also being overwhelmed by delays that should be intolerable in a civilized society – and in prison conditions that are an absolute disgrace. I have written earlier of my increasing anxieties about the administration of the criminal law – and the position of the Law Officers. I can only urge the commissions now studying the matter not to hesitate to call for really drastic reforms. These must restore ultimate authority if not to the Attorney General then to some other officer who is responsible to Parliament for the administration of the law. The leadership of the Bar should also abandon the new practice of multi-count indictments and lengthy trials: they are both unnecessary and inimical to justice.

The multiplicity of cases does, of course, necessitate the appointment of many more judges, some of whom may not be of the highest standard. Of course, there were always some bad judges, although not many; now I am afraid the proportion who are inadequate to the job is considerably greater than it used to be. Too often judges seem to allow unseemly exhibitions by counsel vying with each other in offensiveness in order to gain maximum Press publicity. I yearn for the days when the Goddards, the Rigby Swifts, the Dennings presided over courts and allowed no nonsense, ensuring not only that justice was done but that it was seen to be done. And the Attorney General led the Bar in that philosophy.

The fault for all this I suppose lies mainly with the Bar, which seems to be producing a new type of practitioner. In my time – again I am afraid this is the old man yearning for the good old days – each set of chambers would consist of perhaps six, eight or ten men and women with a head of chambers who had real responsibility for the behaviour and well-being of his tenants. Those were the days when it was the custom often to dine in Bar mess with colleagues in one's Inn of Court; the days when there was serious and even intellectual conversation about this and that, including the conduct of cases; and gossip about the behaviour of judges and those in other chambers; the days when young Juniors coveted the Red Bags that Silks would give them after doing some cases together as a mark of recognition. And the days also when the staff consisted of a trusted clerk – usually someone with great knowledge about the solicitors who were potential clients, some of whom were respectable (and also good payers – by no means the same thing) – perhaps a secretary/typist and possibly a young clerk.

All seems very different today. Chambers may now be located anywhere, not solely within the sacred purlieus of the Inns of Court. There may be forty or more people in a single set. Pupils, instead of paying 100 guineas to their pupil master, are paid by him to devil opinions and pleadings. There is a 'business manager' as well as a clerk. The head of chambers now has much less influence over his tenants than before, and so the risk of departing from recognised standards of behaviour in etiquette is much greater.

Nor do I believe that the radical changes that the go-ahead and active Lord Chancellor, Lord Mackay, has introduced, although amounting to less than the fusion of the two branches of the law, have in any significant way improved the efficiency or the standing of the Bar. It is true that there does not seem to have been any great rush by solicitors into the realm of advocacy. But what I have always considered one of the greatest safeguards of the independence of the barrister – namely that he acts on the instructions of a solicitor and is not in direct contact with his lay client – is becoming eroded. If the lay client has direct access to and contact with the barrister the latter inevitably loses that detachment and objectivity which enables him to give dispassionate advice. This detachment is at the basis of the independence of the Bar and is, as so many distinguished leaders of the American Bar have often emphasized, the envy of the legal profession in other countries.

Some 35 years ago, in a paper I delivered to the New York Bar Association and which they later published in a hardback booklet, I said:

> Let it be said that the lawyer who regards his function as making the worse appear the better case, who devotes his skill to elaborating schemes for frustrating and deceiving the law or the courts, who deliberately pits his wits against the legislature and against the judges is unworthy of his gown

I repeated that observation at the great dinner that Gray's Inn gave me on the occasion of my 90th birthday. I stand by it.

And here again I find myself rashly trespassing into the field of philosophy. Rules, laws and procedures by which they are enforced ought to be a reflection of what is the public interest. The problem here, as it seems to me, is not always to equate the public interest with merely material considerations. Somehow we have got to recover some standard of collective values and individual initiatives, some sense of purpose and destination. As Abraham Lincoln put it, 'a dedication to a proposition'. Our days of military power and empire may be over but our influence in the world need not die with them. We can still possess a certain political genius, qualities of experience, toleration, decency and individualism that we must not only maintain for ourselves but use, at least by example, to promote the welfare of mankind. When Swinburne said that England's past proclaims her future, he was thinking not only of Nelson's might but of 'Milton's faith and Wordsworth's trust in this our chosen and chainless land'. It is for the ordinary citizens to be sure by constant vigilance, discussion and action that their faith and trust is not betrayed by their own indifference and that we can at least continue proudly to proclaim ourselves a chainless land. In this context, I believe we must urgently defend the institution of the family as the mainstay of civilization.

I have always agreed with the philosophy expressed latterly in the international covenant on civil and political rights that 'the family is the natural and fundamental group unit of society and is entitled to protec- tion by society and the state'. And not only protection but constant encouragement. It seems to me, on the contrary, that there has been a complete breakdown in what were accepted as the moral standards of society up to, probably, the Second World War.

It is sometimes said that sexual standards in the Victorian or earlier era were low and hypocritical. But the comparison is nonsense. In every age there were no doubt many transgressions – but they were regarded as transgressions from a standard that sought to condemn promiscuity in normal sexual relations and sternly to forbid perversions. It is difficult to associate today's marked change in moral standards to any single cause – and indeed there are many. But I always felt that a major factor has been sexual licence on the part of the Press, followed by television, in the knowledge that in that way more profit lies. We all have, however we conceal it, a certain degree of prurient curiosity – even if it is only to see 'how far they (i.e. the newspaper, book or play) will go next', and so we buy the paper, the book or the tickets for the show. As a result, sections of the Press, television and the stage are simply a sex-pool. I was being frivolous when I once remarked that 'television was the greatest danger to civilization since the invention of sliced bread'. Yet I do think that its virtually uncontrolled existence is a great danger.

CHAPTER 18

At the End

JOAN and I were blessed with three children. I still call them so although of course they are all adults now, with their own lives. And I mean blessed – for I am proud of them, as Joan would have been. In spite of Joan's death they have remained close to each other and to me. I am grateful for the joy and fun they gave Joan and me as children and for the steadfast support and attention with which they have surrounded me since Joan died.

William was born on 28 May 1946 and he was christened in the crypt chapel at the Houses of Parliament. He grew up in Sussex. I am afraid that I was so much preoccupied with political work and public life that I saw little of him in his earlier years, and although Joan was at home as much as she possibly could be, she also was busy in her various other activities. This made it inevitable that we had to depart from my parents' belief in home education and send him, as we sent the two later children, to boarding school. It is a brutal business which usually – and certainly in our case – causes as much sorrow to the parents as to the child who is sent forth to the care of hitherto unknown masters or mistresses. I well remember how Joan and I took William, at the age of only eight years, to Victoria Station to put him on the school train that was to take him for his first term at his prep school. Joan had fortified herself with a double dose of Valium, but we all wept and missed him terribly. From his earliest years William had a deep religious belief. When it came to the problem of choosing a public school, again it had to be a boarding school. I had convinced myself by this time that the vital thing was the best education and that the social considerations attached to one particular school or another were incidental. We both thought that Eton was the school to go for. He was, I think, happy and successful there. He rowed, and I remember being delighted with his performance as Lady Bracknell in *The Importance of Being Earnest*. We had many happy Fourths of June with him. One of the many good things about Eton is that, within reason, whatever a boy wishes to learn, Eton will find someone to teach him, even if it is not in the curriculum. William wanted to learn sculpture and he was duly taught and produced some very creditable work. Later, unfortunately, he went to one of the leading schools of art in London, and there he was taught in the modern manner, producing, as I remember, what looked exactly like a roll of linoleum. Whether he found this as unsatisfactory as I did I do not know. At all events he gave it up. From Eton he went to Oxford, to University College, my father's old college, which he loved and where he became President of the Junior Common Room. William's sub-sequent career was I think to some extent the result of fortuitous cir-cumstances. Soon after coming down from Oxford he went on holiday with his sister to Prague. Alexander Dubček was then in power and preaching 'Socialism with a human face', only to be overthrown by Brezhnev. William was much affected and wrote his first book, which was entitled *Dubček* and which in 1990 was re-edited and published on Dubček's return to active life. The book was a success. He has a gift for writing and his books have made a marked impression. One – *Sideshow* – about the war in Cambodia which was strongly critical of Henry Kissinger, attracted much attention and praise. But not from Kissinger, who remarked to one of my friends in the Hong Kong Jockey Club that 'Lord Shawcross is all right. It's such a pity about his son.' William's subsequent books have included one on the United Nations and Cambodia, and the Shah of Iran and on Rupert Murdoch.

Journalism and marriage are not easy to reconcile. William has unhappily been twice divorced. But his first two marriages, to Marina Warner and Michal Levin, each produced a child, Conrad and Ellie, to whom William is utterly devoted. They are constantly at Friston for weekends, and we all spend every August together in Cornwall. Conrad has inherited his grandfather's and father's interest in sailing – in Cornwall he races *Vesper* a St Mawes One Design, an 18-foot wooden sloop, and was awarded the Young Sailor of the Year Cup when he was sixteen. He has just finished his A levels and is hoping now to develop his considerable artistic potential. Ellie takes after Joan and is on the way to becoming an accomplished young horsewoman. Apparently she also takes after me in that she wants to become a barrister. William is now happily remarried to Olga Polizzi and has two beautiful stepdaughters, Alex and Charlie.

Our second child was our daughter, Joanna. She soon showed the charm and vivacity of her mother. At her prep school she carried away all the prizes in everything. She went on to Benenden, where the experience was a little different. The headmistress found that she was not only a very keen rider – but also good at other games, particularly tennis and lacrosse. Very much against my advice, Joanna went to Sussex University where, perhaps because she was the daughter of the Chancellor, her life was difficult. She left, changed her plans and entered Barts as a medical student. She did extremely well in her examinations, winning prizes and praise, and became a dedicated NHS doctor with a large and demanding practice in the East End of London. She married Charles Peck, an American lawyer and friend of William's, and in her early-forties produced Henry and Alice in quick succession – charming little children who reproduce all the attractive features of their grandmother and – will not someone say? – their grandfather. In 1994 they went to live in Friston and Joanna now practices in Sussex.

Our third child was in striking contrast to the two elders. I remember well how Joan informed me that he was on the way. She was driving me to Lewes to catch a train to town and said, 'I must tell you something which may make you cross.' I probably remarked, 'Again? – well, what?' She then announced that she was expecting another baby. Cross? I embraced her and said I was delighted. And in due course Hume – so named after Joan's father – was born, his arrival interrupting Joan in the midst of a dinner party. For the first few years he followed much the same course as his elder brother, but quite soon he opted for an independent course; that is to demonstrate that he could make his own way in life without the assistance of any money or influence from his parents. And so he lost interest in Eton.

His relations with Joan and me continued to be friendly and although we were deeply anxious about his plans we understood the motivation and his unwillingness to accept any tangible help. Eventually he reached the age of 18, obtained a passport in a new name and announced his departure with, he said, £130 in his pocket. There was a moving but affectionate farewell at Friston. It was indeed a very sad occasion and turned out much more sadly than we thought for he never saw his mother, nor she him, again. Ostensibly en route to Australia, Hume reached Bangkok and at once obtained a temporary position teaching English. After a time he obtained a job as a radio announcer, on a chat show interspersed with records and advertisements. He became very well known on this programme as 'Joey'. Some kind friend taped one of his programmes and sent it to me. This job continued for several years, after which he worked with a very reputable dealer in antiques with a shop near the Oriental Hotel and acquired considerable knowledge of his subject. Whenever I went to Thailand I had the constant mortification on mentioning my name of being asked about 'Joey', for he seems to have been very popular in a wide circle.

When Joan died he returned for the funeral and reverted to his real name and eventually came back to England for a few years, but still for some time maintaining his independence. But this attitude is now changing and he is more realistic. Our relationship is very good and I see quite a lot of him, trying to put the sad days behind us.

In my half-century of active public life there have, of course, been many world events of a momentous kind which I have witnessed simply as an ordinary citizen affected by developments but not in the slightest degree involved in them: wars, revolutions, undreamt-of scientific and mechanical developments that have altered all our lives but which we individually are powerless to influence.

Nonetheless, in the course of my own life there have been many developments that have been of more personal interest to me because of the various public positions I have held from time to time, including the six years' involvement in government immediately following the war.

I do, on the whole, look back on those six years with pride. Although I am no longer a Socialist, I still feel that the 1945 general election was a golden dawn and that its promise was not entirely belied by the later development of our affairs. We all really believed that we were building Jerusalem in England's green and pleasant land. Of course, as time went on there was much disappointment, disillusion and even bitterness, but the dream of a new Jerusalem lived on. Looking back, with that wisdom which is never with us at the time, I think our mistakes were that at the beginning we thought we were too much at the top of the world: we felt we had won the greatest war ever fought (but without realizing what it had cost us), and believed we would remain the unifying head of the greatest empire the world had ever known in spite of endowing our colonies with independence. We also concentrated far too much on the ideal conditions we thought the new Jerusalem should provide without first dealing with the mundane problems of how to build it. Thus we introduced a free health service. We introduced a more liberal system of general education without realizing that its operation and success would depend upon raising the public teaching profession to at least as high a standard as had been enjoyed by the private schools. We restored very full freedom to the trade unions (and I had some special responsibility for this) without also ensuring that the unions did not restore the old and most damaging restrictive practices which had been suspended during the war or exercise powers that interfered with the proper freedom of their members. We introduced – and here again I had a particular responsibility – a large measure of legal aid without realizing the extent of the need for it or how to cost it.

And so one could go on. We were – in that sunny dawn – idealists. We were not economists. The problem of how to build the new economy was at that time no more than a 'cloud on the horizon no bigger than a man's hand.' It very soon darkened the skies. A realization of our complete impoverishment by our great war effort soon came upon us, although it was four years before we devalued the pound sterling. The complete decay of our infrastructure dating back to long before the war had started soon made its crippling effect felt. The extortions and impositions by the trade unions not only blemished individual freedoms but helped to destroy British competitiveness in world markets – a situation only recovered by Margaret Thatcher's courage and legislation. Equally, on the employers side, there was gross inefficiency, serious detachment from realities, and many leaders of industry remained – as Brendan Bracken called them – blockheads. I wish I could think that things were better in that field now. I fear that cupidity and corruption have crept in to a far greater extent than existed before.

What of those particular matters with which in my oddly varied career I have had some special concern?

I have already referred to my views on the law, to my work on the City Panel and on various company boards, and I have indicated my concern with the change in manners and conduct in the City. It is, I suppose, all part of the pace of modern life; the great amenities that wealth makes available – all the temptations of the Acquisitive Society. It is difficult to swim against this stream and it is small consolation to say that the mass of the people are on the whole materially better off than in my earlier days, although much real poverty remains.

I believe politics is now more openly and honestly conducted than before by parties with recognizable policies and now fairly stable establishments. I regret, however, the fact that politics is becoming more and more a full-time job. This is because of the much greater activity of the State and the constant need for more and more legislation. The result is, however, that politics is becoming a specialist occupation.

It is a good many years since a distinguished and respected Liberal leader remarked that nobody of any distinction had entered Parliament since 1945. I do not like the specialist politician who has had no experience of real life or of ordinary people earning their livelihood in the outside world. The fact that it is so, however, is the great justification for a free, vigilant and fearless Press. Although I deplore many recent cases of press intrusion, I would hesitate to regard them as justifying a law of privacy.

In all this I am naturally thinking of such part as I played in these matters over the years. I certainly do not put myself forward as having in a real sense had a successful life from a public point of view. The kindest verdict might be that I had been seriously lacking in ambition – and in one sense that is true. I look back first at the law. I could certainly have become Lord Chief Justice and Master of the Rolls and, almost certainly, Lord Chancellor had I decided on this course. Certainly the Lord Chief Justiceship – which I regard as probably the most important legal position – did have attractions for me. Should I have taken it? I did not agree with Hugh Dalton's stated opinion that a Socialist in high judicial office (and he said it in reference to me, condemning me for non-acceptance) could have done much good for the law. But I believe I could have filled any of these three offices, and particularly the first, competently. I might have tried to emulate the lawyers I most admired in my day: Lord Atkin, who adumbrated the law as to one's duty to one's neighbour, or perhaps Lord Denning. I might at least have gone down in history as having held high judicial office. As it is I shall go down as nothing, for that is what I am.

As for business I might, I dare say, have gone into full-time chairmanship of some big company and amassed a great deal of money. I do not think, however, that I should particularly have enjoyed such work, nor is it likely that I would have been performing any great service to the public at large.

What of politics? Should I have aimed for the leadership of the Labour Party and so the premiership? Looking back, I certainly find it curious that I did not at the time associate the leadership of the Labour Party with becoming Prime Minister, or realize that many thought, as Harold Wilson did, that nothing could have stopped me. But even if I had appreciated that at the time, I do not think I could have brought myself to use my old friend Herbert Morrison as a stepping stone. I still think personal loyalties are a very important element in life.

Did the public suffer any great loss as a result? Who can say. I doubt whether I would have been the worst Prime Minister since 1945. I suppose it is possible that I might have provided an encouraging leadership and brought about some reforms. I cannot say, for I do not recall giving the matter a thought.

Could I have done more for the public good in politics generally? I do rate myself as having been an efficient and successful law officer; whether that has done any lasting good I doubt. I achieved no very great reforms. I was on the way, I think, to being an efficient President of the Board of Trade. But apart from paving the way for Edward Heath's resale price maintenance legislation, I achieved no great reforms.

Certainly, later on, I could have taken a much more active part in political debate and perhaps helped to promote progressive causes. It is conceivable that I might even have been more effective in this way if I had actually crossed the floor and joined the Tory Party. But I explicitly refused in writing, both to Brendan Bracken for Anthony Eden, and to Walter Monckton, to entertain the possibility of a viscountcy on that basis, and I told Walter Monckton that I would only accept a peerage on the basis that it was known that I remained a member of the Labour Party.

Later, it is true, I was persuaded by Rab Butler to go to the Lords as a life peer and then decided to sit on the cross-benches. I do blame myself for the failure to take any active part in debate, for I might sometimes have had some little influence on policy, as I hope I did when, I think, I helped persuade the Lords to reject the War Crimes bill in 1991.

Looking back over my life, I do seem to have been lacking in the normal ambitions. I certainly do not think that was the case in my much younger days. I suspect it altered when I realized that I had been mistaken about the efficacy of Socialism and lost those early enthusiasms that I sincerely held.

Yet I feel sure that the basic factor was the development of my family life. Although I spent my earlier years in a very happy and quite intellectual family, and was brought up with great fondness and affection, I did not have any very strong intellectual interests that I shared with my parents. We lived quite a modest life. My first marriage was a loving one to an absolutely devoted wife; but it ended childless and in tragedy. Quickly, I married again; we had children and lived very happily for 30 years – until tragedy struck again. Although I was very active in public life during that period I shared my activities with my wife and all my moves were designed to promote the happiness and well-being of my family rather than fame.

Now, in my old age, I have reason to be grateful: my three children care for me and appear to love me, and I have a few friends, one in particular who has been devoted. But I know that in my public life I fell below the standards that I had set myself. I have seen what is wrong but not done enough to put it right. I have been more critical than correct. I have had opportunities of great positions in the service of the state, but I have put them aside. I know that I have not devoted myself enough to promoting the good of others. I am nobody – nor can I be sure that if I had driven myself in another direction I could have been somebody – for the public good. Here I failed, from the standpoint of Galations VI, 3–5.

> For if a man think himself to be something, when
> he is nothing, he deceiveth himself. But let
> every man prove his own work, and then shall he
> have rejoicing in himself alone, and not in
> another. For every man shall bear his own burden.

I thought of all such matters on my ninetieth birthday in February 1992. My children gave me a party at the Café Royal. It was a moving occasion. There were friends from all stages of my life. Chris Mayhew, with whom I did the first TV political broadcast in 1951. Akio Morita, Chairman of Sony, Hugh Cudlipp, and many more. Quintin Hailsham and Margaret Thatcher were amongst those who made very kind speeches.

As well as the dinner at Gray's Inn I have mentioned, other celebrations were held for me – by my legal friends on the Northern Circuit, and by my friends and colleagues at J.P. Morgan. They had a huge cake modelled on the Houses of Parliament in which I have been so proud to serve, and I was once more surrounded by friends and relations of all ages. Dennis Weatherstone, the Chairman of the Bank, presented me with a splendid volume of all my letters to *The Times* over the decades – writing such letters has been a habit which I have never tried to break. In his speech he said that he had made a special "Shawcross rule" – I could stay until I was a hundred! In response I thanked from the bottom of my heart everyone at J.P. Morgan, a great bank and a wonderful institution. By 1995, I had had thirty happy years with them: I fear they have done more for me than I have done for them.

I have now stopped going in to the bank on a regular basis and spend most of my time in Sussex. But every summer I still go to Cornwall with my children and grand-children, and sail on my last boat, *Talisker of Lorne*, a pretty 34 foot mahogany sloop. I rejoice in the happy times. What are those lines?

> Best count the happy moments
> What they gave
> Makes men less fearful of the certain grave
> The happy days are days that make men brave.

There is much that is evil in the world. But there is much that is good. Some more lines

> Two men look out through the same bars:
> One sees the mud and one the stars

I do see some stars. I rejoice in my family. And I cling to the hope that I shall soon find Joan – and Alberta, my first wife – waiting for me 'when I put out to sea'.

Index

Abdul Rahman Putra, Tunku, 22–3, 307

Abercrombie, Sir Patrick, 252

Abs, Herman, 307–8

Abu Dhabi, 241–2

Acton, John Emerich Edward Dalberg, 1st Baron, 188

Addison, Christopher, 1st Viscount, 189

Aden, 272, 307

Adriatic: HWS sails in, 199

AEI (company), 282–3

Aitken, Max, 211, 290

Aix-en-Provence, University of, 307

Albania: and Corfu channel dispute, 165–6, 173–4

Alexander, Henry, 283

Alexander, Robert, 305

Allied Control Commission (Germany), 97

Aluco (tanker), 270

American Bar Association, 153–4, 183, 257, 260

Amery, John, 83–4

Anderson, Sir John (later Viscount Waverley), 39

Angkor Wat (Cambodia), 286–7

Anne, Princess (Princess Royal), 295

Arden-Clarke, Sir Charles, 271

Ariel (yacht), 273

Armstrong, Hamilton Fish, 220

Ashdown Forest, Sussex, 13–14, 39, 47

Assheton, Ralph, 208

Association de Droit Minier et Petrolier, 307

Association for the Promotion and Protection of Private Foreign Investment (APPI), 308

Astor, Gavin, 285–6

Astor, Nancy, Viscountess, 218–19

Atkin, James Richard, Baron, 327

atomic warfare, 135

Attlee, Clement (later 1st Earl): as PM in 1945 government, 63–6; and war crimes trials, 133; insists HWS apologise to Kemsley, 146–7; supports retention of capital punishment, 168–70; and Lynskey Tribunal, 173, 179; congratulates HWS, 179, 201; supports HWS on married women's property bill, 182; criticised as Prime Minister, 184; and Party leadership changes and appointments, 189–91, 237; calls 1951 election, 200; offers posts to HWS, 208–9; asks HWS to wind up debate on East-West trade, 224–5; Churchill's view of, 233; Bevan criticises, 238; resigns, 242–3

Attlee, Violet Helen (*later* Countess), 145

Attorney General: functions and powers of, 66–77, 317–18; prosecutes in poison murder cases, 184

Auchinleck, Field Marshal Sir Claude, 213–14, 216–17

Auschwitz concentration camp, 117

Baden, Switzerland, 14

Bader, Douglas, 264

Balogh, Thomas, Baron, 268

Bar Council (General Council of the Bar), 75, 203, 211, 257–60

Baring Brothers (bankers), 282

Barkley, William, 138

Barran, Sir David, 282

Baruch, Bernard, 154

Batt, Professor Raleigh, 24

Battle of Britain (1940), 46–8

Beaverbrook, William Maxwell Aitken, 1st Baron, 146, 149, 212, 215, 237, 254, 290

Beirut, 249–50

Belcher, John, 175–9

Belsen, 116

Benenson, Peter, 263

Beneš, Edvard, 144

Bentinck, Bill *see* Portland, 9th Duke of

Bents brewery, 31

Berlin, 104

Bernays, Colonel Murray, 88, 136

Besse, Christiane, 272–3, 286, 297, 300

Besse, Tony, 272–3, 286, 297

Beswick, Frank, Baron, 268

Bevan, Aneurin: and dockers' strike, 73–4; threatens resignation over NHS charges, 192; and Labour Party policies, 200, 238; and party leadership, 237; refuses to wear black tie, 287

Bevin, Ernest: asks HWS to chair Catering Wages Commission, 54; dislikes Morrison, 63–4, 189; appointed Foreign Secretary, 64; and trial of Hess, 102; and trade union reform, 140; visits Paris Embassy, 145; in New York, 152–4; and HWS's clash with Vyshinsky, 171; decline, 184; succession at Foreign Office, 184, 189–1

Biddle, Francis, 101, 104–5, 113, 123, 125–6, 128, 132

Bill of Rights (British): proposed, 315–16

Bingham Melcombe, Dorset, 252

Birkenhead, Frederick Smith, 1st Earl of, 23, 73–4, 233

Birkett, William Norman, 1st Baron: defends Dr Buck Ruxton, 29–30; at Nuremberg trials, 99–100, 112–13, 122–6, 129; on Robert Jackson, 111; and Goering's suicide, 130; arranges apology from *Punch* for HWS, 205; chairs London University Court, 266

Blenkinsop, Arthur, 208

Bloch, Sir Maurice, 178–9

Blomberg, Werner von, 119

Board of Trade, 192–4, 236, 327

Bolshoi Ballet, 251

Boncour, Paul, 139

Boothby, Robert, Baron, 281

Bottomley, Arthur, 49

Bowden, Herbert (*later* Baron Aylestone), 66

Bower, Tom: *Blind Eye to Murder*, 107n

Bowser, Gerald, 297

Brabazon of Tara, John Theodore Cuthbert Moore-Brabazon, 1st Baron, 229–30

Brabin, Daniel, 30

Brabin, Mary, 30, 297

Bracken, Brendan (*later* Viscount), 59, 154, 215, 233, 253–4, 263, 325, 328

Braddock, Bessie, 74, 213

Bridges, C.W., 57

Bright, John, 12

Bristol University, 230
Britain: 1940 invasion threat, 45–6; bombed, 47–8
British Empire: dissolution, 46
British Hotels and Restaurants Association, 266, 270
British Information Services, 226
British War Crimes Executive, 98–9
Brooke, General Sir Alan (*later* Field Marshal Viscount Alanbrooke), 45
Brown, George (*later* Baron George-Brown), 193, 243–4, 296
Brown, W.J., 142
Browning, Professor Robert, 275
Bruce, George, 13
Brunei, 263–5
BSA (Birmingham Small Arms company), 293
Bullard, Sir Reader, 241–2
Buraimi Oasis dispute, 240–2
Burgess, James, 80
Bush, George, 164
Bustani, Emile, 250
Butler, Richard Austen (*later* Baron; 'Rab'), 201, 233, 267, 271, 328
Byrne, T.K., 80
Byrnes, James F., 98

Caccia, Sir Harold (*later* Baron), 276
Cadogan, Sir Alexander, 153
Café Royal (London), 263
Caffyn, Sydney, 266–7
Calcutt, Sir David, 305
Caldecote, Thomas Walker Inskip, Viscount, 82
Cambodia, 314
Campbell, R.J., 49
Camrose, William Ewert Berry, 1st Viscount, 148, 215
Canada, 276, 288
capital punishment: abolition of, 30; HWS opposes, 84, 130; discussed in Parliament, 167–9
Carrington, Peter Carington, 6th Baron, 193

Carson, Edward, Baron, 74
Carton de Wiart, Sir Adrian, 139
Caryl (yacht), 35, 148
Casement, Sir Roger, 73, 215
'Cassandra' (William Connor), 212, 255
Cassel, Sir Ernest, 181
Cassell's (publishers), 215
Catering Wages Commission, 54
Catlin, Sir George, 58
Cazalet, Zara, 297
Cecil of Chelwood, Edgar Algernon Robert Gascoyne-Cecil, Viscount, 139
Chamberlain, Neville, 35
Chambers, Paul, 281
Champetier de Ribes, Auguste, 120–1
Chandos, Oliver Lyttelton, 1st Viscount, 282
Chiang Kai-shek, 227
Chicago Crimes Commission, 283
China: UN seat, 227; HWS visits, 298–303
Chorley, Robert Samuel Theodore, 1st Baron, 259
Chou En-lai, 300
Christ Church, Oxford, 23
Churchill, Randolph, 31
Churchill, (Sir) Winston: and 1940 invasion threat, 45; conduct of war, 45–6; and 1945 Labour government, 63; and trial of war criminals, 87, 89; and Potsdam Conference, 98; urges cessation of later war crimes trials, 133; speechmaking, 139; and trade union law, 141; praises Shinwell, 143; involvement in routine administration, 164–5; friendship with HWS, 165, 179; in debate on capital punishment, 168–9; criticizes Shinwell in debate on Hong Kong trade, 194; *Daily Mirror* accuses of warmongering, 203–4; supposed intervention over *Sunday Express*

article on HWS, 211–12; HWS acts for without payment over Dorman-Smith affair, 213–17; awards Bristol degree to HWS, 230; and rearmament of Germany, 231; decline, 233–4; and HWS's appellation 'Sir Shortly Floorcross', 233; and the Other Club, 233; and Bevan, 237

City Panel (London), 290–3, 304–6, 326

Civil Aviation Bill (1946), 145

Civil Defence Staff College, 270

coal industry: nationalisation of, 143

Cohen of Birkenhead, Henry, 1st Baron, 269

Cohen, Professor Henry, 33

Cohen, Lionel Leonard, Baron, 228

Coke, Sir Edward (Lord Coke), 80

Cold War: beginnings, 160

Coleridge, Samuel Taylor: *Biographia Literaria*, 12, 270

Columbia University, New York, 218, 221, 223

Comet (aircraft), 77, 227–9

Commonwealth and Empire Law Conference (1955), 238–9

Communism, 221, 225, 263, 299

Connally, Senator Tom, 149–51, 153

Connor, William *see* 'Cassandra'

Cooke, Alistair, 151

Cooper, Sir Alfred Duff (*later* 1st Viscount Norwich), 145

Cooper, Lady Diana, 145

Corfu Straits, 165–6, 173–4

corruption: in international business, 308–12

Cousins, Frank, 281

Coventry: bombed, 47

Coward, Noël, 195

Crawley, Aidan, 159, 271

Criminal Justice Act (1987), 69

Criminal Justice Amendment Bill (1947), 167

Cripps, Mr Registrar, 26

Cripps, Sir Stafford: and Gresford Mining disaster, 32; supports HWS at St Helens, 62; supports Morrison for PM, 63; antagonism to colleagues, 64–5; at Durham Miners' Gala, 170; supports HWS on married women's property bill, 182; intrigues, 188; resigns, 189

Cromer, George Rowland Stanley Baring, 3rd Earl of, 269, 284

Crosland, Antony, 274

Cross, Geoffrey (*later* Baron), 248

Crossman, Richard H.S., 211–12

Crown Proceedings Act (1947), 162

Cuba: trade pact with, 198

Cuckfield, Sussex, 21

Cudlipp, Hugh, Baron, 289, 329

Cunningham, Sir Graham, 275

Cunningham, Squadron Leader John ('Cat's Eyes'), 48

Curtis-Bennett, Frederick Henry (Derek), 80, 176

Cyrus the Great, Persian Emperor, 294

Czechoslovakia: HWS visits, 143–5

Daily Mirror, 203

Daily Sketch, 148

Daily Telegraph, 268, 279

Daily Worker, 232, 263

Dalai Lama, 301

Dalton, Hugh: as Chancellor of Exchequer, 64; and HWS's Nuremberg fee, 100; praises HWS's speech, 142; at Durham Miners' Gala, 170; and Lynskey Tribunal, 176, 178–9; resigns Chancellorship, 176; political intrigues, 188–9; criticizes HWS for neglect of Parliamentary duties, 208–9; and HWS's non-acceptance of Lord Chancellorship, 326–7

Darbishire, Harold, 24

Darbishire, Hester, 24

Davies, Clement, 262

Davies, (Sir) Edmund, 176
De Havilland aircraft company, 228
Deakin, Arthur, 208
death penalty see capital punishment
Denmark, 235
Denning, Alfred, Baron, 327
Derby, Edward George Villiers Stanley, 17th Earl of, 51
Desert Island Discs (radio programme), 244, 327
Devlin, Patrick Arthur, Baron, 280
Digby, Pamela, Lady, 252
Director of Public Prosecutions, 68–9, 71–2
Docker, Sir Bernard and Norah, Lady, 205–7
Donne, John, 316
Donnedieu de Vabres, Professor Henri, 114, 123, 125–6, 128
Donovan, General William ('Bill'), 105, 154
Dorman-Smith, Major-General Eric ('Chink'), 213–16
Dorset County Council, 252
Douglas-Home, Sir Alex see Home, Baron
Dowding, Air Marshal Hugh (later Baron), 44
Dresden: bombing of, 135
Driberg, Tom (later Baron), 159
Dubček, Alexander, 312, 322
Dudley, William Humble Eric Ward, 3rd Earl of, 50
Dulles, John Foster, 171
Dulwich College, 15, 266
Dunne, Sir Laurence, 206
Durand-Deacon, Mrs, 185–6
Durham Miners' Gala, 170, 225

Eastbourne, Sussex, 42
Economic Commission for Asia and the Far East, 307
Economist, The, 279
ECOSOC (United Nations), 150
Ede, James Chuter, 82, 167

Eden, Anthony (later 1st Earl of Avon): and war crimes trials, 87, 89, 92; makes 1951 election TV broadcast, 200–1; foreign policy, 236; considers viscountcy for HWS, 268, 328
Egremont, John Wyndham, 1st Baron, 287
Egremont, Pamela, Lady, 287, 297, 300–1
Eichmann, Adolf, 117
Eisenhower, General Dwight D.: and war crimes trials, 92, 133
election expenses, 188
Elizabeth II, Queen (formerly Princess), 195
Enemy Alien Tribunal, 36–8
Erskine, Thomas, 1st Baron, 76
Etherington, Sir George, 53
Eton College, 322
European Community, 284–5
European Convention on Human Rights, 316
Evans, Lincoln, 208
Evening Standard, 142, 203, 209
Ewart, Richard, 194
Exner, Professor Franz, 119

Face to Face (TV programme), 272
Falco, Robert, 114, 123
Falkland Islands, 314
Falmouth, 148–9
family: importance of, 320
Festival of Britain (1951), 200
Field, St John, 22
Financial Times, 309
Fletcher, Sir Walter, 224–5
Foot, Michael, 73, 140, 147
Ford Motor Company, 253–4, 257, 263, 274
Fowey, Cornwall, 146, 148
France: HWS visits, 143, 145
Franco, General Francisco, 151
Frank, Hans, 124
Fraser, Canon (of Liverpool), 27–8
Fraser, Sir Ian, 290–1, 305

Freeman, John, 192, 272

Frick, Wilhelm, 124

Friends of Atlantic Union, 208, 257, 263

Friston Place, Sussex, 260, 270

Fritzsche, Hans, 124, 129

Fuchs, Klaus, 190

Fyfe, David Maxwell (*later* Earl of Kilmuir): at Gray's Inn, 19; HWS joins chambers, 24–6; Bar practice, 26–7, 30; supports Conservative candidate at St Helens, 62; and war criminals, 86; replaced on British War Crimes Executive, 98–9; appointed to deputise at Nuremberg trials, 99–100; and Katyn massacre, 103; cross-examines Goering, 112–13; reveals HWS's apology to Beaverbrook, 149; defends Haigh, 185–7

Fyfe, Sylvia Maxwell (*née* Harrison), 25

Gaitskell, Dora, Baroness, 269

Gaitskell, Hugh: as Chancellor of the Exchequer, 189, 192; favours trans-Atlantic cooperation, 208; and HWS's neglect of Parliamentary duties, 208; Bevan attacks, 238; wins Party leadership, 243–4, 247; offers Lord Chancellorship to HWS, 254, 261, and HWS's resignation from politics, 261–2; opposes HWS's life peerage, 267; and HWS's statement on Rhodesia Commission, 272

Game, Sir Philip, 55

Gardiner, Gerald, Baron, 22, 142, 269, 281, 317

Gates, Thomas, 283

Gaulle, Charles de, 145

GEC (General Electric Company), 282–3

Geddes, (Sir) Auckland Campbell, 1st Baron, 40–2, 45, 49–50, 53, 55

General Elections: 1922, 1; 1945, 16, 57, 60, 98, 324; 1950, 189–90; 1951, 200; 1955, 231, 236–8

General Strike (1926), 139

Geneva, 16, 139, 241

Geneva Convention (1949), 315

Genocide Convention, 313

George VI, King, 55

Germany: post-war administration, 156

Gibson, George, 175–6, 178–9

Giessen, Germany, 12

Goddard, Rayner, Baron, 73, 168, 222, 230, 240

Goering, Hermann: trial of, 86, 100, 106–7, 313; cross-examined, 111–13, 117; closing speech at Nuremberg, 122; found guilty and sentenced to death, 124; enmity with Schacht, 127–8; congratulates Fritzsche on acquittal, 129; suicide, 130

Goethe, J.W. von: *Faust*, 12, 269–70

Goodman, Arnold, Baron, 289

Gorbachev, Mikhail, 156

Gore-Booth, Paul (*later* Baron), 153

Gorman, Sir William, 24

Gray's Inn: HWS joins, 17–20; HWS elected a Master of the Bench, 34; HWS elected Treasurer, 232; 90th birthday dinner for HWS, 319

Gresford Colliery disaster (1934), 31–3, 143

Griffiths, James, 190–1

Griffiths, Sir John Norton ('Empire Jack'), 15

Grimond, Joseph (*later* Baron), 208

Gromyko, Andrei, 154

Guardian, The (formerly *The Manchester Guardian*), 147, 279–80

Guernsey, 226

Gulf War, 137, 164, 313–14

H-bomb, 236

Haddock (of Shell), 248

Haigh, John George: trial, 184–7

Haile Selassie, Emperor of Ethiopia, 294–5

Halifax, Edward Frederick Lindley Wood, 1st Earl of, 208

Hall, J.W., 83
Hall, Sir Arnold, 228–9
Hambrow, Carl, 139
Hamburg: bombing of, 135
Hastings, Sir Patrick, 32, 203
Havers, Michael (*later* Baron), 67
Hawker Siddeley Group, 286
Healey, Denis, Baron, 169
Heath, (Sir) Edward, 194, 289, 327
Heilbron, (Dame) Rose, 30
Hemmerde, Edward George, 27–8
Hennessy, Sir Patrick, 253, 257, 263
Hess, Rudolf: tried at Nuremberg, 102–3, 122; sentenced, 124, 129–30
Himmler, Heinrich, 124
Hiroshima, 135
Hitler, Adolf: 1940 invasion threat, 45; early peace proposals, 45–6; and war crimes trial, 90–2; cited at Nuremberg trial, 110, 115, 123; aggressive aims, 124; Speer's disagreements with, 126; Schacht and, 127–8
Hitler Jugend (Hitler Youth), 124
Hobson, Valerie (Mrs John Profumo), 277
Hodges Figgis (booksellers), 215
Hoess, Rudolf, 116–17
Hogg, Quintin (*later* Baron Hailsham), 179, 188, 174, 329
Holland, Henry Scott, 297
Hollom, Sir Jasper, 304–5
Holocaust: denial of, 86
Home Secretary: and administration of criminal law, 71–2
Home, (Sir) Alec Douglas-Home, Baron, 273, 289
Hong Kong: war munitions traded through, 194; HWS visits, 248–9, 301–2
Hopwood, Sir Francis, 252–4
Horner (cartoonist), 289
Horsham, Sussex, 34
Hossbach Conference (1937), 124

House of Lords: HWS's activities in, 168–70
Housewives League, 159
Howard, Gerald, 80
Hudson, John, 194
Hudson, Judge Manley, 241
Huiskamp, Monique, 297
Hull, Cordell, 86
Hull, John Folliott Charles, 305
human rights, 312–13, 315–16
Humphreys, Sir Travers (Mr Justice), 82, 84, 185
Hungary: secret trials in, 255; violation of human rights in, 312
Hunter, Leslie and Margaret, 192
Hussein, Saddam *see* Saddam Hussein

Imperial Chemical Industries, 205
International Bar Association, 226
International Chamber of Commerce, 308–12
International Commission of Jurists, 255
International Court of Criminal Justice: proposed, 137, 312, 314–15
International Court of Justice: and Corfu Channel dispute, 165–6, 173; and expropriations of foreign property, 307
international criminal law, 312–14
International Law Commission, 314
investment, foreign, 306–8
Iran, 293–6
Iraq, 313
Ironside, Field Marshal Sir Edmund (*later* 1st Baron), 45

Jackson, J.C., 29–30
Jackson, Robert: appointed Chief Counsel on War Crimes Tribunal, 90; and setting up of Tribunal, 92–7, 101; and Potsdam Conference, 98; and choice of defendants, 101–2; and Katyn massacre, 103; opens case at Nuremberg, 105, 108–9; qualities

and character, 105, 111; cross-
examines at Nuremburg, 111–13;
closing speech at Nuremberg,
117–19, 126; on Nazi extermination
policy, 117; on von Schirach, 124; on
subsequent trials, 132; son of, 296
Jahrreis, Professor Hermann, 119
James, Eric, Baron, 267
Japan: trade competition from, 198
Jebb, Sir Gladwyn and Lady (*later*
Baron and Lady Gladwyn), 220
Jellicoe, Geoffrey, 252
Jewish Professional Association, 235
Jews: Nazi extermination of, 117, 125
Jodl, General Alfried, 124
Johnston, Sir Alexander, 293, 305
Jones, Elwyn (*later* Baron Elwyn-
Jones), 112, 143
Jowitt, William Allen (*later* Earl), 62,
65, 98–9, 145, 173, 190
Joyce, William ('Lord Haw-Haw'):
trial and execution, 73, 78–83, 140
Justice (organization), 263, 269–70,
272, 308

Kaldor, Nicholas, Baron, 268
Kaltenbrunner, Ernst, 116, 124
Katyn massacre (1939), 103, 121
Kearton, Christopher Frank, Baron,
269
Keeble, Harold, 211
Keeler, Christine, 277
'Keep Left Group', 200
Keitel, Field Marshal Wilhelm, 106,
124
Kellogg-Briand Pact (1928), 119 & n
Kemsley, Edith, Viscountess, 148
Kemsley, Gomer Berry, 1st Viscount,
146–9
Kennan, Melville, 30
Kenya, 273
Kenyatta, Jomo, 213
Kheradjon, Gascon, 309
King, Cecil, 279–80, 289
Kinnock, Neil, 183

Kissinger, Henry, 322
Knollys, Edward George William
Tyrwhitt Knollys, 2nd Viscount, 42
Korea, 194, 314
Kranzbuehler, Otto, 107
Krupp, Alfried, 101–2, 131–2
Krupp, Gustav, 101–2, 131
Kuwait, 313–14

Labour Party: HWS joins, 15; HWS
stands as candidate for in 1945, 57;
1945 election victory, 62; leadership
struggles, 64, 188–9, 200; and trade
union law, 139–41; post-war
government, 158, 325; increasing
moderation, 183; class support for,
200–1; loses 1951 election, 201;
attitude to HWS, 225, 232, 236,
269; loses 1955 election, 238; HWS's
potential leadership, 243–7, 255,
327; leadership succession to Attlee,
243; government under Wilson,
289
Laski, Harold, 63
Law Commission, 317
Law Journal, 173
Law Officers of the Crown, 66–71,
74–5
law reform (Britain), 316–19
Lawley, Sue, 244–5
Lawrence, Sir Geoffrey (Lord Justice),
100–1, 104–5, 114, 122–3, 125–6,
128
League of Nations: dissolution, 139
Leasco (US company), 291–2
Lee Kuan Yew, 248
legal aid scheme (and bill), 143, 162–3,
174, 177
Leggatt, Hugh, 277
Levin, Michal, 322
Lewes, Sussex, 184–5
libel and slander, 163
Liddell Hart, Sir Basil, 215–17
Lincoln, Abraham, 319
Liverpool: bombed, 47

Liverpool University: HWS lectures at, 23–4; HWS's *ex officio* degree, 30; awards honorary doctorate to HWS, 290
Lloyd George, Gwilym, 258
Lloyd's of London, 234
London: bombed, 47–8
London & Continental Bankers, 304
London Fashion Fortnight, 195
London University: Court, 266
Longford, Francis Aungier Pakenham, 7th Earl of, 269
Lonrho (company), 285
Lord Privy Seal, 192
Loudon, John, 271–2
Lynskey, Sir George Justin, 24, 77, 82; Tribunal, 173–9

Mabane, William, 146
MacArthur, General Douglas, 194
McCarthy, Senator Joseph, 221, 278
McCloy, Jack, 87–8
McCloy, John Jay, 154
MacDonald, Ramsay, 16
Mackay of Clashfern, James Peter Hymers, Baron, 74, 163, 318
Macmillan, Harold (*later* 1st Earl of Stockton), 197, 233, 239–40, 267, 271–2, 274
Macmillan, Hugh Pattison, Baron, 82
McNaghton rule (on insanity), 186
McNeil, Hector, 172–3, 254
Magee, Bryan, 244–6, 327
Malaysia, 22–3
Manchester, 49–50, 54
Manchester Guardian see *Guardian, The*
Manningham-Buller, Sir Reginald (*later* 1st Viscount Dilhorne), 248
Mao Tse-tung, 300
Married Women (Restraint on Anticipation) Bill (1949) ('the Mountbatten Bill'), 181–2
Marshall Plan (for European reconstruction), 160–1
Masaryk, Jan, 145, 154

Mather, Joan *see* Shawcross, Joan Winifred, Lady
Mathew, Sir Theobald, 172
Maudlin, Reginald, 282
Maufe, Sir Edward, 260
Maxwell, Elsa, 154, 220
Maxwell, Robert, 235, 291–3
May, Alan Nunn, 142–3, 190
Mayhew, Christopher, 200–1, 329
Mayhew, Sir Patrick, 74
Medical Research Council, 274
Menzies, Robert, 284
Meyer, John, 283–4
Milch, General Erhardt, 125
Miller, A.T., 31, 61
Miners Union, 32–3
Mishcon, Victor, Baron, 235
Mohammed Reza Pahlevi, Shah of Iran, 294–6
Møller, Maersk, 284
Molotov, Vyacheslav M., 87, 149–51, 154–6
Monckton, Bridget Helen, Viscountess, 253
Monckton, Sir Walter (*later* Viscount): at Lynskey Tribunal, 176; and Mountbattens' finances, 181–2; and *Punch* attack on HWS, 204; in Crossman diary as disliking HWS's behaviour, 211; HWS's friendship with, 233, 253; and HWS's decision to leave Bar, 254–5; HWS succeeds as Chancellor of Sussex University, 267; and HWS's lost viscountcy, 268; chairmanship of Rhodesia and Nyasaland constitution commission, 271–2, 274; and HWS's peerage, 328
Monopolies and Mergers Commission, 276, 285
Monsell, Bolton Meredith Eyres-Monsell, 1st Viscount, 49
Montgomery, General Bernard Law (*later* Field Marshal Viscount), 42–4, 133, 214, 231

Moran, Charles McMoran Wilson, 1st Baron, 152, 215

Morgan Guaranty Trust (later J.P. Morgan), 283–4

Morgenthau, Henry, 87

Morita, Akio, 284, 329

Morris, O.G., 37

Morrison, Herbert: at Second Socialist International, 16–17; as wartime Home Secretary, 42; advises HWS against changing job in war, 53; honours Regional Commissioners, 55; pro-Labour speeches in war, 57, 63; supports HWS at St Helens, 61; in Party leadership struggles, 63–4, 189, 191, 243–4, 246–7, 327; speech attacking press, 147; supports retention of capital punishment, 168; criticizes industry's anti-nationalization expenses, 188; Foreign Secretaryship, 191–2, 200; and HWS's Commons speech on East-West trade, 225; as deputy to Attlee, 238

Mosley, Sir Oswald, 79

Mountbatten, Edwina, Countess, 181–2

Muggeridge, Malcolm, 289

Multilateral Investment Convention, 307

Munich agreement (1938), 34

Murdoch, Rupert, 276

Muscat and Oman, 263–4

Mynors, Sir Humphrey, 290

Nagasaki, 135

Nairobi, 230–1, 272

Nation in Doubt, A (TV debate), 280

National Film Finance Corporation, 198

National Industrial Conference Board, Stanford University, 283

National Press Club, Washington, 161

Nazi–Soviet Pact (1939), 121

Nazis: trial of, 86–97

Nazism: revival in modern Germany, 86

Neave, Airey, 134n, 136

Nehru, Jawaharlal (Pandit), 152

Neill, Sir Patrick, 305

New Brunswick, University of, 290

New Daily, 278

New Statesman, 289

New York: HWS visits, 149

New York Bar Association, 319

Nicholson, C.E., 273

Nield, (Sir) Basil Edward, 24, 30

Nikitchenko, General I.T., 94–9, 104, 121, 123–6, 128

Northern Circuit (legal), 24

Norway, 235

Nuremberg Trials (International War Crimes Tribunal): and international law, 85–6; principles and procedures established, 88–90, 93–7, 113–14; British views on, 90–1; site chosen, 97–9; Charter signed, 101, 104; selection of defendants, 101–2; Lawrence appointed president, 104; setting, 105–6; conduct of, 107–8; HWS's opening speech at, 109–11; closing speeches, 117–21; judgments and sentences, 122–30; assessed, 134–7; as 'victors' justice', 313–14

O'Brien, Leslie Kenneth, Baron, 284, 290, 293

Observer (newspaper), 285

O'Connor, Sir Terence, 32

Omar, Sir Muda, Sultan of Brunei, 264

ombudsman system, 270, 272

Other Club, the, 233

Page, Walter, 283, 290

Paget, Reginald, Baron, 289

Paine, Thomas, 76

Pandit, Vijaya Lakshmi, 152

Papen, Franz von: tried and acquitted at Nuremberg, 124, 129

Paris, 145, 170–1

Parker, John J., 114, 123

Paull, Gilbert, 204

Paull, Walter, 28, 35–6, 148, 226

Pearce, Edward Holroyd, Baron, 292

Peck, Alice (Joanna's daughter), 323

Peck, Charles (Joanna's husband), 323

Peck, Henry (Joanna's son), 323

Peck, Joanna (née Shawcross; HWS's daughter): born, 170–1; pneumonia as child, 226; and mother's death, 297; visits China with HWS, 298–9; career and marriage, 323

Peckhams (country house), 192, 196, 260

Pergamon (company), 291

Persepolis, 294–5

petrol rationing, 166–7

Philip, Prince, Duke of Edinburgh, 295

Phnom Penh, 287

Picot, Georges, 309

Plowden, Edwin, Baron, 267

Poland: HWS visits, 143–4; withdraws from Marshall Plan, 160

Polizzi, Alex and Charlie (William's stepdaughters), 323

Polizzi, Olga (William's third wife), 323

Pol Pot, 119n, 287, 314

Ponomareva, Nina, 251

Porter, Samuel Lowry, Baron, 82

Portland, William Cavendish-Bentinck, 9th Duke of, 144

Potsdam Conference and agreements (1945), 98

Powell, Enoch, 289

Prague, 144

Prescott, Stanley, 167

Press Council: HWS chairs, 147, 276, 280, 285; reorganized, 276, 280

press (newspapers): HWS's comments on, 146–8, 161, 183, 212; freedom of, 278; prurience, 320

Pritchard, (Sir) Fred Eills, 24, 27–8

Pritt, Denis Nowell, 210–11, 213

Privy Council, 146, 239

Professional Classes Aid Society, 286

Profumo, John, 277–9

Punch (magazine), 204–5

Qabus Bin-Said, Sultan of Oman, 264

Quebec Conference (1944), 88

Queen Elizabeth, RMS, 149, 154, 251

Queen Mary, RMS, 161, 188

Qureishi (Saudi political officer), 241–2

Rahman, Tunku Abdul see Abdul Rahman Putra, Tunku

Reading, Stella, Marchioness of, 52–3

Recorder, The (newspaper), 190

Reddaway, W.B., 275

Rees-Mogg, William, Baron, 289

Regional Commissioners (wartime): role and function, 39–40, 44, 50; dissolved, 54–5

retail price maintenance, 194

Rey, Jean, 309

Rhodes, Hervey (later Baron), 193

Rhodesia and Nyasaland, Federation of: constitutional commission, 271–2

Ribbentrop, Joachim von, 106, 122, 124

Richardson, Sir Albert, 252

Richardson, Sir Gordon (later Baron), 304

Robbins, Lionel, Baron, 208, 267

Robens, Alfred, 193, 289

Roberts, Geoffrey Dorling ('Khaki'), 113

Robinson, Matthew: as HWS's clerk, 80, 205, 222; death, 250

Roechling (German industrialist), 131

Roll, Sir Eric (later Baron), 285

Rollier, Dr, 28

Roosevelt, Franklin D.: favours prosecution of war criminals, 86–90, 92–3

Rosenberg, Alfred, 124, 126

Rosenman, Samuel Irving, 88–9
Royal Commission on the Police, 271
Royal Commission on the Press
    (1961–2), 274–6, 280
Royal Dutch Shell *see* Shell (group of
    companies)
Royal Institute of International Affairs,
    311
Royall, Kenneth Claiborne, 133
Rudenko, General Roman, 103, 121,
    123
Runnymede Meadow, 260
Russell, John, 220
Russia *see* USSR
Ruxton, Dr Buck, 29–30
'RW' (County Court Judge), 36–7

Saddam Hussein, 119n, 137, 313–4
St Bartholomew's Hospital, London
    (Barts), 16
St Helens: HWS first stands for, 16,
    57–9; HWS wins in 1945 election,
    62; and HWS's resignation from
    politics, 255, 260–2
Salter, Dr Alfred, 59
Samuel, Harold, 221–2
San Francisco, 283
San Francisco Conference (United
    Nations), 92
Sauckel, Fritz, 124–7
Saudi Arabia: and Buraimi Oasis
    dispute, 240–2; and Gulf War, 314
Sauter, Dr Fritz, 121
Savoy Hotel, London, 221–2
Schacht, Hjalmar: tried at Nuremberg,
    101, 106, 113, 117, 122, 124, 127;
    acquitted, 128–9
Schirach, Baldur von, 121, 124–5
Schmitz, Herman, 131
Schnitzler (German industrialist),
    131
Schroeder (German industrialist),
    131
Schuster, Sir Claude, 36–7
Scott, George, 278

Sealion, Operation (1940), 46
Securities Industry Council, 305
Seligman, Douglas, 205–6
Serious Fraud Office, 68–9, 72
Seyss-Inquart, Arthur, 124
Shah of Iran *see* Mohammed Reza
    Pahlevi
Shahnaz, Princess of Iran, 294
Shaw, Sir Run Run, 248–9
Shawcross family, 11
Shawcross, Alberta Rosita (*née*
    Shyvers; HWS's first wife): HWS
    meets and marries, 20; ill-health,
    20–1, 28, 33–4, 50; in Manchester,
    50; death, 51–2
Shawcross, Christabel (Christopher's
    daughter), 62
Shawcross, Christopher (HWS's
    brother): childhood, 13–14; legal
    career, 31, 61–2; wartime service in
    navy, 38, 61; wins Widnes seat in
    1945 election, 61–2; divorce,
    remarriage and death, 62
Shawcross, Conrad (William's son),
    322
Shawcross, Ellie (William's daughter),
    322–3
Shawcross, Emily (HWS's adopted
    sister), 13
Shawcross, Hartley William, Baron:
    peerage, 11, 15, 267–8, 328; birth,
    12; childhood, 14; joins Labour
    Party, 15; schooling, 15; reads for
    Bar, 17–20; wins motorcycle in
    raffle, 19–20; first marriage, 20–1;
    success in Bar exams, 20; motor cars,
    21, 28, 41, 60, 167; early Bar
    practice, 22–30; tutors for Bar, 22;
    lectureship at Liverpool University,
    23; sailing and boats, 28, 35–6, 146,
    148, 187, 198–9, 226, 240, 273–4;
    heads Chambers, 30–1; takes Silk,
    34; presides over wartime refugee
    tribunal, 36–8; assists wartime S.E.
    Regional Commissioner, 39–42;

as North-Western Regional Commissioner, 50–1, 53; marriage to Joan, 53, 328; resigns as Regional Commissioner, 54, 59; earnings, 55, 69, 205, 207, 223, 255–6; post-war return to Bar, 55–6, 59; adopted as St Helens candidate for 1945 election, 57–9; views on socialism, 59, 156, 161–2, 183, 226, 231–2, 237, 258, 269, 328; contests and wins 1945 election, 60–2; appointment and duties as Attorney General, 65, 69–74, 76–7; knighthood, 66; 90th birthday celebrations, 74, 319; prosecutes cases as Attorney General, 78–81; at Nuremberg trials, 99–100; opening speech at Nuremberg, 109–11; closing speech at Nuremberg, 118–20; maiden speech in Commons, 138; speechmaking, 138, 146–7, 158, 160, 164, 183, 217–18, 221, 224, 225–6, 232–3, 270, 288; at United Nations, 139–40, 150–6, 161, 163, 170–1, 183, 187; quotes 'we are the masters' in Commons, 141–2; appointed Privy Councillor, 146; Kemsley threatens to sue, 146–7; views on moral decline, 147–8, 224, 279–81, 320; assists in rescuing drowning child, 159–60; hopes to succeed Bevin as Foreign Secretary, 184, 189–91; disc trouble, 190, 273; appointed President of Board of Trade, 192–4, 236, 327; duodenal trouble, 195; marriage relations, 197, 328; makes 1951 TV election broadcast, 200–1; as opposition spokesman on foreign affairs, 202, 207; resumes Bar practice, 203–7, 213, 234, 240, 247, 251–2; offered and declines judicial office, 208–9, 247, 254, 326; honorary degrees, 218, 220–1, 223, 230, 266, 290; friendship with political opponents, 233;

appendix operation, 234; economic views, 236–7; proposes fusion of Bar and solicitors, 239; as potential Party leader, 243–7, 255, 327; leaves Bar for business, 254–5; savings and investments, 256–7; resigns from politics, 260–3; on Rhodesia and Nyasaland constitution commission, 271–2; chairs Royal Commission on the Press, 274–6; business activities, consultancies and directorships, 282–4, 290–1; on criminal law reform, 288; made GBE, 293; visits to China, 298–302; and foreign investments in developing countries, 306–8

Shawcross, Hilda (HWS's mother): marriage, 12–13; character, 13; death, 49

Shawcross, Hume (HWS's younger son): born, 209, 323; career, 323–4

Shawcross, Joan Winifred, Lady (née Mather; HWS's second wife): as HWS's driver in war, 41–2; Alberta corresponds with, 51; HWS marries, 53; in election campaigns, 60, 236; sailing, 148; and birth of children, 170–1, 209, 323; breaks leg, 177; deputizes for HWS, 195–7; marriage relations, 197, 328; opposes HWS's conversion to Tories, 197; injured on yacht, 198–9; in USA, 218, 220, 251; visits Singapore, 247–8; in Beirut, 249–50; moves to Friston Place, 260; travels with HWS for Shell, 263; launches tanker, 270–1; accompanies HWS to Rhodesia, 271–2; activities and travels, 286–8; at Iranian 2500th anniversary celebrations, 295; death, 297; and children's upbringing, 321–2

Shawcross, Joanna (HWS's daughter) see Peck, Joanna

Shawcross, John (HWS's father): education and career, 11–12; literary achievements, 12–13, 269–70; lectures at Liverpool University, 24; death, 170

Shawcross, Timothy (Christopher's son), 62

Shawcross, William (HWS's elder son): childhood writing, 60; christening, 145; birth, 157, 321; sailing, 226; and death of Dick Stokes, 258; visits China with HWS, 298–300; religious convictions, 321–2; upbringing and education, 321–2; marriages and children, 322–3; writing career, 322

Shell (group of companies): HWS joins, 247–8, 252, 254, 256–7, 263, 272–4; HWS's full-time directorship, 274, 282; HWS leaves, 282

Shemara (yacht), 206

Sherman, Harry, 175, 178

Shinwell, Emanuel (later Baron), 143, 194

Silkin, Lewis, 15

Silkin, Samuel Charles, 66

Silverman, Sydney, 289

Simon, John Allsebrook, 1st Viscount, 25, 73–4, 81; and war criminals, 86; on tribunal of enquiry, 172–3

Simon, William, 309

Simonds, Gavin Turnbull, 1st Viscount, 82

Singapore, 247–8

Singleton, Sir John Edward, 24

Slade, Gerard, 80–1

Smith, Bradley F.: Reaching Judgment at Nuremberg, 116, 126, 134–6

Smuts, General Jan Christian, 152

socialism: HWS's views on, 59, 156, 161–2, 183, 226, 231–2, 237, 258, 269, 328

Socialist International, 2nd, Geneva (1922), 16

Solicitor General: office of, 65, 69, 71, 75, 77

Soskice, Sir Frank, 65–6, 69–70, 172, 174, 189, 193

South Africa: Indians in, 152

Soviet Union see USSR

Spaak, Paul-Henri, 150–1, 155, 163, 171

Spandau prison, 129

Spectator (journal), 279

Speer, Albert, 124–7

Spence, Sir Basil, 266–7

SS (German organisation), 125

Stalin, Josef V.: and war criminals, 87, 98–9, 102; at Potsdam Conference, 98; and Katyn massacre, 103; and Nuremberg judgments, 124; eschews benevolence, 156

Stanford University: Industrial Conference Board, 283

Stanley, Oliver, 182

Stanley, Sidney, 172, 174–8

Steinberg, Saul, 292

Stiarna (yacht), 273

Stimson, Henry: and war crimes trials, 86–8, 133

Stockdale René, 145

Stokes, Richard, 192, 243, 257–8

Stone of Scone (Westminster Abbey), 72

Strachey, John, 184

Streicher, Julius, 116, 124

Suez crisis (1956), 70

Sunday Despatch, 237

Sunday Express: announces article on HWS, 209–12

Sussex University: Lady Reading on Council of, 52; HWS serves on Council and Executive Committee, 266; HWS elected Chancellor, 267; meeting house, 267

Tanganyika, 273

Taylor, A.J.P., 136

Taylor, Colonel Telford, 102, 132,

134n; *The Anatomy of the Nuremberg Trials*, 102

Taylor, Sir Francis Kyffin (*later* Lord Maenan), 26, 34

Teheran, 293, 296

Teheran Conference (1943), 88

telephone tapping, 258–9

Templer, General Sir Gerald, 23

Teng Hsiao-ping, 300

Texas, 183–4

Thames Television, 293

Thatcher, Margaret, Baroness: on Saddam Hussein, 137; and Gulf War, 164; and Shah of Iran, 296; regime, 325, 329

Thomas, J.H., 16

Thomas, Ungoed, 190

Thomson of Fleet, Roy Thomson, 1st Baron, 285–6

Thyssen (German industrialist), 131

Tibet: HWS visits, 301–2

Times, The, 147, 208, 255, 262, 270, 283–4, 305; bought by Thomson, 285–6

Tito, Josip Broz, 199

Tolpuddle, Dorset, 217

Topolski, Feliks, 187

trade unions: law reform, 139–41, 183

Trades Disputes Act (1946), 183

Treath, Cornwall, 28, 35

Trevor-Roper, Hugh (*later* Baron Dacre), 281

Tribunals of Enquiry (Evidence) Act (1921), 172

Tribune (journal), 200, 213, 232

Trotter, Richard, 30

Truman, Harry S.: and war crimes trials, 90; and Potsdam Conference, 98; HWS's friendship with, 154

Tucker, Frederick James, Baron, 80

Tucker, Sir James Millard, 254

Tunbridge Wells, Kent, 39–40

Tweedsmuir, John Norman Stuart Buchan, 2nd Baron, 208

Uckfield, Sussex, 60

United Nations: and international crimes, 137; HWS supports, 160–1, 163–4; China and, 227

United Nations Assembly: HWS attends, 139–40, 149–55, 161, 163, 170–1, 183, 187; achievements, 155–6; disarmament debates, 171–2

United Nations Relief and Rehabilitation Administration (UNRRA), 53

United States of America: and post-Nuremberg trials, 132; anti-communism, 133; HWS visits and travels in, 153–4, 183, 188, 218, 220, 226–7, 251, 283

Universal Declaration of Human Rights (1944), 316

USSR: and war crimes trials, 93, 95, 97–9, 102–4, 114, 121–3; and Katyn massacre, 103, 121; and imprisonment of Hess, 129; at United Nations, 150–1; non-participation in Marshall Plan, 160

V1 flying bombs, 48, 54

V2 rockets, 48–9

Vanity V (yacht), 187, 198–9, 226, 240, 273

Vickers, Geoffrey, VC, 36

Vienna Trade Fair (1951), 199

Vietnam, 136

Visscher, Charles de, 241

Vyshinsky, Andrei, 114, 149–50, 154, 161, 171, 187

Wade, Professor, H.W.R., 277

Wandsworth Labour Party, 57–8

Warburg, Sigmund, 208, 257

Warburg's (bankers), 304

Ward, Stephen, 277

Wareham, Wilfred, 291

Warner, Marina, 300, 322

Washington: HWS considered for ambassadorship, 276

Watson, Dikes, 177
Watson, Sam, 170
Watson, Tom, 269
Weatherstone, Sir Dennis, 329
Webber, W.J., 275
Weinstock, Arnold, Baron, 282–3
Welensky, Sir Roy, 272
Welsh Industries Fair (1951), 196
West, Dame Rebecca: on Nuremberg trial, 135–6; on Lynskey Tribunal, 174; on Klaus Fuchs, 190; supports trans-Atlantic cooperation, 208; *The Meaning of Treason*, 83
White, Sir Thomas, 31
Whitehead, Sir Edgar, 272
Whyatt, Sir John, 270
Widnes, 61–2
Wilcox, Alexander, 234
Wilkinson, Ellen, 58, 62–3
Williams, Lt.-Col. H.F.L. ('The Officer in the Tower'), 38–9
Willoughby de Eresby, Timothy, Lord, 218
Wilson, Harold (*later* Baron): antagonism to Gaitskell, 189; resigns, 192; and HWS's campaign for retirement benefits for Bar, 239; on HWS as potential Party leader, 244–6, 327; ennobles Kaldor and Balogh, 268; premiership, 289

Wilson, Sir Angus, 281
Windyhill, Caldy, Cheshire, 24
Winn, Godfrey, 237
Winn, Roger, 237
Women's Royal Voluntary Service (*formerly* WVS), 52
Wontner, Sir Hugh, 222
Woolton, Frederick James Marquis, 1st Earl of, 174
Wright, Robert Alderson, Baron, 82
Wyatt, Woodrow (*later* Baron), 210–11, 237, 289
Wyndham-Goldie, Grace, 201

Yalta Memorandum (on Nazi war crimes), 89, 92
Yamani, Sheikh, 309
Yasir, Sheikh Yusif, 241–2
Yellowlees, Dr Henry, 186–7
Yorkshire Post, 147
Young, Dr Richard, 242
Yugoslavia: troubles in, 164, 200, 314; HWS visits, 199

Zahedi, Ardeshir, 293–4, 297
Zaid, Sheikh (*later* Ruler of Abu Dhabi), 241
Zorya, General N.D., 131